# MORE THAN MAYOR OR MANAGER

# MORE THAN MAYOR OR MANAGER

## Campaigns to Change Form of Government in America's Large Cities

Editors
**JAMES H. SVARA**
and
**DOUGLAS J. WATSON**

Georgetown University Press | Washington, D.C.

Georgetown University Press, Washington, D.C. www.press.georgetown.edu

Library of Congress Cataloging-in-Publication Data

More than mayor or manager : campaigns to change form of government in America's large cities / James H. Svara and Douglas J. Watson, editors.
    p.   cm.
Includes bibliographical references and index.
ISBN 978–1-58901–709–2 (pbk. : alk. paper)
1. Municipal government—United States.   I. Svara, James H. II. Watson, Douglas J.
JS331.M664   2010
320.8′50973—dc22

                                                          2010007036

♾ This book is printed on acid-free paper meeting the requirements of the American National Standard for Permanence in Paper for Printed Library Materials.

15   14   13   12   11   10      9   8   7   6   5   4   3   2
First printing

Printed in the United States of America

Dedicated to
John Parr, President, National Civic League, 1985–95,
and lifelong advocate of good government
and citizen engagement

# CONTENTS

# ILLUSTRATIONS

# PREFACE

CHANGE IN THE basic organizational structure of large cities and counties has become a major issue in public affairs at the local level in the United States. "Form of government" assigns authority and responsibilities to officials and determines at least formally how they relate to each other and to the public. Charter change in a city where the mayor is "strong" and pulls many levers of government has often been seen as a way to combat the corruption and partisan favoritism. Charter change in a city where the mayor is "weak" and executive authority is assigned to a professional city manager has been seen as an opportunity for aspiring political leaders to expand the scope of their activities. The apparent struggle between "political" versus "professional" executive interests generates political drama but defines the differences too narrowly and overlooks a wide range of important issues.

Different forms present the choice between different kinds of mayors, councils with different authority, and top administrators with differing capacity to use their professional ability. The possibility of charter change to alter or continue the form of government is an important public debate over the constitutional principles that should guide our governing institutions. Form of government has an impact on the leadership of council members and the interaction between all elected officials and large numbers of administrative staff members. It affects how government relates to civic organizations and residents of the community as a whole. It affects the characteristics and performance of administrative staff members, and how they are connected to other governments and to the professional groups from which they come.

Some might argue that the United States has entered a new era of governmental change a century after the civic reform movement that transformed the structure of local governments. In actuality, the dynamics of the earlier movement continue to express themselves with the continuing expansion of the use of council–manager government in cities. A more limited interpretation of the past two decades is that large cities that have used the council–manager form are now switching to the mayor–council form or substantially altering the council–manager form. The evidence we provide indicates that an important but small proportion of council–manager cities are considering change but most are rejecting it. A smaller number of mayor–council cities have moved to the council–manager form. What is happening in our view is that many large cities that face new challenges are taking the occasion to reexamine how they govern themselves. The constitutional contest provides the opportunity to change or reaffirm the form of government and other aspects of city government structure. By examining a number of large cities in which this discussion has occurred in charter change referenda that led to different outcomes, we hope to illuminate the full range of principles and issues that are at stake.

In *More than Mayor or Manager: Campaigns to Change Form of Government in America's Large Cities*, we present the experiences of fourteen large cities in the United States that have dealt with the issue of form of government in the recent past. Through these case studies we expect that students, scholars, and practitioners will recognize similarities of the arguments that are made for retaining or rejecting changes in the basic constitutional format of the cities. While we have identified similarities among the cities, we also recognize the unique histories, experiences, and personalities that impact the form of government in each community. These internal determinants impact importantly the outcome of the debate over form of government. For example, the rise of a charismatic leader who demands more political power may result in citizens granting that authority through a change in form. On the other hand, failure to govern ethically and/or efficiently may result in calls for change in form.

Our interest in this topic arises from both scholarly and applied activities. Both editors of this book have spent years in either the practice and/or study of local government. Jim Svara has taught public administration in North Carolina and Arizona and has examined how formal structure affects political-administrative relations across levels of government and in different countries. In addition, he has worked with charter review commissions in ten cities and counties. During his thirty-year career as a city manager, Doug Watson served three communities, most notably Auburn, Alabama, where he was city manager for nearly twenty-two years. After his retirement as a city manager, he joined the Public Affairs faculty at the University of Texas at Dallas, where he taught and directed dissertations until he retired in 2010. He continues to conduct research on governmental structure and professional roles.

As a result of this experience, we understand the depth of feeling that professional practitioners and elected officials have concerning the two dominant forms of government in the United States. While the two forms of government have taken on characteristics from each other in recent years, they still represent to practitioners, elected officials, and community activists different approaches to governing local communities. In the case studies that follow, the campaigns for change and the defenses of the incumbent systems are explored in detail. We believe that readers will understand the importance of this issue and the commitment that both sides bring to the debate.

We wish to acknowledge the authors of the case studies, local elected officials, professional public administrators in both forms of government, citizens that care how their communities are governed and that become involved in this important discussion, and the professional organizations (National Civic League, the International City-County Management Association, the National League of Cities, the United States Conference of Mayors) that are dedicated to governing on the local level. Special recognition should be given to the state leagues of municipalities that provide information and assistance to cities that are considering a change in their form of government.

We owe a special debt of gratitude to Daniel Ledbetter who applied great energy and care to getting the final manuscript prepared for publication. Danny is a doctoral student in the Ph.D. program in Public Affairs at the University of Texas at Dallas, and a graduate of the Bush School at Texas A&M University.

We dedicate this book to the memory of John Parr, who died in an automobile accident along with his wife and one of his daughters in December 2007. John was the president of the National Civic League from 1985 to 1995. During this time the seventh edition of the Model City Charter was prepared, which replaced the sixth edition of 1964. It was a major revision that continued key principles of civic reform. It also updated the charter to enhance political leadership and strengthen the contribution of citizens in the governmental process. We hope that his commitment to civil and informed debate about the ways that local governments can be designed to best serve the community is reflected in our discussion.

# CHAPTER 1

# INTRODUCTION

## Framing Constitutional Contests in Large Cities

JAMES H. SVARA AND DOUGLAS J. WATSON

THE UNITED STATES is unique compared with most countries in having two different forms of government in widespread use in its cities: mayor–council with more or less strong mayors, and council–manager with usually directly elected but nonexecutive mayors. The two major forms of government are based on different constitutional principles. The mayor–council form, like American national and state government, incorporates separation of powers and formal checks and balances between the executive and the legislature (Newland 1985). The council–manager form, somewhat analogous to parliamentary systems, is based on unified authority assigned to the legislative body that controls the executive branch. In the former the mayor as executive is chosen by the electorate, and in the latter the council appoints the executive officer, the city manager. City managers have been found in local government since 1908, and the form of government in which they are located has become the most commonly used structure in cities except the smallest and the very largest. This expansion occurred because some governments changed their form of government from mayor–council to council–manager and because many newly organized governments used the form from their inception.

This widespread change reflects a characteristic in American local government that is missing in most countries where local structure is imposed by the national government or is uniform throughout the country. The choice of how the government will be structured is a local one that cities can make and revise over time. As Hassett and Watson (2007, 1) observe, "once the structure is determined, it is not permanent." Leaders may propose and citizens may initiate revisions in the city charter. Some argue that change in several of a wide variety of features can fundamentally alter the structure of the city (Frederickson, Johnson, and Wood 2004); these features include how officials are elected, the mayor's voting status or veto power, or the extent of staff support for the mayor or council. In contrast, we agree with Hassett and Watson's distinction between minor changes, such as the switch from at-large to district elections, and what they call "profound change to the basic structure of the city government" by altering form of government.

This book focuses on efforts to change the form of government. There is an additional emphasis on large cities that have a population of more than one hundred thousand. These cities are important as trendsetters and because they have characteristics that test the capacity of a form of government to provide sound governance. In the introductory discussion we examine how the evidence regarding differences related to form of government might shape the arguments that are made in cities where change is being considered. Case studies of fourteen cities are then offered. In the concluding chapter we compare the factors related to efforts to change charters in the case study cities. We examine whether the potential arguments that can be used to support or attack each form of government are actually used and how they are related to the outcome of the referendum. We also examine other claims that have arisen in referenda campaigns as well as the city-specific factors that affected the referendum results. Finally, we consider what these constitutional contests teach us about the forms of government used in American cities and in other countries of the world.

The dominant trend in the choice of form in the United States has been the increased use of the council–manager form of government, but that trend may not apply to large cities. Furthermore, large cities that use the form may be abandoning it or altering it so substantially that it loses the essential features of the form. Whether the council–manager form is suitable for large cities and whether large cities are turning away from the form are the underlying questions that we examine in this book. In addition, we address the implicit counter questions—is the mayor–council form an appropriate design to meet the leadership needs of large cities (as well as smaller ones), and is this form an attractive alternative to cities that have used other structures? In this introduction we examine the characteristics of the two major forms of government in cities of all sizes and the changes occurring in the use of the major forms. The discussion then shifts to the special issues associated with governance in cities over one hundred thousand in population and how the general expectations regarding form might be altered by size. A summary of the positive and negative claims regarding each form based on the research literature and observations by public affairs commentators is provided.

These claims are compared in the concluding chapter to the actual points made in referenda campaigns in the fourteen case study cities. They cover five cities that abandoned the council–manager form of government and converted to the mayor–council form, four cities that rejected the abandonment of the council–manager form, two cities that switched from mayor–council to council–manager form, and two cities that rejected a change to the strong mayor–council form and retained the unusual commission form (in Portland) and an atypical weak mayor–council form of government (in St. Louis). The analysis of positive and negative claims and assessment of the impact of changing or rejecting change in form provide important insights about the future of governance in large cities. The chapter concludes with a summary of the case studies presented in the book.

In the final analysis scholars and observers of local government affairs should be interested in promoting the highest level of performance in cities of all kinds regardless of their form and other features. For most cities most of the time, improving perform-ance will entail working within the characteristics of the existing form of government and acting in ways that are appropriate to the values and roles for officials in that form. This is more likely to happen if there is a better understanding of the strengths to be exploited and the weaknesses to be avoided in each form of government. Given the unique circumstances of American local government, however, it is also important to sort out the arguments and evidence that are offered when the residents must decide what form will be used in a specific large city.

This book, drawing on an examination of the most important recent cases of efforts in large cities to change the form of government, contributes to both the general knowl-edge of the plusses and minuses of forms of government and also provides a guide to understanding the give-and-take in constitutional contests. Across the world demo-cratic national governments may be organized by the principles of presidential or parlia-mentary systems similar to the mayor–council/council–manager distinction. There is no serious discussion of major reorganization of government at the national level (or state level) in the United States, but at the local level Americans can and often do participate in the big international debate about comparative government.

## What Is Form and Does Form Matter?

Before examining the differences in form of government in the United States, there is a basic question to consider: why is form important? In the early days of political science as a scholarly field and in the circle of governmental reformers in the Progressive Era, there was probably the presumption that structure determines behavior and explains how governments perform. The orthodox model of public administration that emerged in the 1920s placed great emphasis of the formal features of organizations (Henry 1975). In the social science revolution after World War II, the importance of attitudes and behavior of individuals and groups inside and outside government was recognized, and the informal features of organizations were seen to be major determi-nants of performance. At the same time, there was a tendency in the behavioral revolu-tion to downgrade the importance of structure and formal provisions in organizations. It was possible to conclude that relationships and behaviors of political actors were more important than formal structure. For example, some might argue that it is quality of leaders that is important to explaining the performance of city governments rather than the structure in which they operate (Ehrenhalt 2004).

A variation on this shift in views is the argument that form of government depends on other institutional features to produce distinctive characteristics. Frederickson, Johnson, and Wood (2004) have argued that a wide range of structural choices deter-mine the extent to which a city incorporates practices and values that politicize the governmental process, on the one hand, or that strengthen administrative values, on the other. These are contrasting sets of consistent practices that they label as political and administrative models. As change in any combination of these features including but not limited to form occurs, cities move from pure to adapted status and may eventually have features that completely intermix the two models. Form, or the constitutional platform, alone does not determine the classification of cities. All adapted cities, in their view, are more like each other than they are like other cities that share their form but differ in using the full model of consistent practices (Frederickson, Johnson, and Wood 2004, 100–101). According to this perspective, one might argue that change in form for an adapted city makes little difference in isolation from other structural features.

The counter position is that form is a structural characteristic of special importance regardless of how it is combined with other structural features (Svara and Nelson 2008). Form is the constitutional and legal basis for assigning authority and functions to officials in government and creates its overall framework. Form shapes the nature of official roles and channels interactions into likely patterns of relationships, that is, who talks to whom, who gives instructions to whom, and how are those instructions interpreted and acted on by the recipient. The essential differentiating characteristic is whether power is divided between the mayor and the council, on the one hand, or resides in the council, on the other.[1] The former is a feature of mayor–council governments and the latter of council–manager governments.

If there is a chief administrative officer (CAO) in the government, the second differentiating characteristic is whether the top administrator is primarily responsible to the mayor or to the council as a whole. The principles of separation of powers and responsibility of the top administrator to the elected executive are found in American national and state government and at the local level in American mayor–council cities and in municipal governments in countries such as France, Italy, and Germany. The principles of unified authority and responsibility of the executive to the legislative body are found in parliamentary systems and at the local level in American council–manager cities and in municipal governments in countries such as Ireland, Finland, and Australia (Mouritzen and Svara 2002). Approximations of the council–manager form are found in Denmark, Sweden, and most English cities.

These distinct forms are used with a variety of other structural features. Mayor–council cities can use nonpartisan elections, as many in the United States have for a long time. The mayor–council cities in Europe universally have CAOs. The council–manager and parliamentary forms are combined in various ways with other structural features across types of governments. Council–manager cities can elect their mayors directly (a long-standing practice that has recently become more common) or select some or all of their council members from districts (a change that became more common in the late sixties) (Svara 1977).[2] Most county governments in the United States, including those with the council–manager form, use partisan elections, and cities in Europe that use parliamentary forms that approximate the council–manager form usually have strong political parties (Svara and Nelson 2008). Rather than seeing the combinations that depart from the pure American models as undermining the distinctions between forms of governments, the diversity of combinations suggests that form establishes some distinct institutional characteristics that persist across settings. Other features can be changed without fundamentally altering how forms of government function. In contrast, changing form of government produces a fundamental alteration in the governmental process.[3]

One final observation is that the basic constitutional features of the council–manager form are widespread in local government special districts and in nonprofit organizations. The governing board–appointed executive model offers the combination of lay leadership and oversight with professional direction of the organization. Corporate organization may also approximate this model, although the possibility of merging the roles of chairperson of the board and chief executive officer (CEO) creates a variation that is closer to the mayor–council form in blending power over purpose and strategy with authority over executive functions. Recommendations for corporate reform in the wake of scandals such as Enron include having a board chairperson who is not the CEO and independent directors with a strong commitment to oversight (MacAvoy and Millstein 2004; O'Neill 2005). The roles of the chairman of the corporate board and the mayor in the council–manager form are similar, as are the policy-making and oversight functions of the corporate board and the city council.

These comparative and cross-sectoral perspectives remind us that a form of government with unified authority and an appointed executive is widely used in the United States and other countries and in governmental and nongovernmental organizations. In city government in the United States, however, it is common to think of the council–manager form as part of a campaign of reform—not as an approach that makes good governing conditions better or a preferred design for a new organization but as a method of correcting serious shortcomings and governmental failure.

## Characteristics of Forms of Government

The debate over forms of government in the United States originally focused on perceived differences in competence—the capacity to operate city governments effectively and efficiently—and corruption. There was a widespread observation that forms of government tended to be found in different kinds of settings—small towns and suburban jurisdictions versus central cities—and reflected different values about how government should be organized and operated. Banfield and Wilson (1963) argued that the council–manager form (and the reform model generally) was accepted not because it won out over the forces of partisanship and particularism in large cities but because it became dominant in the places that had never had party machines and corruption. From this perspective divergent settings and distinctive value systems are the foundation of the two major forms of governments. It is expected that people from different places or with different backgrounds have different ways of looking at how government should be organized and function (Alford and Scoble 1965). To Hassett and Watson (2007) these contrasting viewpoints can be considered separate paradigms. In most communities both paradigms are simultaneously present, but one tends to be dominant at any particular time. The community's dominant paradigm, which is grounded in the unique characteristics of that city, serves as the basis by which local policy decisions are made and governmental affairs are administered.

Underlying these differences is the contrast between viewing the city population as a collection of competing interests or as a community with shared interests that benefit the city as a whole. In the former setting each group is looking out for itself, and a strong leader is needed to contain and channel conflict. In the latter setting all groups can work together, and shared leadership articulates common goals (Banfield and Wilson 1963; Wolfinger and Field 1966). The dominant perspective in the city is likely to shape governmental institutions. The mayor–council form seems to match the large city with extensive conflict, and the council–manager form matches the small, harmonious community. When the characteristics of a community shift, it may lead to a change in the dominant value paradigm and a change in the form of government.

This widely held interpretation of institutional choice in cities does not necessarily apply to conditions observed in the past fifty years. The civil rights revolution, governmental encouragement of citizen participation, the rise in political activism, internal migration across regions, and increased immigration brought new political dynamics to many cities large and small. Not only is the council–manager form increasingly found in large cities (discussed more below), but many council–manager cities of all sizes have also become diverse demographically. As community characteristics shift, other features in the governmental structure may change; for example, district elections put in place to improve the presentation of new (or formerly underrepresented) groups in the community—or the behavior of groups may shift. Browning, Marshall, and Tabb (1984) found that minority and neighborhood groups plus labor unions and liberal Democrats increased the liberal and the minority representation in ten California cities they studied even without district elections or change in the form of government. All but one used the council–manager form during the time of the study, and only one—Oakland—subsequently has changed its form. The political change, however, was dramatic, with a shift from an average of 40 percent Democratic officeholders in 1962 to 80 percent in 1977. Thus, the governmental process may adjust to new demands and expectations and incorporate new groups, but the form of government does not necessarily change.

Corresponding to this broader view, the interpretation of the salient characteristics of each form of government has been expanded as well although it is not clear how much these newer views are reflected in the media or popular perceptions of differences between the forms. It is no longer sufficient to contrast the forms as typically characterized by political responsiveness, political control, and strong political leaders (e.g., Box 1995) as opposed to professional management, apolitical decisions, and efficiency. Commentator Allan Ehrenhalt (2004) expresses this narrow view of the differences between forms as follows: "[A city] can hire a manager to replace wasteful political patronage with nonpartisan administration, but in doing that it gives up the benefits of having highly visible political leadership. Or it can choose a strong mayor, and get the leader it is looking for. But as often as not, that brings in an element of managerial cronyism and politically tainted policy decisions. Either way, something seems amiss." An alternative view argues that the choice is not between a strong mayor or a strong manager and the norms stereotypically associated with each. The two forms offer different kinds of political leaders and relationships between elected officials as well as differences in administrative values and behavior.

There are differences with respect to political leaders based on form as well as a similarity that contradicts the politics versus professionalism distinction. To be sure, the mayor in the mayor–council city is expected to use his separate powers to be in charge of the governmental process (Dahl 1961; Talbot 1967; Ferman 1985). Mayors in council–manager cities, although once dismissed as figureheads (Pressman 1972), can also provide leadership in setting direction (Svara 1994). Many are viewed as visionaries by council members, especially if directly elected (Svara 2008). Their leadership style tends to be facilitative, that is, mayors encourage and coordinate the contributions of council members rather than attempting to control them, as is common among strong mayors. Council contributions are not limited by the powers of a separate political executive, and council–manager councils perform better as a governing body—establishing goals and providing oversight—than their mayor–council counterparts (Svara 2003). Power is divided between the mayor and the council in mayor–council cities, and lines of accountability and clarity of control of administration are unclear (Svara 1990, 11). There is a greater conflict among officials (Svara 1990; Nollenberger 2008). Taken together, these characteristics suggest different models of political leadership—one based on executive democracy with the mayor as a driving force and the council in a checking role, and the other based on representative democracy and shared governance with the mayor in a guiding and facilitative role.

The provisions differ for the administrative dimension of government as well. Professionalism is not absent in the mayor–council form. Most cities of all kinds have civil service systems for hiring personnel, and professionalism is well established at least at the departmental level. Approximately half of the mayor–council cities have appointed CAOs, but the office is organized differently than in council–manager cities. The CAO in mayor–council cities, even if approved by the council, is responsible to the mayor. An overwhelming majority of CAOs approved by the council consider themselves to be the agent of the mayor and agree that their duties generally expand or decrease as determined by the mayor (Svara 2001), and these tendencies are even stronger when the appointment is by the mayor alone. The city manager is responsible to the council as a whole. The unified authority contributes to clear lines of accountability (Montjoy and Watson 1995; Svara 1990). Furthermore, the city manager has always been an important source of policy advice to the city council, not just an apolitical manager, and is concerned with advancing a wide range of professional values, not just efficiency (Nalbandian 1990; Keene et al. 2007).

Finally, there are differences in the relationship of the administrative function to elected officials in the two forms. Despite the common association of the separation of policy and administration with the council–manager form, the unique feature of the council–manager form is the interaction of council members and administrators in both policy and administration (Montjoy and Watson 1995). The form ensures that a professional perspective will be presented to the council by the manager on all policy decisions and that council oversight can be directed to any administrative action (Svara and Nelson 2008). With separation of powers, the mayor can erect a wall between administrators and the council. The mayor can determine the level of professionalism and the extent to which the full advice of professionals is shared with the city council.

The mayor often uses executive power to limit council oversight of administrative performance (Svara 2003). In the mayor–council form, professionalism coexists with particularism and patronage (Montjoy and Watson 1995). In contrast to the council–manager form in which the council has authority over the manager, the mayor in the mayor–council form is a separate and independent executive.

The administrative function in council–manager cities is headed by a trained, professional city manager who serves at the pleasure of the city council. The assessment of options and recommended actions is guided by universalistic standards, and administrators manifest competence that is neutral in relationship to the policy orientation of political leaders (Montjoy and Watson 1995; Svara 1990). City managers are obligated to carry out the policy decisions of the city council but not to slant their recommendations to reinforce the preferences of the mayor or council.

Various distinctions between forms of government have a conceptual or empirical foundation. In the analysis of efforts to change the form of government, it will be important to examine which of the distinctions are used in the arguments made in actual referenda campaigns and to identify themes that have special relevance to large cities.

## Use of Forms of Government

A comparison of the distribution of governmental forms used by U.S. cities with populations over 2,500 and the change over the last twenty-five years is depicted in table 1.1.

Table 1.2 shows that the percentages of cities that use the various forms differ to some extent across cities with different populations. Cities with populations under 5,000 are more likely to use the mayor–council form of government in part because of the resistance to change from traditional weak mayor–council form and the expense of adding a full-time administrator to the city government staff. As population increases in cities up to 250,000, council–manager government is more likely to be employed. Nearly two-thirds of the cities with populations between 25,000 and 250,000 use council–manager government as of 2007. Above this population level, the mayor–council government is used frequently: in just over half of the cities with populations between 250,000 and 499,999 and two-thirds of the cities with populations over 500,000.

The distribution of council–manager cities has expanded overall and has moved into larger cities. The issue that has been raised in a number of cities is whether the form will work in the large cities where it is increasingly found. That question is the focus of our inquiry.

## Form of Government in Large Cities

It has long been presumed that the council–manager form of government faces special challenges in large cities.[4] There are several reasons to expect unique circumstances in such cities (Svara 1999). The range of interests is wider, and the capacity of groups to organize to influence government is more widespread. The media are more developed

**Table 1.1 Distribution of Governmental Forms among U.S. Municipalities over 2,500 population, 1984–2008 (numbers in parentheses are percentages)**

| Form of Government | 2008 | 2002 | 1998 | 1996 | 1992 | 1988 | 1984 |
|---|---|---|---|---|---|---|---|
| Council–Manager | 3,520 | 3,387 | 3,232 | 2,760 | 2,441 | 2,356 | 2,290 |
| | (48.9) | (48.5) | (48.1) | (41.4) | (36.5) | (35.3) | (34.7) |
| Mayor–Council | 3,131 | 3,011 | 2,943 | 3,319 | 3,319 | 3,686 | 3,686 |
| | (43.5) | (43.1) | (43.8) | (49.8) | (49.6) | (55.3) | (55.8) |
| Commission | 143 | 143 | 146 | 154 | 154 | 173 | 176 |
| | (2.0) | (2.0) | (2.2) | (2.3) | (2.3) | (2.6) | (2.7) |
| Town Meeting | 338 | 337 | 333 | 365 | 365 | 369 | 370 |
| | (4.7) | (4.8) | (5.0) | (5.5) | (5.5) | (5.5) | (5.6) |
| Rep. Town Meeting | 62 | 63 | 65 | 70 | 70 | 82 | 81 |
| | (0.9) | (0.9) | (0.9) | (1.0) | (1.0) | (1.2) | (1.2) |
| Total | 7,194 | 6,981 | 6,719 | 6,668 | 6,686 | 6,666 | 6,603 |

*Note:* Totals for U.S. local governments represent only those municipalities with populations of 2,500 and greater. According to the 2002 Census of Governments, there are approximately twelve thousand additional municipalities with populations under 2,500.

*Source:* Data from International City/County Management Association (2002, xii) and International City/County Management Association (2008, xi).

and focused on large city governments in a way not found in smaller places. The problems large cities face tend to be more complex, more interrelated, and more difficult to handle. As a consequence of these conditions, the political environment of the large city is highly charged.

Large cities do not necessarily provide a broader range of functions than smaller cities, but they certainly take on a wider array of activities and are more likely to introduce innovations that may prove to be controversial. Just as place matters in shaping the political process and outcomes (Dreier, Mollenkopf, and Swanstrom 2004), so too does size. Large cities have the potential to shape their own destiny, or at least many cities act on the illusion that they can devise strategies that will improve the city, foster new industries, and strengthen its competitive advantage. Such opportunities create different and higher expectations for leaders and performance. It is natural that large cities should consider how they are organized for governance along with other strategic choices. Big plans can also produce big leaders who want to expand their powers and big disappointments that may produce a demand for change not just in the occupants of public office but also the structure of those offices. Many cities have recently become large because of dramatic growth—especially those that use the council–manager form—and growth itself generates conflict and questions about purpose and direction of the city that could spill over into constitutional contests. It appears

**Table 1.2 Distribution of Governmental Forms among U.S. Municipalities by Population Size**

| | 2500–4999 | 5000–9999 | 10,000–24,999 | 25,000–49,999 | 50,000–99,999 | 100,000–249,999 | 250,000–499,999 | 500,000–999,999 | 1 million & over | Total |
|---|---|---|---|---|---|---|---|---|---|---|
| Mayor–Council | 55.3 | 43.9 | 37.7 | 32.1 | 33.4 | 33.0 | 50.0 | 65.2 | 66.7 | 43.5 |
| Council-Manager | 37.6 | 46.8 | 52.9 | 63.0 | 64.6 | 65.4 | 47.2 | 30.4 | 33.3 | 48.9 |
| Other | 7.0 | 9.3 | 9.4 | 5.0 | 2.0 | 1.7 | 2.8 | 4.3 | 0.0 | 7.5 |
| *Percentage* | *100.0* | *100.0* | *100.0* | *100.0* | *100.0* | *100.0* | *100.0* | *100.0* | *100.0* | *100.0* |
| No. of cities | 2,031 | 1,895 | 1,623 | 704 | 373 | 174 | 38 | 23 | 8 | |

*Source:* Data from International City/County Management Association (2008, xi).

that approximately 3 percent of cities with populations over 5,000 and under 100,000 population have held referenda on change of form since 1990.[5] Based on our calculations, twice that proportion, or 6 percent, of the cities between 100,000 and 249,999 population, have held referenda on form during this period, and 17 percent of the cities over 250,000 in population have done so. The more highly charged political dynamics of large cities produces attitudes and circumstances that contribute to considering change in the form of government. Referenda are far from typical, but they happen more commonly in large cities.

Despite the overall growth in the use of council–manager form, many observers of local government have suggested that the council–manager form is best suited for relatively small, homogenous cities. In the early sixties, Banfield and Wilson (1963) linked the essential characteristics of the council–manager form at that time to the characteristics of the cities that tended to use it. Only three cities with more than a half million residents used the council–manager form at that time (and sixty-eight cities over 100,000 used the form.) Over the past fifty years, the form has increasingly been used in large, diverse places as well. Now 9 governments in cities over 500,000 in population and 140 in cities over 100,000 use the council–manager form. For the most part, growing cities with the council–manager form in place have retained the form while migrating into larger population categories. In comparison, nineteen cities with population over 500,000 and ninety-one with population over 100,000 use the mayor–council form. The council–manager form has become more commonly used in large cities and often used in very large cities.

There are some major variations within each form of government in large cities. Nelson and Svara (2010) have developed an approach to classifying governmental structures that builds on those of DeSantis and Renner (2002) and MacManus and Bullock (2003). They divide council–manager cities into those with the mayor selected within the council, with directly elected mayors, and with empowered mayors who have extra authority such as nominating the city manager to the council for selection. As indicated in table 1.3, direct election is by far the most common approach, and council election (in less than one-sixth of these cities) is used only in cities under 250,000 people. Only five cities have empowered mayors (Hansell 1993).

Almost half of the mayor–council cities do not have a CAO. One-third of the cities with CAOs have council approval of the CAO appointment, and two-thirds give the mayor authority to appoint the CAO.

It is possible that the old truism that the form is not suited for large, diverse cities remains sound, and, therefore, large cities are likely to question the use of the form and often abandon it. An alternative interpretation is that the characteristics and consequences of using the council–manager form identified in earlier research were shaped by the size and demographics of the cities that used the form at that time. As the population characteristics change, the interpretation of what the form means and how it functions should change as well. Support for this view might be found in rejection of the move to the mayor–council form or the adoption of the council–manager form in some large cities.

Table 1.3    Variations in Forms of Government in Large Cities

|  | Population | | | | |
|---|---|---|---|---|---|
| *Variation in Forms* | *Over 1,000,000* | *500,000– 1,000,000* | *250,000– 499,999* | *100,000– 249,999* | *Total* |
| Council (Selects Mayor)– Manager | 0 | 0 | 0 | 22 | 22 |
| Elected Mayor–Council– Manager | 3 | 5 | 12 | 93 | 113 |
| Empowered Mayor– Council–Manager | 0 | 1 | 2 | 2 | 5 |
| Mayor–Council–CAO Appointed by Mayor and Approved by Council | 2 | 1 | 5 | 8 | 16 |
| Mayor–CAO Appointed by Mayor–Council | 1 | 7 | 9 | 15 | 32 |
| Mayor–Council (no CAO) | 3 | 5 | 5 | 30 | 43 |
| Total | 9 | 19 | 33 | 170 | 231 |

*Source:* Variations from Nelson and Svara (2010); data calculated by authors.

Overall, the number of council–manager cities over 100,000 in population represents 58 percent of the total and is growing. Still, the underlying question about the appropriateness of the council–manager form to the large city context is often raised, and the debate has intensified in the past two decades (Gurwitt 1993). Since 1990 local governments in 23 of America's 243 large cities have grappled with the question of whether they should change from one form of government to the other. Thus, almost 10 percent of the large cities have had a charter change referendum.

The council–manager form has been replaced with the mayor–council form in nine cities with population over 100,000 in population (in the following lists of cities, those in bold are the subject of case studies in this book): Fresno, California; **Hartford, Connecticut**; Miami, Florida; **Oakland, California**; **Richmond, Virginia**; **St. Petersburg, Florida**; **San Diego, California**; **Spokane, Washington**; and Toledo, Ohio. The council–manager form replaced the mayor–council form in **El Paso, Texas**; and **Topeka, Kansas**; and the commission form in Cedar Rapids, Iowa. Abandonment of the council–manager form was rejected during this period in nine large cities (Corpus Christi, Texas; **Cincinnati, Ohio**; **Dallas, Texas**; **Grand Rapids, Michigan**; **Kansas City, Missouri**; Little Rock, Arkansas; Pueblo, Colorado;[6] Tucson, Arizona; and Worcester, Massachusetts). In addition, a charter change from the commission to strong-mayor form was considered but rejected in **Portland, Oregon**, and a change from a weak mayor–council form to the strong-mayor form was rejected in **St. Louis, Missouri**.[7]

With these crosscurrents of change, there is not a clear trend regarding public support for the council–manager form in large cities or public preference for the strong-mayor–council form, but it is apparent that the issue of change in form is more likely to be raised in large council–manager cities. They represented eighteen of the twenty-three large cities in which the referenda have been held. Still, the strong-mayor–council option has been replaced or rejected in fourteen of the twenty-three cities in which it was considered.

The process of structural change in a local government is quite complex and has been the subject of numerous articles and decades of academic research (see, e.g., Highsaw 1949; Lyons 1978; Morgan and Pelissero 1980; Fannin 1983; Farnham and Bryant 1985; Adrian 1988; Protasel 1988; Anderson 1989; Box 1992, 1995; Montjoy and Watson 1993, 1995; Parrish and Frisby 1996; Ruhil 1999; Simmons 2001; Simmons and Simmons 2002) and has served as the context in which governmental processes are examined (see, e.g., Kim 1997; Svara 1990; Lineberry and Fowler 1967; Welch and Bledsoe 1986). A large part of the complexity of analyzing cases of change in the municipal form of government is capturing the many influences that shape decisions made by these communities. To address this challenge, this book uses a case study approach to analyze how and why communities change their forms of government, and it offers an in-depth examination of the political dynamics within these communities. The case studies incorporate a substantial proportion of the large cities in which referenda have been held. They represent fourteen of the twenty-two large cities with charter change action since 1990. We are hopeful, therefore, that the analysis of the case studies in the concluding chapter will be representative of the distinctive forces affecting the initiation and outcome of charter change efforts in large cities.

A number of generic arguments can be made to advance major forms of government when they are contested and arguments also can be made that relate specifically to the conditions in large cities, in particular greater diversity and conflict, more complexity, and higher levels of media attention. The points summarized here include both the strengths claimed for a form and the weaknesses that are attributed to the other form. In identifying the claims, it is assumed that the mayor–council form includes a strong mayor who is responsible for appointing the CAO and department heads, formulating the budget, and directing the administrative organization, and that the council–manager form includes an elected mayor and a manager who is responsible to the council as a whole. These are the common provisions found in large mayor–council cities with CAOs and council–manager cities. In addition, the points focus on systemic features that are alleged to be associated with the form of government, as opposed to strengths and weaknesses of specific individuals or the handling of particular challenges.

## The Case for the Mayor–Council Form

Proponents of the mayor–council form stress the need for effective political leadership in city government. In addition, they argue that the mayor is in a position to allocate resources in order to achieve the goals of the platform upon which he or she was elected. Mayor–council advocates claim the council–manager major is weak and ineffective, whereas the nonelected city manager is in a position to become the focal point of the local government.

### *Arguments/Claims That Support the Strong-Mayor–Council Form*

♦ Mayor provides strong leadership.
♦ Mayor can form coalitions on the council and in the community by rewarding supporters and sanctioning opponents.
♦ Voters hold one person accountable.
♦ Strong mayor provides greater capacity to initiate major policy changes.
♦ Large cities can produce effective political executives.
♦ Mayor can allocate resources to support his/her agenda and to respond to demands of supporters.
♦ Council can be supported by staff to serve as counterweight to the mayor.
♦ CAO can provide administrative expertise.

### *Arguments/Claims That Criticize the Council–Manager Form*

♦ Mayor is figurehead; does not have enough power to set direction, form coalitions, or overcome opposition.
♦ City council is prone to dissension; no one can overcome dissension on the city council.
♦ Too many masters brings diffusion of power, accountability.
♦ City manager acquires too much influence if not properly supervised.
♦ City manager is narrowly focused on improving efficiency.
♦ City manager can ignore the mayor.
♦ Turnover in the city manager position can weaken government; city council can arbitrarily remove manager.
♦ Having city manager does not guarantee competence and high ethical standards.
♦ Form is efficient in small matters but not in taking on major initiatives.

## The Case for the Council–Manager Form

Supporters of council–manager government generally offer a series of arguments that stress the leadership role of the mayor and city council members while pointing out the advantages that professional city managers offer city governments in efficiency, accountability, and ethical behavior. In addition, council-manager advocates often point out deficiencies that they believe exist in the major–council form, such as the dominating influence on both policy and administration by a single figure, the mayor.

*Arguments/Claims That Support Council–Manager Form*

- Mayor is a visionary who provides facilitative leadership and builds partnerships.
- Mayor is leader of the council and symbol for the community.
- Council is a governing board that focuses on coherent policymaking and oversight of administrative performance.
- City manager provides policy advice based on objective assessment of trends, needs, and community goals.
- Typically a cooperative relationship exists between the mayor, council, and manager.
- City establishes long-term goals and maintains continuity of commitments.
- City administration is innovative and incorporates leading practices.
- Decisions reflect universal values such as equality, fairness, social equity, inclusiveness, responsiveness, efficiency, and effectiveness.
- City manager is continuously accountable to the council for performance.
- Minority groups are empowered as members of the governing body.

*Arguments/Claims That Criticize the Mayor–Council Form*

- Performance of form is too dependent on one person; effectiveness can rise and fall with qualities of the strong mayor.
- Mayors lack equal levels of political and executive skills.
- Mayors have excessive power and are more prone to corruption; when faced with obstacles, mayors seek more power.
- Council performance as governing board is weak and dominated by the mayor.
- Conflict between the mayor and council is common; there is a risk of impasse between the two seats of power.
- Professionalism of the CAO depends on whom the mayor appoints; mayor can bypass the CAO and undercut his/her professionalism.
- Shortcomings in accountability: separation of powers creates unclear lines of responsibility; review of performance by voters in elections is infrequent; emphasis on election success makes mayor accountable to supporters rather than all voters.

These arguments based on the literature and comments that appear in the media might be made in actual referendum contests. After reviewing the case studies we attempt to identify which ones have been articulated.

In addition to examining arguments and outcomes, attention is also given to the use of initiatives and referenda as the mechanism for changing the constitution of city government. Popular input in a decision of this magnitude is a democratic requirement, but it is possible that the process may be subject to domination by special interests and big money as some contend is the case for initiatives generally (Broder 2000).

## Overview of Cases

The fourteen case studies are grouped under one of four categories: change from council–manager to mayor–council; retaining the council–manager form; change from mayor–council to council–manager; and rejecting the strong mayor to retain other forms.

### Change from Council–Manager to Mayor–Council

In St. Petersburg, Spokane, Hartford, Richmond, San Diego, and Oakland, along with five other large council–manager cities since 1990, political leaders, citizens, and interest groups have led successful efforts to abandon the council–manager form of government and convert to the mayor–council form. The cities are arranged in the chronological order of the final change in their form of government. Although a trial change in form began in Oakland in 1998, it was not finalized until 2004.

Edwin Benton, Donald Menzel, and Darryl Paulson present the case of St. Petersburg, Florida, a medium-sized city that changed its form of government from council–manager to mayor–council in 1993. The authors report that the pro-development city hall was considered hostile to the interests of the elderly, the historic preservationists, and the neighborhood activists, who formed an antigrowth group in the city. Charter change became entwined with policy differences over development, the accomplishments of development, and the behavior of city managers.

Voters in Spokane, Washington, a city of two hundred thousand people, decided in 1999 to switch to a strong-mayor form of government, abandoning the council–manager system that had served it well for most of the forty years that it had been in place. In the late 1990s a number of downtown retail businesses closed, and the city council felt a need to intervene in order to redevelop the downtown. According to Wendy Hassett, a failed development plan and high-profile personnel problems provided the backdrop for a mayor and city councilors who did not support council–manager government to lead the effort to change the form of government in 1999.

Hartford, Connecticut, the state's capital city and the home of many of the nation's largest insurance companies, abandoned council–manager government in 2002 following white flight to the growing suburbs, the alienation of the business community because of high taxes, the partisan bickering between Democrats and Republicans over control of the city government, and extreme racial tension and violence. Hassett notes that a switch by the council to hiring managers from within the city and the emergence of more assertive and popular mayors shaped the conditions for change in form.

Richmond, Virginia, a state capital of two hundred thousand residents, changed its form of government from council–manager to mayor–council in 2003. Nelson Wikstrom notes that Richmond suffered from years of economic decline, conflict with its surrounding suburbs, an adversarial relationship with the business community, and ethical lapses under the council–manager system that had been in place since 1948. In 2002 former Governor L. Douglas Wilder, backed by local business leaders and the daily newspaper, led the effort to abandon council–manager government in favor of a strong mayor.

San Diego is the seventh most populous city in the United States and the largest city to abandon the council–manager form. Glen Sparrow cites a number of factors, some of which developed over several decades, that led to the change in the form of government: the experience with Mayor Pete Wilson, who offered stronger and more visible leadership than his predecessors; the move to district elections in 1988; the efforts of a working group of community leaders; and two mayors who wanted greater powers. A financial debacle in 2004 caused by many years of underfunding the city-run retirement fund provided the final impetus to change. In 1998 Oakland, California, voters elected former Governor Jerry Brown as their mayor and decided to experiment with a change in the form of government from council–manager to mayor–council. Following Brown's election and his campaign for more power in the mayor's office, Oakland residents approved the switch to mayor–council government on a six-year trial basis with 75 percent in favor. Despite an abortive effort by the city council to remove the sunset provision in 2002, voters did approve the continuation of mayor–council government in 2004.

## Retaining the Council–Manager Form

In nine large cities, abandonment of the council–manager form has been rejected since 1990. Four of these cities are profiled: Kansas City, Grand Rapids, Cincinnati, and Dallas. Two of these cities made charter changes to empower the mayor either before the effort to shift to the mayor–council form (Kansas City) or after the referendum on form (Cincinnati).

Kimberly Nelson and Curtis Wood trace the history of council–manager government in Kansas City, Missouri, from its adoption in 1925 until the present. By the late 1980s, citizen dissatisfaction with council–manager government led to a referendum in 1989 to convert to mayor–council government. Even though voters retained council–manager government with 60 percent opposed to change, mayors from that year to recent ones have sought to increase the powers of the mayor. Formal empowerment of the office occurred in 1998, but the issue of changing form continues to surface.

In 1916 Grand Rapids, Michigan, was one of the earliest cities to adopt council–manager government. The council–manager form was not challenged until 1967 when the mayor appointed a committee to study a conversion to strong-mayor government. Change to a strong mayor was rejected in 1970 and in subsequent years as well. Eric Zeemering compares the 1970 effort with the rejection of a proposal in 2002 that would have made the mayors office full-time within the council–manager form.

Karen Jarrell explores the efforts by proponents of mayor–council government to abandon council–manager government in Dallas in 2005. In 1990 the federal court decided that Dallas's five-member city council elected at large violated the requirements of one-person, one-vote rulings of the court and mandated a change to a fifteen-member council with the mayor elected at large and all councilors elected from fourteen separate

wards. In referenda in May and November 2005, the business community supported
the change to mayor–council government, but the minority communities strongly
opposed the conversion, and change was defeated.

Like some other boss-led cities in the early decades of the twentieth century, Cincinnati adopted council–manager government in 1924 in response to the calls of the Progressive reformers. As John T. Spence observes, white flight to the suburbs contributed
to the loss of more than two hundred thousand in population in the post–World War
II period, and the business community in Cincinnati had lost much of its clout to
neighborhood interests. A change to the strong mayor–council form was rejected by
voters in 1995. In 1998, the Build Cincinnati committee sponsored a referendum to
create a "stronger mayor"—a leading example of the effort to empower council–
manager mayors. This proposal was accepted and went in effect in 2001.

## Change from Mayor–Council to Council–Manager

Contrary to the shift away from the council–manager form since 1990, El Paso and
Topeka have switched from mayor–council to this form in recent years, as did Cedar
Rapids, Iowa. It appears that no cities have rejected the move to the council–manager
form during this period, although Miami–Dade County did not approve the form in
2007.

Larry Terry explores the change in form from mayor–council to council–manager
in El Paso, Texas, a city of more than one-half million residents on the Mexican border.
For more than a century, the city's political life was characterized by ineffective and
inefficient city government with periods of corruption and episodes of partisan and
ethnic violence. Multiple sources of dissatisfaction, support for charter change from the
mayor and business elites, and inaction by the majority Mexican American community
led to charter change in the 2004 referendum.

Topeka, Kansas, also converted to the council–manager form as a result of a referendum in 2004. Advocates of council–manager government had sought change for nearly
eight decades, but Topeka voters rejected the form in referenda in 1929, 1952, 1962,
1964, and 1969. In 1998 pro-council–manager city councilors blocked a strengthening
of the mayor's powers and began to push for a change in form. Paul Battaglio indicates
that after initial resistance that continued to block change, problems in the mayor's
office and a scandal in the city's purchasing card system led to acceptance of change to
council–manager government.

### Rejecting the Strong Mayor to Retain Other Forms

In addition to the cases that pitted the mayor–council and council–manager form
against each other, two other cases involve the preservation of less mainstream structures and the rejection of the strong-mayor–council form, although the choice to some
extent reflected the refusal to accept the council–manager option as well. Todd Swanstrom, Robert Cropf, and William Krummenacher examine an effort rejected by voters

in St. Louis in 2004 to strengthen the powers of the mayor, reduce the size of the governing body and the number of other elected officials, and broaden civil service protection. In 2003 Civic Progress, an organization composed of leaders of the thirty largest corporations in St. Louis, formed Advance St. Louis to review and revise the city's charter. Despite extensive support from the business establishment, the political establishment especially in the African American community opposed change and defeated the referendum.

Unlike the other large cities discussed in this book, Portland, Oregon, is governed under the commission form of local government. While the commission form has continually lost favor across the country, Portland voters have rejected efforts to change it on eight occasions since its adoption in 1913. In 2002, through the initiative process, a group of citizens called for consideration of a strong mayor once again without success, and in 2007 a Charter Review Commission recommended the mayor–council form with a strengthened CAO. It too was resoundingly rejected. Doug Morgan, Masami Nishishiba, and Dan Vizzini examine what is distinctive about the commission form used in Portland and about the city itself that keeps Portland as the only very large city using this form of government.

The analysis of the case studies presented in the concluding chapter compares the factors involved in efforts to change charters in these fourteen cities. We examine whether the potential arguments that can be used to support or attack each form of government are actually used and how they are related to the outcome of the referendum. We also examine other claims that have arisen in referenda campaigns as well as the city-specific factors that affected the referendum results. Finally, we consider whether the constitutional content of these contests over form has been adequately developed.

## Notes

1. As Tsebelis (1995) argues about governmental structures generally, when there are two or more "veto players"—president and Congress or mayor and council—whose approval is needed to secure change, the bureaucracy is subject to less control than when there is a single veto player, as in parliamentary systems or the quasi-parliamentary council–manager form.

2. The Model City Charter—once the compilation of the orthodox reform package—accepted district elections as an option starting in 1964, and in 1973 the International City/County Management Association (ICMA) dropped its previous position of advocating at-large elections as part of the reform plan (Svara 1994).

3. There is not necessarily a short-term change in governmental outputs. Morgan and Pelissero (1980) and Ruhil (2003) find that change in form makes little difference in city budgets. Benton (2003) finds that the change is linked to higher spending budgets in counties, but Morgan and Kickman (1999) find no difference in revenue and expenditure policies.

4. In 1922 two speakers at the city managers' annual meeting debated the question "Is City Manager Government Applicable to Our Largest Cities?"

5. The International City/County Management Association tracks referenda that are held on form of government. Its data include 26 cities that adopted the council–manager form, 18 that rejected it, 72 that retained the form, and 21 cities that abandoned it from 1990 through

2008. The total number of cities with over 5,000 in population is 4,838. Form can be changed through council or legislative action as well as through referenda.

6. At the same time in November 2009, Pueblo voters rejected eliminating the council president chosen within the council and replacing this seat on the council with a directly elected mayor.

7. In addition, St. Louis, Missouri, rejected a proposal to eliminate certain county offices from its charter.

# References

Adrian, C. R. 1988. Forms of city government in American history. In *Municipal year book 1988*. Washington, DC: International City Management Association.

Alford, R. R., and H. M. Scoble. 1965. Political and socioeconomic characteristics of American cities. In *Municipal year book 1965*, eds. O. F. Nolting and D. S. Arnold. Chicago: International City Managers Association.

Anderson, E. 1989. Two major forms of government: Two types of professional management. In *Municipal year book*. Washington, DC: International City/County Management Association.

Banfield, E. C., and J. Q. Wilson. 1963. *City politics*. New York: Vintage Books.

Benton, J. E. 2003. The impact of structural reform on county government service provision. *Social Science Quarterly* 84, no. 4 (December): 858–74.

Box, R. C. 1992. The administrator as trustee of the public interest: Normative ideals and daily practice. *Administration & Society* 24, no. 3 (November): 323–46.

———. 1995. Searching for the best structure for American local government. *International Journal of Public Administration* 18, no. 4:711–41.

Broder, David S. 2000. *Democracy derailed: Initiative campaigns and the power of money*. New York: Harcourt, Inc.

Browning, Rufus P., Dale Rogers Marshall, and David H. Tabb. 1984. *Protest is not enough*. Berkeley: University of California Press.

Dahl, Robert A. 1961. *Who governs?* New Haven, CT: Yale University Press.

DeSantis, V. S., and T. Renner. 2002. City government structures: An attempt at clarification. In *The future of local government administration: The Hansell Symposium*, eds. H. George Frederickson and John Nalbandian. Washington, DC: International City/County Management Association.

Dreier, Peter, John Mollenkopf, and Todd Swanstrom. 2004. *Place matters: Metropolitics for the twenty-first century*, 2nd ed., revised. Lawrence: University Press of Kansas.

Ehrenhalt, A. 2004. The mayor–manager conundrum. *Governing Magazine*, October. www.governing.com/archive/2004/oct/assess.txt (accessed June 2008).

Fannin, W. R. 1983. City manager policy roles as a source of city council/city manager conflict. *International Journal of Public Administration* 5, no. 4: 381–99.

Farnham, P. G., and S. N. Bryant. 1985. Form of local government: Structural policies of citizen choice. *Social Science Quarterly* 66, no. 2 (June): 386–400.

Ferman, Barbara. 1985. *Governing the ungovernable city*. Philadelphia: Temple University Press.

Frederickson, H. G., G. A. Johnson, and C. Wood. 2004. *The adapted city: Institutional dynamics and structural change*. Armonk, NY: M. E. Sharpe.

Gurwitt, R. 1993. The lure of the strong mayor. *Governing* 6, no. 10: 36–41.

Hansell, B. 1993. Director's desk. *Public Management* 75, no. 7: 19–21.

Hassett, W., and D. Watson. 2007. *Civic battles: When cities change their form of government.* Boca Raton, FL: PrAcademics Press.

Henry, N. 1975. Paradigms of public administration. *Public Administration Review* 35, no. 4 (July/August): 376–86.

Highsaw, R. B. 1949. City and county manager plans in the South. *The Journal of Politics* 11, no. 3 (August): 497–517.

Keene, J., J. Nalbandian, R. O'Neill Jr., S. Portillo, and J. Svara. 2007. How professionals add value to their communities and organizations. *PM* 89, no. 2 (March): 32–39.

Kim, J. 1997. *Changes in municipal governmental forms and their impact on local government policy outputs: Theory, evidence, and implications.* PhD diss., Cleveland State Univ.

Lineberry, R. L., and E. P. Fowler. 1967. Reformism and public policies in American cities. *American Political Science Review* 61, no. 3 (September): 701–17.

Lyons, W. 1978. Reform and response in American cities: Structure and policy reconsidered. *Social Science Quarterly* 59, no. 1 (June): 118–32.

MacAvoy, P.W., and I. Millstein. 2004. *The recurrent crisis in corporate governance.* Stanford: Stanford University Press.

MacManus, S. A., and C. S. Bullock. 2003. The form, structure, and composition of American municipalities in the new millennium. In *Municipal year book 2003.* Washington, DC: International City/County Management Association.

Montjoy, R. S., and D. J. Watson.1993. Within region variation in acceptance of council–manager government: Alabama and the Southeast. *State and Local Government Review* 25, no. 1 (Winter): 19–27.

———. 1995. A case for reinterpreted dichotomy of politics and administration as a professional standard in council–manager government. *Public Administration Review* 55, no. 3 (May/June): 231–39.

Morgan, D. R., and K. Kickham. 1999. Changing the county form of government: Effects on revenue and expenditure policy. *Public Administration Review* 59, no. 4 (July/August): 315–24.

Morgan, D. R., and J. P. Pelissero. 1980. Urban policy: Does political structure matter? *The American Political Science Review* 74, no. 4 (December): 999–1006.

Mouritzen, Poul Erik, and James H. Svara. 2002. *Leadership at the apex: Politicians and administrators in Western local governments.* Pittsburgh: University of Pittsburgh Press.

Nalbandian, J. 1990. Tenets of contemporary professionalism in local government. *Public Administration Review* 50 (6): 654–62.

Nelson, K. L., and J. H. Svara. 2010. Adaptation of models versus variations in form: Classifying structures of city government. *Urban Affairs Review* (forthcoming).

Newland, Chester A. 1985. Council–manager governance: Positive alternative to separation of powers. *Public Management* 67, no. 1 (July): 7–9.

Nollenberger, K. 2008. Cooperation and conflict in governmental decision making in mid-sized U.S. cities. In *Municipal year book 2008.* Washington: International City/County Management Association.

O'Neill, R. B., Jr. 2005. The conundrum that wasn't. *Governing Magazine*, March. www.governing.com/archive/2005/mar/letters.txt (accessed December 2008).

Parrish, C. T., and M. Frisby 1996. Don't let FOG* issues cloud community's horizon: Models of retention and abandonment. *Public Management* 78, no. 5 (May): 6–12.

Pressman, Jeffrey L. 1972. Preconditions of mayoral leadership. *American Political Science Review* 66, no. 2 (June): 511–24.

Protasel, G. J. 1988. Abandonments of the council–manager plan: A new institutionalist perspective. *Public Administration Review* 48, no. 4 (July/August): 807–12.

Ruhil, A. V. S. 1999. *Explorations in twentieth-century municipal government: The case of civil service commissions and forms of government.* PhD diss., State University of New York at Stony Brook.

———. 2003. Structural change and fiscal flaws: A framework for analyzing the effects of urban events. *Urban Affairs Review* 38 (January): 396–416.

Simmons, J. 2001. Whither local government reform? The case of Wisconsin. *National Civic Review* 90, no.1 (Spring): 45–62.

Simmons, J. R., and S. J. Simmons. 2002. Structural conflict in contemporary cities. A paper presented at the Midwest Political Science Association Conference in Chicago, Illinois. April 25–28.

Svara, J. H. 1977. Unwrapping institutional packages in urban government: The combination of election institutions in American cities. *Journal of Politics* 39, no. 1 (February): 166–75.

———. 1990. *Official leadership in the city: Patterns of conflict and cooperation.* New York: Oxford University Press.

———. 1994. Facilitative leadership in local government: Lessons from successful mayors and chairpersons in the council–manager form. San Francisco: Jossey-Bass.

———. 1999. The shifting boundary between elected officials and city managers in large council–manager cities. *Public Administration Review* 59, no. 1 (January/February): 44–53.

———. 2001. Do we still need model charters? The meaning and relevance of reform in the twenty-first century. *National Civic Review* 90, no. 1 (Spring): 19–33.

———. 2003. Two decades of continuity and change in American City Councils. Washington, DC: National League of Cities, 2003. www.nlc.org/ASSETS/AED3E653151A49D6BF0 B975C581EFD30/rmpcitycouncilrpt.pdf (accessed August 2008).

———. 2008. *The facilitative leader in city hall: Reexamining the scope and contributions.* Boca Raton, FL: CRC Press.

Svara, J. H., and K. Nelson. 2008. Taking stock of the council–manager form at 100. *PM* 90, no. 7 (August): 6–14.

Talbot, Allan. 1967. *The mayor's game.* New York: Harper & Row.

Tsebelis, G. 1995. Decision making in political systems: Veto players in presidentialism, parliamentarism, multicameralism and multipartyism. *British Journal of Political Science* 25, no. 3 (July): 289–325.

Welch, S., and T. Bledsoe. 1986. The partisan consequences of nonpartisan elections and the changing nature of urban politics. *American Journal of Political Science* 30, no. 1 (February): 128–39.

Wolfinger, R. E., and J. O. Field. 1966. Political ethos and the structure of city government. *American Political Science Review* 60, no. 2 (June): 306–26.

# PART I

# CHANGE FROM COUNCIL–MANAGER TO MAYOR–COUNCIL FORM

CHAPTER 2

# ST. PETERSBURG

## Easing into a Strong-Mayor Government

J. EDWIN BENTON, DONALD C. MENZEL AND DARRYL PAULSON

## Introduction

ST. PETERSBURG, FLORIDA (population of 260,000 in 2008), located on Florida's gulf coast, is a relatively new city, only a little over one hundred years old. It was incorporated as a town in 1893 and then as a city in 1903. Like the rest of Florida, St. Petersburg experienced phenomenal growth beginning in the 1930s. Due to the area's warm climate, beautiful beaches, cheap land, relatively low cost of living, low local taxes, no state income tax, and laid-back lifestyle, St. Petersburg quickly became a point of destination for retirees and tourists. But it was the massive waves of retired people (mainly from the Midwest) who migrated to St. Petersburg that drove the city's and area's economy. In spite of attracting some light industry (companies like Sperry Rand, General Electric, and Honeywell that had defense-related contracts), the city's development remained heavily tied to preferences and needs of a large senior citizen population.

Beginning in the 1970s the city population began to stagnate, whereas the population of Pinellas County, in which the city is located, and Florida continued to grow unabated. Also, there was a conspicuous graying of the city's population. By 1990 the median age of all St. Petersburg was 45.8 years, but in the downtown area it was 73 years (44.9 percent of the population in the same downtown was over 75 years old). Moreover, the central city elderly were dying and being replaced by younger people with families and not necessarily more retirees. Subsequently this precipitated a movement to change the image of St. Petersburg from "God's waiting room" to a younger, more vibrant community. As part of this movement, civic and governmental leaders set out on a quest to redevelop the downtown area to become a major league baseball city. Battle lines were quickly drawn between pro-development and antidevelopment groups, and ultimately, the capability of the government to mediate these schisms was called into question. By 1993 these events and the unresponsiveness of city hall to citizens' desire to slow down the relentless and expensive redevelopment efforts prompted a change in the form of government from a council–manager to a strong-mayor type.

We present a chronological accounting and discussion of the factors that persuaded community stakeholders and residents that a change in government structure was necessary. This is followed by a description of the new form of government that was adopted in March 1993. Then we examine how the city's structural changes have resulted in the achievement of the goals advocated by reformers and "good government" groups.

## Background of Change in Form of Government

Given its rapid growth rate, medium-sized population, and the public's desire for the city to employ more business-like principles into day-to-day operations, it was not surprising that the city's residents adopted the council–manager government in 1931, after having a mayor–council structure since the city's incorporation. And, from 1931 to 1993, the operation of the City of St. Petersburg embodied nearly all of the ideas of reform government. By the 1970s, however, the adequacy of the council–manager structure of government began to be questioned as city hall increasingly became unresponsive to the policy preferences and needs of the citizenry.

### Council–Manager Government

The council–manager government adopted in 1931 as part and parcel of the new city charter contained many of the usual reform features. Eight council members were chosen in a nonpartisan process, with nominations being decided by district and elections being conducted on an at-large basis. The mayor, who served as the ninth member of the city council, was also elected at large in a nonpartisan contest. Although the mayor was expected to play a purely ceremonial role, several mayors (especially Robert Ulrich and David Fischer in the late 1980s and early 1990s) made the office into more than a symbolic one. The council functioned as the legislative body and hired a manager to serve as the chief administrative officer and run the city on a day-to-day basis. However, the city's charter also featured some variations from the prototypical reform package. For instance, the ability of citizens to exercise the referendum and recall options was more restricted than in the usual reform package. In addition, the city charter prohibited referenda and initiatives on capital improvement projects until 1988, and state constitutional procedural limits on the recall process made the recall an almost meaningless measure.[1] In short those elements of a reform package that are usually designed to ensure a degree of responsiveness by public officials were missing.

### Demographics and the Social Setting

As noted above, the development of St. Petersburg historically was dictated in large measure by the dominant—mainly white—senior citizen population that was concentrated mostly in a ninety-block area in the downtown (central) area (see figure 2.1).

Several factors account for most senior citizens continuing to live in this area. First, property owners created low-rent apartments for retirees from the large homes built in the 1920s or erected tiny efficiency apartments over existing garages, while public-and church-sponsored high-rise housing projects for the elderly were built downtown (Rigos and Paulson 1996). Second, the downtown neighborhoods area, which had always been the location of social clubs, dances, and sports activities that catered to senior citizens, was the site for a public multiservice senior center built in the late 1970s (Rigos and Paulson 1996). In addition, the downtown featured many cafeterias, thrift shops, and dime stores that served an older clientele. Finally, the social and economic transactions of senior citizens, out of necessity, usually were limited to downtown neighborhoods, since many elderly residents did not have private transportation.

African Americans constituted 19.4 percent of the city's population in 1990 and historically had been confined to the Methodist Town and Gas Plant sections of St. Petersburg. This was the result of the 1931 city charter that established a goal of setting apart "separate residential limits or districts for white and Negro residents" (Arsenault 1988, 265). These neighborhoods were located, literally, on the other side of a set of railroad tracks that bisected First Avenue South about a mile west of the main business district. By the 1960s younger African Americans, however, began to move from the vicinity of First Avenue South and Central Avenue to the southern sections of the city.

Meanwhile, younger whites and the more well-to-do elderly built homes away from downtown, while most of the major light industrial companies that the city attracted during the 1950s and 1960s also located in the outer portions of the city. As in other parts of the country, mobile younger residents began to shop in suburban malls rather than patronize downtown stores. And a new generation of tourists was more captivated by the beaches of the Gulf of Mexico than by the wide verandas and formal dining rooms of downtown St. Petersburg (Rigos and Paulson 1996).

The resultant deterioration of downtown St. Petersburg and the economic and racial segregation of the city portended the formation of several movements to redevelop the downtown area and a ratcheting up of racial tensions.

## Development Movements: Political Actors and Coalitions

Development supporters consisted of the leading newspaper in the Tampa Bay area (*St. Petersburg Times*), the St. Petersburg Chamber of Commerce, Florida Power and Light, key owners of downtown real estate, and most major banks. Downtown business interests were especially well represented by St. Petersburg Progress, a private, nonprofit advisory group of about seventy-five downtown businesses led by Florida Power and Light. The more or less agreeable attitude of the African American community, parts of which would be required to relocate, can be viewed as a type of support. African American elites believed that the black community would be rewarded by city officials if they became part of the development coalition (Rigos and Paulson 1996).

Another driving force in development efforts was found within city government. Almost all of the city's elected officials as well as most of the city's bureaucracy endorsed

the city's development ideas. Especially strong support was found within the city's
housing and planning departments, which were staffed with young, well-trained professionals excitedly hoping to duplicate the northern urban renewal scenario with a different conclusion (Jreisat 1987). There was a genuine concern among some administrators
that the tax base was eroding at the same time that service needs remained constant. In
fact, many believed that the tax rate would increase if redevelopment was not pursued.
A case in point is Miami Beach, another renowned retirement community, which by
1985 had a tax rate well above the Florida tax limitation of 1 percent of property value
(State of Florida, Office of Comptroller 1987).[2]

The role played by the *St. Petersburg Times* was a familiar one that is seen in many
nonpartisan cities where newspaper endorsements can make a major difference in local
elections and influence citizen views on issues. During the 1980s, only two candidates
were elected to the city council without the backing of the *Times*. The *Times* was an
enthusiastic supporter of revitalization and of the pursuit of a major league baseball
(MLB) franchise. One of the *Times*'s executives was an ardent supporter of the stadium
idea and of its downtown location.

Development opponents included elderly residents who wanted to maintain low
taxes, preservationists who wished to preserve historic buildings, and neighborhood
activists who aimed to prevent the commercialization of St. Petersburg's open waterfront. Two groups—Save Our St. Petersburg (SOS) and the Council of Neighborhood
Associations (CONA)—directed the neighborhood opposition to redevelopment
efforts. Within SOS, leaders like Connie Kone, Tim Clemons, and Ray Arsenault and
a number of young local architects led the fight by talking with the *St. Petersburg
Times*'s editorial board, testifying before the city council, engaging in demonstrations
and picketing, and even meeting with the authors of the Means Report (Thomas and
Means 1988).[3]

The clashes that occurred between pro-development and antidevelopment groups
from the early 1960s until 1993 when the citizens of St. Petersburg adopted a strong-
mayor–council form of government can be divided into four phases: predevelopment,
development planning, development implementation phase I, development implementation phase II.

## Predevelopment Phase (1960–79)

Efforts to revitalize downtown St. Petersburg were initiated in the early 1960s with the
start-up of urban renewal projects. As is typically the case in declining central cities,
these projects produced conflict between the business community and older residents.
One can identify the unpopular decision by the city council in 1961 to remove several
thousand green benches from city sidewalks as the first shot being fired in a long,
protracted battle between these two sides. This removal, which was completed in 1969,
marked the beginning of the city government's new direction. According to one close
observer (Vesperi 1985), it signified the beginning of the city's estrangement from
its own social base (i.e., senior citizens) and the embittered polarization between key
constituent groups and the city.

After a decade of growing unrest and increasing insensitivity to older residents, the city council in 1972 created a formal procedure to answer the criticism that citizen input had been neglected and reformulate a more responsive image of city government. This mechanism, known as the Citizens Goal Process, however, appeared to be more of a symbolic gesture to pacify complainants rather than a meaningful process designed to seriously address concerns of the citizenry. For example, meetings to field complaints were held at the discretion of the city council and were not a requirement for decision making. Ironically, the first time that this participatory mechanism was used, it resulted in the endorsement of downtown revitalization as a major city objective.

The city government during this period was unquestionably under the strong influence of the city manager. City Manager Raymond Harbaugh, whose near-decade-long tenure gave him more stature than the usual manager, along with three deputy managers, controlled a well-oiled administrative machine (Rigos and Paulson 1996). Harbaugh subsequently left his job in 1979, six months after an unsuccessful effort was made by disgruntled council members to fire him over the city's purchase of a hotel that was targeted for demolition. He was succeeded by the younger, charismatic Alan Harvey who introduced a number of business-like operations to the city. Consequently, the city administration began to take on more of an image of progressiveness, responsiveness, effectiveness, integrity, youth, and vitality. More than anything else, Harvey had a strong desire to revitalize downtown St. Petersburg (Rigos and Paulson 1996). Throughout the 1970s the city's administrative structure and operations were impressive to outsiders and the epitome of a modern professional and responsive government. Citizen satisfaction surveys and productivity measurements were so impressive that they were the subject of professional journal articles and monographs (see Hatry 1974).

## Development Planning Phase (1980–87)

With the foundation firmly laid, the city was ready to move decisively ahead with redevelopment by the early 1980s. The city embarked on the Intown Redevelopment Plan in 1982, which targeted decaying areas and created a tax-increment financing (TIF) district for the downtown. In 1984, city voters were asked to approve an ambitious $72 million entertainment complex project called Pier Park. This proposed festival marketplace project had the support of the city council, chamber of commerce, the *Times*, and the local NAACP. Opponents, led by Charles Schuh and members of Save Our Waterfront, were adamant about not wanting the commercial development of the waterfront. Voters rejected the Pier Park project by a two-to-one margin. Nonetheless, the city, without voter approval, embarked on a $12.5 million facelift of Pier Park and $25 million renovation of the Bayfront Center and Mahaffey Theater. These bold actions were followed by a push for a $138 million Suncoast Dome (now called Tropicana Field and home to the Tampa Bay Rays professional baseball team) and a $200 million Bay Plaza project.

The 1980s municipal elections produced a solid pro-development coalition on city council that further reinforced Harvey's "cowboy" image, a label given to him by the

*St. Petersburg Times* (Dahl 1985). In fact, Harvey's "make it happen" management style five and a half years later ensnared him in a web of development politics and conflict of interest accusations. In September 1985 Harvey was forced out after the city council sitting as the Ethics Committee learned that he had invested $8,000 (equivalent to $16,000 in 2008) in a downtown office complex that would profit if the deal with the city to purchase a city-owned parking garage next door was consummated. In describing Harvey's fall from grace and how he got caught up in this breach of ethics, the *Times* states that "He got carried away with his sense of power in the community. . . . He thought he was a power broker [referring to the business leaders] just like them" (Maddox 1985). This observation clearly signals the drift toward a super strong executive nine years before one is provided for in the new form of government that was adopted in March 1993. Subsequently, Harvey was succeeded by his chief lieutenant, Robert Obering, who was described as a mild-mannered man in a business suit that conscientiously continued to follow council cues and sought to manage the city's complex and ambitious projects (Olinger 1991).

Efforts to slow the pro-development movement gained momentum in the mid-1980s. The fact that voters were denied the right to vote on these massive and costly revitalization projects produced tremendous resentment, and subsequently, led to a strong voter backlash. Ed Cole, a staunch opponent of the stadium and downtown plans, was elected mayor in January 1986. At the time, his election could have been interpreted as a citywide vote against development and the stadium plans (Rigos and Paulson 1996). In July of that same year, a movement to recall three city council members was initiated. The justification for the recall was misfeasance of office for supporting the development projects and the consecutive property tax increases of 22 percent and 13 percent. In the end, the recall effort failed to survive the complex Florida recall process, in spite of the fact that 56 percent of the voters approved (Tobin 1988). Throughout these challenges, however, the development coalition and rhetoric prevailed and continued to push for redevelopment of the downtown and a stadium (Rigos and Paulson 1996).

The stadium politics, especially the site-selection process, were very controversial from the outset. After considering several possible sites and faced with land costs up to $40,000 per acre, the city offered a sixty-six-acre site known as the Gas Plant area for $1.00 per year (Snajderman and Hill 1991). This created a rift between the city and the predominantly black, poor residents of the area. In 1970 the city decided to use Community Development Block Grant (CDBG) funds to raze houses, relocate the residents, and create a new industrial park. In return for the willingness of residents to agree to this plan, the city promised them a fair share of jobs from the proposed industrial park. When industrial prospects for the park were not forthcoming, the city manager persuaded the city council to offer the Gas Plant site for the stadium. When questioned by the black community and the NAACP, the city leaders were unapologetic in proclaiming that the city's redevelopment plans were a greater priority and that it was willing to pay all sorts of political costs and take large risks to make sure that the stadium project was part and parcel of its downtown strategy (Rigos and Paulson 1996).

In retrospect, placing the stadium in the Gas Plant area in downtown St. Petersburg was a politically unwise decision with huge repercussions. First, it virtually eliminated all hope of an early metropolitan consensus for the pursuit of a major league baseball team. Second, Pinellas County unsuccessfully attempted to break its financial commitment to partner with the city to pay for the stadium. In addition, this precipitated a baseball war across Tampa Bay in Tampa, where the Tampa Bay Sports Authority reacted by deciding to pursue a major league franchise on its own.

A few months later and amid the controversy swirling around the stadium issue and with clear indications of growing opposition from the electorate to downtown redevelopment, the development coalition on the city council relentlessly pushed ahead. After residents voted down the Pier Park project, the council came up with an alternative public/private venture. They moved swiftly and requested the city manager to solicit proposals for a master developer who would redevelop an area stretching ten blocks from Tampa Bay to the newly constructed stadium (later to be called Bay Plaza). The project would connect Pier Park, the city's main tourist attraction, with the newly refurbished Bayfront Center, consisting of an arena, a performing arts facility, and the stadium. The plan featured upscale shops, and success of the project hinged on attracting three upscale tenants such as Saks, Bonwit-Teller, and Neiman-Marcus.

Ominous signs appeared from the beginning. First, consultants questioned whether the Tampa Bay area, with a per capita income below the national metropolitan average, could support such an expensive project (Rigos and Paulson 1996). Second, only one company (the Bay Plaza Development Group) submitted a proposal, and rather than interpreting the interest of only one developer as a negative sign about the viability of the project, the city stubbornly plowed ahead and awarded the contract to the sole applicant (Selz 1989). Under terms of the agreement, Bay Plaza would manage Pier Park, the Bayfront Center, and the stadium and would control the redevelopment. Estimated to cost $200 million, St. Petersburg was responsible for $40 million of the costs and the developer would finance the remainder (Thomas and Means 1988). The project was to proceed in three phases; however, the venture would turn out to be a ten-year fiasco.

## Development Implementation Phase I (1989–91)

Neither the Pier Park two-to-one vote nor the recall efforts, nor even scathing criticism from a larger segment of the public, discouraged the development forces. They continued to press on. By early 1989, the battle lines over redevelopment had been clearly drawn and were played out in the March mayoral election between Dennis McDonald, the leader of the recall movement, and downtown attorney Robert Ulrich, and there was no backtracking. With construction already started on the stadium, it is likely that citizens went to the voting booth wondering whether a vote for McDonald would produce an even worse financial crisis with bonding agencies (Rigos and Paulson 1996). This concern resulted from McDonald's plan to mothball the stadium until a baseball franchise was awarded. Also on the ballot in the March 1989 mayoral election was a citizen-initiated referenda item to change the city charter to require the city to seek voters' approval via referenda of future capital projects. This item was placed on the ballot by the efforts of a group known as CHOICE whose members were unhappy with the fact that the city was able to move forward with the stadium without first seeking voter approval. The initiative was approved with 78 percent voting for it, and Ulrich narrowly defeated McDonald.

From the beginning, development proponents believed that their best opportunity to get one of the two National League expansion teams to be awarded in 1991 by MLB was to have a stadium in place. This was in spite of the fact that MLB had cautioned the city on more than one occasion that the building of a stadium would not guarantee that they would get a franchise. In 1989 there was still optimism that the financial risk the city was taking to build a stadium first would pay off when a franchise was awarded. Upon taking office Ulrich hit the ground running and forged ahead with efforts to land a franchise while greatly expanding the visibility and role played by the mayor in city politics. Previous mayors always played a secondary role, with the council and manager wielding greater influence and power. Ulrich proved to be the exception. He negotiated with Tampa's strong mayor, Sandy Freedman, with the result being the formation of a united front that they believed could not be ignored by MLB. In the words of two close observers: "The achieved unity of the two parts of Tampa Bay gave glitter to the mayoralty" while Ulrich's accession to power marked a period of mayoral supremacy (Rigos and Paulson 1996, 254). Meanwhile, development leaders, more confident than ever about the prospects of being awarded an expansion franchise, began to remind everyone of the wisdom of their aggressive stance for the Gas Plant site. Not surprisingly, these leaders and many city residents were shocked when the city was not awarded one of the franchises. Shock was followed by disbelief when city leaders failed to convince the San Francisco Giants to relocate to St. Petersburg.

At the same time, the Bay Plaza project began to encounter problems. The developers were unable to attract an anchor tenant for the first phase of the project, in spite of continuing reassurances to local officials and the media that the signing of an anchor was imminent. With diminishing hopes of getting a commitment from an upscale anchor tenant, the developers and local leaders sought to convince mall-type chain stores such as J. C. Penney, Belk, and Maas Brothers to locate in the unoccupied first-phase building. These companies, however, showed no interest as they were already in the process of closing their old downtown stores. From that point, lower-end companies such as Walmart and Kmart were unsuccessfully approached and, as a last resort, discussions even turned to opening the first phase as a site for outlet stores—a very different option from the upscale stores and shops originally planned. In 1996, the Bay Plaza developers abandoned their venture never having secured a tenant or ever constructing any buildings on the project site. In addition, a parking garage, which was built as part of the first phase of Bay Plaza and was supposed to be self-sufficient whether the retail stores opened or not, incurred enormous operating deficits. Moreover, it became necessary for the city to begin subsidizing operating expenses at Pier Park at $1.4 million per year, with another $1 million going to the Bayfront Center and about $2 million to the stadium. The city continues to subsidize the operation of these facilities today.

Other problems loomed. The city's tax rate was nearing the state-mandated 10 mill (one-tenth of a cent per dollar of assessed property value) cap on property taxes and bonded indebtedness had skyrocketed. City debt shot up from $117 million to $261 million—or by $145 million—in a little over one year (Olinger 1987). Total debt payments due in the next thirty years jumped from $226 million in 1985 to $590 million the following year (Olinger 1987). To make matters worse, city officials had grossly overestimated economic activity in their tax-increment financing district. In 1985, officials had projected that downtown property values would reach $497.3 million by 1990, when they were actually valued at $260.4 million, or barely one-half the original estimate (Rigos and Paulson 1996). Moreover, property values in the TIF district dropped sharply from $276 million in 1988 to $260.4 million in 1990, a decrease of 7.7 percent (Rigos and Paulson 1996). These erroneous predictions forced the city to transfer approximately $1 million from parking revenues over the next two years to cover bond debt (Rigos and Paulson 1996). The city immediately imposed a hiring freeze. The city also faced the prospect of having to raise property tax rates, because declining property values in the central business district in the 1989–93 period meant that tax assessments would be lower and subsequently produce less property tax revenue. More specifically, the total assessed value of eight of the nine prime buildings in downtown St. Petersburg dropped 30 percent from 1981 to 1991 (Shaw 1991). Originally assessed at $100 million in 1987, the 1991 assessed value plummeted to $70.3 million in the face of 40 percent vacancy rates (Shaw 1991).

### Development Implementation Phase II (1991–93)

The 1991 city elections marked a turning point in St. Petersburg history. For the first time, a majority of the council members were pro-neighborhood and opposed continued funding of the downtown. Of special note was the fact that two past leaders of CONA (Connie Kone and Paul Yingst) joined the council and replaced pro-development council members. Mayor Ulrich, facing a hostile electorate, decided to not seek reelection.[4] The new mayor, David Fischer, a retired municipal consultant, and the newly elected members of the council who ran on the pledge to stop pumping money into downtown revitalization and provide more funds for all of the city's neighborhoods, took office. As the events surrounding development efforts in St. Petersburg from the early 1960s to 1991 illustrate, the true costs of development usually do not come to light until the implementation stage arrives, and by that time, the political actors responsible for the early initial decisions have made their exit. This scenario is consistent with the experiences of other cities that have attempted massive redevelopment projects (Stone 1987).

Two other events occurred in 1991 that affected the city's development policies and contributed to a growing concern about the city's leadership. In June 1991 MLB officials announced that two new franchises would be located in Miami and Denver. This meant that the city was stuck with a stadium (dubbed a white elephant) that ended up costing $200 million and now had no baseball team. Several months after receiving the bad news about not being awarding a MLB franchise, City Manager Robert Obering's six-year tenure ended when a grand jury was convened to investigate what became known as the Fotomat scandal amid allegations that the city had covered up the proposed sale of the city's municipal services building for $2.5 million in 1982 to two businessmen hoping to profit from downtown development plans (Olinger 1991). Several years afterwards, the developers contended that they had offered the city $4 million for the building. This could not be verified since the written offer had been destroyed, and city officials, including former City Manager Harvey, claimed that they did not recall a higher offer. The grand jury, while finding that the allegations were substantially true, did not indict anyone but the report concluded that "the city had selectively destroyed records pertaining to the sale" (Olinger 1991). The concealment of the higher offer by Harvey and Obering was also criticized by the grand jury. Obering's credibility was in tatters as he denied that a deal had ever been struck. He resigned four days after the report was released.

## The Straw That Broke the Camel's Back

By the middle of 1991, citizen discontent and disaffection with city hall mounted daily as revitalization efforts seemed to take on the appearance of a boondoggle and property taxes and city debt escalated to record levels. However, the last straw grew out of a situation with racial overtones involving the acting city manager Donald McRae and the newly hired police chief Ernest (Curt) Curtsinger. After Obering's resignation, McRae, an African American, fired Curtsinger, who is white, for racial insensitivity and insubordination. While housing issues had from time to time evoked the ugly image of racism, the firing of the police chief brought out a degree of racial polarization not seen in St. Petersburg since Jim Crow days (Rigos and Paulson 1996).

Curtsinger, a no-nonsense, tough law-and-order cop who came up through the ranks of the Los Angeles police department, was very popular among white, middle-class, conservative residents of the city. Within a few days thousands of St. Petersburg residents signed a petition calling for the rehiring of Curtsinger and removing the authority of the manager to fire the chief. There was even considerable frustration among a majority of the members of the city council, who, while decidedly unhappy with Curtsinger's firing, were nonetheless powerless to intervene because the city charter gave the manager unilateral authority to hire and fire department heads. In short, neither the council nor the mayor had the legal authority to reverse the manager's decision. The turmoil that ensued was momentarily defused as a result of a large financial settlement to the fired chief and his reinstatement to a different position in the city bureaucracy. This respite, however, did not last. Political and racial conflict intensified even more when Curtsinger decided to run for mayor in 1993, employing an "us versus city hall" campaign theme.

In the midst of this turmoil and mounting pressure from residents for a greater degree of responsiveness from city hall, the city council established a nineteen-person

Charter Review Commission in July 1992 to revisit the city charter and reassess whether the council–manager structure was still adequate. The overwhelming majority of the commission supported the retention of the council–manager structure but with some modifications. Specifically, there was a desire to decrease the authority of the manager and enhance the powers of the mayor and council. A former mayor, Don Jones, who addressed the commission as a witness, succinctly captured the shortcomings of the council–manager plan in St. Petersburg: "The city manager system has been particularly effective in periods when local government's priorities and objectives were building roads, sewers, utilities and other capital improvements . . . [and] has become increasingly inadequate as we have grown in size and sophistication as a city in dealing with the 'people needs' such as police protection, parks and recreation, and other 'people' or social programs that are a part of our city's daily life" (Jones 1992).

The remainder of the members of the commission (five to six) steadfastly believed that the council–manager system was broken and should be abandoned in favor of a strong-mayor–council form. It was argued that the proposal by the commission's majority to weaken the manager and strengthen the mayor was a "prescription for guaranteed paralysis," resulting in a new government that would create dual executives and confuse lines of authority (Paulson 1992). But perhaps the most vocal argument in support of a strong-mayor plan was that in head-to-head competition with Tampa and its strong mayor, St. Petersburg had lost numerous battles such as where the University of South Florida would be located, where the airport for the Tampa Bay area would be built, and who would get professional football and hockey teams. But even this argument was not enough to dislodge the belief among the majority that the council–manager plan could still be saved. Unable to convince a majority to endorse the strong-mayor plan, supporters initiated efforts to get the option on the March 23, 1993, ballot as a referenda item.

By the middle of the fall 1992, it appeared likely that voters in the March 23, 1993, election would be given two choices with respect to the city's form of government. First, per the recommendation of the remaining members of the commission (minus the six members who advocated the strong-mayor–council plan), voters would be able to opt for a reconfigured council–manager plan with less authority granted to the manager and enhanced roles for the council and mayor. Additionally, voters would be permitted to choose a strong-mayor–council system (Amendment 5). Sentiments ran high, and the strong-mayor option survived several court challenges over the next few months, although the organizers of the petition drive to get it on the ballot were able to secure more than fifteen thousand signatures (only a little more than twelve thousand were required per the state constitution) in just a few weeks. Moreover, interest in the election was heightened as it also included the selection of the mayor where incumbent David Fischer faced the popular former police chief Ernest Curtsinger.

Turnout in the election was an amazing 53 percent of the eligible voters. Fischer barely defeated Curtsinger (51 percent to 49 percent) in what turned out to be one of the most brutally fought mayoral contests in St. Petersburg history, while voters narrowly approved (52.6 percent voting "yes") the strong-mayor–council system. Within one week of the election, the new strong-mayor–council system went into effect with

Fischer, albeit an incumbent mayor under the old council–manager plan, becoming the first strong mayor. What appeared to be an odd outcome of the election—election of a mayor who did not favor the strong-mayor–council system—could be explained logically. Supporters of a strong-mayor–council system were not willing to entrust the office of mayor with its greatly enhanced powers to someone who was racially insensitive and often displayed a belligerent and confrontational demeanor (Curtsinger), preferring the mild-manner and even-tempered David Fischer. Furthermore, those who supported retention of the council–manager plan probably felt less threatened by the strong-mayor plan with someone like Fischer occupying the office (Journey 1993).

## Structure of the New Government

As amended by the voters on March 23, 1993, the St. Petersburg city charter provides for a clear separation of powers between the executive (mayor) and legislative (council) branches of city government similar to what exists between the president and Congress at the national level. The council consists of eight members with one elected from each of the city's eight election districts. Elections are nonpartisan and held in November of odd-numbered years with four members who serve four-year terms elected every two years. Council members are limited to two consecutive terms. Like members of the council, the mayor is also elected on a nonpartisan ballot and can serve no more than two consecutive four-year terms.

The council is "the governing body of the City and has all legislative powers" vested in it. This means that all city ordinances as well as the budget must be approved by the council. The council must also approve all appointments made by the mayor and can override (two-thirds vote is required) vetoes of the mayor. In addition, the council is empowered to conduct special elections to fill vacancies in the office of mayor and replace any member of the council who is unable for whatever reason to fulfill his/her term of office.

The mayor is the chief administrative official of the city and is thereby "responsible for the administration of City affairs placed in the Mayor's charge by or under [the] city charter" and to "see that all laws, provisions of the charter, and actions of the council are faithfully executed." Compared with the mayor in the council–manager structure, the mayor has considerably more authority and responsibilities and clearly fits the mold of the prototypical strong mayor. This is evident in several areas. First, the mayor's managerial powers are extensive. He or she has the authority to dissolve, create, or reorganize units that pertain to the "administrative affairs of the City," suspend, demote, or remove all city employees without consulting the council, appoint, subject to council confirmation, several key administrative officers (e.g., city attorney, city clerk, and city administrator), and appoint members to all city boards and commission except the civil service board and charter review commission. In addition, the mayor has significant authority in fiscal matters, since she or he prepares and submits an annual budget and capital improvements plan for council consideration, since March 2003 can exercise the item veto on appropriation and revenue measures, and advises the council on the financial health and future needs of the city in an annual report. Third, the mayor has the opportunity to influence legislation enacted by the council through several venues, such as attending (or sending a representative to) council meetings and being permitted to take part in discussion (she/he cannot vote). Moreover, the mayor has the authority to negotiate and sign contracts and other agreements on behalf of the city.

The mayor is also given the power to appoint, subject to confirmation by the council, a city administrator. However, the mayor has unilateral authority to fire the administrator without consulting the council. According to the city charter, the city administrator is in charge of the daily operations of the city and is expected to have "relevant management, executive, or administrative experience in municipal government." It is noteworthy that, while charter framers recognized the need to retain professional management, they did not believe that educational achievement was a significant criterion for the selection of the city administrator. The framers, of course, certainly were in agreement about bolstering the powers of the mayor.

This arrangement is fully consistent with municipal trends over the past fifty years in the United States. Managerial expertise in local governance is widely accepted as a necessity, not a luxury. Political cities like administrative cities, write Frederickson, Johnson, and Wood (2004a, 2004b), have become adapted cities. In fact, these researchers contend that traditional mayor–council and council–manager cities that have adapted themselves to cope with the complexities of local governance are more alike than unalike.

## New Government in Action: What Changed/What Stayed the Same?

An examination of the operation of the new strong-mayor–council plan in St. Petersburg over the first fifteen years of its existence yields some interesting findings. But perhaps the most intriguing conclusion that can be drawn is that the culture underlying the operation of city government has been slow in changing from the days of the council–manager system, thus giving credence to the old saying "that the more things change, the more they stay the same." Even in the midst of disgruntlement and frustration among neighborhood groups and older residents about the unresponsiveness and lack of accountability in city hall, many citizens initially did not want to abandon the council–manager structure, but rather wished to correct its defects. Indeed, this was the sentiment expressed by a majority of the Charter Review Commission, and it is reflected in its recommendations. This perspective is best captured in the words of a *Times* columnist: "It was like the city wanted to maintain the virtues of the council–manager plan but have more accountability at city hall" (Troxler 2008).

A review of the development of the mayor's role since 1993 supports this perspective. Simply stated, the role played by the mayor did not begin in the typical strong-mayor fashion. In the words of someone very familiar with the transition period, "the new government could be characterized as nothing more than a superficial change in the city's charter, except that the mayor was substituted for the manager" (Stephens 2008). In essence the mayor assumed the role of chief administrative officer and was expected to implement policies enacted by the council. This arrangement satisfied most people because it permitted the electorate to hold the chief administrator (formerly the manager and now the mayor) accountable at the ballot box. Fears of an unbridled strong mayor were further allayed since the mayor was not given the power to veto acts of the council for another ten years (November 2003).

In his eight years in office, Fischer did not rock the boat and made no attempt to stretch the new powers of the mayor. Early on he devoted a considerable amount of time helping to heal the city after a very divisive, nasty campaign against the former police chief, Curtsinger. For the remainder of his time in office, he worked tirelessly to achieve consensus among many groups in the city on a number of issues, but especially economic development in the midtown section of the city, revitalization of neighborhoods, and the Challenge 2001 urban renewal plan. While seeking to win citizen approval for these and other initiatives, Fischer routinely gave considerable autonomy to the four city administrators who served under him and their subordinates. This resulted in heavy criticism from a majority of the members of city council who still saw themselves as having the same oversight role vis-à-vis the bureaucracy that they had under the old council–manager structure. In fact, it was not unusual for "city employees—from the mayor's office on down . . . [to be] frequently dressed down by council members who [were] often skeptical of information they [got] from anyone on the mayor's staff" and were miffed at the fact that most of the city's bureaucracy looked to the mayor, their supervisors, and the city administrator for direction (Ryan 1998). One new member of council in 1998 explained this behavior of council in the following way: "that could be because in the old city manager form of government, the mayor acted as a ninth council member. Then, the council made decisions and directed the manager to carry them out. A manager who wanted to keep his job catered to the council. Now the mayor has the power to hire and fire city employees and a mandate from the voters" (Ryan 1998).

Near the end of Fischer's eight years in office there was significant turnover among the membership of the council. Most of those who had persisted in believing that they still retained oversight authority for the bureaucracy had left office and were replaced by a more congenial group who not only did not try to micromanage the city but "failed to act as an effective check on the mayor in legislative matters" (Troxler 2008). This change in the council's makeup was the perfect setting for the more gregarious Rick Baker when he was elected to succeed Fischer as mayor in 2001. Baker, who campaigned on the four-point Baker Plan (public safety, schools, economic development, and neighborhoods), came across as promoting a collegial approach to governance. In retrospect, he clearly came to office with the desire to fully utilize—and even stretch—the powers of the mayor (Troxler 2008; Elston 2008). Baker had been Fischer's campaign manager in 1993 and 1997, and as a member of the Charter Review Commission in 1992, had, oddly enough, opposed the strong-mayor plan. Over the course of Fischer's tenure, Baker became a staunch advocate of the strong-mayor plan and a defender of Fischer against critics on the council. And after seven years in office,

Baker has unquestionably earned the title of being the city's first modern "strong" strong mayor (Troxler 2008).

By the time Baker took office in January 2002, the perception that most council members had of their role still was not congruent with the projected responsibility of the legislative body in a strong-mayor system. As noted above, the council had shifted from attempting to maintain its oversight role to being a passive player and acquiescing to the mayor's initiatives and rarely questioning his decisions and recommendations, even when the public and civic groups challenged the mayor (Troxler 2008). Some observers even claim that some council members cower in Baker's presence (Arsenault 2008; Troxler 2008). For the most part, the council has given Baker a free hand to negotiate deals with both private and public sector entities and has been willing to accept what in effect amounts to a fait accompli in a number of instances (Troxler 2008).

While the projected role of the executive branch (i.e., the mayor) in a strong-mayor plan has been realized over the last fifteen years, the same has not been the case with regard to the role that the legislative branch (i.e., the council) is expected to play in this type of governmental arrangement. Yet, one has to wonder if the culture that seems to define the current role perceptions of the mayor and council would change if the next mayor were to come from the ranks of the council. Would the mayor be more of a team player vis-à-vis the council and be willing to share both oversight of the bureaucracy and policy initiation with the council? This is an interesting prospect in that the two candidates vying to become the city's third strong major going into the November 2009 nonpartisan mayoral election were two current council members.

However, in light of the outcome of the election, the answer to the question posed above is probably "no." By choosing conservative Republican Bill Foster (regarded by most political observers as the establishment candidate) over Democrat Kathleen Ford (highly touted as the change candidate), voters seemed to have endorsed the status quo (Troxler 2009). After all, Foster had tied himself to the policies and popularity of Baker. Moreover, Foster clearly benefited not only from garnering almost all of the significant endorsements, but also from the fact that most residents were satisfied with the last eight years under Mayor Baker. According to a poll conducted just prior to the election, 59 percent of the city's residents said "the City was moving in the right direction" and only 24 percent thought that "the City was moving in the wrong direction" (Silva 2009).

## Goals and Expectations

This examination of the change in the structure of St. Petersburg's government would not be complete without addressing whether or not the goals and expectations of the proponents of the strong-mayor–council plan were realized. After fifteen years in operation, one would expect to find some evidence that sheds light on a question that political science and public administration scholars have debated for years: "Does government structure matter?"[5]

One major goal was to bring about greater responsiveness and accountability. In what seemed to be a genuine commitment to making city government more responsive and accountable to the public, Mayor Baker chose to employ the title First Deputy Mayor for his city administrator (see figure 2.1). He intentionally chose this title to convey to residents that this person represents him in the community, has the authority to speak for him on most matters, and shares his ideological perspective on community issues (Elston 2008). (It is important to note that newly elected Mayor Bill Foster has announced his decision to retain the incumbent city administrator and to delegate to her the same authority and responsibilities that she had had under Mayor Baker.) The organizational chart also shows that Baker designated two other persons directly accountable to him as "deputy mayors" in matters that cover economic development and neighborhood services. His motivation for opting for these titles was to reassure residents of his desire to be closely attuned to their needs and preferences in these sensitive areas (Elston 2008).

Budgetary data also indicate that city hall has been responsive to the public's call to lower property taxes and reduce the level of city indebtedness. Both Fischer and Baker often articulated their belief that property taxes must be reduced so as to make the city more competitive with surrounding jurisdictions, and each mayor set out on a deliberate campaign to lower them on an incremental basis (Elston 2008). Review of the city's property tax operating millage rate (mill) since 1993 clearly illustrates that they were successful in achieving this goal. At the time Fischer took office in April 1993, the rate stood at 8.5584 mills (the state limit is 10 mills). By the time he left office in early 2001, the rate had been decreased to 7.1500 mills. Under Baker's tenure as mayor, the rate has dropped further to 5.9125 mills in 2008–9. In a similar manner, Fischer and Baker launched a concerted effort to reduce the high level of city indebtedness that had peaked during the late 1980s and early 1990s. This can be seen by examining trends in the outstanding debt accrued under three types of bonding arrangements with most of the proceeds designed to help finance revitalization efforts and construction of the stadium. In all three cases there were substantial reductions between 1997 and 2007—public improvement revenue bonds (tax increment financing) debt dropped from $51.395 million to $29.160 million; utility tax revenue bonds (infrastructure) debt declined from $45.163 million to $9.272 million; and excise tax revenue bonds (stadium) fell from $101.955 million to $60.350 million.

In addition, the city has improved its financial situation in other areas. For instance, St. Petersburg was finally awarded a baseball expansion team in March 1995. The next month the city council approved a thirty-year lease with Vince Naimoli, the leader of the ownership group for the then Tampa Bay Devil Rays, but only after the city spent another $58 million in improvements to the four-year-old stadium. The lease was somewhat of a bittersweet deal since the Devil Rays essentially received everything they asked for. As a former council member commented at the time, the council had lost the ability to negotiate because of the costly stadium (Newsner 1995). The team was to manage the stadium and get all of the revenue from stadium advertising, concessions, merchandising, and parking for all activities at the stadium and most of the money for

**Figure 2.1 St. Petersburg Organization, 2008**

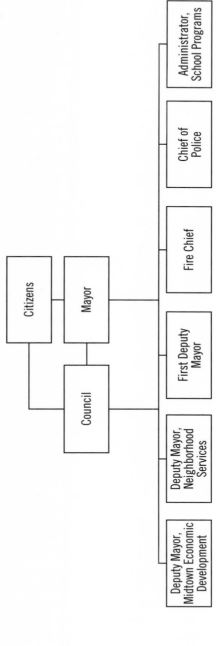

naming rights to the stadium. The city, however, was able to salvage something out of the deal as it was to get fifty cents a ticket at games (Rogers 1995).

Another stated goal of the proponents of the strong-mayor–council plan was that it would give the city a clearly identifiable point person to represent the city and speak for and negotiate on behalf of the city's best interests (Arsenault 2008; Troxler 2008). Many people (both opponents and proponents of the strong-mayor plan) who have paid close attention to this expectation of the mayor agree that this goal has not only been realized but "realized many times over" (Elston 2008). Examples abound. One week after the strong-mayor government was approved on April 1, 1993, Mayor Fischer moved his office to the city manager's office (away from council offices) in order to be on the administrative side of the city instead of the legislative side. The mayor presented his blueprint for the next four years, which included "continuing to ensure taxes go down, seeing that downtown St. Petersburg fulfills its commitment, bringing in new businesses and industry to provide more jobs, continuing revitalization of neighborhoods, continuing the trend of low crime rate to make St. Petersburg a safe city in which to live, and, making sure the city moves together to fulfill its goal of being a good place to raise a family, work, and play" (Elton 2008).

When Mayor Baker took office in 2001, he branded the midtown area and launched a major initiative to create what he called a "seamless" city by investing in midtown's infrastructure and encouraging private development in midtown. As part of this initiative, he used CDBG funds to construct a full-service retail component in the U.S. post office in the midtown, after convincing postal officials of the need to offer services to residents there. He also worked to attract a Jobs Corps site for the city by helping to assemble several parcels of land for its construction. In addition, he persuaded numerous businesses to locate in St. Petersburg, including construction of a Sweet Bay grocery in midtown in 2006, SRI International at the port in 2007, and retention of Jabil Circuit's headquarters in the city's Gateway area 2008. A recent poll of city residents found that 57 percent rated Mayor Baker's job performance as "good" or "excellent" (*St. Petersburg Times* 2008).

In sum there is little question that the mayor's office and its occupants have become a highly visible point to speak for the city and make things happen.

## Conclusions

The strong-mayor–council government of St. Petersburg, Florida, has changed in some ways over the first fifteen years of its existence. Most assuredly, it will continue to evolve and adapt in the years ahead. Therefore, the situation there warrants continued scrutiny by students of urban government and politics, in the hope that we can learn from this city's and similar cities' experiences. However, we can already point to at least three lessons derived from this chapter's review of the history surrounding the change in government form in St. Petersburg, Florida, and its aftermath.

First, in pursuing an ambitious urban development program, a council–manager city will experience powerful pressure to conduct itself as a strong-mayor city. Specifically, the increased visibility and influence of the mayor—and even the city manager behaving as the de facto mayor—during the peak of the development stage were clear indications of that trend. Second, the council–manager system appeared especially disposed to ethical issues previously unforeseen by good government advocates and the professional management community. The latter's great passion for development schemes cost St. Petersburg three managers who were experienced, well-trained professionals eager to innovate and lead. Finally, in nonpartisan, low turnout elections, it is possible for some high-risk schemes to be approved even when presented to the voters. Low turnout improves the potential for a highly organized and motivated minority to turn out and push through a slate of officials that end up making risky policy decisions. Once the mistake is made, it is frequently too difficult even for many astute and careful voters to opt for a change in the development path. Only when the disastrous consequences have begun to take their toll will change occur, and in situations like that found in St. Petersburg, that change could entail the abandonment of an otherwise practical and suitable form of government.

We conclude our assessment of the change in the form of government by highlighting several intriguing questions: Has the change in St. Petersburg really amounted to tinkering with the council–manager structure? Does the new structure merely reflect an adaptation that did not shift the center of governmental gravity much at all? Or is the restructuring a significant change? Strong-mayor–council cities often find the mayor and council locked in heated debate over public policy issues and even personnel matters. The framework of the traditional model invites conflict and adversarial relationships as has been evident across the bay in Tampa. The council–manager plan is designed to promote teamwork and shared responsibility. The culture that emerges then is quite different from that of the mayor–council structure. Has the shift to a strong-mayor plan in St. Petersburg generated a culture change as well? Have the mayors over the past fifteen years found themselves in increasingly adversarial relationships with city council members, as might be predicted? We believe the answer is "no." The council–manager culture continues to influence relationships between the mayor and council and the city administrator. In other words, the change in structure has not resulted in a "political city" nor has it produced an "adapted political city," to use the terminology of Frederickson, Johnson, and Wood (2004b, 139). Rather, it has produced a "conciliated city." In conciliated cities, critical elements of both the separation and unity of powers are combined. For example, a conciliated city has "an independently elected mayor with some executive authority and a professional city manager or CAO who also has executive authority, particularly over city departments . . . in their structural arrangements, conciliated cities provide for both high-profile political leadership in the office of the mayor and for professional management competence in the office of the city manager or the CAO" (139).

Is St. Petersburg on the forefront of the changing landscape of urban America? It would seem so. Are conciliated cities such as Cincinnati, Ohio; Evanston, Illinois; Oakland, California; Hartford, Connecticut; and St. Petersburg more responsive, efficient, and effective governments than others? These are important questions that beg for answers by urban researchers.

## Notes

1. A Florida statute requires that recalls must follow a two-petition-drive procedure and the second one calls for as much as 15 percent of the registered voters.

2. The Florida Constitution permits cities to exceed the 10 mill cap only if the electorate is consulted in a referendum and for very limited purposes.

3. In 1988 St. Petersburg commissioned three urban planners—Mary Means, Ronald Thomas, and Thomas Hammer—to review the feasibility of the Bay Plaza Project. The report concluded that the project was a high-risk venture that could succeed only if the developer was able to secure at least three upscale anchor tenants.

4. Ulrich infuriated St. Petersburg citizens when, soon after leaving the mayor's office, he accepted a position as an attorney with the Bay Plaza Corporation.

5. Although scholars and reform groups certainly discussed and debated the strengths and weaknesses of various local government structural arrangements over the years, the subject became a frequent topic of research among scholars after the publication of Lineberry and Fowler's (1967) seminal work.

## References

Arsenault, Raymond. 1988. *St. Petersburg and the Florida dream: 1888–1950.* Norfolk, VA: Donning.

———. 2008. Interview by the authors of a former member of 1992 City of St. Petersburg Charter Review Commission. December 12.

Dahl, David. 1985. Ethics panel will start investigation of Harvey today. *St. Petersburg Times,* September 9.

Elston, Tish. 2008. Interview by authors of the current City of St. Petersburg city administrator. December 22.

Frederickson, H. George, Gary A. Johnson, and Curtis Wood. 2004a. The changing structure of American cities: A study of diffusion of innovation. *Public Administration Review* 64, no. 3 (May): 295–306.

———. 2004b. *The adapted city: Institutional dynamics and structural change.* Armonk, NY: M. E. Sharpe.

Hatry, Harry P. 1974. *Measuring the effectiveness of basic municipal services.* Washington, DC: Urban Institute and International City Management Association.

Jones, Don. 1992. Testimony before City of St. Petersburg Charter Review Commission on June 15.

Journey, Mark. 1993. Former foes are courting Fischer. *St. Petersburg Times,* March 27.

Jreisat, Jamil E. 1987. Productivity measurement: Trial and error in St. Petersburg. *Public Productivity Review* 11, no. 2 (Winter): 3–18.

Lineberry, Robert L., and Edmund P. Fowler. 1967. Reformism and public policy in American cities. *American Political Science Review* 61, no. 3 (September): 701–16.

Maddox, Martha. 1985. Harvey went too far on course council set. *St. Petersburg Times,* September 13.

Newsner, N. 1995. St. Petersburg OK's Devil Rays lease. *St. Petersburg Times,* April 27.

Olinger, David. 1987. Big projects double city's debt in one year. *St. Petersburg Times,* May 17.

———. 1991. The undoing of Robert Obering. *St. Petersburg Times,* 15.

Paulson, Darryl. 1992. Voters face a hybrid government series; guest column. *St. Petersburg Times*, March 10.

Rigos, Planton N., and Darryl Paulson. 1996. Urban development, policy failure, and regime change in a manager–council city: The case of St. Petersburg, Florida. *Urban Affairs Review* 32, no. 2 (November): 244–63.

Rogers, David K. 1995. City council leases dome to Rays. *St. Petersburg Times*, April 28.

Ryan, Kelly. 1998. Mayor, council battle boosting tension level. *St. Petersburg Times*, August 9.

Selz, M. 1989. St. Petersburg plays a long shot. *Florida Trend* 31 (March): 38–45.

Shaw, Rob. 1991. Property value drops portends tax shortfall. *Tampa Tribune*, May 9.

Silva, Christina. 2009. Mayor Baker's legacy. *St. Petersburg Times*, November 1.

Snajderman, Michael, and Judy Hill. 1991. St. Petersburg's passion proves costly. *Tampa Tribune*, June 30.

State of Florida, Office of Comptroller. 1987. *Financial Report 1984–85*. Tallahassee, FL: Department of Banking.

Stone, Clarence. 1987. Summing up: Urban regimes, development policy and political arrangements. In *The Politics of Urban Development*, eds. Clarence Stone and H. Sanders, 269–81. Lawrence: University of Kansas Press.

*St. Petersburg Times*. 2008. Poll reflects strong feelings about Rays stadium plan. June 2. www.tampabay.com/news/localgovernment/article589128.ece (accessed January 2, 2009).

Stephens, Darrel. 2008. Interview by the authors of a former City of St. Petersburg city administrator. December 30.

Thomas, Ronald, and Mary Means. 1988. *The Bay Plaza project: A feasibility study*. Consultants' report to *St. Petersburg Times*. St. Petersburg, FL: Times Publishing Company.

Tobin, Thomas C. 1988. Fifty-six percent favor recall, poll says. *Tampa Tribune*, January 30.

Troxler, Howard. 2008. Interview by the authors of *St. Petersburg Times* columnist. December 12.

———. 2009. By electing Foster, city stays course. *St. Petersburg Times*, November 4.

Vesperi, Maria D. 1985. *City of green benches: Growing old in a new downtown*. Ithaca, NY: Cornell University Press.

CHAPTER 3

# SPOKANE

## Development Debate Sparks Government Debate

WENDY L. HASSETT

## Background

IN 1810 A TRADING POST was built at the confluence of the Spokane and Little Spokane rivers. This area was an ideal habitat for beaver and other fur-bearing animals. Under the direction of North West Trading Company explorer David Thompson, Finan McDonald and Jacques Finlay were sent to build the small trading post that they called Spokane House. "Spokane" means "children of the sun" or "sun people" and originates from a Native American tribe that made its home in the area.

The first Spokane county government was organized in 1860. Pinkney City, a small trading post, served as the first county seat. Over the next three decades, the county seat was relocated several times. An election finally designated Spokane as the county seat in 1886. Spokane put down roots as a town in about 1873, when James Glover arrived in the area and was enchanted by Spokane Falls. He bought a 158-acre area located approximately where Spokane's business district is today. Over the years Spokane became a grand city with luxury housing and elegant hotels.

In the summer of 1881 the first Northern Pacific Railroad train arrived from the west with six cars full of passengers. The first train from the east arrived two years later in 1883. Northern Pacific regional activity eventually was centered in Spokane.

The Spokane fire department was established in 1884 after a hot, dry summer with several fires, one of which destroyed sixteen businesses along Main Street. In the summer of 1889, a fire burned almost the entire downtown area to the ground, including two of the three fire stations and nearly all of the stately buildings. The city rebuilt quickly, and many of the original buildings from post–1889 are still standing today. The strength of the city was based on the railroads, the proximity to the Coeur d'Alene region with gold, silver, and lead mines, and the natural beauty of Spokane Falls. With the yield of the mines and fortunes from the railroad came the birth of millionaires. Those newfound riches led some to build extravagant homes and elegant theaters. This

47

period in Spokane is known as the age of elegance. Spokane's business district experienced improvements as well. Increasingly, Spokane gained a reputation for its wild side. As many as fifty-one saloons and dance halls were established, which became a breeding ground for drunkenness, gambling, and shootings. Since that time Spokane's expansion and growth have been punctuated with periods of population and economic decline.

The 2000 Census reports the population of Spokane as 195,629, up from 177,196 in 1990. As the county seat, the City of Spokane serves as the hub of the Inland Northwest, a region of thirty-six counties that encompass parts of Montana, Oregon, Idaho, British Columbia, Alberta, and Washington. With such notable events as the annual lilac festival, Lilac Boomsday Run, Hoopfest, and the Spokane International Film Festival, Spokane offers the region a number of interesting activities and attractions. The Spokane Symphony Orchestra recently celebrated fifty years of performances, and the Spokane Jazz Orchestra is the longest-running orchestra performing jazz in the United States. The Spokane Opera House offers Broadway hits, concerts, and dance performances, and the Spokane Arena provides a venue for concerts and sporting events.

## Municipal Government

The Spokane city government operated under a strong-mayor system until 1910 when it switched to a system of five full-time commissioners who selected a mayor from among themselves. In 1960 the city adopted the council–manager form of government with a rotating mayoral position. The council elected at that same time was pro-business.

By all accounts the council–manager form of government served the city well for more than three decades. In the mid-1990s council–manager government was challenged when a referendum was held in September 1996 to abandon it. However, the citizenry was not ready for a change, and the effort failed with 56 percent of the voters wanting to retain the council–manager form.

While operating under the council–manager form, Spokane enjoyed a high degree of stability in the city manager's office. From 1960 through 1999 only five individuals served as city manager. Henry Nabers was Spokane's first city manager and served from 1960 until 1963 when he resigned. F. Sylvin Fulwiler served from August 1963 until July 1977. Terry Novak filled the post from May 1978 to June 1991. Roger Crum, who succeeded Novak, served from September 1991 through May 1996. Bill Pupo, who had served as assistant city manager since 1982, was appointed city manager in February 1997 and served until 1999.

In 1999 the council–manager form was challenged again. The story leading to this referendum is an important one. While many factors have been cited as causes for the challenge, two major public issues contributed to the decline of confidence in council–manager government: the River Park Square development and a dissatisfaction with Spokane's economic development priorities.

# River Park Square

Following the closing of a number of major business establishments in the downtown, including Sears, Montgomery Ward, J. C. Penney, the Crescent department store, and the Davenport Hotel, the Spokane City Council felt that something needed to be done to support the economic vitality of its downtown (Sloane 2001). The number of downtown vacant storefronts had increased, and increasingly the downtown began to show signs of urban blight and decay. This situation affected not only the city's coffers but also the quality of city services. Preserving the retail sales tax base in the urban core became increasingly crucial to city leaders (Pupo 2001).

A focal point for the desire to revitalize downtown Spokane was the River Park Square shopping mall, which was considered to be the lifeblood of downtown Spokane and was located across from City Hall, the public library, and a large public park (Pupo 2001). The mall's anchor tenant, Seattle-based Nordstrom department store, made it clear that it would no longer remain at that location without major improvements made to the shopping facility. River Park Square's developer, a local and influential family in Spokane, was willing to invest in the improvements, and city officials were invited to participate in a public/private partnership.

Former city attorney James Sloane said that the council understood that its involvement would be focused on the parking garage that would serve as a way for the city to show its support for these economic development efforts and encourage the developer to move forward with plans to renovate the complex (Pupo 2001). The council's desire was for this improvement to help maintain the viability of the mall and the greater downtown area (Camden 2004). In light of information from the city's consultant that River Park Square's developer was willing to offer significant concessions to secure a long-term commitment from Nordstrom, the council was interested in participating in the parking garage as the public part of the deal (Connor 2000).

Specifically, the plan was to renovate and expand the existing 750-space downtown public parking garage to 1,304 spaces in order to breathe new life into the River Park Square shopping mall and downtown, and keep Nordstrom in the mall (Connor 2000). In addition, the city assisted the developer to secure a U.S. Department of Housing and Urban Development (HUD) loan guarantee to assist in the financing of the private improvements. In order to make the parking deal work, several crucial decisions were made that had important implications not only for the parking facility and the entire downtown but also for the long-term financial future of the city.

# Parking Consultant's Report

One of these crucial decisions was the faith in and reliance upon the parking consultant's feasibility study. This report has been referred to as the single most influential document in the River Park Square project. It was relied upon heavily not only by the city council and management in making key project decisions but also by the bondholders and investors since it was used in the bond prospectus' official statement (Connor 2000; Powers 2001; McGregor 2002).

A number of issues were raised in regard to the assumptions used in the report, including the appraisal method employed to determine the value of the garage (Connor 2000) and the number of hours that the average shopper might park in the garage (McGregor 2002). Former city manager Bill Pupo acknowledged that many people thought that the assumptions used by the parking consultant to calculate and project the income stream were too aggressive and overly optimistic (Pupo 2001). There have also been questions surrounding the independence of the analysis (Connor 2000; McGregor 2002). Regardless, the resulting feasibility study report from the consultant showed that the garage was "self-sustaining" (Powers 2001).

The outcome was a $26 million price tag used by the developer to sell the garage to the newly created nonprofit Spokane Downtown Foundation that served as a substitute buyer for the city. While the developer received a purchase price of $26 million, the exact amount that it cost the developers to reconstruct the garage is not clear. The parking consultants estimated in late 1996 that to refurbish and expand the existing 750-parking-space facility to a 1,304-space facility would cost $8.7 million. In September 1998 prospective bondholders were told in the official statement that the construction-related costs were $17,516,326. Costs of related professional services increased the total cost to $20.7 million. The remaining net proceeds of at least $5.3 million would be reinvested by the developer in "the retail and development project as an equity or cash contribution" for a total of $26 million (Connor 2000).

## Spokane Downtown Foundation

Still another questionable decision made by the city government was the creation and role of the entity that purchased the garage. Since the city was reluctant to buy the garage, the attorneys representing the seller/developer formed the nonprofit Spokane Downtown Foundation (SDF) to serve as a substitute buyer for the city. The nonprofit status of SDF allowed it to issue tax-exempt bonds, thereby eliminating the direct exposure to loss of Spokane's general fund. SDF used the $31.5 million generated by the sale of the bonds to purchase the garage from the developer for the appraised value ($26 million) and then leased the facility to the Public Parking Development Authority (PDA) that assumed responsibility for managing the garage and paying its bills. Some of the additional dollars were placed in a reserve account. The plan was that after the bonds were paid off in twenty years, SDF would transfer ownership of the garage to the city (Connor 2000; Prager 2004c).

There was no legal question that bonds could be issued to finance this project as long as the garage operated as a public facility and the bond proceeds were used in accordance with the federal restrictions for private profit taking. PDA President Novak explained why the bonds were issued in the amount of $31 million: "The bond sale by the foundation (not by the city) was rated BBB so it couldn't be readily sold without setting up a substantial Reserve Fund. That added $3.1 million to the total [purchase price of $26 million]. Add in sale expenses and legal fees and you get $31 million" (Novak 2001).

Terry Novak, who served as Spokane's city manager for thirteen years until 1991, accepted the position as the PDA president at the request of then mayor Jack Geraghty who "was convinced the deal was appropriate and would be successful." Novak (2001) commented on why Mayor Geraghty felt so strongly about the deal: "Jack was active in the U.S. Conference of Mayors during those years. USCM was pushing this type of project and city after city was doing it around the country, especially Seattle. He was predisposed to believe in the project."

According to the agreement that was reached, PDA was to pay the debt service, ground rent, and operation costs, and then to remit any extra funds to the developer. Novak (2001) said that not long after he took the position, he learned the deal was a "tinderbox."

Although the creation of SDF kept the city technically distanced from the arrangement, there was a significant linkage between the city and the garage. In January 1997 the council unanimously passed an eleven-page off-street parking ordinance that essentially accomplished two things. First, it required the city to pledge funds from its parking meter collections to cover any garage losses. If the garage lost money, the city agreed to appropriate money from its parking meter collections that normally went to the city's general fund, to PDA to cover the shortfall. Second, it required that the city must increase its parking meter fees each year to cover any increases in the costs of the operations or ground rent of the garage. Ultimately, this ordinance created a contingency fund for garage shortfalls from the city's budget, and at the same time, made the garage more competitive by increasing the price for on-street parking (Connor 2000; Prager 2004c; Camden 2004).

## HUD Loan

Another complicating factor was a Section 108 HUD loan guarantee, a federal loan that was used in conjunction with the project's construction. In addition to the $31 million of bonds issued that allowed the Spokane Downtown Foundation to purchase the garage, the city made a separate loan of $22.65 million to the developers linked to the project's construction, which was approved based on the need for economic revitalization in the downtown.

Then Mayor John Powers (2001) noted that the city borrowed $23 million through the credit markets based on a guarantee by HUD. The financing was based on the developer repaying the loan to the city and the city, in turn, amortizing the debt owed to the lenders. The structure of the financial arrangement was that if the city failed to make the debt payments, then HUD would collect any shortfall by withholding the city's share of CDBG targeted for low-income neighborhoods. Powers (2001) expressed concern that the loan was "significantly under-collateralized" because of the problems created by the parking garage and Nordstrom's failure to perform to expectations. He stated that "the HUD money must be protected for additional projects in our low-income neighborhoods" (Powers 2001). Over time, the loan account gradually dipped into these grant funds that normally are used to improve low-income neighborhoods (Prager 2004d, 2005b).

The most serious concern to the city of Spokane was a financial one: if the deal collapsed under the heavy weight of the debt and the garage's inflated purchase price, city funds were pledged to make up any difference. Success of the parking structure was necessary to keep city funds from being siphoned out of Spokane's coffers. As long as the garage was financially strong, the city had no serious financial concerns. However, the moment the PDA could not honor the fiscal commitments of the garage, city funds were in serious jeopardy.

And that unfortunately was what happened. In 2001 then–Spokane Mayor John Powers commented that "from the day the garage opened, actual operations have resulted in massive losses. The parking garage is losing between $1.5 million and $2 million a year, and based on revenue trends, losses of that magnitude can be expected to continue for the 20-year life of the bonds" (Powers 2001).

Powers also commented on the larger issue of income generation for the city: The optimistic projections of increased sales tax revenue from the project were not being realized. "The garage losses, meanwhile, are not being compensated for by increased sales tax revenue. State law protects the privacy of tax records, so the city does not know on a store-by-store basis what additional sales tax revenue is being generated by River Park Square." Mayor Powers stated that the city did have enough information to know that the city was not recouping from the River Park Square area anywhere "near the magnitude of the parking garage losses" (2001).

Years later issues surrounding this project remained riddled with controversy and legal battles. One of the lawyers involved in legal wrangling referred to the River Park Square project as the "'perfect storm of litigation" that has filled a conference room at his office with a half-million pages of documents (Prager 2004c).

Beyond the negative financial implications to the city's bottom line, the issue presented a public relations problem. Even Novak said the deal was based on "bad estimates and improper appraisal methods" (Novak 2001). Increasingly, the citizens grew to perceive this project as a bad deal for the city because the project appeared to be structured at the expense of the city. The public purpose of the parking structure became lost in the ongoing debate. During subsequent years, the River Park Square project was referred to as the "eye of the political storm" (Modie 2000).

This issue did not fade away quickly. Several years later, the local media reported that the city still feels pains from the River Park Square matter. "Arguably, no issue has caused more upheaval at City Hall than the parking garage dispute" (Prager 2004b). Since that issue came to the forefront in the mid-1990s, Spokane has gone through three city managers, three mayors, one acting city manager, a city attorney, and its council–manager form of government (Prager 2004b).

However, the storm finally began to subside in late 2004. The Spokane City Council approved an agreement in December 2004 to resolve the legal issues associated with River Park Square. As a part of that settlement, the developer guaranteed payment of the HUD project loan and was granted ownership of the parking garage. The city was held responsible for paying $43.4 million to cover the outstanding debt from buying the bonds for the garage. It was estimated that the city's financial obligation will cost between $1.4 million and $2.3 million a year through the year 2027 (Brunt 2008a).

## Economic Development Priorities

Spokane residents became increasingly dissatisfied with the misplaced economic development priorities of the city, specifically in the area of technology. Public sentiment focused on a growing economic dissatisfaction that Spokane was not enjoying the economic successes of other Washington cities. The economic chasm in Spokane had widened between high-paid professionals and low-paid employees working in manufacturing and retail areas. The perception was that the city was in "economic stagnation" (Pupo 2001). Many viewed the development of high-tech jobs as the solution (Murphey 1999c). However, the city's decision to focus a significant portion of its economic development effort on protecting existing and creating additional low-paying retail jobs in River Park Square was "forcing its best and brightest minds to look elsewhere for work" (Johnson 1997).

Although the decision to focus the city's efforts on the downtown was supported by the Chamber of Commerce, downtown retailers, and the Economic Development Council, it was not a decision supported by the entire community. To some citizens it indicated the city's contentment with the status quo and low-paying jobs rather than working toward developing new high-paying manufacturing and high-tech jobs (Pupo 2001). Those citizens became increasingly more vocal.

In 1997 local developer John Stone proposed that the city convert a nine-block area on the east end of downtown Spokane into a "technology village," taking advantage of existing fiber optic lines. The proposal also involved partnerships between universities and private industries in support of newly developing technology-based businesses until the fledgling companies became profitable, in an effort to create high-paying technology jobs. Stone reported that the response from the city was that the River Park Square project was its first priority. Stone saw this response as reflecting the city's misguided priority on the creation of low-paying retail jobs in lieu of supporting technology-based companies that had the potential of adding highly paid, high-tech jobs (Murphey 1999a).

Compounding that general sentiment was a *Forbes* magazine article in May 1999 listing Spokane as one of the worst places to do business, especially for a high-tech industry (Connor 2000). In *Washington CEO* magazine Spokane high-tech executive Glen Griffin charged that the priorities of the city were awry if millions were spent on economic development projects that did not support fledgling high-tech companies (Geranios 1999). High-tech company owner Dave Lenartz added: "Instead of competing with everyone else, why don't we do more for the small high-tech companies that are already here?" (Murphey 1999c).

Bernard Daines, founder of high-tech Packet Engines, a company he sold for $315 million in October 1998, also felt strongly about the poor environment for high-tech companies. Daines spent his preteen years in Spokane, and, after living in San Francisco for twenty-five years, moved back to Spokane in 1994 (Murphey 1999b). When he returned, he did not like what he found—a community without the infrastructure needed to support high-tech businesses. His strong desire for change led him to contribute more than $31,000 toward efforts to change the form of government to strong-mayor (Geranios 1999).

In commenting on the future challenges to Spokane, Michael Murphey wrote in August 1999, "The sense that Spokane's existing leadership has somehow failed to guide the city into the high-tech age is becoming a key element in a broader effort aimed at reshaping Spokane's political landscape" (Murphey 1999a). Former city manager Bill Pupo said that one of the frustrations the city had with high-tech companies was that, instead of locating in Spokane, they located outside the city limits in Liberty Lake, a then-unincorporated area of about 80,000 residents where there was a large amount of "vacant and cheap land." To entice the high-end companies to Spokane, the city invested money in a high-quality retail establishment and focused on quality-of-life issues (Pupo 2001).

Novak did not think that the city neglected the high-tech, industrial, and manufacturing sectors during that time. Instead, he saw the city's involvement in those other areas as simply being downplayed by the media: "The Chamber of Commerce, the Economic Development Council, and the Visitor and Convention Bureau continued to push development in other [areas] than downtown. It's just that those activities (all with city financial support) received less press, so it appears downtown was treated specially. I don't think it actually was true" (Novak 2001).

In spite of efforts the city may have made in different sectors, a growing sentiment was that the city bore the responsibility for the health of all sectors of the local economy, but city leaders were not doing all they should to ensure the high-quality economic growth and prosperity desired by the citizens.

## Council–Manager Abandonment

In 1997 retired U.S. Air Force Colonel John Talbott defeated Jack Geraghty, the mayor who served during the River Park Square development. For some time Talbott had criticized the actions of the city, even joining in a lawsuit attempting to stop the city's involvement in the River Park Square project (Johnson 1997). Even before taking office, Talbott thought that the legal restrictions placed on the mayor in Spokane's council–manager government made the position largely ceremonial: "We need a strong mayor . . . who can go out and develop a vision for our citizens. I believe I'm the leader that can cause that to happen" (Johnson 1997). Once in office he made it clear he was not pleased with the limited power he had under the existing council–manager form of government (Geranios 1999).

During the late 1990s a number of controversial issues swirled around city hall while Bill Pupo was city manager. One issue involved the resignation of police chief Alan Chertok, who left office after serving in that capacity for only six months. As a part of his departure, Chertok collected $65,000 as a buyout. Another controversial personnel action involved Pupo's termination of Spokane's engineering director. Pupo learned of a romantic relationship between the official and a consultant employed by the city. The engineer sued the city alleging denial of due process. The city settled for $135,000.

Another lawsuit involved homeowners living near the Colbert compost facility. These individuals claimed that the plant's odor lowered their property values. The city offered to buy the homes of those affected (Mulady 1999b, 1999c).

The council's 1999 evaluation of Pupo was kept private, but local newspapers reported that it was "average." During Pupo's tenure as city manager, the strong-mayor initiative gained momentum. By 1999, the question of form of government had been scheduled for a November referendum (Mulady 1999b). In July 1999 Pupo announced his resignation. At that time he had been an employee with the city in various capacities for twenty-three years (Camden and Mulady 1999).

In commenting on the departure of city manager Pupo, Mayor Talbott stated in a local newspaper: "It was mutually understood that it would be in the best interest of all involved for an amicable change in management. A sense of concern had been voiced." While Pupo and the council commented publicly that there had been no pressure for the city manager to resign, Mayor Talbott was quoted as saying: Pupo "may have gotten a sense it was headed that way" (Welch 1999). Assistant city manager Pete Fortin was appointed acting city manager in August 1999 (Mulady 1999d).

Efforts had begun in the spring of 1999 to change the Spokane city charter. A strong-mayor initiative had been proposed by Coalition for a New Spokane, headed by local attorney Steve Eugster. By mid-July the Coalition acquired the necessary number of signatures to place the proposal on the ballot (Mulady 1999c). The strong-mayor initiative, termed Proposition 2, was a part of a slate of reforms assembled by a number of anti-establishment citizens (Geranios 1999).

Former mayor David Rodgers requested that the council delay its decision to place the issue on the agenda alleging that signatures of 15 percent of voters in the last general municipal election should be required rather than the 5 percent secured by initiative backers (Mulady 1999e). Despite the delay, on August 30, 1999, the council placed the strong-mayor initiative on the November 1999 ballot at the same time as the next general city election (Mulady 1999f). At that election, citizens of Spokane also chose individuals to fill three council positions that were up for reelection.

Supporters of Proposition 2, including then mayor John Talbott, argued that the strong-mayor system would "bring more accountability to city government" and "provide Spokane with a visionary leader able to skillfully pilot the city into the next century" (Mulady 1999g). Under the proposal, the strong mayor could veto actions of the city council within ten days. Mayoral vetoes could be overridden with a vote of a majority plus one of the council members. The salary of the mayor would increase from $36,000 per year to $80,000 per year or the same as the salary of the highest paid department head. The mayor could terminate department heads, assistant department heads, the police chief, the fire chief, the city attorney, and city clerk without consulting the council members. Appointments to these positions would require council approval. The proposal (Initiative 99–1) would also allow the mayor to hire an administrative officer (Mulady 1999g).

David Rodgers, who served as mayor from 1967 to 1978, headed the opposition to the strong–mayor proposal. Rodgers's political action committee (PAC), Citizens for Responsible Government, argued that the city would have difficulty recruiting top-notch professionals to fill the department head positions if their jobs would be in jeopardy every four years (Mulady 1999a). The group also used fliers that warned "absolute power corrupts absolutely" (Mulady 1999g).

The local media noted the importance of the mayor's race in the upcoming election (Modie 2000) by pointing out that the winner would become the "most powerful local-government official in Eastern Washington." Modie (2000) stated that the new mayor would be responsible for running the city and not "merely holding the gavel at City Council meetings." As part of the new mayor's challenge, he will have to govern with a divided council whose members are openly hostile to each other, evidenced by litigation and name-calling. Problems that the press enumerated for the new mayor to address included restoring the city's bond rating and repairing the "bruised civic image" as a result of the lawsuits over the downtown shopping mall and the parking garage (Modie 2000). The *Seattle Post-Intelligencer Reporter* commented that Spokane's citizens could watch the weekly city council meetings on local cable television in what Mayor Talbott identified as "Monday Night Live."

Councilman Rob Higgins offered the media his perspective on a story of the upcoming council–manager election by stating "the council showed 'cronyism in a classic sense' when it voted 4–3 in February to hire a new city manager." The appointee was Henry Miggins, the animal-control director of Multnomah County, Oregon, who was a friend of a friend of the mayor. Higgins and other Talbott critics complained that the majority shoved through the appointment without interviewing or even seeking alternative candidates. A local businessman suggested facetiously that Miggins's animal-control background made him uniquely qualified to deal with the council (Modie 2000).

Of course, the River Park Square matter was also part of the backdrop for the November election. Because revenue from the parking garage was not meeting expectations, the clause in the contract with the developers of River Park Square was invoked that required the city to use other parking meter revenue to subsidize bond and operating deficits. On a 4–3 vote, the city council decided not to lend the money despite the agreement. When the developers sued to enforce the agreement, the Washington State Supreme Court ordered the city to pay the deficits with the parking meter revenue. The city's initial failure to pay the deficits and the loss of numerous key staff members resulted in a lowering of the city's bond rating. Both mayoral candidates, Powers and West, vowed to "negotiate an end to the River Park Square quagmire (Modie 2000).

## Election Outcomes and Analysis

Spokanites approved the entire slate of proposals on November 2, 1999. The most significant of these changes was the abandonment of council–manager government effective in January 2001 (Geranios 1999; WCMA 2000) by a narrow margin. Although council–manager government was abandoned in Spokane by a count of only 29 votes out of more than 54,000 cast on the first count (Spokane County Canvassing Board 1999a) and 164 in the recount (Spokane County Canvassing Board 1999b), the message from the citizens was that they wanted a change from the status quo. As an added emphasis to that cry from the citizens, two pro-strong-mayor candidates defeated two pro-council–manager incumbents on the city council.

Former city manager Novak said that he felt the most "obvious" change resulting from that particular election was "the people elected to the city council, especially Steve Eugster." The composition of the governing body was vastly different than the councils he served under during his thirteen-year stint as city manager (Novak 2001). Attorney Eugster, who had sued the city numerous times in recent years, was one of the new strong-mayor supporters elected to a seat on the council. Eugster was quoted as saying, "The government was in the hands of the bureaucracy and special interests. People in this community are saying they want to be in charge" (Geranios 1999). Novak described Eugster as "a determined character" who "appeals to about 30 percent of the electorate." He explained why he thought Eugster won a seat on the city council: "Spokane is relatively low-income area and we have about a third of the population who are into blame and conspiracy theories. He appeals to those. We also have a rela-tively light voter turnout, so those who are ideologically charged up have the upper hand, since they are motivated to vote" (Novak 2001).

Mayor Talbott stated that the narrow victory has important implications for the city of Spokane: "It means we better be listening to what the people say on both sides" (Camden and Mulady 1999).

## Aftermath

Acting City Manager Pete Fortin, highly respected for his financial abilities, was fired in 2000 by Eugster, two other council members, and Mayor Talbott. City council member Higgins, who opposed that action, later stated, "I was so offended, I left the dais. I could not believe what happened to Pete in front of God and everybody" (Prager 2004a). The abandonment of council–manager government coupled with the election of a number of council members strongly in favor of the change to the mayor–council form was perceived to be a vote of "no-confidence" in the existing local government in Spokane.

John T. Powers Jr. was elected as the first mayor under the new form of government. Describing his new post, he stated, "Serving as Spokane's first strong mayor ranks among the very highest honors in my life" (Prager 2003b). As a candidate, Powers advocated resolving the River Park Square dispute but made little headway during his tenure. Powers spent most of his political efforts behind "One Spokane," an initiative aimed at addressing the issue of poverty. The issue of poverty, although a noble cause, was viewed by some as a futile effort and a waste of time and energy: "One Spokane became known as a series of events in which the well-heeled enjoyed some good cater-ing while paying lip service to the travails of the impoverished" (Weins 2003).

In the months that followed, a number of the long-time city department heads left their posts. Speaking to this issue, Mayor Powers commented that those who left were more concerned about their vacations and benefits than working hard (Prager 2003a). Other reports indicated the split was due to uncertainty with the new form of govern-ment on the part of the upper management.

## Form of Government: Round 2

At the next election in September 2003, the voters were given the opportunity to vote for mayor, three council seats, and council president, and revisit the form of government issue yet once again. City Proposition 1 was the ballot measure to replace the three-year-old mayor–council form with the council–manager form.

"Citizens for Sensible Government," a campaign aimed at returning to council–manager government, was headed by past–city councilman Dick Gow. Interestingly, the effort was financially supported by the city's largest employee union which reportedly spent more than $17,000 to back the change (Prager 2003a). Dave Rodgers, the last mayor in Spokane to win a reelection, also joined the campaign in support of council–manager government. Rodgers's involvement was significant because his tenure as mayor, from 1967 to 1977, was considered by many as "a high-water mark in civic affairs." Members of the Police Guild publicly supported the campaign but did not contribute any funds (Prager 2003a).

Of course, there were still those in Spokane who strongly supported the mayor–council form. Those advocating retention of the existing form organized as Strong Mayor-Spokane and staged a relatively limited campaign (Prager 2003a).

## Election Outcome and Analysis

In the September 16 election, voters chose to retain the strong-mayor form that it had embraced four years earlier. Were Spokane residents going to stand behind the strong-mayor form for the long term? Some suggested that the dissatisfaction with the council–manager form as communicated in the 1999 election was still felt by many. Clearly the majority of voters were not ready to give up on its new governmental structure yet. Discussing Spokane's decision to retain its mayor–council form, a local pollster was quoted as saying: "It sounds like people are willing to give this form of government a chance. But the next cycle's very critical for the system. I think they will give somebody a shot at being strong-mayor this time. But that person's at the crossroads. People will be watching closely" (Camden 2003).

Spokane residents denied Powers the office of mayor for another term in a primary of five mayoral candidates (Prager 2003b). Upheaval in Spokane's mayor's office was not unusual. The city had not reelected a mayor in more than three decades (Prager 2004b). Interestingly, this pattern would continue under the strong-mayor form, resulting in a rocky road for Spokane as various mayors with differing viewpoints pushed divergent agendas, which created lack of continuity in municipal priorities.

## Spokane's String of Strong Mayors

The person that the public would be watching so closely was Republican James Elton "Jim" West, who was elected Spokane's incoming mayor in November 2003. West served two terms in the state House and four terms in the state Senate before deciding to run for mayor of Spokane (Associated Press 2006).

And the public *was* watching. West's first sixteen months in office were viewed quite positively. He championed a voter-approved $117 million bond issue to repair the city's crumbling streets, made a series of necessary budget cuts, settled labor talks with unions, and oversaw the settlement of the River Park Square development, which saved the city from potentially being held liable for additional payments over the matter (Prager 2005a).

However, less than two years after his election, the *Spokesman-Review* began publishing articles about West's online activities in gay chat rooms and allegations of his attempts to get a city hall internship for what he thought was a high school student with whom he had sexually oriented discussions on the internet (Morlin 2005). The West scandal, rooted in a growing number of charges related to West's private life, quickly led to a cry from the citizens, Spokane City Council members, business leaders, and Republican leaders for a resignation or a recall. West, who boasted a twenty-seven-year career in city and state politics, fought these efforts and asked for a second chance (Associated Press 2006; Wiley 2005). Ultimately, the recall was successful. West was the first city official in Spokane to be recalled from office. He later died in July 2006 at the age of fifty-five from complications related to cancer surgery (Camden 2005b; Associated Press 2006). News reports indicate West was diagnosed with colon cancer in 2003 (Associated Press 2006).

In late 2005 Dennis P. Hession was unanimously appointed Spokane's new mayor. Hession, a former business attorney, was elected council president in 2003 (*Spokesman-Review* 2007). His goal was to "restore integrity to the office and a strengthening economy in the city" (Camden and Brunt 2007). In that vein Hession focused much of his time and energy on streamlining the city's budget and improving the efficiency of its services (*Spokesman-Review* 2007).

Local media reported that Hession's strong support shifted when a consultant's report recommended that the city could realize savings by reducing the number of city employees in various departments. This recommendation angered some of the city employee unions, particularly those representing the fire department and city hall. In the next election those unions supported one of Hession's opponents, Mary Verner, by making campaign contributions and volunteering in her campaign (Camden and Brunt 2007). Hession's service as mayor was short lived. Once again, the incumbent mayor failed to win a reelection to the $139,000 per year job as Spokane's mayor (*Spokesman-Review* 2007).

Hession was replaced in November 2007 by Mary Verner, who had served on the city council for four years and had previously worked as the executive director of the Upper Columbia United Tribes, which serves federally recognized Indian tribes in the region (www.spokanecity.org/government/mayor). She told Spokane voters that she represented a "change in the way we do leadership" and would bring to the office of mayor a "collaborative style of leadership" (Camden and Brunt 2007).

Verner's swearing-in ceremony, considered unusual by some, included a solo by her daughter as well as a Native American prayer and drum performance. With a background in law and environmental studies, Verner advocated an environmentally friendly agenda. Clearly Verner represented a vast departure from the career politician elected by the voters in 2003.

Interestingly, the River Park Square debacle continued to rise to the forefront of public discussions. In spite of the settlement of the case in 2004, other issues and lawsuits continued. In 2005 a Spokane County Superior Court judge said the city was negligent in not turning over hundreds of River Park Square–related documents properly requested by the media in 2000. The fine for violating the state's Public Records Act was approximately $21,000. The city must also pay the legal fees and related costs for bringing the lawsuit (Camden 2005a). Even when Verner took office, the question of the release of additional River Park Square documents was in the spotlight.

Verner, commenting on the ongoing financial fallout from the deal, was quoted as saying, "The pay-down of the River Square facilities is far from over." In mid-2008, Verner directed city staffers to draft an ordinance for consideration by the council that would require the developers involved in public–private partnerships to provide letters of credit or bonds in order to protect taxpayers and the city from future projects structured without that protection (Brunt 2008b).

## Conclusion

In Spokane, among other issues, the unpopular economic development priorities, a mayor who wanted stronger powers, and public doubt regarding the extent of the council's attention to its fiduciary responsibility all contributed to a lack of trust in the existing form of government and in some holding governmental positions. Interestingly, this growing lack of trust occurred in spite of a high degree of stability in the city manager's office demonstrated by only five city managers serving during Spokane's thirty-nine years as a council–manager city.

A number of important points emerge from this case. First, elected and appointed city leaders need to be in touch with the community's consensus on the preferred approach to economic development matters. Claims of misdirected economic development priorities and the parking garage controversy led residents to question their governmental leaders and its underlying form of government. If the manager had played a more influential role in guiding these policy decisions the outcomes might have been different. However, in this case economic development policy decisions proved to be powerful motivators for residents to demand a form of government change.

Second, this case emphasizes the simple concept that local elections are always crucial to the future direction of a city. Occasionally, elections serve as decisive turning points for a community. The timing of elections also plays a role. Highly publicized controversies serve as formidable backdrops for the reelection campaigns of incumbents and strongly influence individual election decisions. This is certainly the case when voters elect a mayor or a council majority that does not support their legal roles as happened in this case.

Finally, the bedrock of any form of government is public trust in the system. As demonstrated by Eugster, repeated allegations in the courts, the media, or elsewhere of possible improprieties by local public officials eventually will wear away public trust in its government. The damage done by these allegations was aggravated by the public's dissatisfaction in the city's responses to these charges. Furthermore, it is crucial that the city council and the city manager have sufficient credibility with the media to achieve balanced reporting on these charges.

If some citizens feel disenfranchised and perceive that the city's priorities are not in line with the desires of the citizenry, problems may develop in achieving comprehensive support from the electorate. This concern was articulated by the two candidates running for a council seat in the 1999 election. When asked to identify the "biggest problem facing city government," both candidates addressed the lack of trust and confidence in Spokane's city government (*Spokesman-Review* 1999).

Public trust was again the issue with the West scandal, which occurred while the city operated under mayor–council government. Facing allegations of using the mayor's office for personal gain and solicitation of minors, West was forced to deal with national media attention and Spokane faced negative and embarrassing publicity. Might this incident be the beginning of the undermining of the mayor–council form? Only the future will tell. The policy decisions and achievements of the Spokane City Council, Mary Verner, and her successors will go a long way in determining whether or not the citizens of Spokane will once again revisit its form of government.

## Note

The author wishes to acknowledge the assistance provided by Bill Pupo, Terry Novak, and Jim Sloane. An earlier version of this chapter was published in *Civic Battles: When Cities Change Their Form of Government*, by Wendy L. Hassett and Douglas J. Watson (Boca Raton, FL: PrAcademics Press, 2007).

## References

Associated Press. 2006. James E. West, 55; Ousted mayor of Spokane, Wash. *Washington Post*, July 23.

Brunt, Jonathan. 2008a. City's RPS strategy faces familiar critic. *Spokesman-Review*, June 7.

———. 2008b. Mayor hopes law ends garage debate. *Spokesman-Review*, July 4.

Camden, Jim. 2003. Mayor initiative too close to call. Poll shows measure slightly trailing, but neither side had majority. *Spokesman-Review*, September 10.

———. 2004. City bypasses warning signs. *Spokesman-Review*, March 31.

———. 2005a. City of Spokane fined in RPS battle. *Spokesman-Review*, February 10.

———. 2005b. West recall effort approved. *Spokesman-Review*, June 14.

Camden, Jim, and Jonathan Brunt. 2007. Jubilant Verner in control. *Spokesman-Review*, November 7.

Camden, Jim, and Kathy Mulady. 1999. Slim win for strong mayor. *Spokesman-Review*, November 18.

Connor, Tim. 2000. *Secret deal: The story behind the River Park Square garage*. Spokane, WA: Camas Magazine.

Geranios, Nicholas K. 1999. Rebels win battle to overhaul Spokane government. *Seattle Times*, November 28.

Johnson, Kristina. 1997. Council critic turns conciliatory candidate. *Spokesman-Review*, September 13.

McGregor, Ted S. 2002. Walker talks (finally). *The Pacific Northwest Inlander Online*, August 8.

Modie, Neil. 2000. A bitter battle in Spokane. *Seattle Post Intelligencer Reporter*, September 4.

Morlin, Bill. 2005. West tied to sex abuse in '70s, using office to lure young men. *Spokesman-Review*, May 5.

Mulady, Kathy. 1999a. Strong mayor plan revived. *Spokesman-Review*, March 26.

———. 1999b. Pupo plans to resign this week. *Spokesman-Review*, July 18.

———. 1999c. Council to consider Pupo package. *Spokesman-Review*, August 2.

———. 1999d. Council names Fortin as acting city manager. *Spokesman-Review*, August 10.

———. 1999e. Initiatives on council agenda. *Spokesman-Review*, August 30.

———. 1999f. Council puts three initiatives on ballot. *Spokesman-Review*, August 31.

———. 1999g. Mayor's future in hands of voters. *Spokesman-Review*, October 28.

Murphey, Michael. 1999a. At the crossroads. *Washington CEO*. August.

———. 1999b. High-tech genius. *Washington CEO*. August.

———. 1999c. Three keys for growth. *Washington CEO*. August.

Novak, T. 2001. Personal communication with author. October 17.

Powers, John. 2001. Resolving River Park Square: Commentary by John Powers. *Pacific Northwest Inlander Online*, August 23.

Prager, Mike. 2003a. Voters must wrestle over best kind of mayor. *Spokesman-Review*, September 7.

———. 2003b. Powers says he's grateful for opportunity mayor promises effective transition, draws standing ovation from council. *Spokesman-Review*, October 14.

———. 2004a. Spokane's outgoing city council was, at times, a turbulent bunch. *Spokesman-Review,* January 4.

———. 2004b. 'Yes' man in charge; Mayor sets new tone-and tells staff saying 'no' to residents is no option. *Spokesman-Review*, January 25.

———. 2004c. Legal fees pile up over RPS garage. *Spokesman Review*, February 14.

———. 2004d. RPS problems could cost Spokane grant recipients. *Spokesman-Review*, March 12.

———. 2005a. West has brought new tone, new success to city hall. *Spokesman-Review*, May 5.

———. 2005b. Spokane's link to River Park Square coming to an end. *Spokesman-Review*, September 14.

Pupo, B. 2001. Personal communication with author. October 15.

Sloane, J. 2001. Personal communication with author. October 24.

Spokane County Canvassing Board. 1999a. *Certificate of Election*, November 17.

———. 1999b. Amended *Certificate of Election, Proposition No. 2*, December 1.

*Spokesman-Review*. 1999. Questions for the candidates. *Spokesman Review*, October 21.

———. 2007. Breaking down the primary. *Spokesman-Review*, July 29.

WCMA [Washington City/County Management Association]. 2000. WCMA Regional Representative Reports. *WCMA News* 12, no. 1.

Weins, Richard. 2003. Strong-mayor system survives weak occupant. *Spokesman Review*, September 20.

Welch, Craig. 1999. Pupo gets walking money. *Spokesman Review*, August 3.

Wiley, John K. 2005. Pressure increases on Spokane mayor to resign. *Seattle Times*, May 26.

CHAPTER 4

# HARTFORD

## Politics Trumps Professionalism

WENDY L. HASSETT

## Introduction

THE CITY OF HARTFORD, CONNECTICUT, not only serves as the state's capital but also is home to many of the world's insurance company headquarters. Companies such as Aetna, Hartford Financial Services Group, Phoenix, and Travelers have roots in Hartford. Because of its historical connections with a number of insurance giants, Hartford earned the nickname of "insurance capital of the world."

Another company that called Hartford home was Colt firearms, founded in Hartford in 1847. Colt held the patent on the revolvers used in the Mexican–American War and is perhaps best known for the famous Colt .45. Today, one of Hartford's most prestigious corporate residents is United Technologies Corporation (UTC), a large military supplier known for the Black Hawk helicopter.

Hartford also has a rich cultural heritage. It is home to destinations such as the Wadsworth Atheneum art museum, the Mark Twain House (where Twain wrote *The Adventures of Tom Sawyer* and *The Adventures of Huckleberry Finn*), the Hartford Stage Theater, the Bushnell Memorial, and the Artists Collective.

## History

Hartford was founded in the early 1600s by Dutch fur traders who were attracted to the trade-related benefits of the Connecticut River and established a trading post. A few years later a group of English settlers settled just north of the Dutch trading post and eventually engulfed it. The English settlement was originally called Newtown but was changed to Hartford in 1637 in honor of the English town of Hertford.

In the early 1800s Hartford was home to a number of abolitionist supporters. In fact, Harriet Beecher Stowe, author of the famous *Uncle Tom's Cabin*, lived the last twenty-three years of her life in Hartford. Her house and a research library are located in the city.

Hartford's population steadily increased in the nineteenth and twentieth centuries from just over 17,000 in 1850 to more than 170,000 in 1950, which was the height of its population to date. In fact, Hartford went from being considered one of the wealthiest U.S. cities in the late 1800s to being one of the poorest in the 1970s (McKee 2000, 27).

The story of Hartford's struggle with governmental form played out against a backdrop of heated partisan elections, a politically influential private sector, massive demographic changes, and economic hardships. Undoubtedly, these factors play a role in the city's struggle to return to prosperity and economic health, but the story of Hartford is one that continues to find the city ranking near the bottom of municipalities in Connecticut, and the nation, on many indicators of economic health. A U.S. Census 2000 Brief addressing national poverty in 1999 ranked Hartford as the second poorest city in the country with one hundred thousand or more residents—just behind Brownsville, Texas (U.S. Census 1999).

## Adoption of Council–Manager Government

During the mid-1940s Hartford was an affluent and vibrant city enjoying commercial and industrial growth. Hartford's population was on the upswing as the city saw an influx of workers seeking employment in Hartford and its suburbs. While the industrial, commercial, and retail sectors were thriving, the financial and insurance sectors also were burgeoning (Cruz 1998; Fenton 2004).

In spite of the strong economy at that time, many were concerned with Hartford's long-term economic viability because of the heavy tax burden imposed by the city. This tax burden on Hartford's corporate citizens was attributed to the highly political city administration at the time. If the companies that called Hartford home got fed up, they could relocate to another city where the tax rate was not as burdensome. In fact, Pratt & Whitney Aircraft did just that in 1939. It is believed that the decision to relocate was largely based on Hartford's high taxes (Fenton 2004).

In the early 1940s Hartford was governed by a mayor who was elected every two years and who presided over a twenty-member board of aldermen, most of whom were elected by districts. The aldermen and mayoral candidates were elected from party-endorsed slates. The mayor had veto power over council decisions, which could be overridden by a simple majority (Fenton 2004).

In 1945 Republican Mayor William Mortensen was convinced that the existing government structure needed an overhaul and rallied support for a Charter Review Commission. The goal was to submit revisions to the voters at the upcoming election in November 1946. Mortensen did not seek reelection and was succeeded in December 1945 by Republican Cornelius Moylan who died in office after serving only one year (Fenton 2004).

After holding a series of public meetings where the issue of governmental form was hotly debated, the Charter Review Commission drafted a proposed new charter that was publicly released in May 1946. The proposal recommended a more streamlined government that had a city manager answering to a nine-member city council elected at-large in nonpartisan elections. The title of mayor was given to the individual who received the most votes in the city council election. A merit system was introduced, and most of the long-standing boards and commissions were replaced by individuals who reported to the city manager (Cruz 1998; Fenton 2004).

Once the commission recommendations were released, opponents to the plan became vocal. One such opponent was Democrat John M. Bailey, a young lawyer educated at Harvard Law School and son of a well-known Hartford doctor. In spite of the disapproval of Bailey and others who favored a strong-mayor form, the central recommendations remained intact as the document went to the city council for formal consideration. The aldermen who opposed the revisions threatened to oppose inclusion of the measure on the November ballot and instead push it to a special election. Supporters of the reform, including business and civic leaders, actively fought these delaying tactics. However, by September 1946 it was clear that most of the alderman supported the issue being placed on a special election ballot in December. Voters approved the Charter Review Committee's recommendations by more than two to one. Nonpartisan elections were soon to be the order of the day and a nine-member council elected at large would govern the city (Cruz 1998; Fenton 2004).

While the civic and business community longed for a more professional and streamlined city government, others supported the change for much different reasons. While the overriding rationale behind the community's choice of this form is not clear, one of the prevailing thoughts is described by Clyde McKee (2000, 32): "During the first half of the twentieth century, Connecticut was a Republican state. Republican state officials recognized that the state's cities were becoming growth centers for the Democratic Party. They saw council–manager government, with its at-large, nonpartisan elections and nonpartisan professional management, as an ideal strategy to preserve their hegemony and prevent a rapid rise of the Democratic Party."

According to McKee, Republicans wanted to block attempts by Democratic leadership to take control of the state capital. They viewed council–manager government as a roadblock to these efforts.

In spite of the reasons behind the community's support of the new form, Hartford had a new organizational structure in place by 1947—the council–manager form. Carlton F. Sharpe was selected as Hartford's first city manager. Sharpe enjoyed a long tenure in the position, serving from 1947 to 1963.

## Hartford's Growth

The 1950 Census reported Hartford's population as 177,397—the highest population recorded. However, the decade from 1950 to 1960 was a turning point. In the late 1950s downtown Hartford began to experience economic decline while Hartford suburbs began to flourish. Department stores began to close while suburban shopping malls thrived. Insurance giant Connecticut General (now CIGNA) abandoned a key building in Hartford when it relocated to the suburb of Bloomfield. During this time

minority populations began to grow; between 1957 and 1959 the Puerto Rican population doubled from three thousand to six thousand (Cruz 1998).

Hartford businesses were still thriving, however, and increasingly used the Chamber
of Commerce as their vehicle to push the city government in new directions. In the
mid-1950s a new executive director for the Greater Hartford Chamber of Commerce
was hired—Arthur J. Lumsden. In many ways Lumsden acted as a conduit between
the private and public sectors, actively forging business relationships with the city by
involving the business community in municipal efforts such as urban renewal projects
and regional planning (Clavel 1986).

## Council–Manager Government and Partisan Politics

While Hartford's new form of government brought with it the hope of a more professional and efficient approach to city administration, it did not eliminate partisan and
political struggles that were such a fundamental part of the city's history. McKee (2000,
33) describes city politics following the adoption of the new form of government as
following "the model for council–manager charter in form if not in spirit." Between
1947 and 1969 candidates for city council were nominated by petitions and ran in
nonpartisan elections. The position of mayor was determined by the council candidate
with the highest vote total. The job was primarily ceremonial with presiding at council
meetings and representing the city at meetings as the primary responsibilities, according
to McKee (2000).

However, things changed in 1953 when Democrat John M. Bailey invested a great
deal of money in the local election and endorsed a slate of Democratic candidates.
These efforts paid off. Democrats won eight of the nine council seats. Many people felt
the 1953 election was a subversion of the nonpartisan system formally embraced by the
city (Cruz 1998). Before long a pattern of Democratic control of the city's elected
offices was established that continued for decades.

Bailey had become a strong political force in Hartford. McKee (2000, 33) described
how Bailey, with the cooperation of the local chairman of the Democratic Party, controlled the city council and dictated the policy that he wanted to implement. Bailey
and the party chairman recruited Democrats to run for the nonpartisan council by
assuring them that he would secure the necessary signatures on the petitions and ensure
a strong partisan turnout on election day. Bailey soon became the most influential
political leader in Hartford, controlling party endorsements for state and local candidates. McKee (2000, 33) reported that Bailey would host a meeting of city council
members in the "Bailey Room" of a restaurant situated behind city hall prior to each
council meeting. At this meeting Bailey would discuss with the elected officials the
decisions they were to make at the upcoming meeting, as well as their interests in
patronage appointments. McKee (2000) noted that Bailey and other party leaders were
careful not to interfere with the administrative duties of the city manager.

In the mid-1950s black citizens organized a successful effort to have a voice on the
Hartford council. In 1955 John Clark Jr. was elected as the first African American on

the Hartford City Council. By the 1960s the African American community became disgruntled with their socioeconomic position. Black extremist groups increased in membership. Increasingly the African American community expressed their desire to have a growing number of blacks in key leadership positions (Cruz 1998, 26).

By 1960 Hartford's population dropped to 162,178, and the economic status of its poorest residents looked bleak. Clavel (1986) describes Hartford in the 1960s as "polarized in its economics and demography." He states that while Hartford earned prestige for serving as the state capital and for being home to some of the largest insurance giants employing some 30,000 people, it was also the home to an increasing number of individuals and families living at or below the poverty level. Part of this was due to the decline of the tobacco industry that decades earlier attracted a large number of laborers who were now unemployed. During this same time, many white families left Hartford for the suburbs (Clavel 1986, 19–20). In August 1963 Hartford native Elisha C. "Eli" Freedman, who had served as the executive secretary to former city manager Carlton Sharpe since 1959, stepped in to fill the post of city manager (Morse 1963).

## Republicans Revisit the City's Charter

In light of the partisan control of the city council, Republican leaders revisited their strategy in Hartford in the late 1960s. Clearly the so-called nonpartisan approach did not result in the outcome they had envisioned. While they recognized the value of a professional manager and did not want to abandon a governmental structure that was supported by the citizenry, they wanted to address somehow Hartford's political reality and encourage aspiring and promising politicians to offer themselves as candidates for the office of mayor.

Support grew within this group to reintroduce partisan elections in the hope that this strategy would enable them to secure seats on the council. They reached out to the Democratic leaders with this proposal. In exchange for their support, the Democrats wanted a directly elected mayor. As discussion continued, a trade-off was made that the separately elected mayor would give up a vote on the council, enjoy veto authority over council decisions, have an increased salary of $18,000, and manage a personal staff (McKee 2000, 34; Cruz 1998; Zielbauer 2000).

## Racial Tensions and Changing Leadership

Racial tensions in Hartford grew. For example, one December evening in 1966, a firebomb was thrown on the porch of City Manager Freedman's home (Williams 1966). Soon thereafter, in the summer of 1967, Hartford experienced a series of riots, looting, vandalism, firebombs, shootings, and arson. These episodes had strong racial undertones and challenged the ability of the city to maintain civil order. While the worst riots happened in Hartford, the city was not alone in dealing with these violent outbreaks. New Haven, Bridgeport, Waterbury, and New Britain also experienced riots that year. In spite of attempts to curb the outbreaks and the imposition of curfews, these intense eruptions continued through 1970 (Gansberg 1970; Clavel 1986; Cruz 1998).

Antonina P. "Ann" Uccello had served as a city council member during the riots and, after serving on the Hartford City Council for two terms, won the office of mayor by winning the most votes in the 1967 election. An active member of the Republican Party for many years, Uccello had worked to improve the heavily Democratic-led city government in the early 1960s. Uccello's election as mayor was an important milestone in a number of ways. She became Hartford's first female mayor, its first Republican mayor in twenty years, and the first large-city female mayor in Connecticut (Gizzi 2005).

The destruction caused by the riots deeply affected the city at many levels during this time. Clavel (1989) described the council–manager form as functioning well when the decisions before the council were straightforward and simple. However, the aftermath of the riots deepened the complexity of the issues facing the council. The heated debates with racial overtones presented a problematic environment for city administrators. As Clavel put it, "what existed in 1969 was an authority vacuum in Hartford's political leadership caused by those leaders' inability to deal with the riots" (27).

Interestingly, in spite of the civic unrest, incumbent Uccello was reelected mayor in 1969. This was the first year the rules had changed, providing for a separately elected mayor in partisan elections. Uccello's performance as mayor of Hartford was viewed very positively. She was regarded as a favorite political figure in the state and earned a glowing reputation among Hartford citizens. In fact, in a 1970 poll 81 percent of the Hartford citizenry approved of her performance (McKee 2000). Riding high on the wave of popular opinion, Uccello chose to seek higher office. She resigned from her mayoral post in 1971 to run for the First Congressional District. In spite of her loss in a close race, she continued to serve in the public sector as the director of the Department of Transportation under presidents Nixon and Ford. As of this writing, Uccello was the last Republican to serve as Hartford's mayor.

Upon the resignation of Uccello, then deputy mayor George A. Athanson (Democrat), who was considered a "flamboyant mayor who modeled himself after Fiorello La Guardia" (Martin 2000), assumed the office of mayor. Athanson served 1971–1981, a term of office that was the longest of any Hartford mayor since the early 1800s.

Athanson evolved into a mayor who, once again, allowed other forces, primarily Nicholas "Nick" Carbone, to exert strong influences on the city government. Most of Athanson's time was spent practicing law and teaching college classes. While he wanted to serve as mayor, he did not have the time or energy to be more than a figurehead. As a result the political power was held by Deputy Mayor Nick Carbone and the local Democratic Party machine. Interestingly, Carbone was at one point Hartford's Democratic Party chairman and leader. His influence was felt deeply in the politics, policy, and administration of Hartford's city government. In July of 1977 a *Washington Post* article called Carbone "America's most powerful city councilman" (McKee 2000, 34).

Carbone relished his power in Hartford's municipal government and invested the time and effort to line up the votes necessary to make things happen. Carbone's influence is claimed to have been the reason behind the resignation of City Manager Freedman in the early 1970s. Following the resignation of Freedman, the Hartford City

Council appointed the fire chief, Edward M. Curtin Jr., as city manager. Curtin was the first of a number of short-term managers who "functioned fairly much in Carbone's shadow" (Clavel 1986, 40). Cruz (1989, 31) noted, "The resignation of city manager Elisha Friedman [sic] in 1970 gave Carbone an opportunity to fill a policy vacuum, and he took it. In the process he subverted the council–manager form of government, becoming a de facto strong mayor."

The influences on Hartford's local policy decisions reached beyond Nicholas Carbone. Local business leaders continued to influence the decisions emanating from city hall. In particular, a closely knit group of prestigious corporate executives from the most influential industries and banks in the area came together through their association with the chamber of commerce. This group met regularly at breakfast with city leaders including Carbone to discuss policy directions that would be mutually beneficial to both the business community and the city. In response to requests from the city leaders, these individuals participated in funding a number of key municipal projects including the Hartford civic center, the riverfront recapture project, moderate-income city apartment rehabilitation, and technology upgrades in the schools (McKee 2000).

Meanwhile, city conditions continued to worsen. Welfare and social security payments increasingly supported a growing number of Hartford residents, and unemployment was twice what it was in the mid-1960s. The city's cost to provide basic public services increased while the tax base eroded. The number of abandoned and dilapidated houses grew while property tax was much higher than in other Connecticut cities (Clavel 1986).

Carbone decided to run for mayor against Athanson in 1979. Although he knew that his strong stance on a number of local issues had created political enemies, Carbone longed to serve the city as its formal political head. In an unscientific poll, staff of *Southside Neighborhood News*, now the *Hartford News*, called one hundred randomly selected Hartford residents to ask their opinions about the mayoral race between Athanson and Carbone. Then editor Lee Paquette was quoted as saying, "Support for Athanson was so strong, the race was judged to be over before it started" (Hart 1997). Carbone lost the Democratic primary by a wide margin (Clavel 1986). Athanson was reelected and served until 1981. Carbone moved on to different endeavors, eventually working as a real estate developer (Cruz 1998; Clavel 1986).

In Athanson's last term of office, the city faced a major shift in its population base. By 1980, middle-class flight resulted in a population consisting of roughly one-third Latino, one-third African American, and one-third Caucasian. With these changes came growing and active neighborhood organizations that coalesced around common social and economic concerns (Clavel 1986). The stage was set for an interesting election in 1981.

## New Leadership

Perhaps reflecting the population shift, in late 1981 Thirman L. Milner became Hartford's first African American mayor. Black leadership became a reality in Hartford now that the mayor, deputy mayor, and city manager (Woodrow W. Gaitor) were all African American. In 1982 Aetna decided to move part of its operations outside the Hartford city limits. To some, the decision was viewed as a forewarning of things to come. Many of the insurance and corporate entities located in Hartford had leases that were set to expire in just a few years (Clavel 1986).

When Milner chose not to run for reelection in 1987, he urged state representative Carrie Saxon Perry to run. Perry won and became the first black woman to be elected mayor of a major northeastern city (Simmons 1998). She served three terms. Perry was intelligent, charismatic, and politically ambitious. She had earned a reputation of being an outspoken advocate for minorities and of affirmative action. Once in office she made personnel changes to some of the key departmental positions held by whites. During her final term she ran with a reform slate that won all nine seats (Simmons 1998; McKee 2000). The most significant changes were made during this last term of office; the position of deputy mayor became a rotating position that changed monthly.

While powers granted by the charter had not changed, Perry used her political strength to exert considerable control over the operations of the city. McKee (2000) suggests that Perry not only orchestrated the city manager's resignation, but also strongly influenced the selection of his replacement. In this way she could make sure the person in this position was loyal to her in spite of the form of government in place.

The policies of the 1980s affected Hartford dramatically. This was particularly true in the area of municipal finances. For example, the state passed a law in 1988 that allowed cities to place a very low cap on residential property tax and make up the difference with surcharges paid by business properties. Grasping for any way to keep its middle class from leaving town, Hartford instituted the change, and it was the only Connecticut city to do so. Although a number of businesses paid the additional taxes, many small companies relocated outside the city. This one action more than any other decision has been credited with devastating the city's business appeal.

During 1991–1993, the council and city administration more accurately reflected the new demographics in Hartford. The nine-member council consisted of three African Americans, three Puerto Ricans, and three whites. The female mayor was African American. The city manager was an African American male, and the position of corporation counsel was held by a Puerto Rican (Simmons 1998).

By 1993 the governing situation in Hartford was grim and "the atmosphere at city hall was extremely contentious" (Simmons 1998, 181). McKee (2000) suggests that Mayor Perry's six years in office resulted in a budget that was out of control. Budget cuts to the police department were blamed for the marked increase in gang-related crimes and homicides.

At the urging of Perry, an election was held to revisit the form of government once again. Perry's efforts to replace council–manager government with a strong-mayor plan were defeated by Hartford residents who remained supportive of the council–manager form (Zielbauer 2000). Voters also ousted Perry from office and elected as mayor Mike Peters, a long-time fire department veteran, whose sister was on the council. In many ways, Peters was very different from Perry. Peters was vocal about his support of council–manager government and was supported by downtown businesses (Simmons 1998).

Peters was considered witty, nonconfrontational, upbeat, inclusive, and friendly (Ryan 1993). "Any liabilities or dubious qualities of Peters were transformed into assets: His lack of in-depth knowledge on issues and his use of wisecracks rather than substantive comments were heralded as a down-to-earth approach, spiced with humor" (Simmons 1998, 182).

Prior to stepping down from their public offices and upon learning that Peters and his allies did not plan to reappoint then city manager Howard J. Stanback who had made campaign contributions to Perry's campaign, Perry's supporters on the city council reappointed Stanback. They also approved a severance package of one year's salary plus benefits, which amounted up to $150,000. Peters criticized the move, saying, "Kids don't have proper books in schools here and she's going to give this guy an extra year's salary" (Ryan 1993).

Once in office Peters hired a new city manager, Saundra Kee Borges, an African American woman who was a long-time friend of Peters. Kee Borges had a law background and had worked for the city before Peters was elected (McKee 2000).

According to a State of Connecticut report in 1994, Hartford's population loss of 11.1 percent was the largest in the nation for a large city during 1990–1994 (State of Connecticut 1996). Peters and Kee Borges faced significant challenges. During the Peters–Kee Borges era that spanned eight years, the business elites once again strongly influenced the policy decisions and priorities of the city. The private sector influence was communicated in a White House press release dated November 4, 1999. This official White House statement announced President Clinton's trip to Hartford, where he would see firsthand the significant ways the private sector rather than the public sector addressed the needs of a city in economic distress. The press release mentions corporate presidents and CEOs by name and describes the initiatives they spearheaded in Hartford (Office of the Press Secretary 1999).

Zielbauer (2002b) described the situation this way:

> In spite of projects that represented to many a resurgence of economic health for Hartford, serious problems remained. In the 1980s and 1990s, the city made several questionable policy and administrative decisions. A *New York Times* article mentioned that in the 1980's and 1990's, Hartford allowed top managers to have full pensions after working for only 15 years, granted 25 percent raises to firefighters over a three year period, and hired a city manager who lived in Chicago and commuted to Hartford several days per week. The *New York Times* opined that these ill-advised decisions "would bankrupt any private enterprise."

Public confidence in the city and the role of the city manager continued to erode. Gurwitt (2000) offered two reasons for the failure of council–manager government during this time. First, the city council did not seem to want a strong city manager who could advise it on policy matters and "who might also fend off its incursions into the day-to-day management of the city." Second, the incumbent city manager had been the deputy city attorney and was too conciliatory for a "contentious city like Hartford."

The local economy suffered during these years as the employment base began to vanish. Citizens watched as more than a quarter of Hartford's factory jobs left town. Making things worse, the cornerstone of Hartford's economy, its insurance industry, was devastated when thousands of well-paid, high-skill jobs were eliminated.

Critics also point to a number of festering administrative problems that had not been resolved (McKee 2000; Gurwitt 2000): the unfortunate plight of the city's public school system, scandal in the police force, racism in the city's fire and public works departments, questionable fiscal expenditures, and problematic hiring practices.

For example, in the 1990s Hartford's school system was challenged by poor student test scores, patronage appointments, financial and administrative problems, deteriorating facilities, and divisive racial issues (Burns 2002; Mazzocca 1998). The problems intensified to such a degree that the schools were considered to be dysfunctional. In fact, Hartford made national news when, in a last-ditch effort to improve the schools in 1994, the city hired a private company, Education Alternatives Inc., to run its school system.

Apparently not even outside experts could help. In 1996 the city council fired the company and declared its school system to be "incapable of self-correction" and urged the mayor to declare a state of emergency. Upon receiving a recommendation from the New England Association of Schools and Colleges to revoke Hartford's public high school's accreditation in 1997, the governor stepped in and called for the state to take over Hartford's public schools (Simmons 1998; Burns 2002). Mayor Peters supported that move.

Interestingly, in 1996 *Governing* magazine named Peters one of the year's public officials of the year. While the magazine recognized that Peters had not turned Hartford's economic and social situations around, it hailed him for changing the mood of the city: "Over the past few years, its spirit and sense of confidence have undergone a striking revival. City government, Hartford's residents, its neighborhood groups, its business leaders and, most notably, its suburban neighbors—all have been overtaken by an almost buoyant belief that reversing the city's decline is possible" (Gurwitt 1996).

Increasingly, the structure of the government became a hot issue. The *New York Times* (Zielbauer 2001) made this commentary on the mayoral position in Hartford: "In Hartford, the mayor has no vote on the City Council, holds no power to hire or fire anyone other than his secretary and makes so little money—$30,000, which is a shade more than double the state's minimum wage—that only a handful of city residents qualified to hold the office have even considered running for it."

The declining population base and declining tax base brought with it an increase in crime. In 2004 the local paper reported (Burgard 2004) that Hartford was included in a list of the most dangerous U.S. cities: "A survey by a national research firm has ranked Hartford as the seventh most dangerous city in the United States, alongside such traditional crime hotbeds as New Orleans, Baltimore, Washington D.C. and Detroit." And its options are limited for expanding its geographical territory. Hartford encompasses approximately nineteen square miles. It is surrounded on all sides by land incorporated by other cities, thereby eliminating the option of increasing its tax base by annexing adjacent land. Rusk (1993, 53) identified Hartford as one of the most "inelastic" municipalities in the United States shouldered with some of the most problematic challenges, including severe erosion of its tax base and deteriorating social issues.

## 2000 Form of Government Election

While Peters was mayor, the question of governmental form was once again brought to the forefront. A local Hartford lawyer who served as the chairman of the Charter Revision Commission was quoted in the *New York Times*: "The council has never let the city manager really be the chief executive of the city. We've had a form of government that kind of combines the worst of both worlds. We have a city manager that is unaccountable to the public, and the City Council involves itself in a lot of things that mess up the way the city works." Those who opposed the change included the city's Democratic town chairman, Bob J. Jackson, who was quoted in the same article: "When you go to a strong mayor form of running a government, you have got to have the necessary safeguards in place. I don't think changing the government is the root cause of all of our problems" (Zielbauer 2000).

In December 2000 Hartford voters were faced with a question of whether or not to revise the city charter and establish a mayor–council form. The proposed charter revisions were written by a commission and reportedly designed to make Hartford's government more efficient, less political, and more responsive. In addition to eliminating the position of city manager and making the mayor the chief executive, the proposed revisions would have elected the mayor every four years (instead of two), increased the salary of the mayor from $30,000 to $105,000, increased the number of council members from nine to fifteen, and changed from at-large council elections to elections by ward. The measure also proposed the city's state-appointed board of education be changed to seven members—with four elected by Hartford votes and three appointed by the mayor (Zielbauer 2000).

The matter was to be decided in a special election that required a minimum of 15 percent of all registered voters to approve the measure. While the results of the election supported the charter revision, the votes fell short of the 15 percent requirement. As a result the measure failed (Zielbauer 2000; Burns 2002). Some attribute the failure of the measure to the fact that the form of government question was grouped with several other changes (Stowe 2002).

## Perez Runs for Mayor

Born in Corozal, Puerto Rico, Eddie Perez arrived in Hartford in 1969 at the age of twelve with his family. In his 2001 run for mayor, Perez was the clear favorite. As president of the Southside Institutions Neighborhood Alliance (SINA), a community development association, he helped build the $110 million Learning Corridor, which many thought would never happen. Perez was an advocate for increasing homeownership, improving public schools, and initiating community policing. Perez ran for mayor assured that the voters would approve a charter revision. He felt a strong mayor was needed to recapture the faith of Hartford residents and businesses and to move the city's policy agenda forward in terms of economics and social issues (Stowe 2002).

Perez was elected to a two-year term and became Hartford's first Latino mayor. Soon after taking office, Perez formed a Charter Review Commission to scrutinize the current governmental structure and make recommendations on changes (Frederickson, Johnson, and Wood 2003, 146). Interestingly, in spite of his claim of structural constraints of Hartford's council–manager government, Perez was considered a very powerful leader even though he had no formal authority under the city charter. Pazniokas (2002) pointed out that Perez was "indisputably the most powerful man in city hall" as he approached the midpoint of his first term. At that point in his first term, Perez had installed his choices for school superintendent and city manager, and took control of all school construction (Pazniokas 2002).

Coinciding with the election of Perez, City Manager Kee Borges stepped down from the post she had held under former mayor Mike Peters (Pazniokas 2001). Kee Borges's vacancy was filled for about a year by Albert Ilg, a retired town manager. The transition from Kee Borges to her successor, Albert Ilg, was not without controversy. Upon the end of Kee Borges's contract, the *New York Times* (Zielbauer 2002a) described the transition as one hotly debated among the city council and legal counsel on both sides. The crux of the issue involved Borges's pension, which some considered "hefty," a "performance bonus," and compensation for two months of "consulting services."

Perez's choice for interim city manager, retired Windsor, Connecticut, town manager Albert G. Ilg, served from December 2001 to August 2002 (Simpson 2005). During that temporary appointment, Ilg made a number of changes in the city in an attempt to streamline the overgrown city government. While only serving a short period, Ilg's accomplishments were viewed as impressive (Stowe 2002).

Despite a $47 million budget gap projected in December, Ilg presented a balanced $422 million budget that did not require an increase in Hartford's high property tax rate. It passed with minor changes. Ilg made a number of moves to professionalize city hall. Ilg reorganized public works, fired the finance director, and began the merger of city and school information technology and building services functions. Perez took no credit for the changes, though he was supportive. The council and mayor seemed to leave Ilg to do as he saw fit. In some cases they seemed pleased to be spared the political backlash (Pazniokas 2002).

While city manager Ilg made headway in addressing many of the challenges facing the city, the broad scope of the troubling social, economic, and public safety issues facing Hartford was overwhelming. Thirty percent of the city's population lived in poverty, the school system was one of the worst performing in the country, and each child born in Hartford had an 80 percent chance of being raised by an unwed mother (Stowe 2002).

A Charter Review Commission was already established and holding public meetings to solicit input as to how to improve the city structure. The vote to once again revisit Hartford's form of government was scheduled in the coming months. After the departure of interim manager Ilg, Lee C. Erdmann began his duties as city manager in September 2002. Erdmann had the benefit of having both city management experience and a connection to Hartford. He served as town manager in Wethersfield, Connecticut, for fifteen years. And, in the late 1970s to mid-1980s, Erdmann served as Hartford's budget director and assistant city manager (Hartford Press Release 2002).

## The 2002 City Charter Changes

In September 2002 the mayor and council approved commission recommendations that included changing the form of government from council–manager to mayor–council. The expanded mayoral powers included increasing the term of office to four years, serving as the chief executive officer of the city, appointing all department heads, and serving as the chief operating officer who managed the department heads. The removal of these individuals from their offices required approval of six council members. The mayor would also prepare and present annual budgets to the council for its consideration and appoint a majority of the board of education.

With the backing of Perez and many community activists, voters approved the proposed charter changes on November 5, 2002. Those in favor of changing to the council–mayor form of government were 6,125, or approximately 77 percent. The vote against the change was 1,859, or 23 percent. The other two charter revision questions received the same level of support. The question of establishing a board of education consisting of nine members, five of whom would be appointed by the mayor and the remaining elected at large, received support as well—77 to 23 percent. The last question lumped the remaining Charter Revision Commission's recommendations into one generic question regarding whether the city's charter should be revised to incorporate all additional changes recommended by the committee. This, too, received support of 5,851 to 1,658, or 78 to 22 percent. The changes to the city's charter would take effect in conjunction with the 2003 election (Frederickson, Johnson, and Wood 2003, 146–47; Pazniokas 2002).

### Analysis of Referendum Results

The question of why council–manager government failed to achieve positive results for Hartford is worthy of consideration. Three contributing factors stand out: continuity of leadership, a culture of partisan politics, and a dramatic change in demographics.

#### LACK OF LEADERSHIP CONTINUITY

There is no doubt Hartford lacked continuity in its governmental leadership. The city had fifteen mayors while it operated as a council–manager city (1947–2002) (Mayors of Hartford). Looking back over his service as Hartford's mayor in the mid-1960s, former mayor James Kinsella commented, "Since the late 1940s, the mayor's hands have been tied. It was only through sheer force of the mayor's personality that goals were achieved, a caveat that benefited some more than others" (Stowe 2002).

Interestingly, Hartford records show the city employed fifteen city managers during that period as well. The initial city manager hired in 1947, Carlton F. Sharpe, had a long tenure of sixteen years. The two who followed, Elisha C. Freedman and Edward M. Curtin, enjoyed tenures of eight and five years, respectively. However, the nine city managers who served after Curtin had an unusually short average tenure of 1.8 years. This pattern was broken by Saundra Kee Borges, who was appointed in December 1993 and served for eight years under Mayor Mike Peters, who was Hartford's mayor for the same eight years (1993–2001). With this much change in personalities and leadership style, one might conclude that Hartford is an example of council–manager government faltering within a disjointed leadership environment.

It is interesting that at several points in Hartford's history, leadership came from places other than city hall. McKee (2000, 45) argues, "The overall leadership dynamics in Hartford have subverted and modified the council–manager form of government in ways that inhibit even competent technical and administrative leadership from emerging. Since 1972 Hartford's political leaders have hired and fired ten city managers and ten school superintendents, costing the city hundreds of thousands in contract buyouts. Even more costly was the disruption to the governance of the city. Many of the city's present problems can be traced to a lack of continuity and the hiring and firing of city managers, a number of whom were untrained locals." A *New York Times* article (Stowe 2002) echoed that sentiment: "In the past 20 years, the city has had eight city managers, some of whom are credited with negotiating union and pension contracts that experts said would bankrupt a private business."

Is continuity among a city's top elected and appointed leadership a factor that undergirds a community's form of government? Is continuity such an important factor that the lack of it can undermine confidence in the existing governmental form?

## A PARTISAN POLITICS CULTURE

Frederickson, Johnson, and Wood (2003, 145) categorized Hartford's council–manager government as "conciliated" because in spite of the city's legal structure of council–manager, there was "separation of political powers between the mayor and the city council, and the city manager serves as the chief executive officer." They argue that because the city manager was appointed and dismissed by the council and responsible for appointing, managing, and dismissing department heads, the manager was placed in the unique position of being a "facilitator and bridge between the mayor and the council." Furthermore, because the mayor did not play a legislative role in directing the actions of the city manager, yet enjoyed veto power over council decisions, Hartford's mayor served more as a policy advocate whose power "rests solely on the ability to cobble together a council coalition" (Frederickson, Johnson, and Wood 2003, 145).

Perhaps as an outgrowth of this legal structure, party politics continued to thrive in municipal operations. As history has shown, partisan politics has deep roots in Hartford's culture. A Hartford attorney was quoted in a *New York Times* article (Stowe 2002) as saying, "A strong mayor government is more conducive to an urban environment where patronage politics have a more important role and ethnic politics are more significant than in the suburbs." That sentiment was vocalized time after time as the form of government question rose to the forefront of community discussions. In spite of various efforts and structural adjustments aimed at eliminating party politics from Hartford city hall, citizens viewed partisan politics as the dominate influence on the vast majority of local decisions. Was Hartford's deeply rooted political culture so incompatible with the classic council–manager model that it rendered it ineffective?

### DEMOGRAPHIC AND ECONOMIC CHANGES

Hartford also is a study of population change and increasing diversity. The composition of the council mirrored the increased diversity of Hartford's population. In addition to the demographic diversity, Hartford faced a continual decrease in population and an increase in poverty. These factors have been noted as making cities "ripe targets for a challenge to the form of government" (Hassett and Watson 2007, 142). Is there a tipping point related to demographics and poverty where council–manager government can no longer be the responsive and politically neutral managerial force it was designed to be?

## Hartford under Perez's Leadership

More than fifty years after adopting the council–manager form, Hartford returned to the mayor–council form in the 2003 election, reestablishing municipal authority in an elected mayor. Eddie Perez was reelected in 2003 to a four-year term under the city's new charter. One of the first official acts of the governing body was to approve the mayor's recommendation to name standing city manager, Lee C. Erdmann, as the city's new chief operating officer (Pazniokas 2004).

As Hartford's mayor, Perez was a larger-than-life figure who garnered much attention. In October 2007 he was recognized as one of the "100 Most Influential Hispanics" by *Hispanic Business* magazine. While far from controversial, Perez maintained support from a large segment of the community under the new mayor–council form. However, the *New York Times* endorsed I. Charles Mathews for mayor in the 2007 election. In September 2007 an editorial in the *New York Times* explained its reasoning for not supporting Perez and for endorsing Mathews. The *Times* noted that Hartford is the poorest of the nation's fifty state capitals and that voters in 2003 elected Perez to change the direction of the city. The editorialist agreed that Perez had made some positive moves, such as bringing in a dynamic school superintendent, who appeared to be improving the Hartford schools. New high-end housing was under construction in the downtown, and the city's new civic center was generating activity in the downtown.

However, his poor relationship with the business community resulted in losing two major insurance companies to the suburbs, and his confrontational relationship with the governor appeared to be unwise since the city counted on 50 percent of its budget from the State of Connecticut. Most troubling to the *Times* may have been the awarding of a no-bid contract for a city parking lot to a Democratic Party official who was not recommended by the city's parking authority. The *Times* concluded that Perez showed "a troubling willingness to grant city business to political allies. Hartford can and must do better."

Because Perez's public image had been faltering in the media prior to the election, many were surprised when he was reelected in 2007 (Lavado 2007). Commenting on the election results, one local news columnist attributed Perez's win as simply "effort" rather than a reflection of his leadership style, performance, or ethical decisions (Simpson 2007): "Gotta give Eddie an 'A' for effort. But he gets an 'F' in personal relations. His arrogance under 'strong-mayor' overshadowed his progress and made him unnecessarily vulnerable in an election that he won Tuesday."

In January 2009 Perez was arrested on bribery and corruption charges related to his alleged dealings with contractor Carlos Costa on renovations done at Perez's home (Browning 2009; Pazniokas 2009). Costa was unpaid for a $40,000 renovation job at Perez's home. Perez stated that his wife's health problems led to a delay in payment. Costa claimed that he did not expected to be paid because it was intended to be free. The local news quoted Costa as saying that the work was "the cost of me doing business with the City." Perez reportedly overruled city staff who were determined to pull Costa from a multimillion-dollar city project (Cohen and Kauffman 2009).

How the arrest of such a high-profile, multiterm mayor will affect Hartford's support base for the underling mayor–council form is yet to be seen. Will it plant a seed of distrust in that form of government, or is it just a wrinkle in the fabric of Hartford's city government? Only time will tell.


## Conclusion

Hartford has experimented with the mayor–council and council–manager forms of government. It has elected its leaders with partisan elections, nonpartisan elections, and partisan elections masquerading as nonpartisan elections. It has used both at-large and direct election to select its mayor. It has authorized two-year mayoral terms and four-year mayoral terms. It has employed professionally trained and experienced city managers and city managers with arguably few qualifications. In spite of these adjustments, nothing has cured what ails Hartford.

It is safe to assume that Hartford is far from finished in examining its charter. Will a lack of leadership continuity, partisan politics, or demographic and economic changes once again emerge as trigger points to revisit the question of governmental form? How will corruption allegations surrounding the first mayor serving in the recently embraced mayor–council form affect the future of that form?

What is clear from the story of Hartford is that a unifying local government figurehead and coherent policy agenda are not automatic with any form of government or variations of them. As the city faces present and future challenges, Hartford will likely continue reinventing itself, led by political leaders who closely examine the boundaries within which they must operate in an effort to perfect the structural balance of power, responsiveness, and accountability in Hartford's municipal government.

# References

Browning, Lynnley. 2009. Mayor of Hartford is accused of taking bribe in a municipal corruption plot. *New York Times*, January 28.

Burgard, Matt. 2004. Mayor, police chief dispute survey, say findings skewed. *Hartford Courant*, November 23.

Burns, Peter. 2002. The intergovernmental regime and public policy in Hartford, Connecticut. *Journal of Urban Affairs* 24 (1): 55–73.

Clavel, Pierre. 1986. *The progressive city*. New Brunswick, NJ: Rutgers University Press.

Cohen, Jeffrey B., and Matthew Kauffman. 2009. Hartford mayor arrested on bribery charges. *Hartford Courant*, January 28.

Cruz, José E. 1998. *Identity and power: Puerto Rican politics and the challenge of ethnicity*. Philadelphia: Temple University Press.

Fenton, Donald F. 2004. Politics of change: Mayor vs. manager. *Hog River Journal* 2 (4) August/September/October.

Frederickson, H. George, Gary A. Johnson, and Curtis H. Wood. 2003. *The adapted city: Institutional dynamics and structural change*. Armonk, NY: M. E. Sharpe.

Gansberg, Martin. 1970. Hartford is put under a curfew. *New York Times*, August 1.

Gizzi, John. 2005. Saluting 'Madam Mayor': Former Hartford Hizzoner Ann Uccello. www.humanevents.com/rightangle/index.php?p = 13675&gd = 12262005 (accessed January 7, 2008).

Gurwitt, Rob. 1996. The mayor as showman. *Governing* 10 (3): 31.

———. 2000. Rudderless in Hartford. *Governing* (September).

Hart, Andy. 1997. 20 years with the little paper that could. *Hartford News*. Special 20th Anniversary Issue, October 22–29. www.townusa.com/southsidemedia/1022twenty.html (accessed June 22, 2008).

Hartford Press Release. 2002. Hartford City Manager Lee C. Erdmann Receives National Status as Credentialed City Manager by the International City/County Management Association. October 24. www.hartford.gov/news/pressreleases/icma_award_11-4-02.htm (accessed June 21, 2008).

Hassett, Wendy L., and Douglas J. Watson. 2007. *Civic battles: When cities change their form of government*. Boca Raton, FL: PrAcademics Press.

Lavado, Lillie. 2007. Perez re-elected despite controversy. *Trinity Tripod*, November 13. http://media.www.trinitytripod.com/media/storage/paper520/news/2007/11/13/News/Perez.ReElected.Despite. Controversy-3097909.shtml (accessed June 2, 2008).

Martin, Douglas. 2000. George Athanson, 72, lively Hartford mayor. *New York Times*, January 11.

Mayors of Hartford. www.hartfordhistory.net/mayors.html (accessed on June 2, 2008).

Mazzocca, D'Ann. 1998. Chicago school restructuring and state takeover of Hartford school system. A memo from the Office of Legislative Research, Connecticut General Assembly dated September 25. www.cga.ct.gov/ps98/rpt/olr/98-r-1116.doc (accessed June 6, 2008).

McKee, Clyde D. 2000. Mike Peters and the legacy of leadership in Hartford Connecticut. In *Governing Middle-Sized Cities: Studies in Mayoral Leadership*, eds. James R. Bowers and Wilbur C. Rich, 27–46. Boulder, CO: Lynne Rienner Publishers.

Morse, Charles F. J. 1963. Permanent city managership given Freedman on birthday. *Hartford Courant*, August 13.

*New York Times*. 2007. Our choices in Connecticut: For mayor in Hartford. September 2.

Office of the Press Secretary. 1999. White House Press Release. President Clinton's November New Markets Trip: Highlighting the Need for Investment in Hartford, Connecticut, and America's Inner Cities. November 4.

Pazniokas, Mark. 2001. Perez takes office as Hartford's first Latino mayor. *Hartford Courant*, December 5.

———. 2002. Perez's power play. *Hartford Courant*, November 17.

———. 2004. Strong mayor is sworn in. *Hartford Courant*, January 6.

———. 2009. Keeping a high profile under a cloud. *New York Times*, April 19.

Rusk, D. 1993. *Cities without suburbs*. Baltimore: Woodrow Wilson Center Press, Johns Hopkins University Press.

Ryan, Bill. 1993. In Hartford: Moving from the firehouse to city hall. *New York Times*, December 5.

Simmons, Louise B. 1998. A new urban conservatism: The case of Hartford, Connecticut. *Journal of Urban Affairs* 20 (2): 175–98.

Simpson, Stan. 2005. A cleanup will help fight crime. *Hartford Courant*, February 16.

———. 2007. Perez's win: Effort over arrogance. *Hartford Courant*, November 7.

State of Connecticut. 1996. State of Connecticut the Comptroller's Report: Connecticut's Economic Health, January 30. www.osc.state.ct.us/reports/economic/96cmprpt/crptchgf.htm (accessed June 8, 2008).

Stowe, Stacey. 2002. Can one man make a difference? *New York Times*, October 20.

U.S. Census. Poverty: 1999. Census 2000 Brief. www.census.gov/prod/2003pubs/c2kbr-19.pdf (accessed June 6, 2008).

Williams, Thomas D. 1966. Freedman's son, 14, puts out blast, brings no damage. *Hartford Courant*, December 22.

Zielbauer, Paul. 2000. Change to strong mayor seems to fail in Hartford. *New York Times*, December 6.

———. 2001. Memo from Hartford; well, at least the title is impressive. *New York Times*, May 13.

———. 2002a. A familiar Hartford story about pay and performance. *New York Times*, January 20.

———. 2002b. Poverty in a land of plenty: Can Hartford ever recover? *New York Times*, August 26.

CHAPTER 5

# RICHMOND

## Implementation of and Experience with Strong-Mayor Form of Government

NELSON WIKSTROM

RICHMOND, VIRGINIA, with a population of about two hundred thousand, a majority of whom are African American, is the hub of the Richmond consolidated metropolitan area with a total of one million residents. Over the years Richmond has been plagued by a high rate of poverty (housing approximately 70 percent of the poor of the metropolitan region), a substantial amount of substandard housing, escalating violent crime, and deteriorating public schools. Further adding to the socioeconomic woes of Richmond is Virginia's unique local governmental structure of independent cities and counties. As a result of this arrangement, Richmond is required to provide all social services for its disadvantaged.

In addition Richmond, largely due to past racially inspired annexation attempts (some that met with success and others with failure), has had a rather contentious relationship with its major neighboring suburban jurisdictions of Henrico and Chesterfield counties, both of which have witnessed a large increase in their populations, rising business and political profile, and economic growth. In 1948 Richmond adopted the council–manager form of government, with a nine-member at-large city council, along with a mayor chosen by council members. As a result of this council structure, the vast majority of the members who served were white, with a minimal amount of African American representation. However, the U.S. Department of Justice, as a result of a long, bitterly litigated annexation case involving Richmond and Chesterfield County, ordered Richmond in the mid-1970s to adopt a ward system for city council elections to correct what the courts viewed as a long-standing strategy by the city's white governing elite to dilute the voting strength of African Americans. As a result of this new electoral arrangement, in the 1977 city council elections African Americans captured five of the nine seats and chose Henry Marsh III as Richmond's first African American mayor.

During his tenure Marsh was often opposed by and in conflict with the leaders of the white business establishment; in addition the *Richmond Times-Dispatch* and its then-sister newspaper the *Richmond News Leader*, which went defunct in the early 1990s, relentlessly criticized his performance. Throughout the 1980s and 1990s Richmond witnessed an intensification of its socioeconomic problems, experiencing, in particular, a significant increase in violent crime. The city government, which critics characterized as inefficient, mismanaged, and mired in corruption, appeared to lack the political, managerial capacity and will to respond to these challenges. Critics, largely drawn from the business community, began advocating for a popularly elected strong mayor as a remedy to improve city governance. However, the legacy of racial conflict and politics in Richmond rendered discussion of the merits of the strong-mayor structure more difficult and complicated, and a good share of the African American political leaders argued that the adoption of such a structure would dilute the political power of their community. The latter largely accounted for the General Assembly (state legislature) in 1996 thwarting the popular mandate of the citizenry—as expressed through a popular referendum and city council approval in 1995—to directly elect the mayor. As future events substantiated, it was somewhat ironic that L. Douglas Wilder, the former governor, was instrumental in denying the people's will on the issue.

## Changing Richmond's Form of Government

In a commentary article titled "City Voters Should Be Able to Elect a Strong Mayor," published in the *Richmond Times-Dispatch* on April 7, 2002, Wilder, a somewhat maverick Democrat, initiated the process of changing Richmond's form of government from a council–manager to that of a strong mayor. Wilder argued that under the council–manager form the community was suffering from overall "mediocracy" in its government operations and that recent mayors, in their desire to run the city government, had been instrumental in the resignation of a well-respected city manager and police chief. He also claimed that allegations had surfaced that the mayor's liaison was involved in fixing traffic tickets. Concluding his commentary and in the interest of good government, Wilder advanced, "Why can't we have a 'strong' mayor chosen by all of the voters, rather than a city manager chosen by five of the nine (Council) people?" (Wilder 2002a, E6). The following June, Wilder wrote another newspaper article, titled "Richmonders Have Tolerated Mediocrity Long Enough." He criticized the governmental structure at the time "where city council members could be elected with fewer than 1000 votes in a city of 200,000 people" and again advocated the case for structural reform (Wilder 2002b, E6).

In July Wilder suggested establishing a citizens commission to explore the idea of the citizens directly electing the mayor and other possible changes in the city charter. He proposed that following their deliberations and public hearings, and the gathering of the required 6,702 signatures on a referendum petition, the citizens be allowed to vote on the recommendations of the commission and, if given a favorable support by the citizenry, the recommendations be forwarded to the General Assembly for its approval. In defense of his initiative, he stated that the current affairs in the city "clearly show (that) we aren't attracting the best and brightest to be involved in the governance of our city." He stated that he was simply motivated by his sense of civic duty and desire to help the city and added that he had absolutely no interest in becoming mayor.

Support for Wilder's initiative drew a mixed reaction from state and local political leaders. Lieutenant Governor Timothy M. Kaine, a former mayor of Richmond, voiced strong support and stated that a popularly elected mayor would ensure much stronger political leadership and provide the voters with a clear sense of vision for the city. In contrast Mayor Rudolph C. McCollum Jr. assumed a strong negative stance and stated: "I don't think it will affect the quality-of-life issues that most citizens are looking to enhance. It is being touted as some kind of panacea for a number of complaints that have been more related to individuals (city officials) and how they act than being about a system of government." State Senator Benjamin J. Lambert, a local prominent African American political leader, voiced his skepticism and noted: "At this point, I would like to know who is going to be on the Commission to work it out. And if these people on the Commission would have the best interests of the whole city, not part of the city." And, he added, "When we had the thing come up before, it gave the powers back to the people who ran the city a long time ago" (Williams 2002a, B1).

Wilder's position lamenting the overall lack of political leadership and mismanagement of Richmond's government was provided a significant measure of credence the following August by A. Barton Hinkle, an editorial writer for the *Richmond Times-Dispatch*, who noted that the city government had failed in a number of well-publicized economic revitalization efforts, including the former highly touted downtown Sixth Street Marketplace, and that school and public safety services had "lapsed into drift and decay." He further advanced that the city council was marked by internal bickering and a series of scandals, and that its members were prone to "obstructionism, penny-ante theatrics, and grandstanding." As a result, he said, the council had lost much of its standing with the public (Hinkle 2002, A9).

## Citizens Commission Established

Toward the latter part of August, Wilder, joined by Thomas J. Bliley, a Republican, who served as a mayor in Richmond during 1970s, announced the establishment of a citizens commission with each serving as cochairman. The commission was charged with studying and recommending the manner in which the citizens of the city should choose their mayor and advance other changes in the city charter. Following holding public hearings, soliciting the advice of experts, and their deliberations, the commission had the option of requesting a Richmond Circuit Court to order a special election during the first half of the following year to ask voters to approve their charter revisions. The holding of the special election was contingent upon volunteers gathering 6,702 petition signatures, which represented about 10 percent of the voter turnout in the 2000 presidential election. Pending an affirmative action by the voters, the commission charter revisions were to be forwarded to the General Assembly for its approval (Redmon 2002a, B1).

The nine members appointed to the commission, one from each of the nine electoral wards of the city, represented a wide variety of politically visible and well-connected citizens. It was a biracial group, with members largely drawn from the business, education, and legal sectors of the community. The most prominent of these individuals included Barbara Grey, a long-time educator and former elementary school principal; Melvin D. Law, a former Richmond school board chairman; and James E. Sheffield, a former Richmond Circuit Court judge (Redmon 2000b, B5).

In early September William Ferguson Reid, a cofounder of the largely African American Richmond Crusade for Voters and the first African American to serve in the General Assembly (from 1968 to 1973), voiced strong skepticism about the work of the commission and the possibility that it would recommend that Richmond adopt the strong-mayor form of government. He stated, "You're just creating more bureaucracy. I can't see what the advantage is of having the strong mayor. . . . I can see the reason behind it: that he can be controlled by the power structure. . . . That's what they're trying to do: decrease the power of the City Council. We're getting back to the old spoils system." And, taking a swipe at Wilder, Reid stated, "To each his own. Everybody has a different political philosophy. I don't know how he got involved in it when he doesn't even live in the city" (Williams 2002b, H3).

In the same month, several of the members of the General Assembly from the larger Richmond metropolitan area, and destined to play a key role in approving any commission recommendations advanced to that body, weighed in on the issue of whether Richmond should adopt a strong-mayor form of government. State Senator John C. Watkins and Delegate John M. O'Bannon, both inner suburban moderate Republicans who represented a small portion of Richmond, voiced their favor and noted that such a change would make the government of Richmond more accountable and more in keeping with a healthy democracy. On the other hand, Lambert reiterated his skepticism and was joined by Marsh, who stated: "We have to keep a certain amount of checks and balances in the system. Without that there is going to be chaos. . . . I think it should be given careful study by officials who represent the citizens of Richmond" (Redmon 2002c, B1).

## Commission on Richmond's Government Established

Partly in reaction to the establishment of the Wilder-Bliley–sponsored citizens commission, McCollum, supported by five of his city council colleagues, announced in mid-October the formation of a panel called the Commission on Richmond Government. The commission was composed of seventeen members appointed by the city council and cochaired by Earl H. McClenney Jr., a professor of political science and public administration at Virginia State University, and John B. Thompson, a prominent local attorney who had served on the city council. The commission had a more extensive mandate than the citizens commission led by Bliley and Wilder. It was charged with considering matters relating to the powers and elections of the mayor and council members, expanding their terms of office from two years to four, the benefits of a strong-mayor form of government, and the topics of annexation and revenue sharing among Richmond-area governments. The commission was charged with reporting its findings to the council by March 31, 2003 (Redmon 2002d, B1).

The commission released a report in October. Due to a significant amount of dissention, provoked by racial issues, between its members and their inability to reach a consensus on most of the issues, the commission advanced only its singular recommendation that the term of city council members should be extended from two years to four years.

## Citizens Commission: Developments

In November Wilder and Bliley established a nonprofit fundraising arm for the citizens commission labeled Richmond for the 21st Century. It raised about $60,000 from a dozen large business firms. The donors included BB&T Bank; the Markel Corporation, a large insurance firm; CCA Industries, a holding company, and owner of the prestigious Jefferson Hotel; Swedish Match North America, a tobacco company; and Ukrop's, the dominant grocery store chain in the Richmond metropolitan area. James W. Dunn, president of the Greater Richmond Chamber of Commerce, served as the liaison between the donors and the fundraisers. Richmond for the 21st Century expended funds to compensate several political consultants, taped calls that were made by Wilder and Bliley urging city residents to attend the public hearings of the citizens commission, and paid copying and food expenses (Redmon 2003a, A1).

Following several months of public hearings and deliberations, the citizens commission in a press release issued in April 2003 advanced the city charter revisions that it would seek to place on the forthcoming November ballot. The revisions included that the mayor be directly elected on a nonpartisan basis for a four-year term, limited to a maximum of three terms in office. Concerning the election of the mayor, the recommendation had a unique feature in that it required that a successful candidate had to prevail in at least five of the nine city council election districts; this requirement was designed to ensure that the political power of the African American community was not curtailed. If no candidate met this requirement, a runoff election was to be conducted involving the person receiving the highest number of votes cast in all nine city council districts and the person receiving the second highest number of votes cast.

The citizens commission set forth revisions to provide that the mayor was to be recognized as the head of the city government for all ceremonial purposes, the purposes of military law, and the service of civil process. In addition, the mayor, although lacking veto power, was given the power to appoint a chief administrative officer (CAO), subject to the advice and approval of a majority of the members of the city council. The CAO was to be responsible to and report to the mayor, and the mayor was given the exclusive right to terminate the CAO's services.

An additional charter revision required the members of the city council to appoint from among their ranks a vice mayor to serve a two-year term. The vice mayor was also charged with presiding over council meetings. In addition, if the office of mayor became vacant, the vice mayor was designated as the acting mayor. Sheffield penned in regard to these revisions, "The Future of Richmond needs the adoption of the Commission's propositions for changes to the City's Charter. The proposed changes offer the City's voters what for most of us is a once-in-a-lifetime opportunity to enact meaningful reform in a crucial aspect of the governance structure of the city" (*Richmond Times-Dispatch* 2003, H1; Sheffield 2003, A15).

## Commencement of Petition Drive

On Friday afternoon, June 20, 2003, Paul Goldman, a political consultant to the citizens commission, and a rather flamboyant off-and-on political aide to Wilder, standing outside of city hall, commenced the petition drive designed to provide Richmond with a strong-mayor form of government. Upon the approval of the voters, under the petition proposal, requiring a total of 6,702 signatures from qualified registered voters, the citizenry would directly elect a mayor to a four-year term. The administrative and budgetary powers of the mayor were not specified other than he was given the right to appoint a CAO, subject to the advice and consent of a majority of the members of the city council. Council members would appoint a vice mayor to preside at their meetings and serve as an acting mayor in case of a vacancy in the mayor's office (Redmon 2003b, B5).

Several weeks later Robert C. Bobb, a well-respected former city manager of Richmond in the 1990s who resigned from his position to become the city manager of Oakland, California, expressed support for the petition drive and the need for Richmond to adopt the strong-mayor form of government. Bobb asserted, "Clearly, the mayor should be elected at large. Someone needs to represent the community in the broader context and help shape public policies beyond the narrowness of district-wide elections." Somewhat prophetically, Bobb warned that whether such a mayor would succeed would depend to a substantial degree upon the personality of the individual, his mode of operation, and ability to establish a governing consensus. In contrast to Bobb, Marsh expressed his disdain for the petition drive, stating, "The person who is elected mayor would be able to fire the city manager (administrator) without answering to anybody because he doesn't like the color of his necktie or because he doesn't do what the mayor says" (Williams 2003a, H3).

## The Battle Joined

The petition drive on behalf of the strong-mayor form of government provoked a perfect political storm between community political actors and groups who favored the plan and those who were opposed. Leading those who favored the petition drive were Bliley and Wilder, the other members of the citizen commission, business leaders, and the *Richmond Times-Dispatch*. Proponents of the petition drive perceived the city as lacking in strong political leadership and management, and devoid of a sense of vision, floundering, and mired in corruption. They also noted the declining quality of city services, particularly in regard to policing and public education. Further, they noted the relative lack of economic development and growth in the city, and the steady migration of city businesses to the suburbs. Reflective of the latter, Wendy L. Hassett and Douglas J. Watson in their work *Civic Battles: When Cities Change Their Form of Government* report in a wider sense that efforts to change the form of local government usually involve economic development and growth issues (2007, 2). Proponents argued that a directly elected mayor would provide strong visionary citywide political leadership and management, serving to unify the various interests of the city, and provide for more democratic, effective, and accountable government.

McCollum and Marsh provided the political leadership for urging the citizenry to vote a resounding "no" on the petition referendum. Denying the claims of the petition advocates that the city government was a "cesspool of corruption," mismanaged, and not effectively governed, McCollum noted the strong financial position of the city, with a $35.6 million rainy-day fund, the fact the Moody's Investors Service had recently upgraded the city's general obligation bond rating from A1 to Aa3, and that Fitch Incorporated had increased the city's public utility debt revenue bonds from A-plus to AA-minus rating. Further, he reported that "under his watch," Calvin D. Jamison, the city manager, supervised the successful completion of the downtown convention center expansion, the construction and operation of the major regional Stony Point Shopping Center, anchored by a high-end department store, and the design of plans for an $80 million project on Brown's Island, located in the James River in the downtown area (Redmon 2003c, B1). Further, he credited Jamison for providing the leadership and savvy business skills that resulted in the construction of the headquarters for a large bank, a major research facility, a new federal district building, the first Walmart superstore to be located within the confines of the city, the renovation and operation of a downtown train station providing Amtrak service to Washington, D.C., and a host of other capital investments. In addition to these rather sizable economic gains, McCollum noted that during Jamison's tenure the city witnessed a steady decline in its homicide rate.

Marsh was the leading member of Citizens Alert: At-large Mayor, a grassroots coalition of clergy, community leaders, and neighborhood activists organized to defeat the proposal. The coalition adopted the simple, straightforward slogan of "Just Say No." It raised funds, conducted a massive voter registration drive, and carried out a door-to-door campaign. Marsh and the other members of the coalition argued that the direct election of the mayor would turn back the hard-won political gains won by the African American community over the last quarter century and further polarize the community along racial lines. He noted that the beneficiaries of the petition proposal would allow the "old powers-that-be" (the business community) "to take back the city." The latter was the case Marsh asserted since: "Wealth alone would determine who the next mayor would be. . . . Money wins elections" (Williams 2003b, H3). In a display of public defiance, Vashti Mallory-Minor, president of Citizens Alert and the president of the Richmond Education Association, in September held a news conference in the parking lot of a Ukrop's grocery store to showcase who, she said, was behind the petition effort and stated, "We are here in the parking lot of

Ukrop's supermarket as a symbol of those who are behind this proposition to change our local government for their own benefit—we believe for political and financial greed" (Shepherd 2003, B3).

Toward the closing days of October, other prominent African American political leaders weighed in against the strong-mayor proposal. City councilman Walter T. Kenney Jr., a former mayor, supported by Vice Mayor Delores L. McQuinn and councilwoman Gwen C. Hedgepeth, sought the city council to adopt a resolution opposing the proposed change and stated that the ballot issue was a "feel-good thing" that would not necessarily result in positive changes in the city's public schools and increasing homicide rate, and would only serve to dilute the political influence and power of African Americans (Redmon 2003c, B9). Dwight C. Jones, a member of the House of Delegates (and who later was elected mayor in 2008), voiced his opposition to the proposal, and U.S. Representative Robert C. Scott argued that passage of the proposal would dilute the African American vote and, therefore, would be in violation of the federal Voting Rights Act (Redmon 2003d, B7). On the eve of the balloting to change Richmond's form of government, McCollum contributed an op-ed piece to the *Richmond Times-Dispatch* titled "Government Structure Isn't Real Issue," in which he decried the movement for the city to adopt the strong-mayor form of government and stressed the economic progress that had been made under his regime (McCollum 2003, A15).

## Electoral Outcome: The Advocates Prevail

On November 4, 2003, Richmond citizens went to the polls and by a large margin of 4 to 1 endorsed the ballot initiative calling for at-large mayoral elections and other government reforms. The vote was 22,122 in favor to 5,518 against, or 80 to 20 percent, respectively. The measure received a majority of votes in each of the city's nine council districts. In the Sixth District, having the largest majority of African American residents at 92 percent, the ballot issue carried five of the eight precincts; the measure passed by almost 30 to 1 in the city's First District, which contains the greatest majority of white residents at 92.8 percent. The racial card that was used by the opponents to governmental change had little impact, even among African American citizens. Viewed in a positive perspective, the petition results may have signaled the declining significance of race in structuring Richmond politics. We should note, however, that some observers have speculated that if the citizenry had been offered a ballot proposal, which had mandated a complete structural change of government to that of the strong-mayor form rather than simply that of whether they wanted a popularly elected strong mayor, the initiative might have met with defeat.

Reaction to the ballot results by the major political actors involved in the ballot issue was predictable. Wilder noted, "This is a victory for the people of Richmond and Virginia. We've said these bogus racist charges are just not going to work. We are fed up with it, the wolf tickets have been sold out . . . this was going to be a race war, you know? It's over. A new leadership has to take place." In contrast, Marsh asserted, "It's a power grab by wealthy business interests, who have been sitting at the table with African American leaders for 20 some years, sharing the power, and all of a sudden they decide to seize the power." And, McCollum conceded, "The voters have expressed a desire for change, clearly. What that change is going to be is yet to actually be known. . . . The voters have now spoken and the process continues. This by no means has come to a conclusion" (Redmon 2003e, A1).

## Analysis of Referendum Results

A number of factors accounted for the passage of the referendum. First, reform advocates were successful in convincing the electorate that the city government was a "cesspool of corruption and inefficiency," resulting in badly performing public schools, a high crime rate, poor community public health, the highest real estate taxes in the metropolitan region, and a tepid rate of economic development. Reform advocates had some measure of truth on their side, since during the 1990s four city council members and two city administrators were imprisoned for misusing government funds, taking bribes, selling votes, distributing drugs, and various other infractions of the law. Further, questions were raised by the public concerning the alleged mismanagement of the sheriff's department. In response to these ills of governance, the electorate was persuaded that the adoption of a strong-mayor form would provide Richmond with more honest, democratic, accountable, and vigorous government, with the mayor providing strong political and managerial leadership.

Second, the argument of Marsh, Scott, and McCollum, along with the other members of the Citizens Alert coalition, that the reform proposal was, in effect, an attack on the political leadership of the African American community and that the adoption of the strong-mayor form would serve to dilute the political power of African Americans did not resonate with that segment of the electorate. The proposal garnered a majority of votes in all nine of Richmond's city council districts and proved successful in sixty-five of the city's seventy-two voting precincts, many of which have a majority African American population. More specifically, in sixteen precincts where 90 percent or more of the voting-age residents are African American, 53 percent of the voters approved the change to a strong-mayor form of government (Redmon 2003f, A1). The highly visible leadership role of Wilder in the reform effort, who is viewed by many in the African American community as *their* political hero, served to blunt the charge that changing the form of government was racially inspired.

Third, another reason accounting for the passage of the proposal was that the Citizens Alert coalition and their political allies conducted essentially a racially charged negative campaign, failing to cite the substantial economic development and financial accomplishments of the city under the leadership of McCollum and Jamison. The opponents of the proposal made a crucial mistake by simply centering their campaign on the slogan "Vote No."

Fourth, strong financial backing by the business community proved to be instrumental in the passage of the proposal. The Mayor-at-Large Referendum Committee raised approximately $69,000, whereas the Citizens Alert coalition garnered only about half of that amount, specifically $33,000. The Mayor-at-Large Referendum Committee received its largest contribution—$20,000—from Richmond for the 21st Century, the nonprofit organization established by Wilder and his allies. It raised the vast majority of its funds from the business community. A major financial contributor to the Mayor-at-Large Referendum Committee was James E. Ukrop, the chairman of a local super-market chain, along with his wife, Barbara. Ukrop defended his large contribution to the committee by noting, "Having an elected mayor selected by all the people would give that person a mandate to take more of a leadership role in the region. It would also create a better voice for us in the legislature to deal with urban issues." Commenting upon the large financial contributions made by the business community on behalf of the reform effort, Marsh noted, "That confirms our concern and our statements that a small group of businesses are financing this operation. . . . They are the ones who, if this is successful, will play a lead role in electing an at-large major and therefore have a decided influence on the policies the city will be making" (Redmon 2003g, A1).

In contrast, Citizens Alert received about one-third of its funding from five Richmond-area Democratic state legislators. In addition to Marsh, Lambert, and Jones, they included Fenton L. Bland (Petersburg) and Franklin P. Hall (Richmond). Citizens Alert also received financial contributions of $5,000 from a host of African American business leaders and firms including A. Hugo "Al" Bowers, of Bowers Family Enterprises, a general contractor; Dwight Snead Landscaping & Paving Company; Johnson Incorporated, a marketing and public relations firm; and Kelsey and Ashley Management Company, an urban retail consulting firm (Redmon 2003g, A1).

Fifth, passage of the reform proposal was also due to the strong editorial and commentary support provided by the *Richmond Times-Dispatch*. In its news reports and editorial columns, the newspaper repeatedly noted the transgressions of a few city officials and took scant note of the economic progress of the city, except for the invited contribution of McCollum. Wilder was able to utilize his position as a monthly guest contributor to the newspaper as a bully pulpit to advance the cause of reform.

Finally, the high-profile political personages of Wilder and Bliley proved to be instrumental in the passage of the reform proposal. Wilder's endorsement and strong political leadership on behalf of reform served to curtail the fear in the African American community that the proposed change of government would be inimical to their interests. In addition, his long-standing style of practicing transracial politics, which he perfected in his previous successful race for governor in 1989, served to gain support for the proposal from the predominately white business community. Bliley provided legitimacy for the proposal for the business leadership and the minority white segment of community.

## Approval by the General Assembly

Since Virginia, in terms of its relationship to local governments, is structured by "Dillon's Rule," the charter revisions providing for a strong-mayor form of government required approval by the General Assembly and the governor, which was granted by the governor and the General Assembly in the 2004 legislative session. The initial revised charter provisions mandated the direct nonpartisan election of a full-time mayor, for a term of four years, with eligibility to be reelected for two additional terms. Rather unusually, a successful candidate in order to be elected to the office of mayor had to receive the most votes in each of at least five of the nine city council districts. This provision, as previously noted, was inserted into the charter to counter the charge that the citywide procedure of electing the mayor would be politically detrimental to the African American community. Should no candidate be elected, a runoff election was to be conducted between the two persons who received the largest number of votes throughout the city. The charter revisions stipulated that the mayor is the chief executive officer of the city and is responsible for the proper administration of the city government; further, the mayor is assisted by a CAO, appointed by the mayor, subject to the advice and consent of a majority of the members of the city council. The CAO serves at the pleasure of the mayor. The leader of the city council, chosen by council colleagues, is designated the vice mayor. Pursuant to the requirements of the Voting Rights Act of 1965, on June 21, 2004, the U.S. Department of Justice approved Richmond's citywide plan to elect a strong mayor (Jenkins 2004a, B7).

Largely at the behest of Wilder, the charter was again revised by the General Assembly and the governor in 2005. The most important of the revisions provided the mayor with additional powers, including the veto authority over certain budget and fiscal measures, along with the power to appoint and remove department heads. In addition, the mayor and city council were given greater control over the school budget. Finally, the title of the vice mayor was changed to president of the city council.

In 2006 the General Assembly and governor made further revisions to the city charter. These revisions included granting the mayor the right to employ special counsel in instances where the city attorney has a conflict of interest; clarified that the mayor or his designee may attend closed meetings of the city council, unless the latter determines that such inclusion would be detrimental to the purpose of the council's deliberations; and required the CAO to attend, or be represented at, all open meetings of the city council.

## Campaign for Mayor

Under its new strong-mayor form of government, which became official on July 1, 2004, Richmond conducted its elections for the offices of mayor and city council on November 2, 2004. Despite his earlier repeated disavowals that he would not be a mayoral candidate, Wilder did a complete about-face, supposedly at the urging and encouragement of community leaders and residents, and announced on May 29 his candidacy for mayor. Soon thereafter, three additional individuals pronounced their bids: McCollum, the incumbent mayor; Charles Nance, a former school board member; and Lawrence E. Williams, an architect.

Wilder, who moved back into the city from a rural county to establish his required legal residence, Nance, and Williams basically ran on a similar campaign theme focusing on the need to "turn-around-a-decaying-city," by cleaning up the city government, lowering the crime and poverty rate, improving the public schools, and securing business investment and economic growth (Kalita 2004, C1). Nance also argued rather innovatively that the city should raze all public housing and find alternative housing arrangements for its residents (Jenkins 2004b, C6; Jenkins 2004c, B1).

McCollum, as expected, although acknowledging some of the shortcomings of the government in Richmond and the indiscretions of a few elected and appointed officials, stressed the economic accomplishments and financial well-being of the city during his administration, as a result of his political leadership and the able management of the city manager.

Wilder was elected by a large margin, winning 80 percent of the vote and carrying all nine city council districts. At his downtown victory party, Wilder stated that he would work to return Richmond to its days as a vibrant urban hub and noted, "This is a new beginning. . . . There is an opportunity for all of us to reach out and reclaim and rebuild. I want to see a Richmond that doesn't just have a post office address to designate us, but rather a community that unites us" (Jenkins 2004d, A33).

Wilder's landslide victory was due to a variety of factors, including his prominence in the local, state, and, indeed, the national African American community. McCollum noted that running against a politician as prominent as Wilder was an uphill battle and added, "To say that we were the underdog is an understatement." In addition, Wilder benefited from his long-adopted strategy of practicing transracial politics, designed to garner the support of white voters. And, finally, Wilder's victory was ensured by the endorsement of his candidacy by the *Richmond Times-Dispatch* and his overwhelming support from the business community, which provided him with a campaign chest of somewhat over $360,000, more than ten times as large as any of his competitors (Jenkins 2004d, A33).

## Wilder Sworn into Office

Wilder was sworn into office at the downtown convention center on Sunday, January 2, 2005. In his approximately twenty-minute speech, Wilder declared that he was going to turn Richmond into a model city for the commonwealth and said, "It is a special moment for me as we embark on a new course—a new day—in our city's rich history. . . . We begin a new form of government at a time of many serious challenges and even greater opportunities. I accept the task ahead." Although short on specific policy goals, Wilder added, "We have much to do, and the goals we seek will require the energies of us all. . . . Jobs must be created. . . . Corruption must be eliminated." However, several astute political observers noted at the time that Wilder's role as mayor would be just as unpredictable and controversial as when he served as governor (Jenkins 2005a, B1).

## Accomplishments of the Wilder Administration

Wilder can rightly claim a number of significant accomplishments. Most significantly, these accomplishments include the hiring of Rodney Monroe, formerly of Macon, Georgia, to serve as chief of police. Michael Paul Williams, a newspaper columnist, declared that Wilder's hiring of Monroe was the smartest thing that he did and that Monroe's strategy of police administrative decentralization, along with "sector policing," resulted in a much better "linkage" of the police with the various neighborhoods in Richmond, realizing a 22 percent reduction in crime and an 82 percent crime clearance rate. Williams hailed this reduction in crime as Wilder's signature accomplishment (Williams 2008b, B1). As a result of Wilder's leadership and the professional efforts of Monroe, Richmond lost its reputation of being among the most dangerous cities in America.

In addition, Wilder spurred the economic development of Richmond's downtown, guided by a newly developed master plan. The master plan was the product of a significant amount of professional and citizen involvement. In addition to the construction of a new federal courthouse, begun before he assumed office, Wilder's other economic achievements included the completion of new buildings housing the headquarters of MeadWestvaco, a Philip Morris research facility, and a large downtown hotel. As a result of these economic gains, approximately 2,500 new jobs were created in the downtown area. In addition, numerous condominiums were constructed and occupied, resulting in a significant increase in downtown population growth.

Third, Wilder allocated about $300 million for infrastructure improvements throughout the city. Some of these funds were used to assist in the construction of a downtown arts facility, along with the renovation and reopening of the renowned National Theatre. Other funds were expended to repair and rebuild neighborhood streets and sidewalks, improve parks and recreation facilities, and upgrade the computer facilities in each of the city's libraries.

Wilder also launched a vigorous program for cleaning up blighted neighborhoods throughout the city. Through a neighborhood revitalization strategy identifying spot blight, his administration demolished 280 buildings and, as a result, enhanced the overall quality of life in numerous neighborhoods throughout the city.

And, finally, Wilder, seeking to reinforce his image as a tight-fisted manager of the city budget, claimed that his administration saved more than $330 million through city hall refinancing and cost-avoiding measures (Krishnamurthy 2008a, B1, B4).

## The Mayor and City Council: Struggle over Powers and Authority

A considerable amount of political tension, rancor, and conflict developed between Wilder, the city council, and the school board throughout his tenure in office. School board members are elected on a nonpartisan basis by the citizens in each of the nine precincts (wards). To some degree this political tension and conflict was a product of the somewhat ambiguous powers initially allocated by the charter to the mayor, city council, and school board, and therefore were subject to different interpretations. The latter situation continues to persist to some degree even though Wilder upon assuming office was successful, as noted previously, in persuading the General Assembly to further revise the charter, providing the mayor with the veto power over city council actions and broad authority over the city budget. In addition, from the perspective of Wilder, the political tension and conflict among himself, the city council, and the school board was due to the fact that the members of these bodies could not accept their more limited roles: "Because this is a new system there were bound to be clashes about power and authority. It can be hard for persons who once held power to cede it, or to allocate it differently—even though the voters have told them to do so." On the other hand, some city council and school board members felt that the mayor was overstepping the bounds of his powers and authority (Wilder 2007, E1). Somewhat reflective of his combative authority, Wilder noted, "I guess they (City Council members) thought I was going to just sit around and cut ribbons, that I wouldn't have the energy to do what I've been doing. . . . I know a lot of people are wondering . . . what's the old bastard going to do next" (Kumar 2007, B1)?

## Budget Conflict

Throughout his tenure in office, Wilder had repeated conflicts with the city council over the details of the city operating budget. Illustrative of this conflict was Wilder's proposed budget for the fiscal year (FY) 2008, commencing on July 1. Wilder, who described his budget proposal as modest, sought to hold the tax rate at $1.23 per $100 of assessed value. He argued that maintaining the city's tax rate was required because of the steady, tough economic environment, the need to retain the current level of city services, and to continue to provide adequate assistance for the disadvantaged. In response, city council members criticized Wilder for providing large increases, ranging from 13 to 20 percent, to his top administrative officials and suggested that the tax rate could be reduced as much as 4 cents, to $1.19 (Ress 2008a, A1, A12). Responding to this criticism, Wilder stated that the city needed to increase salaries in order to attract and keep superior executive talent and that the bottom-line question is always, "What do they (City Council) do? I'm not concerned with tit for tat, quid pro quo. . . . Up to this point we haven't done that. . . . But I'm here to tell you I'm sick and tired of anybody on Council demeaning our public servants. . . . It's finished. . . . Tell me anytime you've seen any member of Council speak to me. . . . Never. But they'll tell you he's this, that and the other, you know why. They're cowards" (Ress 2008b, B12).

Public reaction to Wilder's hefty pay raises for his top administrative officials was swift and pointed. Williams in the *Richmond Times-Dispatch*, noted, "The same city that meted out 2 percent raises to its work force grunts ladled out hefty pay raises—13 percent to 20 percent—to the power-suited executives at the top of the pay scale. . . . Everyone is being asked to do more with less. . . . But Wilder's inner circle is livin' large. Apparently, Wilder tapped a vein of oil at Ninth and Broad while rooting around for that "cesspool of corruption" he pledged to unearth. Wade Ellegood, president of the Richmond Education Association, volunteered that he was "shocked" by the raises provided to top administrators while the school system remained underfunded (Williams 2008a, B1). Disenchantment with Wilder's budget priorities was further magnified when it was learned that Wilder, who received a $700 per month car allowance, was being driven around the city by his $1.3 million per year security detail. Wilder later paid back the car allowance money to the city (Ress 2008c, A1, A15).

The conflict between Wilder and the city council over the budget for FY 2008 continued into the second week of June 2007 when Wilder stated that the council failed to meet its statutory deadline to deliver a balanced budget by May 31. He declared, "It saddens me that [the Council] . . . once again failed not only to meet its required obligations but, also, in my judgment, failed the people they represent" (Jones 2008a, A1, A6). The following day, city council president William J. Pantele denied Wilder's allegation and claimed that the council had met its fiscal responsibilities (Jones 2008b, B6).

## The Richmond Public School (RPS) Offices Fiasco

Upon assuming office, Wilder adopted an aggressive pro-active posture regarding the need to improve Richmond's public schools. In his City of the Future Plan, he boldly promised to construct or restore fifteen public schools. In seeking to implement his plan, Wilder soon found himself in an adversarial position with the school board, school superintendent Deborah Jewell Sherman, who later resigned her position, and the city council. Wilder blamed the school board and school superintendent for delaying his school program. Somewhat in response, Wilder's administration in January 2008 froze more than $1.4 million scheduled for school maintenance and several months later in March withheld school board funding until it agreed to an outside audit. A second audit of the school system found widespread problems in purchasing and bill paying.

The most visible and explosive public event resulting from the struggle over powers and authority among Wilder, the city council, and the school board stemmed from Wilder's attempt in 2007, after failing to reach an agreement, to relocate the offices of the school board from the city hall to a commercial office building. Wilder justified his initiative by asserting that by moving the school board offices from the city hall, the city would save more than $1 million a year because it would allow several city departments scattered around downtown to move into the city hall. Wilder set several deadlines for the school board to vacate its city hall offices; the initial deadline was January 2006. However, the school board refused to vacate its offices, especially after learning that the city council had passed an ordinance in the summer of 2007 allowing the school board to maintain its offices in the city hall for five more years at the fee of $10 per year. Rather than vetoing the ordinance, Wilder declared it invalid and demanded that the school board vacate its offices by September 30, 2007.

Impatient with the school board not moving its offices out of city hall, Wilder had an administrative official sign a lease on behalf of the school board designed to transfer its offices to the commercial building. Wilder issued a final ultimatum requiring the school board to move its offices out of the city hall by September 30, 2007. When the school board failed to vacate its offices, Wilder, on September 21 at 6:30 p.m., in an event that the press labeled Black Friday and then the Friday Fiasco, ordered the city police to seal the city hall and had about 150 movers from three different companies transfer the school board offices, along with their contents, to the purported new location. In response the school board sought a temporary restraining order to stop the move, and by midnight, a Richmond Circuit Court judge issued an injunction that halted the eviction of the school board offices from city hall and later ruled that the offices could remain in the city hall (Kumar 2007, B1). On April 10, 2008, the CAO signed a lease allowing the school board to occupy space in the city hall for a nominal fee of $10 per year, which may be renewed annually for four additional years with the approval of the city council (Jones 2008c, B7). After Wilder's attempted eviction of the school board from its offices, Carol Wolf, a school board member, noted that Wilder's actions were stimulated by an element of revenge and noted, "It began when we refused to cede to him the power to hire and fire the Superintendent of Schools." She added that her experiences with Wilder were "one unrelenting psychodrama of nonstop negativity" (Bacon 2007, 15).

## Performing Arts Center Controversy

In his quest to spur downtown economic development, Wilder cooperated with and, on other occasions, engendered conflict with the members of the city economic elite. The business elite, referred to informally as the Main Street crowd, had, over the years, played the dominant role in shaping the economic development and growth of the city. Upon his ascension as mayor, Wilder flexed his muscle as a strong mayor by asserting his objections to well-developed plans developed by the civic elite for an expansive downtown performing arts center. Underscoring his objections, Wilder refused to release city funds, established by a meal tax in 2003, to the Virginia Arts Foundation because of its failure to meet private and regional funding goals and asserted that foundation leadership was involved in a "shell game" with regard to the funds that they had supposedly received (Jenkins 2005b, B1). For a long time, a large hole in the downtown area provided a visual reminder of the conflict that continued for months between the mayor and the economic elite over the foundation's plan to revitalize the area with multiple arts facilities. Ultimately, the stalemate led the foundation to downsize its plans and to provide the city with a larger stake in the ownership and leadership role of the renovated Carpenter Center and allied arts ventures. This new arrangement frustrated many members of the economic elite who had supported a larger scale project.

## Departure of the Richmond Braves

The Richmond Braves Triple-A baseball team, owned by the Atlanta Braves, commenced operations in Richmond in 1966 and in 1985 began playing in a new stadium called the Diamond. By 2000 the Diamond had deteriorated and was lacking the popular amenities of more recently constructed sports stadiums. Negotiations between Wilder and Braves officials began in earnest in 2003 concerning the location and building of a new stadium. Numerous proposals were set forth by both sides, including building a new stadium on the site of the Diamond, moving the stadium to a downtown site adjacent to the James River, or constructing a stadium in suburban Chesterfield County. However, no official plans or a timeline for resolving the issue emerged from the discussions or the mayor's office. Much to the surprise and dismay of Richmond's business and political leaders and the general public, in January 2008 the Atlanta Braves abruptly announced that their Richmond franchise was moving to the Atlanta suburb of Gwinnett, Georgia, where a new stadium was already under construction. The Braves leadership became increasingly impatient with Wilder's failure to move ahead more decisively on the stadium issue. In reaction to the move, Wilder quickly promised the public that he would bring to the city another Triple-A baseball team, an impossibility since none of the other Triple-A teams was seeking to relocate. Wilder's statement failed to assuage angry Braves fans throughout the metropolitan region (Pearrell 2008, C3). Jeff E. Schapiro, a political columnist for the *Richmond Times-Dispatch*, penned, "The Braves exit may be for Richmonders what the New Year's blizzard of 1978–79 was for Chicagoans: snow-clogged streets became a symbol of a city that didn't work" (Schapiro 2008a, B1). The Richmond Braves played their last season in Richmond in 2008.

## Assessment and Conclusion

Proponents, led by Wilder and Bliley, and heavily backed by the business community, along with the *Richmond Times-Dispatch*, were successful in their goal of Richmond abandoning its council–manager form of government in favor of that of a strong-mayor system. Against a legacy of racially charged politics, their initiative won the support of an overwhelming majority of citizens. Reform advocates convinced the citizenry that Richmond needed a strong mayor who could provide resourceful political and managerial leadership to better cope with the various problems confronting the community, especially in regard to the excessive crime rate and deteriorating public schools. Also, proponents argued that a strong mayor, assisted by a CAO, could more effectively and efficiently manage the city government. In addition, reform advocates stressed that a strong mayor, elected by all of the citizenry, could provide better policy leadership for the city council, which over the years had pursued a strong district orientation in terms of policymaking, and been ridden by factionalism and some measure of personal indiscretions. And, finally, they argued that a strong mayor could be a highly visible spokesman for the entire metropolitan region, and constitute a significant political force for advancing the interests of Richmond and its suburban neighbors in the General Assembly.

In contrast, those opposing the change of city governmental structure argued that Richmond was making significant progress in attracting downtown development and investment, reducing crime, and improving public education. And, crucially, most of the traditional African American political leadership perceived that the change to a strong-mayor system would dilute, or undercut, the political strength of their community. Their reasoning was based on the belief that the overwhelming white business community with its greater access to financial resources would be in a better position to fund its preferred candidate and thus would play the dominant role in mayoralty contests.

Although the proponents of change prevailed in the civic arena, they committed a serious mistake in not initially specifying the precise powers and duties of the mayor; incrementally changing the structure of Richmond's government to that of a strong-mayor form proved to be a significant political misstep. This major structural deficiency was, in part, responsible for setting the stage and parameters for unrelenting conflict among the mayor, the city council, and the school board, throughout the regime of Wilder. To some degree, this conflict has been moderated by revisions made to the city charter in 2005, 2006, and 2007. Nevertheless, a representative poll of voters carried out in February 2008 found that a large number of citizens viewed the governing process of Richmond in a less favorable manner and, more specifically, an overwhelming majority—78 percent—viewed the relationship between Wilder and the city council in a "somewhat dissatisfied" or "very dissatisfied" light (Ress 2008d, B4).

The conflict and tension between Wilder and the city council, and Wilder and the school board, was also a function of the civic political culture and a set of political routines that had structured and shaped the governing process in Richmond since the city adopted the council–manager form of government in 1948. Although under the old system the members of the city council were the dominant actors in policymaking, the new strong-mayor system required them to adjust to a more inferior policymaking role. Some council members found this adjustment somewhat difficult to do. On the other hand, Wilder, often leading by his well-reputed strategy of confrontation, eschewed a cooperative and collaborative approach to governance, and was accused of seeking to be a strong man rather than a strong mayor in the governing process. In this regard it is of interest to note that Hassett and Watson have asserted that mayors often feel a need to dominate other actors in the governing process (2007, 80).

Somewhat reflective of his mode of operation, in a poll conducted in February 2008 Wilder received a rather mixed opinion from the public, with 53 percent of the respondents viewing his performance as either "very favorable" or "somewhat favorable," while 43 percent viewed his performance as either "somewhat unfavorable" or "very unfavorable" (Ress 2008d, B4). Throughout 2008 Wilder's approval rating declined even further. A poll conducted in October found that 61 percent of the city-wide voters rated his performance as either "fair" or "poor," including almost a majority—48 percent—of the African American electorate (Ress 2008e, A1, A4).

Changing from the council–manager form of government to the strong-mayor plan proved to be a costly political experiment for Richmond, specifically approximately $13.4 million. Executive branch expenditures increased from $1 million (FY 04) to $2.8 million in FY 09. These expenditures included $7,253,000 additional cumulative spending for the offices of the mayor and the CAO, $1,680,000 costs associated with the mayor's attempt to evict the school board offices from the city hall, along with various hefty legal fees associated with Wilder's conflicts with the city council and school board. Expenditures by the city council increased from $1.8 million (FY 04) to $3.4 million (FY 09), an increase of 85 percent. The increasing expenditures by the city council were largely due to the retention of additional staff and various legal fees. Council members justified increasing their staff largely because Wilder refused to let his administrative staff conduct for the city council evaluative activities relating to the budget and proposed ordinances. Spending by the executive and legislative offices was well above the overall growth of 21 percent for city governmental expenditures (Ress 2008f, A1, A8).

The overall performance of Wilder and his administration in terms of political leadership and management was decidedly mixed. Without doubt, his major success was that of hiring Monroe as his police chief—who eventually left Richmond to assume a similar position in Charlotte, North Carolina—which led to a reduction in crime. Although, obviously, Richmond still has its share of crime, it is a much safer city than before Wilder assumed office. He may also be credited with bridging and forging an effective, though at times a troubling, working alliance with the white business establishment, resulting in substantial downtown growth and economic investment. In addition, Wilder provided for his successors a strong executive office and may be credited with forcing the civic business leadership to amend their plans and adopt a less costly performing arts complex.

In contrast, Wilder's aggressive leadership and confrontational style failed Richmond on a number of counts. His bellicose attitude toward the city council and the school board resulted in political chaos and eroded the confidence and trust of the public in the city's governing institutions and process. Wilder's failure to act more decisively led the Richmond Braves to abandon their turf in the city. Neither did Wilder emerge as a public policy leader for the Richmond metropolitan area in the General Assembly.

In addition, while serving as mayor, Wilder lost some of his past reputation for being a tightfisted budget manager, which he earned as governor, who budgeted for the "necessities and not the niceties." He was severely criticized for providing excessive raises for his department heads and for the expense of his large security detail; in addition, it was reported in March 2008 that the city's purchasing system was widely vulnerable to fraud and abuse (Krishnamurthy 2008b, B1, B2). Further, it was alleged in 2008 that administrative overhead spending per resident in Richmond was higher than anywhere else in the state, with the exception of a few wealthy communities in Northern Virginia, and the decidedly smaller cities of Williamsburg, Fredericksburg, and Charlottesville (Ress 2008g, A1, A8).

Due to his personality and confrontational style, Wilder derailed the process of ushering in collaborative and cooperative governance in Richmond under the strong-mayor form of government and the wider public acceptance of that structure. The Wilder years were marked by continual bickering, tension, and turmoil among the various political actors of the city government, which led to the resignations of several CAOs, including an especially respected long-time Virginia public servant (Ress and

Jones 2008, A1, A7) and a much admired superintendent of schools, lawsuits, and a decline of civic confidence and trust in the local institutions and process of government. Carol A. O. Wolf, a school board member, asserted in 2005 in regard to Wilder, "It's been very, very disappointing thus far. He's governing like a dictator, and what we need is a consensus builder. Someone who builds not tears down. Doug only knows how to tear down" (Jenkins 2005b, B1). In a parallel sort of vein, Schapiro penned about Wilder in 2008, "Usually petty and petulant to a fault, Wilder promised a cooperative approach to governance. Instead, he tried booting the school board from city hall and slowed a downtown arts complex pushed by the wealthy big shots who backed him for mayor" (Schapiro 2008b, B1). Toward the end of Wilder's tenure, Bob Rayner, an associate editor of the *Richmond Times-Dispatch*, noted, "Many were disappointed—often bitterly so—when Wilder brought to city hall not salvation but, well, Wilder. He was often sloppy, imperious, and baffling. He seems at times to undermine his own agenda with unnecessary confrontations and power plays. He was charming, determined, and uncompromising" (Rayner 2008, A13).

We are all aware that structure and rules are important in the civic realm, since they largely structure the great game of politics. However, as the case of Richmond demonstrates, there is no guarantee, as the reform advocates strongly suggested at the outset of their movement, in almost a giddy sort of fashion, that by changing the form of city government, the community would be the beneficiary of strong and unified political and managerial leadership, ensured a much brighter future, and a more productive inclusive governing process. Personalities and personal styles matter. As Blaine Garvin has reported about strong mayors: "The chief lesson that we have learned is the strong-mayor works or doesn't work depending upon who the strong mayor is" (Ress 2004, B1). The concluding point is simply this: The strong-mayor system, marked by confusion, conflict, and chaos, fared rather poorly under the Wilder regime and, hence, Richmond's experience with the strong-mayor form of government is still in the birthing pains stage. Since Wilder did not run for reelection, whether the new form of government will succeed and gain a strong measure of community acceptance and legitimacy will depend upon the governing style of Jones who, in an especially competitive four-way mayoralty contest conducted on November 4, 2008, won the right to succeed Wilder.

## References

Bacon, Lisa A. 2007. In Richmond, critics say L. Douglas Wilder has overreached. *New York Times*, October 21.

Hassett, Wendy L., and Douglas J. Watson. 2007. *Civic battles: When cities change their form of government.* Boca Raton, FL: PrAcademics Press.

Hinkle, A. Barton. 2002. Governor's Commission on the future of Richmond—Final Report. *Richmond Times-Dispatch*, August 6.

Jenkins, Chris L. 2004a. Richmond mayoral election approved. *Washington Post*, June 22.

———. 2004b. For Wilder, a return home to politics; former governor campaigns for mayor and a chance to rebuild Richmond. *Washington Post*, July 25.

————. 2004c. Richmond's urban decay dominates mayoral race. *Washington Post*, September 27.

————. 2004d. Wilder triumphs in mayor's race: After charter change, former governor is elected to lead troubled home town. *Washington Post*, November 3.

————. 2005a. In office again, Wilder lays out Richmond's path. *Washington Post*, January 3.

————. 2005b. Ever the gadfly in Richmond, this time at city hall: Wilder makes waves in 8 months as mayor. *Washington Post*, August 22.

Jones, Will. 2008a. Wilder declares budget invalid. *Richmond-Times Dispatch*, June 11.

————. 2008b. Richmond council insists budget is valid. *Richmond Times-Dispatch*, June 12.

————. 2008c. Richmond school board gets lease. *Richmond Times-Dispatch*, April 11.

Kalita, S. Mitra. 2004. Wilder runs for mayor of Richmond; former governor to return to city. *Washington Post*, May 30.

Krishnamurthy, Kiran. 2008a. Wilder believes you're better off. *Richmond Times-Dispatch*, January 27.

————. 2008b. Wilder, city council face budget struggle. *Richmond Times-Dispatch*, March 11.

Kumar, Anita. 2007. Power struggle rattling Richmond. *Washington Post*, October 1.

McCollum, Rudy. 2003. Government structure isn't real issue. *Richmond Times-Dispatch*, October 31.

Pearrell, Tim. 2008. Richmond's Triple-A options limited. *Richmond Times-Dispatch*, January 24.

Rayner, Bob. 2008. Doug Wilder: Virginia's premier politician never left well enough alone. *Richmond Times-Dispatch*, May 21.

Redmon, Jeremy. 2002a. Wilder, Bliley join forces; goal: Strong mayor for city by 2005. *Richmond Times-Dispatch*, July 26.

————. 2002b. Panel to study electing mayor: Wilder, Bliley appoint nine city residents. *Richmond-Times Dispatch*, August 27.

————. 2002c. Lawmakers disagree about electing mayor. *Richmond Times-Dispatch*, September 6.

————. 2002d. City creates study panel. *Richmond Times-Dispatch*, October 15.

————. 2003a. Businesses give to Wilder panel; $60,000 to help study reform ideas. *Richmond Times-Dispatch*, January 6.

————. 2003b. Mayoral petition drive set. *Richmond Times-Dispatch*, June 20.

————. 2003c. Mayor plan opposed; Kenney to introduce resolution Monday. *Richmond Times-Dispatch*, October 11.

————. 2003d. Scott opposes proposal for at-large city mayor. *Richmond Times-Dispatch*, October 29.

————. 2003e. City voters embrace at-large mayor plan; Wilder declares vote victory for city, state. *Richmond Times-Dispatch*, November 5.

————. 2003f. Support crosses racial lines/at large mayor plan prevails in 65 of the 72 Richmond precincts. *Richmond Times-Dispatch*, November 6.

————. 2003g. Backers of at-large mayor outspend foes; corporate donations boost the reformers' bid, but Marsh rips influence. *Richmond Times-Dispatch*, October 31.

Ress, David. 2004. Strong feelings and strong mayors: around the U.S., it's anger that often prompts cities to switch. *Richmond Times-Dispatch*, December 19.

————. 2008a. Top Wilder aides' pay up 13–20%. *Richmond Times-Dispatch*, March 2.

————. 2008b. Wilder hits council on budget. *Richmond Times-Dispatch*, March 28.

————. 2008c. Costs mounting for Wilder security. *Richmond Times-Dispatch*, May 4.

————. 2008d. Mixed feelings about Wilder. *Richmond Times-Dispatch*, February 27.

———. 2008e. Support for Wilder declines. *Richmond Times-Dispatch*, October 27.

———. 2008f. Mayor shift has a price. *Richmond Times-Dispatch*, April 20.

———. 2008g. Costs to run city near top in state. *Richmond Times-Dispatch*, February 17.

Ress, David, and Will Jones. 2008. Top city official quits post. *Richmond Times-Dispatch*, July 31.

Richmond Times-Dispatch. 2003. Charter Commission releases its questions. April 9.

Schapiro, Jeff E. 2008a. Braves, Redskins, and Wilder. *Richmond Times-Dispatch*, January 20.

———. 2008b. For Wilder, risk topped the reward. *Richmond Times-Dispatch,* May 18.

Sheffield, James E. 2003. City voters need to make charter changes. *Richmond Times-Dispatch*, June 6.

Shepherd, Lauren. 2003. Group fights at-large mayor; encourages voters to say no to proposal. *Richmond Times-Dispatch*, September 9.

Wilder, L. Douglas. 2002a. City voters should be able to elect a strong mayor. *Richmond Times-Dispatch*, April 7.

———. 2002b. Richmonders have tolerated mediocrity long enough. *Richmond Times-Dispatch*, June 2.

———. 2007. The charter invests the mayor with administrative authority. *Richmond Times-Dispatch*, October 21.

Williams, Michael Paul. 2002a. Wilder bids to revise city charter; seeks popularly elected mayor. *Richmond Times-Dispatch*, July 18.

———. 2002b. Co-Founder of crusade opposes a strong mayor. *Richmond Times-Dispatch*, September 4.

———. 2003a. Despite own misfortune, Bobb backs strong mayor. *Richmond Times-Dispatch*, July 9.

———. 2003b. Group sounds alarm on mayor-at-large plan. *Richmond Times-Dispatch*, July 16.

———. 2008a. Fat raises are wasted on a few. *Richmond Times-Dispatch*, March 5.

———. 2008b. Losing Monroe would be a loss for Wilder. *Richmond Times-Dispatch*, May 9.

CHAPTER 6

# SAN DIEGO

## Switch from Reform to Representative

GLEN W. SPARROW

THE DENIZENS OF "America's Finest City" were shocked upon waking on September 7, 2004, to find that the *New York Times* equated San Diego with one of the nastiest financial disasters in U.S. business history. *The Times* outed the city nationally as "a Kind of Enron-by-the-Sea." In the article following the Enron headline, the city's financial debacle became news nationwide. San Diegans had grown comfortable having their city referred to by the national press as "sleepy," "laidback," or even "a navy town" and bristled at this negative reference, even if it was deserved. The city faced a mounting pension deficit, federal investigations into its retirement system, and subsequent allegations of illegal accounting and public corruption. Paragraph seven laid out the extent of the catastrophe materializing in the city: "And the Securities and Exchange Commission and the United States attorney's office in San Diego opened investigations this year into possible fraud in the city's financial statements and potential political corruption. Subpoenas were served on a number of city offices and several people confirmed that they had been interviewed by the F.B.I. in connection with the inquiry" (Broder 2004).

Why this fiscal calamity occurred and how it affected the choice city voters made in November 2004 to replace the council–manager form with a mayor–council system is a significant factor in this account of San Diego's decision to switch. In order to explain the reasons for the shift, some background needs to be provided: first, a brief description of the city as it appeared in 2004, then a look at the ten-year history of charter change in the city, followed by a discussion of how the mayor produced the final charter and what it contained; then a brief look at how the city's financial crisis led to reduced support of the city government, a description of the campaign for the charter, the election, and an analysis of the vote and the reasons for it; and finally, an epilogue to bring San Diego's switch to the present.

## SAN DIEGO 2004

Although classified as a reform city, San Diego is not generally considered a progressive city in terms of governance, so it is of more than passing interest that it is the largest

U.S. city to have recently undertaken a major change in its governing structure. Until the late twentieth century, the political culture of San Diego was that of a city not ready or willing to make lurching changes in its public policies or governing structure. Since its inception as a major Pacific port for the U.S. Navy in the 1920s, San Diego—unlike its fellow California cities to the north, San Francisco and in the past decades Los Angeles—has been considered conservative in the classic sense. It refuses to embrace rapid or even moderate governmental progress, it is frugal in its taxing and spending policies—ranking close to fiftieth in U.S. cities in the ratio of city employees to population—and although embracing the economic impact of the navy, it continues to believe the private sector superior to the public sector, tends to vote Republican—and usually for the candidate furthest to the right—and is not inclined to move rapidly or imprudently toward change. However, rapid modification of demographics in the past decade has nudged the city toward a Democratic plurality and a somewhat more progressive stance, making change in San Diego often dependent upon the voting turnout of the more recently arrived. San Diego voted for Kerry in 2004 and Obama in 2008, the first Democratic presidential candidates to receive a majority since Johnson in 1964.

In 2004 San Diego was the seventh-largest city in the United States and second largest in California, with a population of 1.2 million and rapidly changing demographics. According to the San Diego Association of Governments (2008), the city no longer has a racial or ethnic majority, and the 27 percent Hispanic and 14 percent Asian populations will continue to increase at a rate faster than the 47 percent White. This diversity increase is due to in-migration and a population below eighteen years old that is only 5 percent White but 34 percent and 21 percent Hispanic and Asian, respectively. The African American population is projected to continue to hold at about 7 percent as it has for the last two decades.

Economically, the city (and regional) economy has rebounded well from the 1990s recession; it has diversified and added increased service, tourism and information sectors to a shrinking manufacturing sector. This diversification could be a model for a modern city overcoming a lopsided economy too dependent on military and defense industries. In the late 1990s leadership from local governments, institutions of higher education, the Chambers of Commerce, and business community worked together to re-create the region's economy. Using a cluster analysis process that recognized the value of the border with Mexico, the potential of research and development of the biotech and biomedical industry, tourism and the climate as attractors for jobs and employees considered "value added," the region has remade itself as a "global city-region" (Scott 2001).

San Diego is the largest U.S. city to have changed from council–manager to mayor–council form. The original city manager structure was established in the city charter in 1931 following a series of interesting experiments in local government. Since incorporation as California's third city in 1850, the city embraced, at one time or another, a mayor–council form, a bicameral council, a commission form, and in 1915 a "manager of operations" who reported to the city council. Following the proposal of a board of freeholders in 1930, voters adopted the council–manager form. The 1931 charter was amended a number of times, changing, for example, the number of council districts from six to eight (1963) and making the mayor and council full-time (1974) (San Diego City Clerk's Office, n.d.). The most significant is a 1988 amendment that changed the system of election of council members from nomination by district and election citywide to nomination and election by district. Noting that the communities were now represented and citing the need for a strong mayor to represent a citywide perspective, progressive leaders and pundits waited for the second shoe to fall: the charter revision that would produce a mayor–council system. It would take until November 2004, however, for San Diegans to have the opportunity to make that change.

## Changing the Charter

The idea of changing from the council–manager form is not novel. As early as 1973 Mayor Pete Wilson, riding a wave of support during his first term, sought to change the chief executive from city manager to mayor (Sparrow 1984). Even though he was highly regarded as the new and very effective mayor, the voters did not support his charter amendment. An appointed 1989 charter commission recommended to the city council a plan to increase council seats to ten and expand the mayor's power, specifically, a veto power, but the council never allowed the proposals to reach the ballot. An unofficial and informal 1994 endeavor by a member of the city council and a local civic leader brought together scholars from the region's major academic institutions, who spent three or four months modifying the San Diego charter from its council–manager form to a mayor–council form. Except for an op-ed piece appearing in the *San Diego Union-Tribune* (Mitrovich and Sparrow 1994), the draft languished. Informal discussions occurred among progressive leaders off and on for the next five years, which kept the idea and the draft alive.

In January 1999 a meeting of what could be described as many of the influential leaders in San Diego was held on a Saturday morning at a city hotel. A decision to pursue a mayor–council form of government was made at that meeting. The gathering and its leadership was an outgrowth of the Committee of 2000, a citizen group that had been created to promote the building of a downtown baseball park in San Diego. Voters passed the ballpark proposal in 1998; however, the experience convinced some of its supporters that the form of government in San Diego was, at least, partially to blame for a lack of political leadership and the difficulty in getting the city to support the effort. The primary protagonists for this strong-mayor effort were the owner of the San Diego Padres baseball team, and a local businessman and civic leader, who together, for the next five years, financially supported the effort; a small Committee of 2000 staff supplied administrative assistance.

Over the years on various Saturday mornings at a local law school, a rotating group of interested participants met to debate, adapt, and draft the concepts and language of a mayor–council charter using as a base the draft prepared by the 1994 group. These meetings were open to anyone who was interested in attending, but eventually a group of fifteen to twenty showed up with some consistency. The basic changes made to the charter provided for a separation of powers with an elected chief executive—mayor—who would have veto power, appoint and remove a chief administrative officer and department heads including the chiefs of the police and fire departments, be responsible for creating and implementing the city's budget, and be responsible for the operation of city services. The other half of the government—the legislative branch—would consist of a city council of nine members elected from districts—a ninth district would have to be formed because of the removal of the mayor from the council—approve the mayor's budget, select its own president, establish its own rules of operation, and appoint a budget analyst to assist in its work. The public election of the city attorney was carried over from the 1931 charter without modification.

During the course of the dialogue and meetings representatives of Oakland and Fresno—both California cities that had recently modified their forms of governance from manager to mayor—were sought for advice and support. An individual who had worked on the recent Los Angeles charter effort was hired to draft the changes into the San Diego charter. Although undertaking the task of creating a strong-mayor form, the charter underwent a needed reduction and modernization—sexist language was eliminated, old and outdated sections were redrafted, and portions that were no longer relevant were removed. A completely modernized mayor–council charter was produced by the effort.

The group that undertook this work adopted the title of Committee on Charter Change (CCC) and began to consider a strategy for getting the changes adopted. California law allows two methods for getting charter changes before the voters: the city council could place the amendments on the ballot—but could also make any modifications its members desired. Or the charter changes could be placed before the voters through the initiative method—this would require the collection of signatures, estimated at about $1.50 to $2.00 each for approximately one hundred thousand signatures (15 percent of the 571,060 registered voters plus 20 percent margin of error). Since the cost of the initiative process seemed prohibitive, the members of the committee decided to approach the council. Over the next four years—June 1999 to March 2004—the members of the committee, which eventually became the Better Government Association (BGA), worked with Mayor Susan Golding, her successor Dick Murphy, and various members of the city council to get the proposed charter to the voters. A council majority never chose even to study, let alone place before the electorate, a mayor–council charter. Among the reasons for this are: a stronger mayor might reduce the power the council and the neighborhoods had acquired since the advent of the district-only elections, and retaining the status quo meant retention of control of policy by the council. At one point the leading members of the BGA and Mayor Golding made a strong push and the item was placed upon the council agenda. Following significant presentations by business and academic leaders the council still refused to even docket the concept.

## Mayor Murphy's Charter

As the BGA moved toward a decision to undertake a signature-gathering campaign to place the charter before the voters, Mayor Murphy invited a group of business and civic leaders—mainly the BGA leadership—to a March 15, 2004, meeting in his office. Before the guests could make their pitch, Murphy declared that he was interested in supporting a stronger mayor and was prepared to develop a draft and obtain council approval. The assembled guests were stunned because the mayor and his chief of staff, John Kern, had been staunch opponents of the strong mayor concept, at least up to this point.

Kern noted, in a 2008 interview, that the change in Murphy's support for increasing the power of the mayor was due to: first, the experience of his first term during which there seemed to be a continual increasing expectation of voters and oversight bodies in the ability of the mayor to solve city problems yet the mayor continued to lack sufficient legal authority; and second, Murphy would, by championing this issue, exhibit leadership, thus satisfying these "influential San Diegans" who desire a leader with greater mayoral power. In return Murphy would secure their political and monetary support for his upcoming reelection (Kern 2008).

The process of getting the proposal to the ballot was taken over by Murphy who determined the policies, the language, and the strategy. The BGA was consulted and discussions continued at those Saturday morning meetings, but control clearly shifted to the mayor's office. The proposal was now a single item; basically it was to add a new article XV to the charter. This allowed for a brief, approximately eleven-page ballot measure requiring a single yes vote to switch the charter from a council–manager to a mayor–council form.

The legal strategy ensuring that a single vote was required to modify the existing charter called for substituting "Mayor" in each place "City Manager" appeared in the charter. This was explained in proposed section 260 (b): "All executive authority, power, and responsibilities conferred upon the City Manager . . . shall be transferred to, assumed, and carried out by the Mayor." This effectively made the chief executive of the city the mayor. In addition, the charter changes clearly noted that the "new form of governance [would be] commonly known as a Strong Mayor form of government." This strategy also meant that although the government would be changed the seventy-year-old charter would not be updated.

In following the recently successful Oakland charter, the proposal called for a sunset provision for the changes:

(a)  The date for the provisions of this Article to become operative is January 1, 2006.

(b)  After January 1, 2006, the provisions of this Article shall remain in effect for a period of five years (until December 31, 2010) at which time this Article shall be automatically repealed and removed from the Charter. However, the Council and the people reserve the right to propose amendments to the Charter at the November 2010 election or sooner to extend, make permanent, shorten or repeal the effective period of this Article and to consider increasing the number of Council districts to nine at the time of the next City Council district reapportionment, which follows the national decennial census in 2010. (*San Diego City Charter* Article XV)

This became, of course, a potent political argument to vote in favor of the change because as was noted in the arguments in favor of the measure: "This change has been debated for decades and reviewed by a variety of citizen committees and commissions. Now it's time to give voters a chance to decide. As an additional safeguard, voters will have the choice in five years to make Proposition F permanent, or return to the old City Manager form" (San Diego City Clerk's Office 2004). The mayor as the chief executive of the city has specific administrative powers provided in the charter. In the realm of appointments the mayor will be able to:

♦ Appoint the chief administrative officer with council confirmation and dismiss this officer without recourse. Some confusion exists over this title as the charter refers to this officer as city manager but the only two persons to hold this office have been called the chief operating officer.
♦ Select and appoint the city's agency and department directors.
♦ Appoint the city auditor and controller, subject to council confirmation.
♦ Dismiss the city auditor, controller, the chief of police, or the chief of the fire department, subject only to a right for these city officials to appeal to the city council to overturn the decision. Exempted from mayoral dismissal are the offices of city attorney, clerk, council, and independent budget analyst.
♦ Appoint members of city boards, commissions, and committees, subject to council confirmation.
♦ Appoint city representatives to boards, commissions, committees, and governmental agencies, unless controlling law vests the power of appointment with the city council or a city official other than the mayor.

In relation to the budget:

♦ Propose and, following approval by the council, implement the city's budget.
♦ Have the power to veto the city's budget, as approved by the city council, or eliminate any line item thereof.

As to other veto power:

♦ Have the power to veto any legislative action of the council.

Finally, due to Murphy's desire to preside over the council's executive/closed sessions—a special class of closed meeting allowed for selected issues under California's open meeting law—the mayor will be allowed to attend, preside, and be heard at any closed session meeting of the council but not have the right to vote at such meetings.

The city council is the legislative branch of the city government and will operate without the mayor as a member.

Under the new charter, the council will:

- Be composed of eight council members elected by district.
- Annually elect a presiding officer (who will be called the council president).
- Establish an office of independent budget analyst.
- Set its own rules and determine its docket.
- Establish such committees as it deems necessary.
- Confirm, by majority vote, the mayor's nominees for chief administrative officer, city auditor, and controller.
- Summon any city official or department head in the administrative service to appear before the council or any committee of the council to provide information or answer any question.
- Set, by majority vote, the city's budget.
- Have the right to override, by five votes any mayoral veto.
- Be responsible for all land-use decisions.

As a holdover from the council–manager reform era, noninterference language was modified and retained (*San Diego City Charter* Article XV).

There are some operational problems with the proposed charter changes. The first is a council composed of eight members; no consideration (other than the suggestion of adding an additional district at the time of the next reapportionment) is given to bringing the council to an uneven number. Of greater importance, however, is the issue of the veto override. The charter as proposed requires the same number of council votes to pass an item as the number needed to override the mayor's veto, five votes. Also, due to state law, the mayor will not be able to participate directly in city land-use decisions, among the most important functions municipal governments in growing Sunbelt cities undertake. Additionally, the sunset of five years could produce an inconsistent and unstable future for city government. Finally, the mayor's presence in the council's closed sessions could prove to be awkward for the separation of powers.

## San Diego Chronology of Charter Change, Financial Disaster, and Corruption

To understand the how and why of this process, it is necessary to undertake a brief review of events that moved San Diego toward its charter change. A good place to start is the 1988 charter amendment that modified the method of selecting council members for the city. The method in place prior to the change had been one where candidates in the eight council districts were nominated by vote in the district and then were elected at large, an attempt to accommodate both district and at-large concepts. Revision had been attempted by African American organizations and neighborhood and progressive groups but had been soundly defeated on a number of occasions. In 1988, because of citywide concern over issues of land-use planning, development, and zoning, a coalition of environmental and community groups joined with minority groups to pass the amendment that produced the district-only elections. They launched a successful attack upon those so-called downtown interests that are often felt to have too much control of San Diego government. It is also worth noting, because the issue is raised again later when analyzing the election of November 2004, that the 1988 ballot was typical of California ballots in its complexity and length. This ballot contained a number of competing initiatives at both the county and city levels that would either tighten or loosen controls over land use. The competition and money spent was dramatic and dominated the local political scene. Additionally, the San Diego Unified School District proposed a multimillion-dollar bond issue—the largest in its history—that also sought attention in this busy election season. The postelection analysis generally concluded that the district election initiative that passed 51 percent to 49 percent was underwhelmed in the attention it received, raising the question: was this a move toward a new reform or merely an afterthought by voters?

Regardless of the intent of the voters, district elections, within a few election cycles, changed the makeup of the city council and public policy in San Diego. The Democratic Party, minorities, community groups, environmentalists, and labor unions all contributed to and were beneficiaries of the realignment on the council, and the shift reduced the power of the old guard, downtown business interests. With greater concern and interest in the neighborhoods, the worry became: who represents the whole city? The mayor was still elected at large, but he or she had neither the political nor the executive power to carry citywide issues. The concern was probably overrated as many council members continued to take a broad perspective, but when push came to shove the dollars might go to district and not to citywide projects. This was, of course, the turnaround the district elections were expected to produce. After years of neglect the neighborhoods began to feel the largess of the city government.

Given this greater demand to spend money on district projects, the city manager as chief budget officer found himself each year searching for additional district monies. Often this money came from one-time-only revenues, sale of city land, savings from deferred payments, or other city projects. This quest, along with the effect of Proposition 13—California's 1978 property tax reduction and limitation on future tax growth—San Diego's stingy political culture, and a series of costly large scale city projects—a refurbishing of the football stadium, a Republican National Convention, a Convention Center, and others—made each budget a struggle.

With these demands and structural limitations on revenue during the 1990s and into the new century, San Diego began to drift into debt. One of the methods used to hide these shortfalls was to shift revenues to the general fund by underfunding the city's pension contribution. Unlike most California cities that use the California Public Employees Retirement System (CalPERS), San Diego has its own system—San Diego City Employees Retirement System (SDCERS). Through a series of manipulations of retirement benefits and underfunding of the city's payments—begun in 1991 and expanded in 1996 and 2002 under three city managers and a series of council members—plus, a significant drop in the value of pension fund investments—the burst of the dot-com bubble—by late 2002, the city's pension fund had serious actuarial problems. Shortfalls of between one and a half billion and two billion dollars were projected. In his analysis of San Diego, Roger Lowenstein notes the city's flaw is its aversion to taxes and that the pension crisis occurred because city policymakers choose to tap into the pension to avoid raising taxes (Lowenstein 2008).

In early 2004 it was discovered that the pension underfunding had not been properly reported on the city's Certified Annual Financial Report (CAFR) as well as documents utilized for bond underwriting (Kroll Report 2006). The city's auditor resigned, and days later "city officials disclose[d] reporting errors and omissions about the pension system in past bond documents" (Hall 2008). Because of these problems with financial reporting, annual financial audits could not be certified, and the city's ability to borrow money in the public markets was withdrawn (Kroll Report 2006). Standard & Poor's Ratings Services suspended its ratings for San Diego, followed a few days later by Fitch Ratings placing the city on its watch list, and a day later Moody's Investors Service placed San Diego on negative credit watch (in March 2008 Fitch Ratings changed the city ratings from negative to positive, and in May 2008, Standard and Poor's restored the city's credit rating although it is now A down from the AA it had been before its financial troubles). Before the upgrades in 2008, the city was effectively shut out of the bond market. In April 2004 the city manager resigned "two months after city's credit ratings fall and federal authorities investigate city finances" (Hall 2008). The path leading to the election in November is strewn with indications of city incompetence.

Why did the city drift into this financial quandary, a dramatic pension underfunding, inability to borrow money, and substantial budgetary ills? According to Phil LaVelle, a longtime reporter for the *San Diego Union Tribune*, "Th[ese] schemes were engineered by city managers and approved by councils led by successive Republican mayors Susan Golding and Dick Murphy. These arrangements gave policymakers budget relief, allowing mayors and councils to pay for big-ticket items, such as expanding Qualcomm Stadium and hosting the 1996 Republican National Convention, without raising taxes" (2006).

Meanwhile, in events unrelated to the city's financial woes, in May 2003 the FBI raided the offices of three San Diego city council members, and on August 28 they were indicted by a federal grand jury "charged with wire fraud, wire fraud conspiracy and extortion" (Thornton 2005). The trial "involving an estimated 100,000 wiretap intercepts, two cities, 12 lawyers, six defendants and five years of investigation and trial preparation" (Thornton 2005) would not be held until May 3, 2005, but the corruption case would be closely followed by the media both locally and nationally. At issue in this sad tale is the offer and acceptance of campaign contributions to change city policy in strip clubs. In the final outcome, one council member was convicted, one had his conviction overturned, and one died before going to court (the two former cases are currently on appeal to the U.S. Supreme Court). However, the fallout in the year and a half leading up to the November 2004 election helped the reputation of neither the city nor its government.

## The 2004 Elections

The year 2004 offered San Diegans two opportunities to cast ballots, the primary and general elections and the challenge of long, crammed ballots with national, state, and local candidates. For the city, there was the mayor's race, a city attorney contest, and four council races, plus an assortment of measures. The primary election was held in March (earlier than normal as the state legislature tried to ensure that California would have a say in the Democratic presidential nomination) and produced a 46.5 percent turnout countywide. In the San Diego mayor's race, Mayor Murphy had caused some confusion early when he had said he would not be a candidate for reelection, then about a week later was talked into running—"the reluctant candidate" (Kern 2008). The hesitancy, however, brought two strong opponents into the race, thus assuring a runoff since no candidate was likely to receive 50 percent of the vote in the primary. Murphy led with 40 percent of the vote and the opportunity to face County Supervisor Ron Roberts in November. It was two weeks following the primary that Murphy and his chief of staff met with the "influential San Diegans" he needed to assist him in his reelection bid and agreed to get the mayor–council measure on the November ballot. The move was meant to be a "signal to the business community that there was leadership" (Kern 2008).

Murphy took the draft charter that the influentials had been debating and drafting for the past ten years and gave it to Kern and a Strong Mayor Steering Committee that proceeded to mold the charter to the mayor's liking. Murphy and Kern got the item through the council—six to three—and then stepped away and left the campaign up to the influentials.

The city continued to struggle with its financial condition. The day following Murphy's decision to support the charter change, city manager Michael Uberuaga resigned and left a month later in mid-April 2004. There was no indication that the city manager knew of the Murphy decision or that there was any connection with his decision to leave. In May a federal grand jury began taking testimony from city officials, and in September a report commissioned by the city provided more bad news: "San Diego city officials persistently misread the depth of a growing pension system deficit and their failure to disclose the problem has left the city's reputation on Wall Street 'seriously tarnished,' a law firm hired by City Hall concluded in a report issued yesterday. The 268-page report by Vinson & Elkins LLP said city officials improperly spent money from pension fund earnings that should have been plowed back into the system while adopting a minimalist approach to public disclosure" (LaVelle 2004). In the midst of this chaos. city council member Donna Frye announced her intention to become a write-in candidate for mayor.

Meanwhile, the mayor–council proposal moved forward. The proponents, calling themselves Citizens for Strong Mayor Reform, retained two of the most successful campaign consultants in the city and, with superior fundraising efforts, got off to a quick start. Their focus group and polling results indicated "strong mayor" resonates better with voters than mayor–council. Thus "Strong Mayor Government" was used by proponents in titling the proposal, when it was designated Proposition F by the County Registrar of Voters.

The opposition was composed of two organizations created for the campaign: Neighborhoods for Accountable Government, A Committee against Prop F—the major opposition—and Citizens against One Man Rule—a single-person organization—and two labor union groups, the Committee on Political Education (COPE) of the San Diego-Imperial Counties Labor Council—the AFL-CIO organization—and San Diego Police Officers Association. They experienced difficulty consolidating their messages and efforts. The union opposition was based upon the assumption that this was a Republican effort to reduce the power of the council and take back clout that had been lost in the move to district elections. The unions had learned very soon after the district election change how to operate politically in the new environment. The unions would come together enough at election time to ensure that they maintained a majority on the council. Even in the San Diego milieu with its conservative and Republican base, the unions had controlled the council; they did not want to lose this advantage.

In the ballot argument for Prop F, proponents gave five reasons why voters should support the strong-mayor proposal: San Diego's governmental structure was outdated (the current system was not up to contemporary needs), the mayor needed authority to make changes (the mayor should be able to lead and be held accountable), it had checks and balances to protect taxpayers (the separation of powers structure would position a strong mayor against a strong council), city government would be accountable to neighborhoods (the district council system would not be diluted), and the voters should be allowed to voice their views (the debate had been going on for decades, they said, and it was time to vote, and besides, there is always the protection of the five-year sunset provision) (San Diego City Clerk's Office 2004). The arguments made no mention of the city's financial woes; the statement was a very traditional argument that might well have been utilized ten years earlier. Its main points were those of mayoral leadership and responsibility and protection of taxpayers and communities.

The opponents in their arguments identified negative aspects of Prop F: takeover of the neighborhoods by special interests, and the power grab by those who would "drain public services away from our neighborhoods to subsidize powerful developers," loss of accountability, and calling it a backroom deal to make San Diego like Los Angeles (arguments that a few "downtown business interests" wanted to dilute the district elections and the fear of becoming like Los Angeles always have resonance in San Diego elections) (San Diego City Clerk's Office 2004). Again, no mention was made of the financial crisis, and there was little defense of the council–manager system.

Financially, the proponents were well funded, outspending the opponents almost 10 to 1, raising and spending $524,362 to $37,071. A few large contributions were significant for the proponents as seven contributors provided over half of the money, with two husband-and-wife contributors donating over 30 percent of the money and three other contributors providing over 25 percent. For the opponents, the International City/County Management Association (ICMA) supplied the largest single amount, $15,000, and the union contributions equaled slightly over $12,000.

The proponents spent money in the normal manner, on TV and radio, direct mail, printing, billboards, lawn signs, and salaries. The opponents were limited to focusing on over fifty public debates, having limited radio advertisements, and including notices on union slate mailers. Prop F was not the central issue in the election; in fact, it was overshadowed by many of the other items on the same ballot, including presidential, mayor, city attorney races, and a very competitive race in Council District One. Plus, sixteen state issues and six other city items—including ethics and retirement system reform, a tax increase, and a very emotional issue dealing with the presence of a cross on city property—pushed the "strong mayor" issue to the periphery of the ballot. The complexity and breadth of the ballot diluted the effort of the unions; they were spread thin and thus were not able to devote full attention and dollars to Prop F. In the final tally, Prop F Strong Mayor Government won 51.43 percent (209,773 votes) to 48.57 percent (198,097 votes), almost 50,000 fewer votes than were cast in the mayor's race, and fewer than were cast for the tax increase and "cross" issues.

I offer some notes on the mayoral contest: Murphy won with 34.5 percent of the vote, but the election was not decided until a state court declared enough of write-in challenger Frye's ballots invalid for Murphy to win by 2,108 votes. She would have won by 3,439 if the disputed ballots had been counted. Roberts ran a disappointing third. Six months later, Mayor Murphy, the "reluctant candidate," announced his intention to resign in July 2005. In April *Time Magazine* had declared Murphy one of the three "worst mayors in America" (Gibbs 2005, 16).

## Why Did San Diego Switch?

Some of the local experts who watched closely or participated in the process provided a number of reasons for the vote to switch in San Diego. According to Mayor Murphy's chief of staff, there were four reasons for the passage of Prop F: Murphy was popular as a candidate and voters related the strong-mayor measure to him (although the number of votes he received seem to refute this assertion), poor campaign by the opposition, significant funds of proponents ("all things being equal the money will win"), and lack of attention by the voters because of the other issues that captured their attention (Kern 2008).

One of the consultants who ran the campaign for the Citizens for Strong Mayor Reform offered these reasons: proponents had money to provide focus groups and polling so they knew what issues people were concerned about. Three critical ones were, first, the city's financial meltdown, making "anything that showed accountability or leadership or change . . . attractive;" second, council members for the most part did not feel threatened and except for one did not take a strong interest in opposing; and finally, most of the public employee unions felt, due to a number of compromises in the mayor's proposal, that the districts would be left unchanged—police was the exception. Additional reasons included "no funded opposition," a strong speakers' bureau blocked the only attempt at a campaign by the opposition, and it being a "low profile issue, other more important things were on the ballot" (Shepard 2008).

A city manager who left prior to the financial breakdown felt that 70 percent of the reason for the success of Prop F was lack of leadership and performance of the whole city government, including serious mistakes, and the financial dark cloud over the city—all leading to a lack of confidence, and 30 percent was weakness of the council–manager system (McGrory 2008).

Until the financial debacle, San Diego embraced the council–manager form and felt comfortable with the business-oriented, low-taxing, efficient government it provided. But over the years, the council members become too dependent on the manager and his recommendations and were negligent in their oversight and control of the manager. A good part of the reason for the pension crisis was overreliance by the council on the advice of the manager and his staff, a dependence that had evolved over the years. Following the disclosure and the attendant investigations, reports, indictments, and other matters, the views of some of the council members changed regarding the role the city manager played in the fiscal meltdown. The opinions held by some members of the council may be instructive as to how this revisionist view of his performance affected the election. Of Michael Uberuaga, who held the city manager office during a majority of the discovery of the pension and financial troubles—1997–2004—there have been some harsh criticisms. One councilmember believed the city manager was overmatched in the position and he did not believe him "to be all that competent" (Kroll Report 2006). Another called the manager a "weak leader" whom he thought should be fired and who at times was "misleading"(Kroll Report 2006). As to the previous city manager, one council member noted: "[Jack McGrory] was effective but . . . he tended to do things outside of the Council's sphere" and recalled that the manager "once told him that he did not tell Council members where *all of the money was* because he believed they would just go out and spend it" (emphasis in original, Kroll Report 2006). As the election approached the council–manager system lost its luster and respect due to the pension and other problems the city was enduring.

The conclusion I reach in explaining the San Diego switch is that what occurred and why it happened is typical of San Diego's political culture and its municipal history. The issue of leadership and how it is viewed and appreciated is important in explaining the change in governing systems. This analysis began in 1971 when, following a scandal that cast a pall over the mayor and council, a young state assemblyman returned to San Diego from Sacramento to run for mayor. Pete Wilson was subsequently elected three times and changed the way San Diegans viewed the mayor's office and the role of the person holding the job; he also established a threshold of performance that no successive mayor has been able to duplicate. Through his intelligence, political acumen, personality, diligence, and ability to surround himself with and learn from talented people, Wilson changed the way San Diego is governed, not by changing the council–manager system but by manipulating it to allow Wilson to become, in fact, the city's chief executive (see Sparrow 1984 and 1994 for more detailed accounts of Wilson's terms as well as some of the mayors who followed him).

For future holders of the office and the electorate, the result of the Wilson mayoralty was that the bar was raised and expectations established. The concept of a strong elected leader at the helm became expected even if the governmental structure contradicted it. Every subsequent mayor was measured against the Wilson standard or, at least, the myth that was created and found laudable by successive generations. Each mayor that followed Wilson was found wanting, but the desire for replication of the Wilson years and its prototype of strong leadership endured.

The 1988 change to district elections altered dramatically the city council and hence city policies. The control of the old guard was reduced, and neighborhoods, Democrats, environmentalists, ethnic and racial minorities, and labor unions challenged, and within a decade controlled, the council. In the view of most citizens who paid attention, along with the district vote, came the assumption that strengthening the mayor's powers would be a next step. District elections established anticipation for the next charter change, a strengthening of the mayor's office. Of course, the old guard saw this potential change as an opportunity to regain some of the power lost in 1988. They saw the potential of capturing in a citywide election what they seemed unable to control in the district arena. "Old guard" is used here to describe those influential San Diegans mentioned above who helped to institute and drive the strong-mayor proposal as well as the downtown business interests, the Chamber of Commerce crowd, and those who felt the loss of power that occurred with district elections.

Working in conjunction with these desires and assumptions was an unofficial ten-year charter drafting exercise that proposed a structure anticipating a leader in the mayor's office. The ongoing drafting discussions allowed a public dialogue to occur, intensify, and educate. This decade-long process, at times focused and at others dormant, allowed an exchange of ideas to occur in the city that included representatives of the old guard and progressives both seeing the mayor's office as being important to their goals. The dialogue was often intense and heated and at other times intellectually stimulating and educational. In the final analysis it was a valuable exercise in civic reform that was engaged in, for the most part, by people of differing political, economic, and ideological views that proved that dialogue when free and open will work. A good deal of the credit for the maintenance of the process as well as the civility and progress can be attributed to the leadership of George Mitrovich. Thus, when those influential San Diegans were seeking solutions to what they viewed as a lack of leadership, a document proposing a mayor–council form that had been well vetted was available. Subsequently, when Mayor Murphy decided he needed to show leadership in his 2004 campaign, the concept that had been discussed for a decade was available in written form: very convenient for the mayor.

Finally, by 2004 the city found itself in the midst of a financial muddle, the pension underfunding was estimated at $1.5 billion; there was the possibility of another billion in medical costs for city retirees; city audits were not completed for past years due to mismanaged reports; the city was not able to borrow money through the municipal bond market; the SEC, FBI, U.S. Attorney, and county district attorney were investigating and were about to or had indicted members of the city staff; a city manager, auditor, and other city financial officers had resigned; and revenues were inadequate to meet expected expenditures in the city budget. Discussions of bankruptcy were common, and serious people were proposing it as a solution to the city's financial mess. And three members of the city council were facing a trial in federal court for wire fraud, wire fraud conspiracy, and extortion.

The convergence of these four conditions—the Wilson legacy, district elections, the decade-long discussion of a mayor–council charter, and the financial morass and corruption—was critical to the success of the vote. These issues were especially important, when added to the issues surrounding the election mentioned by observers: proponents' money, lack of substantial opposition, and other issues crowding Prop F from public attention. All these contributed to the success of the mayor–council charter switch in November 2004. But what pushed the voters over the edge? Given San Diego's traditional discomfort with change, it seems unlikely that barring the financial chaos of the city, and to a lesser extent the indictment of the three council members in the strip club case, the strong-mayor proposal would have passed. San Diegans have historically been hesitant to modify their governing structure, but the fiscal fiasco reduced their faith in their government enough to bring about its downfall.

## Epilogue 2006–2008

The unfortunate constant in this updating of San Diego's experiment with mayor–council government is that the economy will not allow the experiment to be analyzed as a single event. Just as the city was beginning its climb out of its fiscal nightmare under the new system, the global economy began to self-destruct. It has been impossible to evaluate the change in the city's governing structure without the overlay of these global economic woes. Mayor Jerry Sanders took office on December 5, 2005, following a special election in November to fill the vacancy that occurred when Murphy resigned. Since the mayor–council government was not to become effective until January 1, 2006, his choice as chief operating officer—retired Rear Admiral Ronnie Froman—was made city manager for the last twenty-five days of 2005—San Diego's last traditionally appointed city manager had left the city in November. The first orders of business were getting the mayor's team in place and operating, addressing the fiscal problems, and becoming apprised of the condition of the city government.

Getting the audits from four previous years became the financial goal; the money markets would not open up until these were successfully submitted. It would be 2008 before the ratings agencies were satisfied. Of course, the irony of finally securing the positive ratings was that by then the global meltdown had shut down the municipal bond market not just to San Diego but also to most governments. The concurrent deflation of the stock market also further damaged the pension system's investments leaving it dangerously underfunded with just a bit over 50 percent of the money needed for its obligations. Additionally, in October 2008 Mayor Sanders announced that the loss of sales, tourism, and property tax had produced a midyear deficit of at least $43 million. The overwhelming financial crisis facing the city certainly makes difficult any analysis of the implementation of the mayor council form in San Diego. Not only did the economy occupy Sander's new administration, it took away valuable time and attention that should have been focused on the transition. COO Froman likened her first months to "performing open heart surgery on a marathon runner—while she was competing in a race."

The creation of the Independent Budget Analyst (IBD) office was authorized in the charter amendment that created the mayor–council structure, and became an important addition to the legislative branch of the city. With this addition, the council had the staff to review the mayor's budget and policies. Andrea Tevlin, deputy city manager of Phoenix, Arizona, was hired and became the first, and thus far only, IBA; her office currently contains nine additional staff positions.

In the June 2008 primary election, the mayor won reelection winning outright with 54 percent of the vote against four opponents. A charter amendment ushered through the process by the president of the council passed easily and cleared up some of the structural problems of the mayor–council system. It required the placement on the ballot in June 2010 of the question of making permanent the new structure, required the creation of a ninth council seat following the 2010 census—at the time of the reapportionment of the council—and made the veto override two-thirds, or six of the nine, council members at the time of the addition of the ninth seat. Another amendment made permanent the office of the Independent Budget Analyst. After two-and-a-half years of operation often obscured by the city's fiscal crisis, the most obvious flaws left over from the hasty original proposal were ironed out. The voters will decide in 2010 if they want to continue with their experiment in switching governance systems.

After nearly three years of mayor–council government, what is the state of the San Diego switch? The economy, of course, has made San Diego's financial situation even more fragile, and it affects any analysis of the mayor–council system. Any comments regarding the effect of the switch, therefore, must take for granted the dismal financial conditions of the city and their impact upon its government.

The first mayor under the new structure, Jerry Sanders, has leaned more toward the caretaker model than the leader model. He is a classic conservative and does not rush to make changes or take on new projects, let alone windmills. His tenure has been steady and cautious. His first months were defined by trying to describe and understand the fiscal situation. He left to his COO the management side of the city, and there were attempts made to "reengineer" the city workforce and administration. Following the election Sanders began to indicate a greater attention to policy issues and has even indicated some limited leadership positions on some of the long-term issues facing the city—water, airport, football stadium, fire protection, convention center, central library, and civic center.

Sanders's report card is mixed; he is not the leader and innovator envisioned by those who led the strong-mayor campaign. Sanders is not the "man on the white horse" that the promoters of the strong mayor promised or imagined, but he has been a steady, calm executive who has shown that he is in charge of the city. He has guided the city through some very difficult times.

The legislative side is more mixed as one might expect from a body of eight politicians not used to working together. Five members of the body were holdovers from the council–manager years, and they had a difficult time realizing that on controversial issues they were not going to get recommendations and cover from the manager. Even though the first president of the council tried hard and defined the position better initially than the mayor did his, the council has not been able to speak with a single voice or even with a few voices. They did not take well to herding. In December 2008 four new members were added—term limitations removed four holdovers. But there has not been cohesion of the council or the clear realization that this new form is a separation of powers. The presence of a very bright, knowledgeable, and assertive Independent Budget Analyst office has enabled the council to keep track of and challenge the executive branch. The council needs to begin to develop policy and not just react to the mayor's proposals; it is hoped that this will come as the new members become acclimated.

At this stage of the transformation the picture is mixed, primarily because of the economic times and the people involved. The winners thus far have been the people of San Diego who have realized the promised benefit of greater transparency. Perhaps the best example of this is the budget. In San Diego under a series of city managers and councils the budget was like a black box that only the staff seemed to understand; little was shared with the council and the council asked few questions or knew what questions to ask. Now, however, the budget is much more open as the adversarial relationship between the mayor and council produces information and openness. The IBA provides analysis and is not fearful of making opposition to the mayor's proposals public. For the mayor's part, the financial crisis has brought forward both one- and two-year budgets as well as five- and more-year-projections. The information is now an expected part of the governance, far different from the past.

Where do we go from here? The system will be up for renewal in June 2010, and the referendum on the mayor–council will be in the hands of the voters. This is too early to know about the opposition, but no doubt it will occur and the debate will be fierce. The city's financial situation will, no doubt, play a major role in the perception of the voters as they analyze the quality of their experience with mayor–council government.

Postscript: On June 8, 2010, voters in San Diego renewed the mayor–council form with 61 percent voting in favor.

# References

Broder, John M. 2004. Sunny San Diego finds itself being viewed as a kind of Enron-by-the-sea. *New York Times*, September 7. www.nytimes.com/2004/09/07/national/07diego .html?_r=1&oref=slogin.

City of San Diego Strong Mayor Form of Governance. 2005. www.sandiego.gov/mayortransi tion/index.shtml.

Gibbs, Nancy. 2005. The 5 best big-city mayors. *Time Magazine*, April 25.

Hall, Mathew T. 2008. SEC complaint says they misled investors about pension system. *San Diego Union Tribune*, April 8.

Kern, John (Chief of Staff of Mayor Dick Murphy 2000–2005). 2008. Interview with the author. May 2.

Kroll Report. Levitt, Arthur Jr., Lynn E. Turner, and Troy A. Dahlberg. 2006. *Report of the Audit Committee of the City of San Diego: Investigation into the San Diego City Employees' Retirement System and the City of San Diego Sewer Rate Structure.* www.sandiego.gov/mayor/news/break ingnews.shtml (accessed April to November 2008).

LaVelle, Philip J. 2004. Document: Errors rooted in confusion and dysfunction. *San Diego Union Tribune*, September 17. www.signonsandiego.com/news/metro/pension/20040917.

————. 2006. A major-league player. *San Diego Union Tribune*, June 18. www.signonsandiego .com/uniontrib/20060618/news_mz1n18labor.html.

Lowenstein, Roger. 2008. *While America aged: How pension debts ruined General Motors, stopped the NYC subways, bankrupted San Diego, and loom as the next financial crisis.* New York: The Penguin Press.

McGrory, John (San Diego city manager 1991–97). 2008. Interview with the author. April 22.

Mitrovich, George, and Glen Sparrow. 1994. Change with the times: San Diego needs a new form of city government. *San Diego Union Tribune*, May 8.

San Diego Association of Governments. 2008. *Fast Facts.* 2008. www.sandag.org/resources/ demographics_and_other_data/demographics/fastfacts/index.asp (accessed April to May 2008).

San Diego Charter Review Committee. 2007. *Final Report.* www.sandiego.gov/charterreview /index.shtml.

*San Diego City Charter.* www.sandiego.gov/city-clerk/officialdocs/legisdocs/charter.shtml (accessed April to November 2008).

San Diego City Clerk's Office. n.d. *A history of San Diego government.* www.sandiego.gov /city-clerk/geninfo/history.shtml (accessed April 21, 2008).

————. 2004. *Prop F: Strong mayor trial form of governance.* www.sandiego.gov/city-clerk/elec tions/city/props041102.shtml (accessed April to May 2008).

San Diego Regional Economic Development Corporation. 2007. *Industry sectors.* www.sandiego business.org/marketintelligence.asp (accessed April to May 2008).

Scott, Allen J., ed. 2001. *Global city-regions: Trends, theory, policy.* Oxford: Oxford University Press.

Shepard, Tom (campaign consultant for Prop F campaign 2004). 2008. Interview with the author. April 22.

Sparrow, Glen. 1984. The emerging chief executive: The San Diego experience. *Urban Resources* 2, no. 1 (Fall). Reprinted in *National Civic Review* 74, no. 11 (December 1985).

————. 1994. The emerging chief executive 1971–1991: A San Diego update. *Facilitative leadership in local government*, ed. James Svara. San Francisco: Jossey-Bass.

Thornton, Kelly. 2005. City hall investigation: San Diego corruption trial likely to present an unflattering picture of the business of politics. *San Diego Union Tribune*, May 1.

CHAPTER 7

# OAKLAND

## The Power of Celebrity?
## Explaining Strong-Mayor Charter Reform

MEGAN MULLIN

IN NOVEMBER 1998 voters in Oakland, California, overwhelmingly approved a city charter reform to increase the formal authority of the mayor's office, despite having rejected similar proposals in the past. Following the 1998 election, political insiders and the press attributed public support for the reform to the celebrity of the mayor-elect who backed the measure. According to this story, he succeeded where others had previously failed because voters were enthused about his leadership background and his agenda of rebuilding the city's downtown. In short, it was the popularity of the incoming mayor that built support for strengthening the office.

This chapter challenges the conventional story explaining the transformation in Oakland residents' support for reform. Using precinct-level voting returns from the 1996 and 1998 elections, I show that support for the newly elected mayor in 1998 does not account for the outcome on the constitutional question. Instead, I argue that the public responded to the positions of elites and the way they framed reform proposals. The timing of the 1998 proposal and the specific reforms it offered created a consensus among journalists and political and community leaders that had not existed for previous reform efforts. Unity among the city's opinion leaders was necessary to win majority support among the public, and the same held true several years later when Oakland's strong-mayor system came up for renewal.

## The Setting

Oakland's council–manager form of government dated back to 1931, when garbage and street-paving scandals caused the city to abandon the commission model (Oakland Public Library 1986; Williams 1996a). Over subsequent decades the city charter underwent several revisions to provide for direct election rather than council selection of the mayor, four-year instead of two-year terms, and district elections for all but one council member, but the council–manager form remained intact. In the Oakland system, the mayor served as presiding officer of the nine-member nonpartisan city council and had no veto privileges. The council appointed a city manager who prepared the annual budget and oversaw all city departments. The manager served at the pleasure of the council and could be removed at any time by a majority vote.

The council–manager structure caused considerable frustration for Oakland mayors, who felt that limitations on the authority of the mayor's office hindered their efforts to improve service delivery and enact policy change (Pressman 1972). The mayor possessed only one of the five council votes needed to provide direction to the city manager, and bypassing the manager was not an option. Under the noninterference clause of Oakland's charter, it was a misdemeanor offense for the mayor or any other council member to "give orders to any subordinate of the City under the jurisdiction of the City Manager." Lionel Wilson, elected in 1977 as the city's first black mayor, found upon entering office that he could exercise no influence over the person responsible for directing the city's departments and staff. As one member of the Wilson administration recalls, "Lionel Wilson was confronted with a city manager who said, 'Well, I don't need to talk to you. Make an appointment. Get in line.'"[1]

Wilson eventually was able to replace the city manager, but still the mayor's authority fell short of his expectations. In 1984 he backed a charter reform proposal that would have strengthened the mayor's office. Although Wilson was a popular incumbent who easily won reelection to a third term the following year, the charter change measure received just 43 percent of the vote, falling short of the majority needed for approval. Wilson was able to win voter support for more incremental reforms, including a significant increase in the mayor's salary and a shift in local elections from odd- to even-numbered years, and he continued to pursue reform of Oakland's form of government throughout his tenure in office. During his third term, the mayor suffered a loss of popularity because of a weakening state economy, criticism for how he handled the city's drug and crime problems, and his support for an unpopular deal to provide taxpayer subsidies to the Raiders professional football team. He was unable to win support for a major charter change before his defeat in the June 1990 primary election by his former protégé, Elihu Harris.

Harris went on to win the runoff election and took office in January 1991. The new mayor quickly grew frustrated with the Oakland council–manager system and made several unsuccessful attempts to increase his authority. Early in 1992 he proposed a charter amendment that would allow the city to take control of the autonomous and financially troubled Port of Oakland. Harris backed down after port officials, shipping companies, and major airlines pressured the council to oppose the plan (Halstuk 1992c). That summer a citizens' group called Citizens for Responsive Government announced its intention to place a charter amendment on the November 1992 ballot that would eliminate the city manager's position and give the mayor full responsibility for city administration. Although Harris was not publicly associated with the group, it consisted of many of his political supporters (Halstuk 1992a). Again, Harris could not obtain enough council votes to place the measure on the ballot. Later that year Harris attempted to wrest control of the Office of Economic Development and the Redevelopment Agency from longtime city manager Henry Gardner (Halstuk 1992b). This effort also failed to win council support.

Although the council did not back his structural reform proposals, during his first two years in office Harris maintained a council majority on most policy issues (Halstuk 1992d). But after the election in 1992 of three new council members over incumbents he had endorsed, the mayor's relationship with the council changed. Unable to build a new majority coalition, Harris insisted that the formal limits on the authority of his office were to blame for his failure in exercising leadership on city policy. In fact, this might have been the most promising time for the mayor to provide policy direction, because Henry Gardner's resignation in mid-1993 created room for new administrative leadership.

As city manager for twelve years, Gardner had accumulated substantial influence over the city council. Although Gardner denied it, many observers believed that he resigned because of a power struggle with Harris (Halstuk 1993). Undoubtedly his absence removed a major obstacle to the mayor carrying out his own agenda. Harris did not take advantage of the opportunity provided by the introduction of a new city manager, however, and Gardner's replacement quickly established a working relationship with the council in which the mayor was in the minority. Says one observer about Harris's relationship with Gardner's successor Craig Kocian, long-time assistant manager: "I know Elihu was often extremely frustrated because it was clear to him that he could not get the city manager to do what he wanted the city manager to do because the city manager, if he didn't want to do it, would then go and talk to a few council members, and work the council. And the mayor ultimately was just a city council person." Both city managers might well contend that they were following the direction of a majority of the city council, but from the mayor's perspective, the managers were not following his lead. Harris eventually placed a sign on his desk reading, "The buck doesn't stop here. See the city manager."

Despite these difficulties Harris maintained enough public support to win election to a second term. After the election Harris and the city council jointly appointed a fifteen-member citizens' committee to recommend changes to the city charter that would appear before voters in 1996. The committee had more credibility than Citizens for Responsive Government, due to the council's participation in appointment of its membership, its lower proportion of Harris contributors, and its open public hearing process (Staats 1995). The Charter Review Committee insisted that it did not begin its deliberations with any specific plan or goals in mind, and it considered a wide range of city issues apart from the balance of power among the mayor, council, and manager (Staats 1995; Winnie 1995). In October 1995 the committee released its recommendations in three areas: form of government, city employment practices, and city involvement in the waterfront. After several months of discussions and postponements, the city council voted in July 1996 to place the committee's strong-mayor proposal on the November ballot, at the last minute eliminating mayoral veto power from the package of reforms (Walker 1996; Williams 1996e). After an active campaign on both sides, Measure F won the support of just 47 percent of the city's voters.

Harris did not run for reelection when his second term expired in 1998. Eleven candidates ran in that year's election, including former California governor Jerry Brown. Popularly known as Governor Moonbeam, Brown had a reputation for promoting innovative ideas but failing to follow through on his promises. Brown's celebrity was based on his family's name as well as his own political biography. Brown's father served as governor of California in the 1960s, and his sister served as state treasurer and ran unsuccessfully for governor in 1994. After seeking the 1992 Democratic presidential nomination, Jerry Brown moved to Oakland, started a daily talk radio program, and hosted classes at his communal converted downtown warehouse. Brown's celebrity, combined with a strong grassroots campaign organization, helped launch him past opponents to earn 59 percent of the vote in the June primary, winning the mayoralty outright without a runoff election.

Less than three weeks before the primary, Brown began to circulate a petition to submit his own strong-mayor measure to voters in November 1998. Over the next month, Brown collected nearly fifty-four thousand signatures—more than a quarter of the city's registered voters—to qualify his proposal for the ballot. By choosing the petition route, Brown did not have to win council support for his proposal or negotiate over its contents. Despite the 8–1 council vote in support of Harris's strong-mayor proposal two years earlier, no council members were supporting the Brown measure when he started to circulate it because Brown was running against a sitting council member for the mayor's office.

The campaign around Measure X was less heated than it had been for Measure F two years earlier, and even one of Brown's opponents in the mayoral election campaigned on behalf of the measure (Wells 1998b). When voters made their decisions in November, Measure X passed overwhelmingly with 75 percent of the vote. Measure F had won 47 percent of the vote in 1996; in just two years, electoral support for institutional reform rose by 28 percentage points. With nearly twenty thousand fewer voters at the polls in 1998, support for a stronger mayor increased by more than twenty-four thousand votes. Oakland joined many of the nation's big cities that amended their charters to enhance the formal power of the mayors. The remainder of this chapter attempts to explain this dramatic shift in the attitude of Oakland residents toward a strong-mayor form of government.

## The Personal Vote Hypothesis

After the vote in 1998, press accounts and political insiders attributed the rise in support for charter reform to voters' feelings about the mayors who would benefit from increased power. According to this explanation, voters were wary of granting more authority to Harris, who had failed to make significant progress in solving the city's economic and social problems and had overseen costly and mismanaged deals related to the Raiders football team and a downtown ice rink. When voters faced Measure X on the ballot, Brown had just been elected and sought to strengthen the office he was about to enter. Voters responded to Brown's celebrity and promise of urban rejuvenation, and they wanted to give him the tools to get the job done. As the *San Francisco*

*Chronicle* reported, "With his strong-mayor initiative, Brown succeeded where three mayors had failed before him. His popularity cut through the policy-wonk haze that made previous strong-mayor proposals intriguing to Oakland voters but slightly frightening" (DelVecchio and Holtz 1998).

This is a compelling story. Because the most immediate effect of both ballot measures would be to empower the sitting mayor, we might expect that attitudes toward the incumbent would play a role in shaping opinion about charter reform.[2] To test the personal vote explanation for the success of Measure X, I conducted a precinct-level analysis of the vote on the 1996 and 1998 strong-mayor ballot measures.[3] Figure 7.1 plots precincts by their level of support for measures F and X. As the figure demonstrates, the city was more conflicted about charter reform in 1996 than two years later; not only was the vote more evenly divided citywide, there also was more variation across communities within the city in their attitudes about strengthening the mayor's office. Precinct vote for Measure F ranged from a low of 27 percent to a high of 71 percent, with a mean support level of slightly less than 50 percent. Two years later the

**Figure 7.1 Precinct Support for Charter Reform Measures**

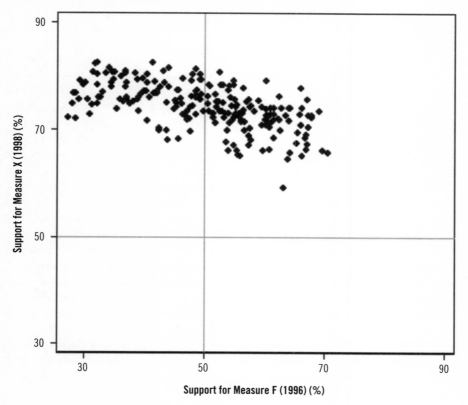

mean level of precinct support for Measure X was higher (74 percent), and there was less variation across precincts. In addition, the figure shows an inverse relationship between support for Measure F and support for Measure X, suggesting that short-term political factors may have played a role in influencing neighborhood-level support for charter reform.

My analysis of the personal vote hypothesis involves regressing precinct vote for each of the two reform proposals on precinct support for the incumbent mayor in his previous election. For Harris the previous election was in November 1994, when he was reelected to a second term. For Brown I used the 1998 primary election, in which he won a majority of the vote over ten opponents. Of course, a multicandidate primary election conducted five months prior to the Measure X vote is not directly comparable to a two-candidate runoff two years before the vote on Measure F. Nonetheless, without public opinion data disaggregated to the precinct level, vote choice in the previous election is the best measure of support for the incumbent mayor.[4] Also included in the model are measures of the racial composition of the precinct.[5] If voting is racially polarized in Oakland, then a neighborhood's racial composition might affect levels of support for Harris, who is African American, and Brown, who is white. Race also may influence opinion about city form of government (Northrop and Dutton 1978; Maser 1985).

Results from ordinary least-squares analyses of voting patterns appear in table 7.1.[6] The fit statistics offer a nuanced comparison of the model's performance in the two elections. The model provides a neater fit for the vote data on Measure X, as revealed by the smaller standard error of the estimate for the 1998 model. However, this is partly a consequence of the lower variance in precinct-level support for charter reform in 1998. The adjusted $R^2$ for the 1996 data is nearly twice as large as for 1998, indicating that racial composition and support for the incumbent mayor explain more of the variation in the vote on Measure F than on Measure X. The adjusted $R^2$ in the 1998 model is 0.45, indicating that over half the variation across precincts in support for Measure X remains unexplained.

The explanatory variables all have more influence over support for the 1996 charter change proposal. The three indicators of precinct racial composition have large and statistically significant positive effects on Measure F support, demonstrating that precincts with larger percentages of white residents were less likely to endorse charter reform while Harris occupied the mayor's office, even while holding support for Harris constant. Support for the mayor has a strong positive effect as well. Among precincts with the same racial composition, every percentage point increase in the precinct vote for Harris boosts support for Measure F by 0.19 points. In contrast, a point difference in support for Brown produces only a 0.07-point increase in precinct vote on Measure X, an effect that is only marginally significant. The strongest result in the 1998 model is a negative effect for African American precinct population. Among neighborhoods that equally supported Brown's election, those with larger black populations were less supportive of changing the charter to strengthen the new mayor's office, an opposite result from two years earlier.

**Table 7.1   Precinct Vote on Measure F: 1996, Precinct Vote on Measure X: 1998**

|  | Precinct Vote on Measure F: 1996 | Precinct Vote on Measure X: 1998 |
|---|---|---|
| *Racial Composition (%)* | | |
| Black | 0.29 | −0.09 |
|  | −0.02*** | −0.01*** |
|  | 0.23 | −0.05 |
| Latino | −0.03*** | −0.02* |
| Asian American | 0.2 | −0.01 |
|  | −0.03*** | −0.02 |
| *Support for Mayor (%)* | | |
| Vote for Harris | 0.19 | |
|  | −0.04*** | |
| Vote for Brown | | 0.07 |
|  | | −0.04* |
|  | 19.7 | 74.71 |
| Constant | −2.2*** | −2.76*** |
| N | 213 | 218 |
| Adjusted $R^2$ | 0.85 | 0.45 |
| Standard error of the estimate | 4.2 | 3.06 |

Table 7.2 uses Achen's "level-importance" technique (1982) to show the aggregate impact of incumbent support and racial composition. Cell entries report the net contribution of each independent variable to the overall level of support for the charter change measures, calculated as the mean value of the variable multiplied by its coefficient. In 1996 the charter reform measure received a mean support score of almost 50 percent across precincts, and only 20 of those 50 points are left unexplained by the model. In contrast, the model does little to explain the overwhelming 74 percent support across precincts for Measure X. Support for the mayor contributes four percentage points to the overall yes vote on Measure X, and nonwhite populations at the precinct level detract approximately the same magnitude of support for the measure. These are marginal contributions to the outcome, however, leaving much unexplained by this model.

In sum, race and support for the incumbent mayor go far in explaining the vote on Measure F in 1996, but they do not account for the strong support of Measure X in

**Table 7.2   Contributions to the Yes Vote on Measures F and X**

|  | Measure F | Measure X |
|---|---|---|
| *Racial Composition (%)* |  |  |
| Black | 11.89 | −3.65 |
| Latino | 2.58 | −0.13 |
| Asian American | 2.57 | −0.54 |
| Support for Mayor | 13.03 | 3.88 |
| Constant | 19.7 | 74.71 |
| Total (Average Precinct Vote) | 49.82 | 74.27 |

1998. If the conventional wisdom were true—that is, if Brown's fame and popularity propelled his strong-mayor measure to victory—then support for Brown in the primary election six months earlier should be a strong predictor of support for Measure X. Instead, precinct-level vote for the mayor has an effect on support for Measure X that is substantively small and only marginally significant. Important factors explaining the Oakland electorate's changed attitude toward charter reform are missing from the model. The next section explores alternative hypotheses to explain this shift.

## Campaign Effects and Elite Influence

If the shift in support for charter reform in Oakland cannot be explained by racial polarization and support for the mayor who would benefit from the reform, perhaps the ballot measure campaigns played a role. A change in the balance of campaign spending or endorsements might have influenced the aggregate election outcome. For either to have any explanatory power here, the balance of support should have shifted between 1996 and 1998. In the case of campaign spending, in both years the proponents of charter reform outspent the opposition (Tramutola 1996; Williams 1996d; DelVecchio 1998). In 1996 the "yes on F" campaign raised more than twice the amount collected by opponents and sent five times the number of mailers (Tramutola 1996). Yet the measure failed to win over a majority of voters. In short, there is no evidence to suggest that campaign spending influenced Oakland's support for a strong mayor system.

Turning to endorsements, individual and organization endorsements on both sides of the issue played a more important role overall in the 1996 campaign than in 1998. Endorsements were featured in campaign literature, newspaper articles, and columns about the ballot measure (Stinnett 1996a; Williams 1996b), op-eds (Gough 1996; Wieland 1996), and editorials (*Oakland Tribune* 1996). Both sides collected an attractive set of endorsements and highlighted them throughout the campaign. Featured supporters of Measure F included a long list of high-profile Democratic politicians, including U.S. senators and members of Congress, state legislators, and the San Francisco mayor. Jerry Brown also endorsed the measure. Organizational endorsements included business and labor groups, the NAACP, and local Democratic clubs. The opposition to Measure F focused more on organizational endorsements from good-government and tax reform groups and a competing set of local Democratic clubs. Supporters and opponents of charter change were successful in projecting an image of community support for their position.

Two years later individual and organizational endorsements played no role in the debate over Measure X. Newspaper articles, editorials, and campaign literature mentioned only the campaign organizations and primary spokespeople for each side of the debate. The single exception was a newspaper article noting opposition from the Alameda County Green Party (DelVecchio 1998). The contrast is dramatic. Whereas the high level of endorsement activity in 1996 suggests a hotly contested political battle, two years later political and community elites did not see a need to get involved.

Newspaper endorsements also indicate more controversy over the 1996 proposal. The *San Francisco Chronicle* endorsed the strong-mayor system in both years (*San Francisco Chronicle* 1996, 1998). The *Oakland Tribune* switched its endorsement between 1996 and 1998, however, moving from opposition to Measure F to support of Measure X (*Oakland Tribune* 1996, 1998). Studies of candidate races have shown that a newspaper's editorial position affects its coverage of candidates, and the overall coverage can influence voters' decisions (Kahn and Kenny 2002; Druckman and Parkin 2005). A shift in position by the hometown newspaper therefore could have important ramifications for ballot measure outcomes. In addition, the "no on F" campaign cited the *Tribune*'s opposition in its campaign literature (Oaklanders for Responsible Government 1996b).

The pattern of endorsements suggests a division of opinion among elites in Oakland over the 1996 charter change measure that did not exist two years later. Indeed, the available evidence indicates that differences in the substance and political timing of the ballot measures caused a shift in attitudes among opinion-makers, which was then reflected in the tone and intensity of the debate over charter reform. Elites played a role in shaping the debate over charter reform by translating the two measures to the public.

Although both proposals abandoned the council–manager form of government and significantly strengthened the powers of the mayor, the similarities end there. Measure F was a detailed thirty-six-page revision of all the charter codes that govern the division of powers in Oakland; Measure X was three pages long. Consistent with the origins of each proposal, the earlier measure represented a comprehensive and detailed approach to changing the governance of Oakland, while Brown's effort was rougher and more oriented toward creating favorable conditions for his own tenure. Although Measure X appeared to at least one observer as a "sloppy cut-and-paste," it demonstrated Brown's determination to avoid the pitfalls of the earlier measure.

Both proposals aimed to remove the mayor from the council and to limit the autonomy of the city manager. Supporters of a strong-mayor system deemed these goals as essential for increasing accountability. Measures F and X took different approaches to achieving these goals, however, which in turn produced different arguments against the two proposed amendments. The 1996 proposal added a second at-large seat to the city council in order to maintain an odd number of council members and avoid deadlock. Opponents of charter reform attacked this element of the proposal for its cost, estimated by the city auditor at $250,000 per year. The opposition also tapped into Oakland's strong support for district elections in arguing that the additional council member "would not be accountable to any neighborhood or district" (Oaklanders for Responsible Government 1996b). Measure X in 1998 avoided these criticisms by allowing the mayor a vote on the council in the case of a tie.

The larger and more consequential difference lay in approaches to reducing the role of the city manager. Measure F proposed to eliminate the manager's position entirely, shifting all of its responsibilities to the mayor. The mayor would be authorized to hire a chief administrative officer, but that position would be administrative rather than substantive. Measure F opponents fiercely attacked this concentration of power in the mayor's office, calling it "an invitation to corruption" (Oaklanders for Responsible Government 1996b) that would result in a "politically controlled administration highly susceptible to graft" (Oaklanders for Responsible Government 1996a). Newspapers picked up on this argument, and debate over the measure came to be framed in these terms. Peggy Stinnett, editorial page editor of the *Oakland Tribune*, wrote in a column about the charter change that it would make the mayor "the fiscal dictator of the city's treasury . . . the judge and jury of all fiscal affairs" (Stinnett 1996b). Articles cited opponents arguing that the measure would lead to "political patronage" (Williams 1996b) and "power-mongering" (Williams 1996c). Opposition op-eds that appeared in the *Tribune* followed the same theme. Consistent with the frame that a strong-mayor form of government would be more vulnerable to patronage and corruption, the opposition pointed to pro-F campaign contributions from local businesses and developers as early evidence of machine-style politics (DelVecchio 1996; Williams 1996d).

Two years later Brown managed to escape the arguments about patronage and corruption that had plagued Measure F by maintaining the city manager's position but making it answerable to the mayor rather than the city council. Measure X gave the mayor authority to appoint the manager, subject to confirmation by the council, and more importantly to remove the manager without council approval. The ballot measure also removed the noninterference prohibition that had prevented the mayor from providing direction to city employees. Consequently, although the manager would continue to direct city administration and finances, he or she would be under the exclusive watch of the mayor. By keeping the position of the manager and making the mayor's control over city finances more indirect, Measure X largely avoided the criticism that it would create a system of patronage and graft. In fact, the pro-X campaign was able to shift the special interests argument to its own advantage. In an op-ed supporting Measure X, Brown wrote, "Tragically, critical challenges in Oakland have been neglected as paid lobbyists and insiders work the current system and its invisible form of politics" (Brown 1998). Brown pointed to the "insiders" who benefited from the

Raiders deal and the bankruptcy of a downtown ice rink as evidence that more authority needed to be concentrated in the mayor's office. In 1996 the same two issues had been used to demonstrate that the city could not risk a concentration of power.

In addition to differences between the proposals in council membership and treatment of the city manager, Measure X included several provisions that were popular among elites: a two-term limit on the mayor, an elected city attorney, and a requirement that all city council pay raises be approved by the voters. Perhaps most important, Brown included a sunset provision requiring voters to reaffirm support for the charter reform after six years. These extra provisions responded to the concerns of Measure F critics that the enhanced stature of a strong office would encourage mayors to serve indefinitely (Oaklanders for Responsible Government 1996b), and the *Tribune* pointed to the provisions as a reason for its endorsement in 1998.

These substantive differences between the 1996 and 1998 proposals helped influence the opinion of elites and shaped how they framed debate over the measures. Community leaders, the press, and some elected officials had concerns about accountability mechanisms under Measure F, leading to a debate dominated by issues of corruption, special interests, and the salaries of council members. Because Measure X addressed some of these accountability concerns, discussion of the proposal rarely addressed potential abuses of power.

The timing of the measures also had an influence on elite opinion. Measure F appeared on the ballot six years into Harris's tenure, by which time the mayor had established a reputation as being ineffectual. Political elites were hesitant to endorse giving the mayor more power when he had not been successful in using the informal authority he already possessed. Furthermore, the mayor's weak political position allowed elites to criticize him and the reform proposal without fear of retribution. Stinnett's columns in the *Tribune* about Measure F were littered with criticisms of Harris, saying that he had "been on the sidelines" (Stinnett 1996c) and that "a change in the charter won't create leadership where there is none" (Stinnett 1996b). The paper's editorial opposing the charter reform argued, "Perhaps, if the city manager has been wielding too much power, it's because the mayor has not consistently and clearly exercised his leadership, thus creating a void, which in government is always quickly filled" (*Oakland Tribune* 1996).

Harris's management of the Measure F campaign did not help his reputation. The mayor's conflicted attitude about publicly backing Measure F reinforced the popular view that he could not stay focused and follow through on his priorities. A backer of Measure F described Harris's difficult relationship with the proposition this way: "He was very much of approach-avoidance on this issue. He felt that he was controversial, or he felt that it would look like a power grab if he was too close to the measure, so he would stay away from the measure. But then he would see the campaign going sideways and he would then step up and he would try to help it and he would help insofar as to get something started . . . and then just backed off."

This attitude had tangible effects on the campaign supporting Measure F. The proposal's backers failed to submit a ballot argument in favor of the measure. They missed two scheduled appearances in front of the city's largest Democratic club, leading the club to endorse a "no" vote on the measure (Stinnett 1996a). In the final days before the election, the campaign received negative press attention for mailing out a leaflet that violated election laws, because it looked like a real sample ballot and did not include accurate campaign committee information (Schorr and Brand 1996). The disorganization affected Measure F's success by reinforcing the impression among political insiders that Harris was distracted and indecisive.[7]

Two years later the debate over Measure X occurred before Mayor-elect Brown entered office. Few elites were willing to risk their relationship with the new mayor before he had begun his term. In the series of debates between Brown and former city manager Gardner over the proposal, Gardner emphasized that his opposition was not directed against Brown (Wells 1998a).

Perhaps most telling, the council member who led the two previous campaigns against strong-mayor charter reform decided to sit out in 1998. The council member later recalled, "While I was in opposition, I didn't really fight it too much because I was going to be working with the mayor and I didn't want to be out there antagonizing him." Like Harris, Brown had a reputation for being unable to stay focused, but he ran a vigorous campaign in support of the charter proposal. Moreover, attentive elites knew that the mayor-elect had agreed to retain newly hired city manager Robert Bobb, a widely respected administrator. The assurance that he would continue to serve as manager under Brown was cited as an important safeguard in editorials supporting Measure X (*Oakland Tribune* 1998; *San Francisco Chronicle* 1998).

## Sunset and Reauthorization of Strong-Mayor Reform

Timing and the substance of specific proposals continued to influence public attitudes about charter reform when Measure X came up for renewal. Although the provisions of the measure did not expire until the end of 2004, Brown decided to act early and ask voters in the November 2002 election to strengthen the mayor's office permanently. Brown had had a successful first term, working closely with Bobb to make progress on the mayor's primary goal of redeveloping Oakland's downtown area, and he was reelected in March 2002 with overwhelming support. That summer, without forewarning, the city council placed a measure on the November ballot that would eliminate the sunset on Measure X. The council president, who was allied with Brown and hoped to succeed him in office, led the effort to bring the sunset clause to a vote.

Good government groups such as the League of Women Voters and Common Cause were blindsided by the move; they had planned to hold forums the following year to consider the system's success. In addition to evaluating the strong-mayor system overall, they wanted to examine the performance of specific aspects of the Measure X reforms, including the size and composition of the council and the relationship between the council and the mayor (DeFao 2002). With two years remaining before the provisions would expire, the groups formally opposed early renewal and ran a modest campaign against the measure (Burt 2002). The *San Francisco Chronicle* editorial board agreed that Oakland should take more time to evaluate the reforms (*San Francisco Chronicle*

2002). Despite a positive endorsement by the *Oakland Tribune* and a campaign that outspent the opposition (Burt 2002; *Oakland Tribune* 2002), the proposal to end the sunset on Measure X fell 375 votes short of winning approval. In the same election voters also rejected three Brown-backed proposals to raise funds for expanding Oakland's police force.

Again, elite signals about the importance of considering reform alternatives seemed to resonate with Oakland residents. Although Brown enjoyed public approval ratings of 70 percent and higher (Counts 2002), journalists and political and community leaders criticized him for being inaccessible and inattentive to administrative issues such as filling committee vacancies. Throughout his tenure Mayor Brown relied too heavily on the formal powers he had designed for himself and failed to dedicate the time and attention needed to maintain support within the political establishment (Mullin, Peele, and Cain 2004). Many elites viewed the strong-mayor extension as an opportunity to send signals to Brown and possibly compel him to work more closely with the council. Because two years remained before the office would be weakened, voters were swayed by the call for public deliberation.

The mayor heard the call for more community input, and before the final vote had been finalized he started planning for a more collaborative approach to reintroducing the measure in 2004. Together with the city council he appointed a citizens' committee that held public hearings to consider issues of city structure. The committee developed a new proposal that responded to complaints brought by both Brown and his critics. The proposal further strengthened the mayor's office by giving the mayor power to hire and fire department heads. At the same time, it required the mayor to hold four public meetings a year and provided the council with authority to make committee appointments when the mayor fails to act. It also removed ambiguity in the charter by changing the city manager's title to city administrator. As the citizens' panel was reviewing the Measure X reforms, Brown exercised his powers his powers as a strong mayor to force out powerful city manager, Robert Bobb, who had been clashing with the mayor over their competing visions for downtown development. In particular Bobb was promoting construction of a downtown baseball stadium on a site that Brown had tagged for housing development. The job title of city administrator better matched Brown's vision—and the reality under Measure X—that the mayor alone holds decision-making authority.[8] Brown called the renewal measure imperfect but noted, recalling his predecessor's complaint about mayoral power in Oakland, "at least the buck stops somewhere" (MacDonald 2004). The council voted to put the new proposal on the March 2004 city ballot.

Having addressed the substantive and procedural criticisms brought by good government groups, and with a looming deadline that would end the strong-mayor system, Brown and his allies had an easier time winning support for their proposal. Some community groups formally opposed the ballot measure, as did former city manager Henry Gardner, but no organized opposition campaign emerged. Supporters of the measure did not take any chances, however, and spent almost $100,000 on a campaign to win voter approval (Brand 2004; Counts 2004; MacDonald 2004). Both the *Tribune* and the *Chronicle* (*Oakland Tribune* 2004; *San Francisco Chronicle* 2004) endorsed the renewal, arguing that although Brown had fallen short of achieving some of his goals, at least it was possible to hold him accountable for his successes and his failures. With near consensus among elites, the measure passed with almost 70 percent of the vote.

## Conclusion

Given the complexity of city structural reform and the uncertainty about its potential impacts, it is reasonable to expect citizens' opinions about a reform proposal to be shaped by their attitudes toward the mayor who stands to gain or lose power in the short term. Indeed, most political observers attributed the success of the 1998 proposal to strengthen the Oakland mayor's office to the celebrity of mayor-elect Jerry Brown. I have argued that Brown's popularity does not on its own explain the Oakland electorate's variable response to charter reform proposals. An analysis of vote returns indicates that support for the previous mayor, Elihu Harris, contributed to support for his failed effort to increase mayoral power in 1996, but the same pattern does not hold for Brown's successful attempt two years later. Similarly Brown was unable to capitalize on his popularity in 2002 and convince the public to act early in removing the sunset on the strong-mayor system.

The Oakland case suggests instead that local elites play an important mediating role that helps shape public response to a structural reform proposal. Both the 1996 ballot measure and the 2002 proposal for strong-mayor renewal elicited a mixed response from journalists and community leaders. The proposals earned support from high-profile Democratic officeholders, but community and civic organizations opposed the measures based on dissatisfaction with the incumbent mayor's performance in office and concerns about the substance of the specific proposals. These groups and the press successfully attached a frame to each measure that influenced public opinion: they framed Measure F as a gateway for corruption and the 2002 renewal proposal as a premature grab for power by Mayor Brown. In both cases the proposals that followed two years later addressed critics' substantive concerns and appeared at a more opportune political moment. Elites were united in their support for the measures, and citizens responded with a majority vote for reform.

My argument about the importance of elite consensus and framing does not discount the importance of a mayor's governing style. How a mayor performs in office helps shape elite perceptions about weaknesses in the existing structure and the likely consequences of reform. Moreover, although a strong-mayor system can help remove some obstacles that impede motivated mayors from achieving their goals, there is no structural reform that will overcome a mayor's lack of interest or leadership skill. Succeeding Brown in the office is Ron Dellums, a longtime member of Congress who made a last-minute decision to run for mayor in 2006. Dellums got off to a rocky start during his first two years in office. The city faced serious challenges, including an upsurge in violent crime and a major budget shortfall brought on by a downturn in the housing market. Dellums offered a weak response to these issues and proposed few new policy initiatives. He drew criticism for being inaccessible and showing more interest in national politics than in the city.

By summer 2008 the city faced a crisis that called for strong leadership. Oakland was grappling with ongoing crime problems, a $50 million budget deficit with millions of dollars in reserve funds unaccounted for, and a federal investigation of city administrator Deborah Edgerly for charges of nepotism and interfering with a police investigation of an Oakland gang. Dellums fired Edgerly but only after drawing criticism for his refusal to discipline the city administrator. Journalists and residents alleged that the mayor was missing in action, and petitions began circulating for his recall. A poll conducted in October 2008 showed the mayor's approval rating had dropped to 27 percent (Rayburn 2009).

As Dellums entered the third year of his term, Oakland's problems continued to mount. A series of scandals rocked the police department, including a bungled investigation into the murder of a newspaper editor, a sexual harassment complaint against a deputy police chief, and an allegation that the chief abused his power in interfering with a police union vote. The department came under federal investigation focused on the beating and eventual death of a suspect at the hands of the department's chief of Internal Affairs. In January 2009 demonstrations and vandalism swept through the city after an officer with the independent transit agency shot and killed an unarmed passenger. Through these events Dellums continued to struggle to exercise the leadership his constituents demanded. The mayor took seven months to fill the city administrator position; many other openings for department heads and other senior city positions also remained vacant for months. In an effort to get a handle on Oakland's problems, Dellums hired former city manager Robert Bobb as a consultant to recommend changes to the operation of city government. Bobb also became Dellums's top choice to fill the vacant city administrator position, but Bobb turned down the job. Dellums finally appointed a longtime aide who had filled the role on an interim basis.

Bobb's review of city government performance under Mayor Dellums concluded that "the strong mayor form of government has not been fully operationalized in Oakland" (*San Francisco Chronicle* 2009). Among a long list of recommendations appeared basic measures such as a more accessible press office, regular performance evaluations for department heads and other top staff, and the mayor improving communication with the council and working a more predictable schedule. Even with the powers of a strengthened office, a mayor needs to exercise strong leadership. Structural design can help promote mayoral effectiveness, but ultimately it is the lack of personal skills or interest that prevents a mayor from governing successfully.

## Notes

1. Uncited quotations come from a series of interviews conducted by Megan Mullin, Gillian Peele, and Bruce Cain in April 2001 with former mayors and members of their staffs, current and former city administrators, and city council members.

2. I consider Brown the incumbent for Measure X because it would take effect upon his entering office.

3. The precinct analysis includes only polling-place voters, because the county registrar does not allocate absentee votes back to their home precincts. Absentee voters were substantially less

supportive of both Mayor Harris's reelection and Measure F than their polling-place counterparts were. Differences were smaller in 1998: absentees voted for Brown at a rate somewhat higher than polling-place voters, and support for Measure X was approximately even between the two groups.

4. If the difference in time spans produces a bias, the bias should favor finding a stronger relationship between mayoral support and ballot measure support for the case in which the time span between measurements is shortest. In fact, the results I report show the opposite: mayoral support has a larger effect on support for Measure F than Measure X.

5. Data on precinct racial composition come from the California Statewide Database (SWDB), which takes precinct-level electoral returns and matches them to Census geography for each election.

6. All results are similar when using a Tobit model that accounts for the limited range of the dependent variable.

7. In 2001 the state Fair Political Practices Commission issued five counts against Harris and two committees associated with Measure F for failing to disclose Harris's involvement in running the committees. Harris and the committees agreed to pay a $10,000 fine.

8. In explaining his reasons for firing Bobb, Brown told the press, "I feel I can be more engaged with the directors and more effective. Robert comes from a background where he picks the department heads and they report to him. I feel the need to communicate with them with no barriers between us. I want a team that works closely together, and I want to do it my way" (Johnson 2003).

# References

Achen, Christopher H. 1982. *Interpreting and using regression.* Newbury Park, CA: Sage.

Brand, William. 2004. OCO rejects mayor's Measure P. *Oakland Tribune*, February 8. News-Bank database (Access World News).

Brown, Jerry. 1998. A strong mayor for Oakland? Yes [Op-ed]. *Oakland Tribune*, October 16. NewsBank database (Access World News).

Burt, Cecily. 2002. Brown's approach to strong mayor softens: He promises to get more input in 2004 if this year's initiative fails. *Oakland Tribune*, November 7. NewsBank database (Access World News).

Counts, Laura. 2002. Oakland mayor's race: Brown cites practicality, his impact on city's future. *Oakland Tribune*, February 26. NewsBank database (Access World News).

———. 2004. Brown tells how strong mayor won. *Oakland Tribune*, March 4. NewsBank database (Access World News).

DeFao, Janine. 2002. Mayoral strength on Oakland ballot: Voters can extend powers given Brown. *San Francisco Chronicle*, October 18.

DelVecchio, Rick. 1996. Referendum on "strong-mayor" system. *San Francisco Chronicle*, October 28.

———. 1998. Jerry Brown wants power of Measure X. *San Francisco Chronicle*, October 23.

DelVecchio, Rick, and Debra Levi Holtz. 1998. Measure X victory for Jerry Brown. *San Francisco Chronicle*, November 4.

Druckman, James N., and Michael Parkin. 2005. The impact of media bias: How editorial slant affects voters. *Journal of Politics* 67, no. 4 (November): 1030–49.

Gough, Leila. 1996. Oakland loses if "F" passes [Op-ed]. *Oakland Tribune*, October 28. News-Bank database (Access World News).

Halstuk, Martin. 1992a. Idea to shift power in Oakland. *San Francisco Chronicle*, July 2.

———. 1992b. Oakland Redevelopment Agency chief resigns. *San Francisco Chronicle*, November 3.

———. 1992c. Oakland's Harris gives up on city takeover of Port. *San Francisco Chronicle*, February 26.

———. 1992d. 2 Oakland council incumbents ousted. *San Francisco Chronicle*, November 5.

———. 1993. City manager talks about resignation. *San Francisco Chronicle*, March 16.

Johnson, Chip. 2003. Moonbeam blew it on Bobb. *San Francisco Chronicle*, July 7.

Kahn, Kim Fridkin, and Patrick J. Kenney. 2002. The slant of the news: How editorial endorsements influence campaign coverage and citizens' views of candidates. *American Political Science Review* 96, no. 2 (June): 381–94.

MacDonald, Heather. 2004. Brown fights to maintain muscle in Oakland. *Oakland Tribune*, February 25. NewsBank database (Access World News).

Maser, Steven M. 1985. Demographic factors affecting constitutional decisions: The case of municipal charters. *Public Choice* 47, no. 1:121–62.

Mullin, Megan, Gillian Peele, and Bruce E. Cain. 2004. City Caesars?: Institutional structure and mayoral success in three California cities. *Urban Affairs Review* 40, no. 1 (September): 19–43.

Northrop, Alana, and William H. Dutton. 1978. Municipal reform and group influence. *American Journal of Political Science* 22, no. 3 (August): 691–711.

Oakland Public Library. 1986. Major Oakland charter changes: An overview. Presented at the City of the 21st Century Conference, Mills College, Oakland, January 25.

*Oakland Tribune*. 1996. Vote no on Measure F [Editorial]. October 20. NewsBank database (Access World News).

———. 1998. Vote Yes on Measure X [Editorial]. October 29. NewsBank database (Access World News).

———. 2002. Oakland should reaffirm strong mayor [Editorial]. October 25. NewsBank database (Access World News).

———. 2004. Keep city mayor strong [Editorial]. February 18. NewsBank database (Access World News).

Oaklanders for Responsible Government. 1996a. Vote no on F. Campaign pamphlet.

———. 1996b. Vote no on Measure F. Campaign pamphlet.

Pressman, Jeffrey L. 1972. Preconditions of mayoral leadership. *American Political Science Review* 66, no. 2 (June): 511–24.

Rayburn, Kelly. 2009. Criticism grows in Dellums' second year. *Oakland Tribune*, January 3, NewsBank database (Access World News).

*San Francisco Chronicle*. 1996. Oakland should employ strong-mayor system [Editorial]. October 22.

———. 1998. Oakland's X Factor [Editorial]. October 26.

———. 2002. Oakland's mayor and cops [Editorial]. October 30.

———. 2004. Chronicle recommends: Oakland's strong mayor [Editorial]. February 23.

———. 2009. The Bobb report: Oakland city manager offers strong recommendations [Editorial]. January 26.

Schorr, Jonathan, and William Brand. 1996. Pamphlet looks like real ballot. *Oakland Tribune*, November 5.

Staats, Craig. 1995. Oakland's charter gets the once-over. *Oakland Tribune*, March 13.

Stinnett, Peggy. 1996a. Demos don't want to change charter. *Oakland Tribune*, September 25. NewsBank database (Access World News).

————. 1996b. Following your tax money in the proposed new charter. *Oakland Tribune*, August 28. NewsBank database (Access World News).

————. 1996c. Why not a strong city council instead of a strong mayor? *Oakland Tribune*, June 21. NewsBank database (Access World News).

Tramutola, Larry. 1996. The dramatic defeat of Oakland's Measure F. *Oakland Tribune*, December 12. NewsBank database (Access World News).

Walker, Thaai. 1996. Power of veto left off Oakland mayor proposal. *San Francisco Chronicle*, July 12.

Wells, Stacey. 1998a. Brown debates "strong mayor." *Oakland Tribune*, September 18. NewsBank database (Access World News).

————. 1998b. Mayor-elect Brown, old foe on same side in debate. *Oakland Tribune*, October 22. NewsBank database (Access World News).

Wieland, Cynthia. 1996. Look at the women who support Measure F. *Oakland Tribune*, October 28. NewsBank database (Access World News).

Williams, Diana. 1996a. Battle opens to bring back strong mayor role. *Oakland Tribune*, July 8.

————. 1996b. A difficult choice at the polls. *Oakland Tribune*, September 9.

————. 1996c. Empowerment or empire? *Oakland Tribune*, October 13.

————. 1996d. Strong-mayor Measure F brings out strong feelings. *Oakland Tribune*, October 25.

————. 1996e. Voters to decide on Oakland government revamp. *Oakland Tribune*, July 10. NewsBank database (Access World News).

Winnie, Richard E. 1995. Important questions about Oakland city government. *Oakland Tribune*, April 7. NewsBank database (Access World News).

# PART II

# REJECTED CHANGE FROM COUNCIL–MANAGER TO MAYOR–COUNCIL FORM

CHAPTER 8

# KANSAS CITY

## The Evolution of Council–Manager Government

KIMBERLY NELSON AND CURTIS WOOD

IN THIS CHAPTER we use historical data, newspaper accounts, and personal interviews to describe the successful and unsuccessful attempts to modify the city charter in Kansas City, Missouri, since 1925 that relate to the powers of the mayor, city council, and the city manager. We examine the arguments for and against these modification attempts, analyze the factors contributing to successful and failed charter change attempts, and assess the contemporary state of council–manager government in Kansas City, Missouri.

## A Brief History of Kansas City, Missouri

Kansas City, Missouri, lies at the confluence of the Missouri and Kansas rivers. In 1821 Francois Chouteau established a trading post in the area that is now the northeast industrial district (City Manager's Office 2008a). In 1833 another trader, John Calvin McCoy, opened an outpost four miles inland (Ellis 1930). McCoy and thirteen other men later formed the town that would become Kansas City's downtown district. The town was incorporated and granted a charter on June 1, 1850, and in 1889 the town officially became known as Kansas City.

In 1853 the city elected its first mayor, William S. Gregory (City Manager's Office 2008b). Between 1853 and 1908 there were a number of significant changes made to the structure and function of the Kansas City government (see table 8.1). Under the 1889 Kansas City Home Rule Charter and its subsequent revisions, the city government operated with a large bicameral council. A series of powerful commissions, headed by patronage-appointed leaders, performed major administrative functions of city government (Flack 1909). In 1925 the city charter returned to a unicameral legislature, with the mayor serving as a council member, a city manager, and a small city council. For the first time, the mayor had the same appointment powers as the city council and had no veto power.

**Table 8.1  Kansas City, Missouri, City Charters (1853–1925)**

| City Charter | Council Structure | Number on Council (Excluding Mayor) | How Administrative Officers Were Chosen | Mayoral Power over Council |
|---|---|---|---|---|
| 1853–state | Unicameral | 6 | Register, treasurer, assessor, collector/marshal (elected)—others were appointed by mayor | Veto |
| 1859–state | Bicameral for less than one year | 12 | Register, treasurer, engineer (appointed by mayor with council confirmation)—city attorney and marshal (elected) | Veto |
| 1875–state | Unicameral | 12 | Clerk, assessor, comptroller, counselor, engineer (appointed by mayor with council confirmation)—auditor, treasurer, city attorney, supervisor of registration of voters (elected) | Veto |
| 1889–home rule | Bicameral | 10 per house | Clerk, assessor, comptroller, counselor, fire chief, two assistants, physician (appointed by mayor with council confirmation)—auditor, treasurer, city attorney, supervisor of registration of voters (elected) | Veto |
| 1908–home rule | Bicameral | 14 per house | Clerk (elected by council); comptroller and treasurer (elected); auditor and counselor (appointed by mayor); assessor and purchasing agent (mayor with council approval) | Veto |

*Source:* Tabulated from Ellis (1930, ch. 4).

At the beginning of World War I, the era of the Pendergast family rule began. In 1881 tavern owner James Pendergast was elected alderman. When James died in 1912, his brother Tom, owner of a concrete company, took up the reins of power. Until his indictment by a federal grand jury and subsequent imprisonment in 1939, Boss Tom virtually ruled the city. Using patronage appointments to buy loyalty and election fraud to win votes, Pendergast and other machine bosses dominated the political landscape. Finally, in 1940 reform forces hired L. P. Cookingham as city manager, realizing the goal of a professionally managed government envisioned in the 1925 city charter.

After World War II Kansas City continued to grow (City Manager's Office 2008b). However, with the decline of the railroad industry, Kansas City began to experience urban decay, particularly in the inner city. The city's population peaked in 1970 (U.S. Census Bureau).

After decades of decline, Kansas City entered a period of regrowth in the 1990s. The U.S. Census Bureau estimated Kansas City's 2008 population at 451,572. Efforts to revive downtown Kansas City have resulted in the completion of the Sprint Center Arena, an expanded convention center, the formation of a new entertainment district, and new retail development. Despite the burgeoning downtown renaissance, much remains to be done for the city to prosper.

## Realizing the Promise of the 1925 City Charter

In the early 1920s reformers led by Walter Matscheck, director of the Kansas City Public Service Institute, promoted the concept of a nonpartisan, professionally managed city (Larsen and Hulston 1997). The proposed form of government was intended to eliminate patronage, thus reducing a primary inducement for machine supporters. The new council would have eight members, four elected by ward and four elected at large. Tom Pendergast chose not to oppose the new charter; he believed that a smaller council might be easier to control than a large one (Gabis 1964).

In 1925 the new charter referendum passed by a vote of 37,504 to 8,827 (Reddig 1947). It was the third try since 1917 to change the city's government (Geary 2008). The 1925 charter created a modified council–manager government with the mayor elected at large in a nonpartisan election. Under the 1925 charter, there were no term limits for the mayor and council members. The mayor and each member of the council had a single vote on council decisions. Appointments to the positions of city clerk, city auditor, and city manager were made by majority council vote, and the mayor and council shared authority for commission and board appointments. Department heads and other administrative officers were appointed by the city manager (Kansas City 1925).

Observers at the time noted that the mayor's position was stronger in Kansas City than in other council–manager cities (Story 1926). For example, mayors in the council–manager plan were typically selected from among the council; however, the citizens elected the mayor in Kansas City. In addition, the Kansas City mayor's salary was significant relative to the city manager. The mayor's annual salary of $5,000 was equal to one-third of the manager's annual salary.

Despite the hopes for an end to boss rule in Kansas City, Tom Pendergast's power increased under the new plan (Gabis 1964; Larsen and Hulston 1997). Although party identities were not disclosed on the ballots, the election process remained highly partisan. The new primary system made it easier for one party to dominate the election than the former system did because there were no limits on the number of candidates who could run in the primary and the two candidates who received the most votes would be placed on the ballot. The Pendergast machine was skilled at getting fraudulent votes for their candidates. If a number of additional candidates were on the ballot, it diluted the opposition vote even more.

The first election following the adoption of the 1925 charter resulted in the reelection of the Republican Party Mayor Albert Beach and a five-member Democratic Party council majority (Dorsett 1968). Because of the Democratic Party's five-member council majority, Pendergast saw his influence rise to new heights. Mayor Beach, although an ardent supporter of council–manager government, had little influence in the face of the machine-dominated council.

The first city manager, Henry McElroy, was a loyal member of the Pendergast machine (Larsen and Hulston 1997). Given his alliances, perhaps it was no surprise that all of his appointees were also loyal Pendergast Democrats (White 1927). Throughout the remainder of Pendergast's reign, McElroy held the post of city manager in Kansas City (Gabis 1964).

Leonard White, in his 1927 case study of Kansas City's new council–manager form of government, stated that McElroy "came to his present office with the conception that he was the representative of the Democratic Party" (51). White argued that the prospects for true reform in Kansas City were minimal. In his examination of documents from the first year of operation under the council–manager form, White found increasing personnel costs, an unprofessional budget, and problems with the accounting system. White concluded that Kansas City represented "the type of government which may be expected under the council–manager plan when spoils politicians are put in power by popular vote. It is difficult to say that any fundamental improvement has been made or to expect that it will be made until the voters of Kansas City elect a different type of councilman" (57–58). Unfortunately, White was uncannily accurate in his assessment; Kansas City continued on a downward slide of increasing debt, overspending, inaccurate bookkeeping, and hiring based on partisan consideration until the end of the Pendergast era.

In 1939 Pendergast's hold on Kansas City ended with his indictment, and subsequent guilty plea, for federal tax evasion (Dorsett 1968). After Pendergast and his allies were indicted, facts about the truly desperate situation Kansas City was facing became public. The city had a $20 million deficit and six thousand employees on its payroll—twice as many as were needed (Gilbert 1978). Additionally, there was evidence of rampant police department corruption, including illiterate police officers, partisan-driven appointments, and shoddy record keeping. In 1939 the city's police department was taken over by the state of Missouri, and the governor appointed a board of Kansas City citizens to oversee the department and appoint the chief of police. Kansas City never regained full control over its police department.

In 1940 a group of reformers called the Forward Kansas City Committee campaigned for a charter amendment that would allow for an election of a new mayor and council. Their success led to an April election in which eight out of the reformers' nine candidates (including the mayor) were elected. The interim city manager, Kenneth Midgley, fired the remaining Pendergast department heads (Larsen and Hulston 1997).

In 1940 fifteen years after the approval of council–manager government in Kansas City, L. Perry Cookingham was appointed permanent city manager. Cookingham, the former city manager of Saginaw, Michigan, and the founder of the national association of city managers, was a steadfast supporter of nonpartisan, professionally managed city government (Larsen and Huston 1997). Under Cookingham's leadership Kansas City enjoyed professional management, free from partisan influence, for the first time. Cookingham immediately began cleaning house by appointing new department heads to replace those fired by the interim manager, then he directed the new department heads to terminate employees who were not qualified or who had engaged in partisan, illegal, or unethical activities. Approximately two thousand employees were fired (Cookingham 1981).

In addition to addressing personnel issues, Cookingham instituted budgetary and accounting reforms in order to correct the budget deficit and introduced competitive bidding for city contracts. By 1946 Kansas City finished its fiscal year with a surplus of more than $3 million (Reddig 1947). Thomas F. Maxwell, who worked under Cookingham in Kansas City, believed that Cookingham transformed the city "from the worst-governed city to the best of its size in the nation" (Maxwell 1981, 271). Kansas City continued to experience tremendous growth and success throughout Cookingham's nineteen-year tenure.

## City Managers from 1974 to 2009

Since 1974 six persons have served as manager in Kansas City. All but Wayne Cauthen received academic training in public management and served as the city, county, or an assistant city manager prior to becoming the city manager in Kansas City, Missouri. Cauthen has a master's degree in political science and served as the mayor's chief of staff in Denver, Colorado, before becoming the Kansas City manager.[1]

## Reaffirming the 1925 City Charter

On April 5, 1989, 60 percent of the voters cast their vote against a charter amendment that would have put more power into the hands of one person than anyone had exercised in Kansas City since the days of Tom Pendergast (Robbins 1989a). The unsuccessful charter amendment would have provided for a full-time mayor, raised the mayor's salary by $24,000 to about $70,000, and given the mayor the right to name committees and chairmen, veto power that would extend to individual items in city budgets, and the authority to nominate the city manager subject to concurrence by the city council (Robbins 1989a,1989b). To the extent that the mayor's power would have been

**Table 8.2  City Managers, Kansas City, Missouri (1974–2008)**

| City Manager | When Hired | Internal/ External Hire | Years Served as City Manager | Educational Background | Previous Government Manager Experience (Prior to becoming KC City Manager) | Remained in KC Area after Serving as KC City Manager? |
|---|---|---|---|---|---|---|
| Bob Kipp | 1974 | Internal | 9 | MPA | planning director in Newton, KS; assistant city manager in Lawrence, KS; city manager in two Ohio cities; department director in KC; assistant city manager, KC; deputy city manager in KC | Yes |
| A. J. Wilson | 1983 | External | 1 | BD, 1966, Yale University, CT | city manager, Santa Ana, CA; city manager, Portland, ME; executive assistant to mayor, St. Louis; executive director, St. Louis County Municipal League; director of human resources, University City, MO | Yes 4/85 – 2/88 |
| Dave Olson | 1984 | Internal | 9 | MPA | assistant city manager and city manager, Gladstone, MO; assistant city manager, KC | Yes |
| Larry Brown | 1994 | External | 3 | MA | assistant county manager, NC; county administrator, VA, NC, and WI; administrator at state of Wisconsin; county manager, MN, VA, FL, and MI | No |
| Bob Collins | 1997 | Internal | 5 | MA | department head in KC; assistant city manager, KC | Yes |
| Wayne Cauthen | 2003 | External | Current manager | MA, political science | chief of staff to mayor, Denver, CO | N/A |

strengthened, the authority of the city council would have been curtailed (Robbins 1989a, 1989b).

The 1989 election was a victory for the council–manager plan and professional management; however, it is unclear whether citizens were more interested in preserving the council–manager plan or in ensuring that three of the four black council members and the only Hispanic council member were able to run for reelection in 1991. There was a heavy turnout in the 10 predominantly black wards, where the vote was 8 to 1 against the charter change, while in the 20 predominantly white wards, the voters were almost evenly divided for and against the charter change (Robbins 1989b).

## The Reform of the Reform: The Cleaver Years (1991–99)

No sooner had Emanuel Cleaver become mayor in April 1991 than his transition commission proposed adding four people to the mayor's staff (Abouhalkah 1991).[2] Cleaver promised that his staff would work closely with city staff for a better government (Abouhalkah 1991). Former mayor Cleaver indicated that additional staff was needed because an archaic form of government that favored professional administration over elected officials left Kansas City unprepared to enter the twenty-first century. Additionally, Cleaver stated that civic and labor leaders were outraged at the slow pace of government action with regard to inspections and building permits (Cleaver 2008).

In 1993, while the mayor was out of town, a slim majority of council members forced the city manager, Dave Olson, to resign. In reaction Mayor Cleaver resurrected the idea of giving the mayor formal responsibility commensurate with citizens' perception of mayoral authority and accountability (Fitzpatrick 1993). Cleaver said that if he was to be blamed for poor government performance, he should be given the power to influence and control government performance (Fitzpatrick 1993). Mayor Cleaver proposed that (a) a majority on the city council could fire the manager only with the approval of the mayor; otherwise it would take a supermajority council vote; (b) a mayoral veto of council ordinances should be subject to a three-fourths council override (nine of twelve council members); and (c) the mayor could unilaterally hire and fire the city manager.

Cleaver's idea won partial support from former mayor Ilus W. Davis (1963–71), who was a staunch supporter of the council–manager plan, former mayor Charles B. Wheeler (1971–79), and Robert A. Kipp, city manager in Kansas City from 1974 to 1983. Mayor Wheeler, however, predicted that Kansas City voters would never give the mayor any significant power because around here "anything that changes the status quo is considered revolutionary—and slightly subversive" (Fitzpatrick 1993, C4). Davis, Wheeler, and Kipp endorsed additional mayoral empowerment, but they did not support the idea of the mayor being able to unilaterally hire and fire the manager (Fitzpatrick 1993). Kipp said, "It's time for a measured shift of power from the council to the mayor, but to do that by eliminating professional management would be a big mistake. It's not a matter of having to choose between professional management or a strong mayor—you need to have both" (Fitzpatrick 1993, C4). Dave Olson stated that such unilateral mayoral power would lead to widespread patronage and a return to the strong-mayor form of government (Fitzpatrick 1993; Olson 2008).

According to Kipp and Olson, the necessity for more centralized political power in the position of the mayor rests in part with an increasingly heterogeneous city council (Fitzpatrick 1993). Olson stated, "Forty years ago, they [council members] all wore the same suit; they all thought alike; and they would get in a meeting and come to a consensus. In the 70s and 80s, the make up of city councils became increasingly diverse with the election of more women and more black and Hispanic members. The result was a fragmentation of power and frequently, stalemate" (Fitzpatrick 1993, C4). Kipp said that while diversity on the council was good for city government and the different groups that gained representation, the interest groups tended to be "self-canceling," and mayors capable of leading, such as Cleaver, found themselves stymied (Fitzpatrick 1993). Kipp suggested it was necessary to do everything possible to enhance mayoral leadership capability, especially when there is a capable political leader (Fitzpatrick 1993, C4). Despite the support from former mayors and city managers, Cleaver's 1993 ideas were not supported by a majority on the city council and thus were never submitted to the citizens for a vote to change the charter.

In June 1997 Mayor Cleaver issued a clarion call for a strong-mayor government, saying that City Manager Larry Brown, who had just resigned amid widespread council dissatisfaction with his performance, would have benefited from the mayor's political instincts (Morris and Lester 1997). The 1997 proposal was even more radical than Cleaver's 1993 proposal by creating a separation-of-powers model of governance and turning the mayor into the chief executive officer who could unilaterally hire and fire the manager and prepare and present the budget to the council (Morris and Lester 1997).

Cleaver's ideas won the support of former mayor Wheeler, who said, "I'm watching Mayor Daley in Chicago trying to get on top of things. Even the school system [in Chicago] is being improved by his strong-mayor form of government" (C1). Rich Hood (1997), the editorial page editor of the *Kansas City Star*, argued that the ghost of Tom Pendergast would not suddenly reemerge to contaminate city hall if the mayor's powers were enhanced. "After all," said Hood, "we've managed to produce a disgustingly healthy crop of corruption inside City Hall under the present [council–manager] form of government. How would Pendergast make the situation worse?" (K1). Hood argued that the greater risk would be to do nothing and continue with "our all-too-typical stick-in-the-mud plodding approach" (K1).

However, Association Chairman Dan Cofran, a former council member and mayoral candidate, argued against the 1997 proposal, saying, "It's not the form of government but the people you have in it" (Morris and Lester 1997, C1). Councilman Ed Ford also believed a strong-mayor form of government was not justified because under the council–manager form of government Mayor Cleaver had been able to act as a strong mayor by successfully pushing his agenda (Morris and Lester 1997). In the end the 1997 Cleaver proposal suffered the same fate as the 1993 proposal.

In 1998 Mayor Cleaver proposed that a charter amendment creating a stronger mayor but not a strong mayor be placed on the August 1998 ballot (Abouhalkah 1998a,

C7). His proposal included (a) mayoral veto authority subject to council override with two-thirds vote; (b) mayoral appointment of all boards and commissions except when provided otherwise in the charter, by statute, or members of the Public Improvement Advisory Committee and Neighborhood Tourist Development Fund; (c) mayoral authority to review and comment upon the city manager's budget before going to the council; and (d) nomination of a city manager upon completion of a joint mayor and council search (Abouhalkah 1998a, C7; Morris 1998a, C1; City Charter 2006).

Cleaver argued that the proposed charter amendment would give future mayors sufficient political strength to get things done and responsibility commensurate with the citizens' desire for enhanced mayoral authority and accountability (Abouhalkah 1998a, C7; Morris 1998a, C1). Former mayors Charles B. Wheeler (1971–1979) and Richard L. Berkeley (1979–1991) endorsed Cleaver's proposed charter changes (Morris 1998b). Wheeler noted, "This is a great day for me. I've been working for a more accountable mayor since I took office in 1971. The changes were long overdue that would allow residents to judge the city by the performance of the mayor" (C1). Berkeley described Cleaver's charter proposal as "reasonable, realistic, well thought out and well done. It's all positive" (C1).

Robert Kipp and Dave Olson supported the proposed charter changes because they left intact the basic elements of the council–manager plan in that the city manager would continue to manage the day-to-day operations at city hall and appoint department heads (Morris 1998b; Kipp 2008; Olson 2008). Kipp was supportive of boosting the mayor's policymaking role through the veto and making budget recommendations to the city council (Kipp 2008). According to Kipp, permitting the mayor to nominate the city manager subject to council approval would make it more likely that the mayor and manager would closely work together (2008). In addition, mayoral appointment of most boards and commissions would reduce political fragmentation (2008).

Former city manager Olson stated that he was much more supportive of Cleaver's 1998 charter changes than the 1993 and 1997 proposals that would have undermined or replaced the council–manager form of government (Olson 2008). Olson also stated that charter changes were necessary because some issues languished under the current distribution of political power (2008). Olson, however, suggested that increasing the formal powers of future mayors would not be a magic bullet. According to Olson, mayors who possessed good leadership and interpersonal skills would be more likely to gain influence and prestige regardless of their formal authority (2008).

Other supporters of a stronger mayor but not a strong-mayor government were the Kansas City Area Chamber of Commerce and the Civic Council (Kipp 2008; Olson 2008). Both organizations have been longtime supporters of professional government in Kansas City but also have favored more centralized mayoral leadership to enhance government accountability.

The *Kansas City Star*, a longtime supporter of the council–manager plan, endorsed a stronger mayor who was indisputably the leading spokesperson for the city and the most powerful politician at city hall (Hood 1998). The *Star* acknowledged the new reality that strong mayors led cities like New York City, Philadelphia, and Cleveland that were making the most dramatic improvements in their citizens' lives. The *Star* acknowledged there had been some mayors who, through the force of their personality, had risen above the restrictions of the 1925 charter, but even these dynamic leaders, including Mayor Cleaver, had at times been too limited in their ability to deal with vital public issues. However, the *Kansas City Star* stopped short of endorsing a boss mayor, the type embraced by Chicago, by arguing for the value added of professional management.

E. Thomas McClanahan (1998), a member of the *Star*'s editorial board, character-ized Cleaver's proposed charter changes as "an odd hybrid—a mayor-manager-council system" that would "muddy the waters" by not eliminating fragmentation or clarifying who was accountable. Councilwoman Aggie Stackhaus argued that "city government isn't broken; if a mayor wants to take the bull by the horns and push his agenda hard, the last eight years is an example of how it can be done" (Morris 1998a, C1). Yael T. Abouhalkah (1998b) argued that "the structure of a city's government is far less impor-tant to a city's fate than the quality of persons serving in that government" (K3), referencing how the financial condition of Cleveland and Philadelphia were improved over the past decade under the leadership of a good mayor but deteriorated under the leadership of a poor mayor—without a change in form of government.

Despite the opposition of some elites, there was little organized citizen opposition to Cleaver's 1998 proposal (Geary 2008; Kipp 2008; Olson 2008). Former mayor Cleaver recalled that the city council unanimously approved his proposed changes for a stronger mayor for several reasons (Cleaver 2008). First, the city council believed that the citizens expected enhanced mayoral responsibility commensurate with their perception of mayoral accountability. Second, a minority of council members believed that the city manager system was not efficient enough. Third, some members of the city council had ambitions to run for mayor in 1999. On August 4, 1998, 62.4 percent of the voters (28,709 to 17,315) approved the structural modifications to Kansas City's form of government—marking the first such changes in seventy-two years (Campbell 1998).

According to Bill Geary (2008), the citizens approved the charter amendment for several reasons. During the mid-1990s three council members were convicted of brib-ery, and more control was sought to strengthen the office of the mayor as a counter-weight to the city council. "The specter of council members marching to jail was reason enough to 'do something' about city hall," he wrote. According to Geary, allowing the mayor to nominate the city manager with the consent of only six city council members while requiring nine council members to approve the termination of the manager when the mayor was opposed was an attempt to pressure the city manager into becoming more accountable and responsive to the mayor (2008).

Mayor Cleaver contends that but for the 1999 charter change, the mayor's office would not have been strengthened and mayoral leadership credibility enhanced. According to Cleaver, enabling mayors to nominate city managers and place their fin-gerprints on the budget makes it more likely that mayors and managers will work closely together (2008). Mayor Cleaver was satisfied that with the 1999 city charter changes in place, the right balance of power has been struck between the mayor, city council, and city manager, and that no further form of government charter changes are necessary (2008).

Former mayor Cleaver also argued that enhanced formal mayoral power is not the sole answer to improving the quality of local government. He argued (2008) that a successful mayor must work harmoniously with the city council and civic leadership and that most city council members will back the mayor with limited formal authority provided the mayor has "keen political skills." Cleaver mentioned that when he returned from out of town to learn that the city manager had been terminated by seven council votes, he was able to use his interpersonal skills to convince at least one council member to retract his vote—thus making it possible to nullify the termination. The city manager, upon hearing he had been saved by one vote, decided to retire anyway (2008). Mayor Cleaver also confessed he had fired two city managers with no opposition among the city council or ripple in the community (2008).

## The Reform of the Reform: The Barnes Years (1999–2007)

It was only fourteen months after Kay Barnes became mayor and the empowered mayor charter changes became effective that she created a seventeen-member Charter Review Commission, headed by Herb Kohn, to consider her idea of switching to a strong-mayor form of government. The Barnes plan would devolve even more administrative power to the mayor than Cleaver's 1997 proposal, including the power to appoint and remove department directors and manage the day-to-day operations at city hall (Horsley 2001c; Abouhalkah 2001). Barnes blamed the city manager system of government for chronic inefficiencies in the delivery of services (Horsley 2001a) and the lack of city administration leadership and credibility (Barnes 2008). According to Barnes, "Accountability appears to be lost in the abyss of an increasingly sluggish bureaucracy and responsiveness suffered as a result" (Kansas City Star 2001a, B8).

Surprisingly, the Kansas City Star (2001b) supported the thrust of the mayor's arguments. So did the greater Kansas City AFL-CIO, and Herb Kohn, the chair of the Charter Review Commission (Horsley 2001a). However, two of Kansas City's most influential business groups—the Greater Kansas City Chamber of Commerce and the Civic Council—argued that the charter changes effective in 1999 were sufficient and that the mayor's proposal created an imbalance of power between the mayor, legislature, and bureaucracy (Horsley 2001a).

Before a final recommendation from the Charter Review Commission, the city council approved a resolution 8–3 to reaffirm its support for the council–manager form of government (Horsley 2001b). Among the concerns about a strong-mayor system were the potential abuse of power, partisan bickering, staff turnover at each mayoral administration, and the rush to fix a system that was not broken (Horsley 2001c). According to Councilman Ford, who introduced the resolution, "We need a change not in government [form] but in the way we do business at City Hall" (Horsley 2001b).

Faced with a choice between a strong mayor and a council–manager form of government, the Charter Review Commission opted for a compromise (Horsley 2001d). The commission recommended that the mayor have the authority to prepare the budget (presumably with the assistance of the city manager and budget director) and present his or her budget to the city council (Geary 2001); however, all other city manager duties and responsibilities would remain the same, including supervisory authority over department heads and the day-to-day operations at city hall (Geary 2001). In addition, the mayor could nominate the city manager without involving the city council in the recruitment and interview process, and the mayor could terminate the city manager, but the council could overrule the mayor's decision with eight votes (Geary 2001; Horsley 2001d). "It's another notch closer to the line [strong-mayor form] but it doesn't go across the line," said James H. Svara (Horsley 2001d).

After months of contentious debate about how much and what powers to give to the mayor, the city council voted 12–0 to present to the voters charter reforms that did not include any of the charter commission or the mayor's suggestions pertaining to mayoral powers or form of government (Horsley 2001e). According to Councilman Ford, "All 12 of us believed that either of these issues [the Barnes and commission proposals] would hurt the chances of the Charter getting passed. Everyone was on the same page that maybe the best thing was to do neither" (B2). However, the city council supported the commission's recommendations to overhaul the 1925 charter by eliminating archaic language; removing outdated or contradictory sections; giving city administration more flexibility and discretion in bond sales and purchasing; and changing certain departmental functions (Horsley 2001e). "I think what the council did will allow the voters to consider a modernization of the charter without the controversial issues attached to the Charter" (B1), said City Manager Bob Collins.

Despite the council's vote to remove form of government charter reforms, Mayor Barnes remained upbeat, maintaining that the primary objective was to revamp an outdated document (the 1925 charter) that was "getting in the way of our doing our business" (B1–2). Barnes resolved to work within the existing system that "will get at substantial basic service issues" (B2). The *Kansas City Star* (2001b) lamented that citizens would not have an opportunity to vote on the suggested changes proposed by the mayor and the Charter Review Commission pertaining to the change in the form of government. Nevertheless, the *Star* advised citizens to approve the recommendation to modernize and streamline the 1925 charter, reducing the length of the charter from 385 pages to 72 pages.

On November 6, 2001, the voters of Kansas City narrowly defeated a modernized and streamlined city charter by 69 votes (6,776 in favor, 6,845 opposed, with 7.3 percent turnout) (Kansas City Board of Election Commissioners 2001). According to Mayor Barnes, the voters did not understand the language of the modernized and streamlined charter, and supporters of the new charter were not able to raise the campaign funds to explain the charter to the voters (Barnes response to questionnaire 2008). "A few gadflies in the community who opposed almost everything were able to plant doubt in the minds of voters as some type of conspiracy to take away their rights, and we did not take them seriously" (Barnes 2008).

Mayor Barnes remained undaunted by the defeat in 2001, and in early 2005 she appointed another charter review commission, headed by Terry Ward, to hold hearings on giving the mayor more power, including the ability to hire the manager without council approval. The commission also considered expanding term limits for the mayor and council from two to three consecutive terms, tightening the initiative petition process, eliminating some city departments, and creating a modern and streamlined city charter (*Kansas City Star* [Editorial] 2005). The charter commission recommended, and the city council approved, placing seven separate questions on the August 8, 2006, election ballot. Question 2 involved almost the same comprehensive overhaul of the city's 1925 charter that was narrowly defeated by the voters in 2001. In addition, Question 2 called for (a) the city to appoint a Charter Review Commission every ten years to reexamine the city charter, (b) the city manager to have the authority to transfer departmental functions, and (c) the city to develop a comprehensive code of ethics, debt policies, and economic incentive policies. The Charter Review Commission and the city council did not recommend any charter changes to be considered by the citizens pertaining to mayoral powers vis-à-vis the city manager or city council. On August 8, 2006, on the second attempt, the voters approved Question 2; 67.38 percent voted for and 36.62 percent voted against the measure, with approximately 14 percent voter turnout (Kansas City Elections Board of Commissioners). Former mayor Barnes articulated a distinction between the 1998 and 2006 charter vote: the 1998 vote was about reforming the political process whereas the 2006 vote was more about reforming the administrative process (Barnes 2008).

City Manager Wayne Cauthen claimed the 2006 city charter modernized and streamlined administrative processes and policies, has improved government performance, and permits the city government to be more nimble in reacting to changing conditions (Cauthen 2008; Geary 2008). When asked why he thought the citizens approved virtually the same modernized and streamlined city charter in 2006 that they had rejected in 2001, Cauthen stated that between 2001 and 2006 the city had successfully embarked on a major downtown redevelopment project and there was a strong belief in the community that the eighty-one-year-old charter was creating barriers to further progress and success (2008). He also said there was pent-up demand in the community for change, and recent redevelopment and development successes fueled the desire and possibility for more change. According to Cauthen, there was a perception that the approval of the new city charter would make it possible to continue the momentum of progress (2008).

In retrospect, former mayor Barnes was satisfied the city struck the right balance between professional management, council representation, and mayoral prerogatives (2008). She asserted that the 1999 expansion of the mayor's constitutional powers had increased the city manager and city council's accountability to the mayor, thus making the mayor more accountable to citizens. "Allowing the mayor to nominate the city manager gives the mayor a tremendous rapport and working relationship with the manager provided the mayor has at least six council members who support the manager," she said (2008). Barnes believed that the 1999 charter changes were in part responsible for the "dynamic relationship" she had with Wayne Cauthen because "he knew that I was in large part responsible for his nomination and continued employment, and I knew he was still the chief administrative officer" (2008).

Although Barnes agreed that mayoral veto authority and the veto threat can enhance the mayor's leadership credibility and policy success, she admitted that the secret to her effectiveness as mayor was her ability to build and sustain relationships with members of the city council, citizens, and city administration (Barnes 2008). Because she relied on a facilitative leadership style and political skills to build consensus on the council and in the community, she never used the veto during eight years as mayor.

## Contemporary Leadership at the Apex

Mayor Mark Funkhouser was elected mayor of Kansas City in April 2007 with a commitment to make city government more accountable to the citizens and effective in the delivery of public services. He indicated that the 1999 city charter changes enhancing mayoral formal authority increased political and administrative accountability; however, he contended that these changes did not go far enough (Funkhouser 2008). According to Mayor Funkhouser, diffused political and administrative power, or "cul-de-sacs of power," creates division, gridlock, and finger pointing that make it difficult to innovate but easy to prevent change (2008). When the city manager wields too much executive power, he becomes too political and is not able to function adequately as a professional administrator who must focus on effective implementation. Only by changing the city charter to become a mayor–council city, Funkhouse said, would it become possible for the city manager and the city council to follow the priorities and vision of the mayor—thus achieving the goal of a more accountable and effective city government (2008).

The following case is an example of the divisiveness that existed between the leaders at the apex in Kansas City.[3] In 2007 and 2008 a dispute erupted between the mayor and city council pertaining to the scope of charter mayoral and city council powers in reappointing or not reappointing the city manager when the city manager's contract comes up for renewal. A major disagreement was whether the 2006 city charter applied only to the initial appointment of a new city manager or whether the city charter also applied to the renewal of the manager's contract.

Part 3 of the 2006 Kansas City Charter addresses the appointment, term, and the suspension or permanent removal of the city manager. Section 3 of the charter requires the city council and mayor to jointly conduct a search for the city manager, authorizes the mayor to nominate a city manager subject to the appointment by the council (presumably by a vote of at least six council members), and permits the mayor and at least six council members (or nine council members without the approval of the mayor) to remove the city manager from office. Section 3 of the city charter is not explicit as to the charter authority of the council and mayor to reappoint (or not reappoint) the city manager upon the renewal of the city manager's contract. In fact, neither the charter nor the municipal code mentions a contract for the city manager. However, the charter states that the manager "shall serve at the pleasure of the mayor and council." Consequently, the city council and mayor may remove the city manager prior to or at the end of the contract.

Funkhouser and a minority of council members argued that only the mayor has the authority to propose a new contract with the city manager (Smith and Horsley 2008). The city attorney's office concurred with Mayor Funkhouser's interpretation that the mayor has the sole authority to introduce a resolution to renew the manager's contract (Horsley, Campbell, and Smith 2007; Funkhouser 2008).

However, a supermajority of council members argued that the mayor might not unilaterally remove the city manager and that in a council–manager form of government the mayor *and* city council jointly rehire and terminate the city manager (Horsley 2008a). Per the charter the city manager would need to be terminated by the mayor and at least six council members or by at least nine council members without the support of the mayor before the mayor could nominate a new city manager.

While the mayor and city council were in the middle of negotiating the renewal of the city manager's contract in December 2007, Mayor Funkhouser indicated that he was opposed to the renewal (Smith and Horsley 2008). However, nine of the twelve city council members voted to extend Cauthen's contract (Smith and Horsley 2008). Three council members and Mayor Funkhouser voted against the renewal of the manager's contract. After consulting with his attorney, Cauthen signed the contract that runs from April 30, 2008, through October 31, 2011, six months after Mayor Funkhouser's first term ends (Smith and Horsley 2008). The mayor pro tem, who sided with Funkhouser, filed a lawsuit in an effort to overturn the new contract. The Jackson County Court ruled in favor of the nine city council members. The mayor pro tem then appealed to the Missouri Court of Appeals (Smith and Horsley 2008).

On September 30, 2008, the three-judge Missouri Court of Appeals panel upheld without dissent the lower court's ruling that the mayor's power to nominate the city manager applies only when the city manager is initially hired (Horsley 2008b). According to the appeals court ruling, "The city manager continues to serve unless and until removed from office" (Horsley 2008b, B2). Mayor Pro Tem Bill Skaggs said he would not appeal the Court of Appeals ruling to the Missouri Supreme Court (Horsley 2008c). "That's good news," a smiling City Manager Wayne Cauthen said (Horsley 2008c, B2).

The mayor indicated that if the Missouri Appeals Court upheld the lower court's ruling he would propose new charter language to give the mayor sole authority to reappoint or not reappoint the city manager upon contract renewal (Funkhouser 2008). Assuming the balance of voting power on the city council remains unchanged, it is unlikely that there will be six council votes to support an ordinance calling for a referendum on the mayor's desired charter reform. Thus, the current 2006 charter language would not change and the city would be legally obligated to follow the case law established by the Missouri Court of Appeals.

A solution that can avoid a protracted battle between the mayor and council would include charter language that addresses reappointment of the city manager upon contract renewal. The new language could specify that the city manager can be reappointed by the mayor and at least six city council members or by at least nine city council members without the mayor's consent; otherwise, the city manager's contract would lapse and the city manager would not be reappointed. If the manager's contract were not renewed, the mayor would be able to nominate another manager after a joint recruitment effort had been made with the council. Such charter language would be consistent with the process used during the initial hiring of the city manager, does not abandon the council–manager form of government, and recognizes the mayor's preeminent role in the reappointment of the city manager.[4]

## The State of Council–Manager Government in Kansas City

Kansas City provides a fascinating case study of the evolution of council–manager government in the United States. From the inception of the council–manager charter in 1925, Kansas City has not fit the classic model of a council–manager government in that the mayor was always elected at large, the mayor had the power to appoint members of several commissions, and half the council members were elected by district instead of at large.

Since the adoption of the council–manager form in 1925, formal mayoral political and executive powers have been significantly expanded. Do the city charter changes to expand mayoral powers mean the city council and citizens support the strong-mayor form of government and reject the council–manager form? We believe the answer is a resounding "NO"! In 1989 citizens overwhelmingly rejected a proposed city charter that would have created a strong-mayor system, and nine years later citizens overwhelmingly approved a more modest expansion of mayoral political and executive prerogatives that stopped short of crossing the line. Although mayors Cleaver and Barnes initially wanted to cross the line while in office, former mayors and city managers, the business community, and a majority on the city council did not support their ideas. Consequently, mayors Cleaver and Barnes settled for having an empowered mayor rather than a strong mayor. While the mayors (in office) and a minority on the council see the value in centralized political and executive authority in the office of the mayor, it seems that almost everyone else in Kansas City places more value on shared and balanced governance at the apex of leadership.

It is not surprising that mayors, while in office, led the call for reforms empowering the mayor. By expanding the authority of the mayor vis-à-vis the other members of council and the city manager, accountability is more squarely placed on the mayor's shoulders where many citizens believe accountability does and should reside. However, mayors have not been alone in support of an empowered mayor. Business leaders, editors of the *Kansas City Star*, and former city managers have also publicly supported centralized political leadership that would reduce the opportunity for and the likelihood of impasse, gridlock, finger pointing, and inaction.

The charter revisions to expand mayoral powers that were approved by the council and the citizens in 1998 have not fundamentally altered the council–manager form of government. The mayor does have a larger role in policymaking because of the veto and the ability to review and comment on the manager's proposed budget. However, the mayor still serves on the council; the council can override the mayor's veto; and the city manager continues to prepare the budget, unilaterally hire, supervise, and terminate department directors, and manage the day-to-day operations at city hall. Although the mayor can nominate the city manager, at least six council members must agree with his or her choice, and nine city council members can terminate the manager without the approval of the mayor.

While the expanded scope of mayoral empowerment in Kansas City may not have been significant enough to cross the line from a council–manager to a mayor–council form of government, such expanded mayoral powers may have adversely affected how the leaders relate to each other at the apex. An empowered mayor in a council–manager form of government may be more inclined to think of himself or herself as a super-council member and a partial executive and begin to use an executive (power-based) leadership style instead of a facilitative leadership style, thus creating more competition and conflict with the council and the city manager.[5] It may seem logical for mayors who have the power to nominate the city manager to believe they have greater authority over the manager than does the council. Because the mayor plays a preeminent role in hiring and firing the city manager, the mayor may also think the city manager "owes me one." The prominent mayoral role in the manager's appointment may also lead the city manager to consider the mayor as a super-council member and thus more worthy of respect and loyalty than the other council members.

A major lesson learned from this study of Kansas City is that the use of informal, or "soft," power by the mayor may be equally or more important and effective than the possession or use of formal, or "hard," power. Mayors Cleaver and Barnes initially supported a strong-mayor form of government so that the mayor would have the necessary power to set the agenda, realize their policy goals, and achieve a more accountable and effective city government. Ironically, a power-based, or executive, style of mayoral leadership style vis-à-vis the city council and administrative staff "provides the foundation for a conflict pattern of interaction among officials who have incentives to compete with one another to accomplish their agendas" (Wheeland 2002, 60) that renders the mayor less effective, not more effective (Wheeland 2002; Svara 2002; Mullin, Peele, and Cain 2004). This theory was born out when, in 2001, the city council members rejected what they felt was an overreaching move by the mayor to upset the balance of power between the leaders at the apex. Under the strong-mayor form, the mayor may be successful in implementing policy that represents his or her vision of the public interest. However, in a community that continues to be supportive of the council–manager plan, the idea of one person's vision being appropriate for an entire city is anathema to the citizens and many of the leaders at the apex.

The second irony is that although mayors Cleaver and Barnes failed to obtain the formal powers associated with a strong mayor, they were nevertheless able to use their leadership and interpersonal skills to build, nurture, and sustain relationships at the top that made it possible to achieve many of their policy goals. These results are not surprising as there is empirical evidence that mayors in a council–manager form of government are the most effective when they practice a facilitative leadership strategy that creates a culture of collaboration and cooperation to achieve a common vision (Svara 1990). Mayor Kay Barnes never used her veto authority, in part due to the threat of the veto and her ability to lead and achieve consensus among council members—a critical skill of a facilitative leader. By avoiding the use of the veto, she avoided the hard feelings and divisiveness created by using the veto.

The evidence from the interviews suggests that the answer to effective governance in Kansas City, or perhaps any city, may be the quality and nature of the relationship between the leaders at the apex. According to James Svara (2001), when the elected officials and the city manager operate within the zone of complementarity there will be greater likelihood of mutual agreement, collective action, and high achievement;[6] however, when there is an imbalance characterized by the dominance, autonomy, or stalemate/laissez faire between elected officials and the city manager, it will be difficult to reach consensus on even the smallest policy issue. Thus, government will perform less efficiently and effectively. We also believe that council members and the mayor and city council must operate within the zone of complementarity for a municipal government to work efficiently and effectively.

Perhaps in Kansas City (and elsewhere), advocates of a strong-mayor form of government are seeking the wrong solution to their city's woes. Instead of focusing on form of government as a magic bullet, leaders should first consider how they could build stronger relationships that will make it possible to take advantage of opportunities and overcome challenges.

## Notes

1. Prior to his retirement in 2004, Bob Kipp served twenty-one years as the group vice president of Hallmark Cards Inc. During his career Kipp earned a Distinguished Service Award (1984) and a Management Innovation Award (1978) from the International City/County Managers' Association (ICMA), and he served on the ICMA Executive Board from 1975 to 1978. David Olson currently serves as the interim city administrator in Parkville, Missouri, and the Business Development Manager of Olson Associates, a consulting firm serving local governments in the Kansas City region. Olson was awarded a thirty-year service award from ICMA in 1999. Bob Collins is an economist, planner, and instructor in public policy at the University of Missouri–Kansas City (UMKC), and he is a cofounding partner of Collins Noteis and Associates, a Kansas City consulting firm in community planning, development, governmental management, and public policy (Noteis and Collins 2006).

2. Since 2004 Emanuel Cleaver has served as a U.S. congressman in the Missouri Fifth District.

3. Poul Erik Mouritzen and James H. Svara borrowed this term from Peter Self (1972). "The apex of leadershp is where the top-level officials [Mayor, City Manager, and City Council] come in contact with each other" (Mourtizen and Svara 2002, 7).

4. On November 19, 2009, the Kansas City City Council dismissed Wayne Cauthen as city manager on a 7 to 6 vote, with the mayor supporting his removal.

5. In the executive, or power-based, model of political leadership, leadership is competitive and is focused on individual goals, and relationships are conflictual (Svara 2002; Wheeland 2002). In the facilitative model of political leadership, the mayor serves as a liaison between groups, strives to communicate from multiple vantage points, works with the professional manager as a partner, and emphasizes a culture of collaboration and cooperation (Svara 2002; Wheeland 2002).

6. Leaders at the apex (politicians and administrators) function within the zone of complementarity when (a) politicians blend control and delegation while administrators blend independence and accountability to legislators, (b) politicians respect administrative competence and commitment while administrators are committed to accountability and responsiveness, (c) leaders at the apex play separate roles and parts but come together in a mutually supportive interdependent way with reciprocal influence, and (d) the relationship between the leaders at the apex is viewed as a partnership rather than an independent or hierarchical relationship (Svara 2001).

# References

Abouhalkah, Y. T. 1991. A questionable idea. *Kansas City Star*, June 2.
———. 1998a. A stronger mayor beats a boss mayor. *Kansas City Star*, February 26.
———. 1998b. My road map for the local ballot issues. *Kansas City Star*, August 2.
———. 2001. Time to boost KC's mayor? *Kansas City Star*, March 18.
Barnes, K. 2008. Interview by Curtis H. Wood, July 14.
Campbell, M. 1998. New mayoral power backed. *Kansas City Star*, August 5.
Cauthen, W. 2008. Interview by Curtis H. Wood, July 14.
City Charter. 2006. Kansas City, Missouri. 2006 Charter.
City Manager's Office. 2008a. City Communications Office. http://www.kcmo.org/manager.nsf/web/kycg1?opendocument.
———. 2008b. City Communications Office. http://wwwkcmo.org/kcmo.nsf/web/kchistory?opendocument.
Cleaver, E. 2008. Interview by Curtis H. Wood, by telephone. August 12.
Cookingham, L. P. 1981. Setting the course. In *Servants of all*, ed. LeRoy F. Harlow. Provo, UT: Brigham Young University Press.
Dorsett, L. W. 1968. *The Pendergast machine*. New York: Oxford University Press.
Ellis, R. 1930. *A civic history of Kansas City, Missouri*. Springfield, MO: Elkins-Swyers Co.
Fitzpatrick, J. C. 1993. Previous leaders favor Cleaver vision for KC. *Kansas City Star*, July 10.
Flack, H. E. 1909. Municipal charter revision—Kansas City, Missouri. *The American Political Science Review* 3, no. 3 (August): 413–16.
Funkhouser, M. 2008. Interview by Curtis H. Wood. July 15.
Gabis, S. T. 1964. Leadership in a large manager city: The case of Kansas City. *Annals of the American Academy of Political and Social Science* 353 (May): 52–63.
Geary, W. 2001. *Summary of proposed substantive changes to the current city charter*. Unpublished internal document. Kansas City, MO.
———. 2008. *Organization of Kansas City, Missouri government*. Letter to Bill Bates, American Century Investments, May 15.
Gilbert, B. 1978. *This city, this man: The Cookingham era in Kansas City*. Washington, DC: International City/County Management Association.
Hood, R. 1997. Stronger mayor could boost KC's fortunes: Mayor Cleaver has right idea about change. *Kansas City Star*, June 22.
———. 1998. A stronger mayor would benefit Kansas City. *Kansas City Star*, July 25.
Horsley, L. 2001a. Mixed day for mayoral proposal: Opposition and support announced. *Kansas City Star*, June 9.
———. 2001b. Council backs current form of KC Government. *The Kansas City Star*, June 22.
———. 2001c. Council split on Barnes proposal. *Kansas City Star*, April 13.

————. 2001d. KC Commission favors compromise plan: Moves closer to strong-mayor form. *Kansas City Star*, June 30.

————. 2001e. Council adopts charter proposal. *Kansas City Star*, August 24.

————. 2008a. Opposing arguments filed. *Kansas City Star*, January 19.

————. 2008b. Court supports contract extension. *Kansas City Star*, October 1.

————. 2008c. Skaggs declines appeal of ruling. *Kansas City Star*, October 3.

Horsley, L., M. Campbell, and D. Smith. 2007. Angry crowd, council put mayor under siege. *Kansas City Star*, December 14.

Kansas City Board of Election Commissioners. 2001. Election results for Question 1: Amend the City Charter.

Kansas City, Missouri. 1925. Charter of 1925.

*Kansas City Star*. 2001a. Welcome push for stronger KC mayor [Editorial], March 18.

————. 2001b. New KC charter would provide more flexibility [Editorial], October 20.

————. 2005. Charter revisions return for fourth round [Editorial], February 11.

Kipp, R. A. 2008. Interview by Curtis H. Wood, by telephone. July 28.

Larsen, L. H., and N. J. Hulston. 1997. *Pendergast! Missouri biography series*. William E. Foley, ed. Columbia: University of Missouri Press.

Maxwell, T. F. 1981. The power of example. In *Servants of all*, ed. LeRoy F. Harlow. Provo, UT: Brigham Young University Press.

McClanahan, E. T. 1998. An odd plan to boost KC mayor. *Kansas City Star*, July 21.

Morris, M. 1998a. Cleaver outlines proposed stronger role. *Kansas City Star*, February 26.

————. 1998b. Plan to boost mayoral role introduced. *The Kansas City Star*, March 20.

Morris, M., and C. Lester. 1997. Strong mayor advocated: Cleaver suggests tinkering with charter to boost clout. *Kansas City Star*, June 14.

Mouritzen, P. E., and J. H. Svara. 2002. *Leadership at the Apex: Politicians and administrators in Western local governments*. Pittsburgh: University of Pittsburgh Press.

Mullin M., G. Peele, and B. E. Cain. 2004. City Caesars? Institutional structure and mayoral success in three California cities. *Urban Affairs Review* 40, no. 1 (September): 19–43.

Noteis, V., and B. Collins. 2006. Opening eyes on what a good neighborhood is. *Kansas City Star*, December 9.

Olson, D. 2008. Interview by Curtis H. Wood, by telephone. July 29.

Reddig, W. M. 1947. *Tom's town: Kansas City and the Pendergast legend*. Philadelphia: Lippincott.

Robbins, W. 1989a. Kansas City to vote on return to a strong role for mayor. *New York Times*, April 3, Special to *New York Times*.

————. 1989b. Kansas City to vote on return to a strong role for mayor. *New York Times*, April 6, Special to *New York Times*.

Self, P. 1972. *Administrative theories and politics: An inquiry into the structure and processes of modern government*. London: George Allen and Unwin Ltd.

Smith, D., and L. Horsley. 2008. Cauthen, 9 council members sign pact. *Kansas City Star*, March.

Story, S. B. 1926. City manager progress. *The American Political Science Review* 20, no. 2 (May): 361–66.

Svara, J. H. 1990. *Official leadership in the city: Patterns of conflict and cooperation*. Oxford University Press.

————. 2001. The myth of the dichotomy: Complementarity of politics and administration in the past and future of public administration. *Public Administration Review* 61, no. 2 (March/April): 176–83.

————. 2002. Mayors in the unity of powers context: Effective leadership in council–manager governments. In *The future of local government administration: The Hansell symposium*. ed. H. George Frederickson and John Nalbandian. Washington, DC: International City/County Management Association.

U.S. Census Bureau. 1940, 1950, 1960, 1970, 1980, 1990. Population of the 100 Largest Urban Places.

Wheeland, C. M. 2002. Mayoral leadership in the context of variations in city structure. In *The future of local government administration: The Hansell symposium*, ed. H. George Frederickson and John Nalbandian. Washington, DC: International City/County Management Association.

White, L. 1927. *The city manager.* Chicago: University of Chicago Press.

CHAPTER 9

# GRAND RAPIDS

## A Lack of Enthusiasm for Change in the Council–Manager Form

ERIC S. ZEEMERING

FOLLOWING A PUBLIC HEARING on the draft of a new city charter in 1971, William Johnson, a member of the Grand Rapids charter revision commission, observed that public comments reflected "a controlled lack of enthusiasm" for change (Hensch 1971b). Voters expressed the same lack of enthusiasm by rejecting the revised charter at the polls later the same year. Minor amendments have been made to the 1916 Grand Rapids city charter, but voters have a history of rejecting proposals that would significantly modify the form of government.[1] Grand Rapids provides a case of public opposition to change in the form of municipal government, despite a variety of calls for reform among active participants in city politics.

What explains the defeat of city charter changes in Grand Rapids? This chapter examines three city charters proposed by a charter revision commission in the early 1970s, ranging from minor enhancements of mayoral power to the adoption of the strong-mayor form. These proposals are compared to a 2002 amendment offered by Mayor John Logie to expand the mayor's power within the council–manager structure. Coalitions to support change have been motivated by a variety of goals, while opposition arguments consistently emphasize the importance of a professional manager unhampered by city politics. A strong council–manager coalition emerges to defend the existing charter when proposals for change emerge. Grand Rapids demonstrates a stable constitutional form because voters appear unconvinced that the city should pay for full-time political leadership, and defenders of the council–manager form issue warnings about the danger of change.

## Charter Politics in Grand Rapids

The current Grand Rapids city charter was adopted in 1916. Historian Jeffrey Kleiman (2006) vividly portrays the personalities and shifting political coalitions of the era.

Kleiman highlights a 1911 labor strike in the city's furniture industry as a focusing event for change in the governance structure. Incumbent Mayor George Ellis was unpopular with furniture manufacturers, the city's dominant industry, because of his support for labor during the strike. A charter commission that began work in 1910 assembled a proposal to enhance mayoral power by consolidating services and expanding the mayor's appointment power. Kleiman explains the reforms were supported by the city's business groups who hoped to expose Ellis' mismanagement (2006, 16). The changes failed when put to a vote in early 1912. Ellis remained a target of the city's business interests. Dissatisfaction with the mayor's management of relief programs during the 1913–14 recession spurred new discussion of reform, and another charter reform commission began work (121). They proposed the creation of a small city commission, holding both administrative and legislative authority. The city commission, elected at large, would appoint the mayor and the city manager. This reform won support from voters (Travis and Mapes 1971).

Grand Rapids voters have consistently supported the city manager form of government laid out in the 1916 charter. Between 1916 and 1923, the Grand Rapids Citizens' League campaigned to support the new governance structure (Kleiman 2006, chapter 7). A report in the *National Municipal Review* conveys that a series of amendments to restore "aldermanic" government were defeated in 1922. The campaign against the amendments highlighted achievements under the commission–manager form, including increased inspections, improvements in the police department, centralized purchasing, and collection of past due taxes. The Grand Rapids Citizens' League argued that the form of government provided "a compact, orderly, smooth-working governing body composed of conscientious, intelligent men who are directing the affairs of this community for the best interests of all the citizens" (Griffen 1922, 204). One significant change in government came in 1923 with a move from at-large to ward-based election of the city commission, and at-large election of the mayor, rather than appointment by the city commission (Travis and Mapes 1971). These reforms were championed by former mayor Ellis, union officials, and a loose-knit group of "amenders" who sought greater democratic control of city government (Kleiman 2006, 141–43).

The city's current governance structure includes a city commission composed of six members elected from three wards, with each ward electing two commissioners on a staggered schedule. A vestige of the structure established in the 1916 charter, Grand Rapids uses the term *city commission* rather than *city council*. This should not be confused with the commission form of government in which the commission exercises administrative power. The city commission is the legislative body for the city. The city manager reports to the city commission. The mayor is elected at-large, chairs meetings of the city commission, and votes as a member of the commission. Grand Rapids also elects the office of comptroller, responsible for auditing city finances.

Although voters have not supported significant change to the form of government since early in the twentieth century, political elites, occasionally joined by voters, have engaged in extended discussions about charter revision. Some of these discussions have focused on democratic accountability, an extension of the arguments advanced by former mayor Ellis and other "amenders" following passage of the 1916 charter. The question that has drawn out more debate is whether or not the city needs stronger political leadership in the office of mayor. Under the Michigan Home Rule City Act, the question of impaneling a charter revision commission can be placed on an election ballot.[2] If a majority of voters endorse a charter revision commission, a nine-member charter revision commission is selected in a second election. Once elected the charter revision commission has three years to complete its work and submit a new charter to the voters. The commission may submit up to three proposals to the voters within the three-year time limit. Since adoption of the 1916 charter, Grand Rapids voters have supported reform discussion by electing charter revision commissions in 1951 and 1970.

Mayors, managers, and city commissioners have also promoted debate about the structure of government. Amendments to the city charter can be initiated by citizen petition or by action of the city commission. In 1967 Mayor Christian Sonneveldt appointed a committee to review the city charter and propose amendments. Sonneveldt encouraged the committee to scrutinize the form of government. He explained, "As elected officials we (the mayor and six commissioners) don't have the controls over the city government that we should have, and which the people expect" (*Grand Rapids Press* 1967). At the same time, City Manager Julian Orr formulated a plan to reorganize the city's financial management structure (Allbaugh 1968). A controversial aspect of Orr's plan was elimination of the elected comptroller. Orr argued changes were needed to modernize the city's financial management and give the manager a better picture of the city's financial status. The amendment package received support from city commissioners, but incumbent comptroller Jack Harper defended his job performance. Harper argued the city manager had access to financial information and described himself as a citizen watchdog and a check on bureaucrats in city hall. Orr's proposal met an overwhelming defeat at the polls, with over 80 percent of voters saying "no" to the elimination of an elected comptroller (Allbaugh 1969b). Shortly after the defeat, the citizen study committee appointed by Mayor Sonneveldt resigned.

After these events, a variety of reform proposals began to circulate. Supporters of Harper recommended a twelve-ward city commission with higher pay for the mayor and commissioners (Allbaugh 1969a). A group that came to be identified as the 11-Ward Committee began efforts to amend the charter to expand the city commission. While the 1916 reforms sought to enhance management capacity in city hall, the reformers of the late 1960s argued that professional managers in city hall were out of touch, unresponsive, and unaccountable to the public.[3] The group successfully submitted petitions, but the proposals ignited a flurry of legal controversy because of unclear wording. The 11-Ward Committee finally asked the court to remove the proposals from the ballot. Over the course of the year in which the 11-Ward Committee was at work, the city commission took action to place on the ballot a proposal for the election of a charter revision commission. The multiple calls for change to the city charter and the failure of the 11-Ward Committee dovetailed into the election of a charter revision commission in 1970. As detailed in this chapter, the proposals from the charter revision commission also failed.

How can the debate about charter revision in Grand Rapids inform our understanding of charter politics and constitutional change in large cities? This chapter compares the work of the 1970 charter revision commission with a 2002 charter amendment proposed by Mayor John Logie. While the 1970 debate was much broader in scope, both events prompted public discussion about the power relationship between the city manager and the mayor. Specific attention is given to the arguments for and against change. After reviewing these details, we can reflect on several factors that suppress voter enthusiasm about charter change in Grand Rapids, and we can attempt to understand Grand Rapids in the context of research on city charter reform. The case study was developed by referencing newspaper coverage from both time periods, as well as the charter revision commission files and primary source documents at the Grand Rapids City Archives.[4]

## The 1970 Charter Revision Commission

In February 1970 Grand Rapids voters approved the election of a charter revision commission (CRC). Interest in charter reform was so high that ninety-seven candidates filed to run for the nine-member board.[5] Emerging from this field, the nine citizens elected to the CRC almost all had links to city government. Leonard Anderson, Harold Hannah, Edward McCobb, and Berton Sevensma were former city commissioners. Donald Oakes had served as city manager. William Johnson was a former police chief, and Thomas Shearer had been a deputy city attorney. Clarence Fuller, a teacher, and Roger Slykhouse, an engineer, were the two members without links to city government (Lloyd 1970).

The CRC invested its first several months of existence in receiving public comment, hearing from experts, and discerning how the group should approach the task of writing a new charter. Many critiqued the performance of council–manager government. Some pointed to problems and inefficiencies with the 1916 charter. Several recommended revisions to the city's financial structure. Others pointed to problems with the political climate in Grand Rapids. A failed CRC candidate warned the commission, "People have a strange idea about city managers; that they are octopuses imported here to siphon the monies from the citizens" (Mohney 1970). Former city treasurer Charles Lawyer pointed to the historically short tenure of city managers in Grand Rapids and argued the political climate would not allow for stabilization of the "commission–manager philosophy of government." He suggested a strong mayor as the alternative. The strong-mayor form of government was also promoted by former mayors, including the recently defeated Christian Sonneveldt (*Grand Rapids Press* 1970).

Supporters of council–manager government also made their voices heard. Former city manager George Bean wrote to the commission, "The strong mayor concept places too much emphasis on personality as contrasted with program and the needs of the city and guarantees internal conflict of interest in the government itself." Z. Z. Lydens, former city treasurer, blamed city council members for the short tenure of managers in Grand Rapids and suggested managers should be given a secure tenure of at least four years. A radio editorial warned that a stronger mayor would encourage "boss-ism" and the development of a political machine. Numerous letters and public comments advocated changes to the city commission. Yet the question of strong-mayor government emerged as a central feature in the public debate.

## The First Charter Proposal

CRC members' differing perspectives on the question of government form began to emerge. Former city manager Donald Oakes forwarded an article about Detroit to his colleagues on the CRC with a note indicating "even the Strong Mayor form is not working well these days." Clarence Fuller shared information with his colleagues about strong-mayor systems with a chief administrative officer (CAO) appointed by the mayor. By mid-July, the division on the CRC was clear. Six members supported council–manager government, with Fuller, Slykhouse, and Johnson forming a faction in support of a strong-mayor system. Despite a clear council–manager majority, the group did not settle the question of form at the beginning of their work. Instead, they began to cobble together a new charter on a proposal-by-proposal basis.

Meetings occasionally involved heated exchange. At one meeting, Oakes declared, "I've been cast in the role of defending the council–manager system since we first began meeting. . . . Why haven't the strong-mayor advocates come up with constructive suggestions?" Thomas Shearer defended the strong-mayor faction and suggested the CRC was building a hybrid system (Hensch 1970a). By November the council–manager faction moved to adopt its preferred form of government in the new charter. Shearer joined the strong-mayor faction, but the council–manager plan was approved by a 5–4 vote. This did not ease tensions. Strong-mayor advocate Johnson argued, "There was a lot of political dissatisfaction that resulted in the creation of this body. The people want a strong executive leader." Chairman Anderson replied, "I can't understand how the political leadership of this city has to go hand in glove with autocratic and dictatorial control by one man" (Hensch 1970b).

The council–manager faction members made occasional concessions, continuing to enhance the role of mayor within the council–manager framework. They moved toward granting the mayor full-time compensation and a larger role in budget preparation. The CRC scheduled a November 2, 1971, election date for the proposed charter and continued to make revisions until the deadline for submitting official language. The final charter proposal included a council–manager system in which the mayor had veto power and the power to appoint the city manager, with council approval. The document eliminated the position of elected comptroller, in the interest of clearer organization of financial management under the city manager. The document also expanded the city commission (Hensch 1971a).

With their work done, CRC members offered the public conflicting advice on adoption of the new charter. Chairman Anderson offered an editorial in support of the document (1971). He described the CRC's lengthy work and the value of a document that incorporated a balance among the competing perspectives. The value of compromise was also the focus of the *Grand Rapids Press* editorial endorsing the proposed charter. More endorsements came from the Kent County Democratic Committee, the League of Women Voters, and the Greater Grand Rapids Chamber of Commerce. Others saw opportunity in the proposed changes, including the higher salary for the mayor. City commissioner Richard Schwaiger announced he would seek the office of mayor if the new charter was approved.

Others found the hybrid document distasteful. Donald Oakes described the charter as a strong-mayor proposal that watered down the powers of the city council (1971). He emphasized that the CRC had the opportunity to make two more proposals, and he suggested a vote against the charter. More numerous were the complaints of those who believed the proposed charter rearticulated the existing charter. Strong-mayor advocate Mary Jane Morris (1971) argued the document contained a stronger city manager and "no new effective power" for the mayor. Morris pointed to the CRC's elimination of the elected comptroller in direct opposition to the will of the voters in the 1968 charter amendment vote. Advocates of strong-mayor government, including former mayor George Welsh, campaigned against the charter. A preelection panel revealed significant disagreement among participants in city politics regarding how the proposal would alter the roles of mayor and manager (Allbaugh 1971b).

On election day, the proposed charter was defeated by a vote of 27,646 to 12,282 with a 49 percent voter turnout (Allbaugh 1971a). After the defeat *The Grand Rapids Press* conducted an unscientific telephone inquiry of voters to identify complaints. The comments revealed concern about the higher pay for elected officials, the potential for increased taxes, and limited mayoral power (*Grand Rapids Press* 1971c). Voters appeared unwilling to pay a full-time mayor if the office did not hold executive responsibility. Yet there appeared to be no simple explanation for the defeat. Some members of the CRC reconvened shortly after the election to discuss the outcome. Attacks by former mayors and CRC member Donald Oakes, the potential mayoral candidacy of Richard Schwaiger, and a lack of public understanding about the proposal were posited as explanations for the defeat (Allbaugh 1971c). The CRC had two more attempts to offer a charter, but a limited time frame in which to work.

## The Second Charter Proposal

The CRC returned to work almost immediately. McCobb offered his resignation, and Mary Lou Heard was appointed to replace him. The group members determined that they required more insight into voters' preferences for the charter and commissioned an opinion survey. Some members opposed this move, and the *Grand Rapids Press* editorialized that a poll was unnecessary. At question was whether or not public opinion supported a change to strong-mayor government. The *Press* argued, "We find no evidence of a widespread demand for basic changes and certainly little to indicate that a majority of local voters favor going to a strong-mayor form of government, particularly one in which mayor and councilmen would be paid substantially higher salaries despite the fact that the city would have to continue to employ experts to run the city's business" (*Grand Rapids Press* 1971a). Consistent with its preelection editorial, the *Press* sought only minimal revision to the 1916 charter.

With the CRC's plans for a second charter unclear, other groups attempted to claim the mandate for reform. Former mayor Welsh identified himself as a spokesman for those who voted against the charter proposed by the CRC. He urged the city commission to place two amendments on the city's next election ballot to expand the city commission to eleven wards and to expand the powers of the mayor (*Grand Rapids Press* 1971d). The Municipal Action League, a community group opposed to the first charter proposal, urged similar action. Mayor Lyman Parks refused to take up the proposals and directed the city clerk to refer the matter to the CRC (*Grand Rapids Press* 1971b). Elected officials at city hall appeared supportive of giving the CRC a second chance at charter writing.

As the CRC awaited the results of the public opinion survey, it returned to work. Its new approach was influenced by former city manager George Bean. Although a supporter of council–manager government himself, Bean proposed offering the public a clear choice: "If the problem of form is to be resolved by the people, it would appear to be a logical procedure for the Charter Commission to write two charters to be submitted one at a time with the two remaining votes allowed under the law. The public should be fully informed as to the procedure and permitted to make the choice at the polls. These charters should be written as unified documents expressing the best elements of the Council–Manager Plan and the Strong Mayor Plan" (Bean 1972).

The CRC agreed to this approach. The next important question, which charter would go to the voters first? Results of the public opinion survey were made public in March of 1972. An overwhelming 88 percent favored a full-time mayor, with 58 percent stating that the mayor, rather than a city manager, should be in charge of the day-to-day operations of the city. Survey results also showed that the public preferred a nonpartisan council with eight wards, and election by ward. Respondents believed mayoral salary should be set between $20 thousand and $25 thousand (Allbaugh 1972c). The findings were an important endorsement for the strong-mayor faction on the CRC. The panel continued its work on both a strong-mayor and a council–manager charter and targeted the next election date for November 7, 1972. By May the panel members concluded they would send the strong-mayor proposal to the voters first.

The second proposed charter offered a very different structure for city government than the 1916 charter. As outlined in figure 9.1 from the *Grand Rapids Press*, the city council would contain nine wards with members elected by ward. The mayor and comptroller would also be elected to two-year terms. The mayor would assume the policy leadership of the city, serve as the executive of city government, prepare the budget, present an annual message, and appoint boards and commissions with council approval. The mayor would have veto power over ordinances enacted by the council but would not be a voting member of the council. The administrative officer of the city would be appointed by the mayor with council approval. The administrator would be responsible for day-to-day administration under the direction of the mayor. The administrator would appoint and remove department heads, with the exception of the city treasurer and attorney (appointed by the mayor with council approval), and the clerk and assessor (appointed by the council).[6]

**Figure** 9.1    Strong-Mayor Structure in the 1972 Charter Proposal

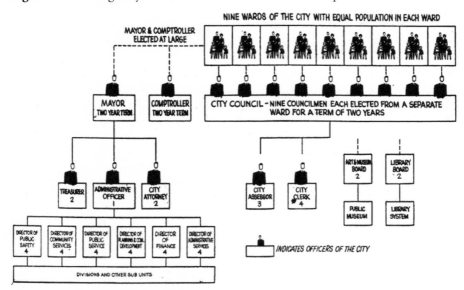

*Source:* Drawing by *Grand Rapids Press* artist Charles Albright, October 11, 1972. *Grand Rapids Press.*

As voters read about the details of the new city charter, they might also have been speculating about the political personalities that would fill the new positions. If the charter passed, several candidates were rumored. Former mayor Boelens expressed interest in the strong-mayor post. CRC members Fuller, Shearer, and Slykhouse were mentioned as potential candidates for city office (*Grand Rapids Press* 1972d).

Many of those dissatisfied with the first charter proposal found the second document acceptable. Strong-mayor proponents from the Municipal Action League praised the document, along with the local political parties and the Grand Rapids Education Association. The Chamber of Commerce endorsed the document but expressed concern about two-year terms for elected officials. The *Grand Rapids Press* editorial page urged a "no" vote. CRC member Oakes was again a vocal opponent, joined in opposition by Hannah. City commissioners were asked to endorse the document, but several expressed a preference for making minimal changes to enhance mayoral power within the existing council–manager structure (*Grand Rapids Press* 1972c). Despite the opinion survey's revelation of support for a stronger mayor, many community groups appeared to prefer minor modifications to the 1916 charter.

Election day brought defeat again—30,911 voted in favor of the strong-mayor charter, and 40,287 voted against the change. The charter vote occurred along with national and state elections, meaning a higher voter turnout than the 1971 contest. The CRC had signaled to the public that it embraced George Bean's proposal to offer voters distinct choices in the form of government for the second and third charter elections.

Voters who defeated the strong-mayor charter likely anticipated a council–manager charter as their next option. One week after the election, the CRC met to discuss its next steps. The members equivocated on the strategy. Slykhouse, Shearer, Fuller, and Heard supported the notion of submitting a strong-mayor charter to the voters again.

## The Third Charter Proposal

Shortly after the CRC expressed interest in another strong-mayor charter, the *Grand Rapids Press* editorial page weighed in with its strongest statement against strong-mayor government. Another strong-mayor charter proposal was identified as a "waste of time." Interpreting the election, the *Press* argued that "the voting public will no longer listen to the naggers and complainers who insist that Grand Rapids city government is basically bad." Further, city government "could probably be made even more account-able with a broadly represented council and mayor overseeing professional managers along the lines of the original charter proposal last year" (*Grand Rapids Press* 1972b). This warning seemed to have little impact on the CRC.

Leonard Anderson's shift from the council–manager to the strong-mayor faction was a turning point in CRC deliberations. Anderson concluded the election on the strong-mayor charter had been influenced by unspecified external events. With the majority, the strong-mayor faction pushed the CRC to submit another strong-mayor charter. The most significant change in the document was the addition of partisan elections. Oakes, the staunch council–manager supporter, was outraged and argued that the CRC was not "keeping faith with the people as there will be no opportunity for them to vote on an updating of the present charter" (Allbaugh 1972b). The CRC's conclusion to three years of work was described as a bitter meeting in which Hannah, Oakes, and Sevensma voted against the third charter (Allbaugh 1972d).

The CRC's abandonment of a "pure" council–manager option for their third attempt prompted criticism and competing reform efforts. Shortly after the defeat of the second charter, city commissioner Richard Schwaiger suggested that the city's legis-lative body should gradually forward charter amendments to the public. When the CRC's plans to advance another strong-mayor charter became clear, more city commis-sioners and citizens endorsed the idea of gradual amendment. City commissioner Barr suggested the CRC and city commission jointly meet to craft amendments to the exist-ing council–manager form. Barr was particularly concerned about the $30,000 price tag for a February 13 special election for the charter (*Grand Rapids Press* 1972a).[7] Shortly before the election, city commissioners Barr and Sypniewski suggested that if the third charter failed, they would support the creation of a citizen committee to offer amendments to the current charter (Malone 1973a). Supporters of various amendment proposals gathered under the umbrella of the Nonpartisan Committee for Effective Charter Amendment to campaign against the CRC's third charter proposal.

The maneuvering of city commissioners drew a fiery response from strong-mayor advocates. CRC member Fuller suggested city commissioners were engaged in "a con-spiracy to discredit the charter commission in order to cover up their own poor record"

(Allbaugh 1972a). Mary Jane Morris of the Municipal Action League described the city commission as "inept" and argued that the commission consistently worked to block changes to the charter (Morris 1972). For supporters of strong-mayor government, clear policy responsibility was lacking in the existing political structure.

Opponents of strong-mayor government remained active in the debate. The *Grand Rapids Press* suggested the presence of an administrative officer in the strong-mayor charter was synonymous with the professionalism already offered in the council–manager form. The paper argued that partisanship and two-year terms for elected officials would harm city government (*Grand Rapids Press* 1973). Voters were also critical of the third charter on election day—12,717 voted against the document, with only 4,887 in support. The *Press* reported the voter turnout of about 16 percent was the lowest for a city election in eleven years. Some city residents had likely grown tired of the three-year-long debate on city government form. After the election some groups proposed amendments to the existing charter, but reform discussions gradually faded (Malone 1973a, 1973b).

The CRC's failure to follow through on the Bean plan results in a gaping hole in our understanding and analysis of Grand Rapids charter politics. The so-called pure city-manager charter becomes part of a counterfactual world that we cannot study. We can hypothesize that the reaffirmation of city-manager government would have passed because strategic city voters rejected the second charter proposal with the knowledge the third proposal would be closer to their preferences. Equally believable, the pure city-manager form would not have received the endorsement of voters. The 1972 survey of city voters suggested a majority supported a stronger mayor. Throughout the CRC's work, regular complaints were heard about the responsiveness of the city commission and accountability in city government. The cumulative coverage in the *Grand Rapids Press* would lead us to believe that a general consensus existed around expanded mayoral power within the council–manager form of government, but this did not pass when proposed in the CRC's first charter. We can conclude that the voters rejected change, but we cannot discern if they would have supported another council–manager charter. Voters were given another opportunity to expand mayoral power almost thirty years later.

## The 2002 Full-Time Mayor Proposal

The charter amendment proposed by Mayor John Logie in 2002 seemed limited in comparison to the changes proposed in the two strong-mayor charters crafted by the 1970–73 CRC. Logie proposed an amendment that would shift the existing "part-time" office to full-time status by adding mayoral power within the council–manager structure. Specifically, the mayor would continue to chair the city commission but would only vote in case of a tie. The mayor would have a veto, which could be overturned by the vote of five city commissioners. The mayor would share responsibility for budget preparation with the city manager. The line for appointment of the city manager, clerk, attorney, and treasurer would shift from the city commission to the mayor but would still require commission approval (Harger 2002e).

Logie had served under the constraints of part-time status since taking office in 1992 but approached the job as if it were a full-time engagement. He immersed himself in public policy, serving on numerous local boards, staking out leadership positions on such metropolitan issues as transportation, and articulating the interests of the state's large cities at the state capital. The Grand Rapids mayor also faced more demands for his time at civic and community events as Grand Rapids revitalized during the 1990s. A variety of observers expressed the opinion that Grand Rapids grew to expect a full-time mayor during Logie's tenure. During the time of the 2002 charter amendment discussion, compensation for the mayor's office was set at $35,000 plus use of a city vehicle. Most candidates running for mayor would have to continue their outside career to maintain an adequate income. Anyone seeking the office would also have to have very flexible work hours. Observers suggested that quality candidates might be discouraged from running for elected office because of the challenge of maintaining an outside career and serving the city (Zeemering and Durham 2009).

The city commission was sympathetic to the idea of defining the mayor's job as full-time; however, commissioners disfavored the parts of Logie's plan that would shift power from the city commission to the mayor (Harger 2002b). Logie responded by conceding the veto and appointment powers. With these revisions Logie gained the support on the commission necessary to approve the amendment. The ballot language pointed to how the mayor's job would be expanded within the existing city structure: "This amendment sets forth additional duties of the Mayor as executive head of the City, including a leadership role in inter-governmental relations, reviewing and commenting on the budget and major public improvements proposed by the City Manager before their submission to the City Commission, recommending salaries of the City Manager, City Attorney, City Clerk, and City Treasurer to the City Commission, making a state of the City address in January and an Annual report to the City Commission, assigning City Commissioners to committees, and maintaining regular office and working hours" (Kent County Election Returns 2002). With the city commission blocking veto and appointment power, the question before voters focused on a formalization of the full-time expectations for the office of mayor.

As in the early 1970s, a coalition emerged to defend the council–manager system from any enhancement of mayoral power. The "No Charter Amendment Committee" included city notables from the past including former manager Joe Zainea, former mayor Lyman Parks,[8] and former comptroller Robert Jamo (Harger 2002a). The Michigan Local Government Management Association argued that the amendment was a "dangerous experiment in mayoral politics" that would alter the balance of power among the mayor, council, and manager (Renando 2002). Arguments against the amendment emphasized that nothing was wrong with local government management, and change could only create problems for the city. Former city manager Zainea and incumbent manager Kurt Kimball advanced the argument that enhanced mayoral power would detract from the intended performance of council–manager government (Zainea 2002; Harger 2002c). Additional opposition came from the Grand Rapids Employees Independent Union and the Grand Rapids Area Chamber of Commerce.

Logie was committed to enhancing the office and announced that he would not seek a third term as mayor in 2003. He dedicated his sizable campaign chest to advance the charter amendment (Harger 2002d). By removing himself as a potential beneficiary of an enhanced mayor's office, Logie was in a better position to argue for the amendment. However, the uncertainty of who would hold the office next raised questions about how future mayors might use their power. Detractors of the amendment argued that changing the charter might alter the balance of power that Logie and Kimball successfully exercised. Logie rejected this argument, stating, "whether or not there is going to be friction between the mayor and city manager has nothing to do with whether my job is full time" (Wilson 2002).

Logie and those offering comments in favor of the amendment emphasized the city's need for policy leadership in the twenty-first century. The *Grand Rapids Press* editorial page described the opposition as "a small band of ex-city officials, mostly retired and from distant yesteryears" and argued the proposal formalized the full-time work already done by Logie. The editorial also emphasized the importance of political leadership in interactions with Grand Rapids' suburban neighbors and in relations with state government (Crawford 2002).

The voice of the opposition was louder. Grand Rapids voters rejected changes to the city's governing structure again, with 29,714 voting against the proposal and 19,550 (less than 40 percent) favoring a stronger mayor. The charter vote took place along with state and national elections. Post-election comments suggested some voters were unclear about what a full-time mayor would do, or how someone other than Logie would approach the responsibility (Harger 2002f). While the city commission recognized the significant gap between the formal definition of the office and the actual workload of the incumbent mayor, perhaps the public campaign did not successfully communicate this message to voters. Even if voters did recognize Logie's investment in the job, why would the voters agree to pay more for government if, as opponents argued, the existing arrangement worked?

## Analyzing Charter Politics in Grand Rapids

How can we explain the rejection of charter changes in Grand Rapids? We can compare the 1970–73 and 2002 debates to help answer this question. The two debates can be compared with reflection on five points: the need for change, public concern about the cost of government, the politics of the moment, coalitions supporting the council–manager form, and how the debate compared governance in Grand Rapids to other cities.

### *The Need for Change*

The two debates appear to differ most when considering the impetus for change. The 1970 CRC was elected in the aftermath of the failure of two different calls for change

in city government. The first call for change emphasized the need for improved management at city hall. Mayor Sonneveldt and elected officials in the late 1960s complained about their level of influence over city government. Others focused criticism
on the short tenure of city managers and the quality of government management. City
Manager Orr advanced an amendment to alter the financial management of the city,
centralizing responsibility under the city manager and eliminating the elected comptroller. Voters rejected Orr's amendment and postelection interpretations indicated that
citizens desired an elected "watchdog" to check up on the manager and city commission. Elected officials and city managers exhibited tension over the balance of power in
city government. This tension animated the debates of the CRC, and after the failure
of three proposals remained unresolved.

A second impetus for the 1970 CRC was the question of representation. Citizens
from the 11-Ward Committee argued for a more representative and responsive city
commission, proposing amendments to increase the number of wards. During the late
1960s and early 1970s discussions about improving representation and policy responsiveness in the legislative branch was widespread in U.S. cities (Heilig and Mundt
1984). In Grand Rapids, technical problems with ballot language and a lack of enthusiastic support at city hall kept these proposals from reaching voters. Some actors explicitly used the failure of the 11-Ward Committee to argue for the election of a charter
revision commission. While the CRC became fixated on the question of mayoral
power, the record of deliberations suggests general support for a slightly larger council,
and the three charter proposals reflect this. Thus, reform to the representative and
legislative institutions of city government was a more broadly embraced goal, but suffered because of its incorporation in a full-scale charter revision debate that divided the
public.

In 2002 Mayor Logie asked voters to recognize changes that he had brought to city
government over the last decade. The amendment process sprang from Logie's State of
the City speech, and the final amendment was approved through discussion at the city
commission table. The controversial aspects of the proposal, specifically veto power,
were stripped away by the time the proposal reached voters. For city hall insiders,
Logie's performance as a "part-time" mayor stood in contrast to predecessors. For the
general public, the need for change may have appeared more unclear. If Logie had
served in the office successfully, change appeared to be unnecessary for future mayors
to be successful. In sum, the events prompting debates about change were distinct. The
public perception of a need for change was present in 1970, but the CRC could not
identify a package of proposals to respond to the demand for change. In 2002 the
public appeared uninterested in an elite-driven proposal. While the demand for change
helps us better understand individual "no" votes, this does little to help us understand
Grand Rapids's consistent pattern of "no" votes.

## Cost of Government

Because the debates in Grand Rapids emphasized expansion of the city commission
and expansion of mayoral powers, voter concern about the cost of government must

be considered as part of the explanation for voters' rejection of charter changes. Grand Rapids voters have demonstrated a keen interest in keeping the salaries of elected officials low. The 1916 charter fixed salaries that went largely unadjusted until 1972 when the state authorized local governments to adopt Local Officers Compensation Commissions to set elected officials' pay. Debate about elected officials' pay occupied hours of the CRC's time. While a specific salary for the mayor was not discussed in 2002, shifting the position to full time implied higher salary and extra costs. Lacking detailed public opinion data for both time periods, a relationship between cost of government and "no" votes should be considered speculative. Still, the 1971 postelection documentary evidence offers tentative support for this argument. As noted earlier, the *Press* queried citizens about their "no" votes immediately after the election and found complaints about higher pay for elected officials. The CRC's first charter included a $25,000 salary for the mayor. The 1972 survey of voters found 44 percent supported a salary of between $20,000 and $25,000 (Allbaugh 1972c). This left a sizable percentage preferring lower pay. We should not reject the argument that increased salaries for elected officials helped shape Grand Rapids voters' aversion to charter change.

## The Politics of the Moment

The politics of the moment appear to bog down long-term constitutional questions. In the 1970s former mayors, incumbent city commissioners, and even charter revision commission members were eyed as potential officeholders. Concern about political personalities is illustrated by the CRC's decision to include a series of questions in the 1972 survey about the credibility of various community members and public officials.[9] Logie attempted to prevent this from happening in 2002 by removing himself from the upcoming campaign for mayor. Still, citizens' conceptions of a stronger mayor may be influenced by those who are active in city politics rather than abstract questions about governance structure. Even Logie's successful operation under part-time constraints might have depicted to voters that a change to the office was unnecessary. Voters' understanding of the existing city structure and their unwillingness to support change is explained in part by the political personalities of incumbents and potential office holders.

## Support for the Council–Manager Form

Both charter debates included coalitions supporting council–manager government. In both time periods, former city managers were leaders in crafting public perceptions about how council–manager government had served the city. The coalitions supporting council–manager government rearticulated the traditional reform argument of business-like administration. The debate in the early 1970s exhibited a variety of warnings about the rebirth of partisan machines and patronage in city government. In 2002 the organization of city management as a profession and as an interest group was displayed through the involvement of the Michigan Municipal Management Association.

Defense of the council–manager form and campaigning by the council–manager coalition help explain Grand Rapids' tendency to vote "no" on charter change.

Although the presence of the council–manager coalition persisted, the 1970 and 2002 coalitions worked under very different conditions. In the 1970s council–manager supporters had to confront the question of why Grand Rapids experienced frequent turnover of city managers. The job appeared impossible, and the power relationship between the mayor, commission, and manager appeared unstable. In 2002 Kurt Kimball had been in the city manager's office for fifteen years and maintained a stable working relationship with mayor and commission. Kimball developed this balance during a time of growing public expectations for policy leadership in local government and increasing interest by elected officials in the administrative affairs of large council–manager cities (Svara 1999; Nalbandian 2005). In recent years Grand Rapids officials have accommodated public expectations for policy leadership in city government without structural change. Competent balancing by manager and mayor may affirm public satisfaction with the current government form. Yet current stability does not guarantee that existing administrative arrangements resolved the political questions discussed in previous charter amendment campaigns (Durant 2000, 104). The long-serving Kimball's retirement in 2008 will make Grand Rapids an interesting city to watch in the years ahead. This leaves open the potential for new discussions about city form if future managers and mayors do not achieve balance or if political leadership is perceived to be necessary for the city's continued economic prosperity.

## The Charter in Context

Finally, the charter debates differed in the degree to which the governance structure of Grand Rapids was compared to the practices of other cities. CRC members began their work in 1970 by seeking out expert opinion from Dr. Arthur Bromage of the University of Michigan. They frequently bolstered their debate by placing Grand Rapids in the context of other cities, referring to research such as Alford and Scoble's (1965) study of political and socioeconomic characteristics of American cities. Donald Oakes sent regular notes to his CRC colleagues, sometimes attaching articles about mayors and governance structure. CRC member Johnson prepared extensive research about chief administrative officers working in strong-mayor governments. Politically active members of the public also turned to social science to place Grand Rapids in context, as demonstrated by a report of the Local Government Study Committee of the Democratic Party (Monsma et al. 1971).

However, this context was absent in coverage of the 2002 debate. Few cities were highlighted for comparison. Renando (2002) raised the specter of Flint, Michigan, as an example of a city that increased mayoral power with negative consequences. He also pointed to Phoenix as an example of a large council–manager city to reply to the argument that growth necessitated change in Grand Rapids. The language of opponents of the 2002 amendment depicted the Grand Rapids charter as offering an ideal-type of council–manager government.[10] Voters in 2002 received much less comparative information about local government form, and the information they did receive was framed by council–manager advocates to help shape a "no" vote. Attention to research did not seem to help the passage of charter amendments in the early 1970s, so we cannot say that a lack of comparative information explains voters' opposition to charter amendments. Based on the evidence, we can say that the council–manager coalition seems more adept at using comparative information in public debate to influence "no" votes.

## Conclusion

Recent research on city form recognizes many cities have blurred the structural lines between the council–manager and strong-mayor form (DeSantis and Renner 2002; Frederickson, Johnson, and Wood 2004; DeSoto, Tajalli, and Opheim 2006). A study of charter change in Michigan found strong-mayor cities have been more likely to adopt reforms that move them toward a "conciliated" structure than are council–manager cities (Carr and Karuppusamy 2009). In other words, taking steps away from the "ideal-type" council–manager structure may be difficult for Michigan cities. The case study of Grand Rapids, including observations of three change proposals in the early 1970s and one change proposal in 2002, illuminates some reasons why voters have consistently said "no" to change. In the early 1970s broad public interest seemed to exist in the expansion of the city commission, but political elites and the public seemed divided on whether strong-mayor or council–manager government would serve the city best. In 2002 Mayor Logie unveiled a proposal similar to the first charter proposed by the CRC in 1971. The city commission revised the proposal to eliminate expansion of mayoral power but recognized the full-time nature of the office. Voters still rejected the amendment.

The most consistent explanation we can offer for the rejection of the four proposals discussed in this chapter is the consistent organization of coalitions in support of the existing council–manager form of government. With clear defenders of the status quo, and uncertain costs and political personalities surrounding change proposals, Grand Rapids voters are unenthusiastic about change. Despite this history, we should not anticipate that Grand Rapids voters will always reject changes in form. Former mayor Logie and current mayor George Heartwell have, in many ways, been filling a part-time job on a full-time basis. If future mayors fail to perform in this way, the recognition of the need for full-time status may become apparent to voters. Significant change in form appears unlikely because of the strong coalition supporting council–manager government.

## Notes

1. The charter's comparative table lists thirty-nine modifications. See www.grandrapids.mi.us/3984 (accessed July 9, 2008).
2. See Michigan P.A. 279 of 1909, §117.18.

3. The resurgence of concern about democratic control might reflect broader concerns about decentralization and representation (e.g., Kaufman 1969).

4. The files for the 1970 CRC include meeting minutes, public correspondence addressed to the CRC, notes circulated among commission members, transcripts of some statements made in public meetings, and a variety of supplementary documents and reports about charter reform. I extend my thanks to city archivist William Cunningham for facilitating access to the archive in March 2008.

5. The candidates who won the election included figures with experience in Grand Rapids politics. Equally interesting are the candidates who would be important in the city's political future, including Mayor John Logie (1992–2003) and Congressman Vernon Ehlers (1993–present), who failed to win spots on the CRC but received 4,580 and 4,719 votes respectively.

6. The second and third proposed charters were printed in *The Grand Rapids Press* on October 16, 1972, and January 24, 1973, respectively. This suggests the CRC took seriously criticism about the lack of information about the first proposed charter.

7. Because of the three-year time limit, the CRC could not align its final attempt with a regularly scheduled election.

8. Lyman Parks served as mayor from Robert Boelen's resignation in 1971 until 1975. Interestingly, Parks endorsed the first charter proposed by the CRC, which was a larger expansion of mayoral power than Logie's 2002 proposal.

9. The responses to these questions were neither released to the media nor included in the archive file.

10. Carr and Karuppusamy (2009), using the adapted cities framework of Frederickson, Johnson, and Wood (2004), classify Grand Rapids as an adapted-administrative city.

# References

Alford, Robert R., and Harry M. Scoble. 1965. Political and socioeconomic characteristics of American cities. In *Municipal year book*. Washington, DC: International City Managers Association.

Allbaugh, Floyd. 1968. Changes in charter will take selling job. *Grand Rapids Press*, August 25.

———. 1969a. Sonneveldt blasts proposal for 12-ward government. *Grand Rapids Press*, February 21.

———. 1969b. Victorious Harper proffers cooperation to city leaders. *Grand Rapids Press*, February 18.

———. 1971a. It's back to conference room for stunned charter authors. *Grand Rapids Press*, November 3.

———. 1971b. Mayor versus manager-roles under proposed charter spark forum debate. *Grand Rapids Press*, October 28.

———. 1971c. What went wrong? Charter writers ask in postmortem. *Grand Rapids Press*, November 10.

———. 1972a. Charter writer accuses city fathers of conspiracy for opposing election. *Grand Rapids Press*, December 15.

———. 1972b. Charter writers switch to strong-mayor version. *Grand Rapids Press*, December 6.

———. 1972c. Poll finds voters want strong mayor. *Grand Rapids Press*, March 27.

———. 1972d. Strong mayor vote due despite ill-will. *Grand Rapids Press*, December 12.

Anderson, Leonard W. 1971. Chairman Anderson recommends approval of proposed charter. *Grand Rapids Press*, October 20.

Bean, George E. 1972. A council–manager or strong mayor charter: What do they *really* want? *Grand Rapids Press*, January 30.

Carr, Jered B., and Shanthi Karuppusamy. 2009. Beyond ideal types of municipal structure: Adapted cities in Michigan. *American Review of Public Administration* 39 no. 3 (May): 304–21.

Crawford, Joseph. 2002. Grand Rapids needs a full-time mayor to handle full-time duties. *Grand Rapids Press*, October 12.

DeSantis, Victor S., and Tari Renner. 2002. City government structures: An attempt at clarification. *State and Local Government Review* 34, no. 2 (Spring): 95–104.

DeSoto, William, Hassan Tajalli, and Cynthia Opheim. 2006. Power, professionalism, and independence: Changes in the office of mayor. *State and Local Government Review* 38, no. 3:156–64.

Durant, Robert F. 2000. Whither the neoadministrative state? Toward a polity-centered theory of administrative reform. *Journal of Public Administration Research and Theory* 10, no. 1 (January): 79–109.

Frederickson, H. George, Gary A. Johnson, and Curtis H. Wood. 2004. *The Adapted City: Institutional Dynamics and Structural Change*. Armonk, NY: M. E. Sharpe.

*Grand Rapids Press*. 1967. Manager system may be out in updating city charter. *Grand Rapids Press*, October 6.

———. 1970. Ex-officials disagree on charter. *Grand Rapids Press*, May 13.

———. 1971a. Charter by consensus? *Grand Rapids Press*, December 8.

———. 1971b. Charter changes don't make ballot. *Grand Rapids Press*, December 22, 1971.

———. 1971c. Mayor's high pay, low power apparently was key to charter defeat. *Grand Rapids Press*, November 4.

———. 1971d. Welsh fights commission delay. *Grand Rapids Press*, November 24.

———. 1972a. Barr would like to avoid costly charter election. *Grand Rapids Press*, December 6.

———. 1972b. The charter—One more time. *Grand Rapids Press*, November 15.

———. 1972c. City commission cool to back-charter plea. *Grand Rapids Press*, October 3.

———. 1972d. Municipal Action League backs charter. *Grand Rapids Press*, October 6.

———. 1973. Vote 'No' on the charter. *Grand Rapids Press*, February 9.

Griffen, Russell F. 1922. Grand Rapids refuses to revert from the commission-manager plan. *National Municipal Review* 11, no. 7 (July): 200–4.

Harger, Jim. 2002a. Committee opposes bid to change mayor's job to full-time. *Grand Rapids Press*, October 4.

———. 2002b. GR commissioners reject veto power that mayor wants. *Grand Rapids Press*, June 26.

———. 2002c. Kimball lines up against full-time mayor bid. *Grand Rapids Press*, October 8.

———. 2002d. Logie cash backs mayor plan. *Grand Rapids Press*, October 8.

———. 2002e. Logie lobbies for stronger powers in mayor's office. *Grand Rapids Press*, January 31.

———. 2002f. Part-time work will go on for mayor. *Grand Rapids Press*, November 6, 2002.

Heilig, Peggy, and Robert J. Mundt. 1984. *Your voice at city hall: The politics, procedures, and policies of district representation*. Albany: State University of New York Press.

Hensch, Steve. 1970a. Charter body defines manager's role. *Grand Rapids Press*, September 16.

———. 1970b. Council–manager system accepted by 1-vote margin. *Grand Rapids Press*, November 4.

———. 1971a. Charter revisionists approve their work, set Sept. 21 vote. *Grand Rapids Press*, July 20.

———. 1971b. New charter draws fire as writers pledge to reconsider controversial parts. *Grand Rapids Press*, June 17.

Kaufman, Herbert. 1969. Administrative decentralization and political power. *Public Administration Review* 29, no. 1 (January/February): 3–15.

Kent County Election Returns. 2002. *Proposal Text* [cited August 22, 2008]. Available from www.electionmagic.com/archives/mi/2002/novgen/K41results/proptext.htm.

Kleiman, Jeffrey. 2006. *Strike! How the furniture workers strike of 1911 changed Grand Rapids.* Grand Rapids, MI: Grand Rapids Historical Commission.

Lloyd, Mike. 1970. Familiar figures dominate city charter commission. *Grand Rapids Press*, April 7.

Malone, Brian. 1973a. Citizen group urged for charter changes. *Grand Rapids Press*, February 5.

———. 1973b. Fear of confusion prompts dropping charter proposal. *Grand Rapids Press*, February 23.

Mohney, Linda. 1970. Charter race losers get chance to speak. *Grand Rapids Press*, May 27.

Monsma, Stephen V., Barbara Higbee, H. Rhett Pinsky, H. David Soet, Daniel Waters, Douglas Evans, and Friley Johnson. 1971. Municipal government in Grand Rapids: A plan for action. Grand Rapids, MI: Local Government Study Committee of the Democratic Party.

Morris, Mary Jane. 1971. 'Strong-Mayor' proponent seeking rejection of charter. *Grand Rapids Press*, October 20.

———. 1972. Blasts city commission turnabout on charter. *Grand Rapids Press*, December 30.

Nalbandian, John. 2005. Professionals and the conflicting forces of administrative modernization and civic engagement. *American Review of Public Administration* 35, no. 4 (December): 311–26.

Oakes, Donald. 1971. Oakes cites 'strong-mayor' provisions. *Grand Rapids Press*, October 20.

Renando, Warren D. 2002. Don't tinker with mayor-manager setup. *Grand Rapids Press*, October 17.

Svara, James H. 1999. The shifting boundary between elected officials and city managers in large council-manager cities. *Public Administration Review* 59, no. 1 (January/February): 44–53.

Travis, Anthony, and Lynn Mapes. 1971. Charter revision: It wasn't easy the first time, either. *Grand Rapids Press*, December 19.

Wilson, Rick. 2002. Full-time mayor debate raises questions on overlapping duties. *Grand Rapids Press*, October 25.

Zainea, Joe. 2002. No reason to change city charter. *Grand Rapids Press*, October 26.

Zeemering, Eric S., and Roger J. Durham. 2009. Expanding the scope of policy leadership through networks: Grand Rapids, Michigan. In *The facilitative leader in city hall: Reexamining the scope and contributions*, ed. J. H. Svara. Boca Raton, FL: CRC Press.

CHAPTER 10

# DALLAS

## The Survival of Council–Manager Government

KAREN M. JARRELL

## Introduction

DALLAS IS THE NINTH LARGEST CITY in the United States and the third largest city in Texas. It is one of three cities in the United States with a population of more than one million people that continues, despite years of talk about changes to its governance structure, to utilize a council–manager form of government (Ramshaw 2005a, B1). The idea of a strong-mayor system of government and the role of the mayor has been debated and discussed for years in Dallas (Sweany 2005). *Governing* online highlighted the call for this shift in 1988, 1993, 1997, and again in 2006 (Gurwitt 1993; Gurwitt 1997, 20; Gurwitt 2006, 42; Mobley 1988).

Dallas operates under the council–manager plan with a professional city manager reporting to a fifteen-member council, composed of fourteen single-member district council members and a mayor elected at large. Because of infighting on the council since the adoption of the current electoral system in the early 1990s, disagreements between the city manager and a strong-willed mayor, racial politics, ethics violations, and other allegations of fraud, citizens of Dallas in 2005 voted in two referenda calling for a shift to a mayor–council form of government. Although both efforts aimed at city government change failed, the question of form in Dallas is likely not settled for the long term. As Hassett and Watson (2007) pointed out, where a community is nearly divided on the question of form, the issue will be revisited.

## Racial Relations and Representation in Governing Dallas

African American leaders from the Progressive Voters League (formerly the Progressive Citizens League), in concert with other stakeholders including the Dallas Express, the National Association for the Advancement of Colored People (NAACP), the Negro Chamber of Commerce, African American ministers and activists, and supportive

183

Anglos were committed to increasing equal rights and opportunities for minorities in Dallas (Graff 2008, 171–72) despite a charter amendment in 1930 that "restricted African-Americans' access to [public] office by requiring all candidates to run at large and on a non-partisan basis" (Graff 2008, 169). Leaders of the civil rights movement challenged the hold that the Dallas Citizens Council (DCC), an organization of Dallas's top business leaders, had on Dallas politics for many decades (Hanson 2003). Dallas, like many southern cities, opposed the Supreme Court's mandate for desegregation (Leslie 1964, 70). However, city leadership, under the direction of R. L. Thornton, took lessons from negative outcomes in other cities to work on a purposeful integration plan with black leaders (Leslie 1964, 72). "It was not an argument over whether Negroes should be integrated or not. It was simply a matter of dollars and cents" (Leslie 1964, 72). According to the U.S. Census Bureau, Dallas's total population in 1960 was 679,684 (Graff 2008, 87). Although 19.6 percent[1] of Dallas's residents were African American during the 1960s and for the last thirty years, Dallas's African American community was advancing and gaining a national reputation (Graff 2008, 172), no minority had ever been elected to the city council because of the at-large voting system controlled by the DCC (Hanson 2003, 72).

The mayor and council members ran citywide, and it was possible for well-organized sectors of the voting public to maintain a majority on the city council. These groups, traditionally white businessmen organized by the Dallas Charter Association, funded and backed specific candidates allowing the Alliance to run the city. These actions created an atmosphere of discrimination and racial exclusion for African Americans and Hispanics in Dallas politics (Hanson 2003, 48–49, 62, 66–73). In fact, "Blacks and Hispanics were excluded from elective office until the 1960s, and when some were finally elected, it initially was with the endorsement of the Anglo business leaders. Only 'safe' minority candidates received endorsement and financial support from the entrepreneurial regime, a necessity for success in the at-large election system" (Hanson 2003, 72). According to Graff (2008, 168–69), "Dallas leaders . . . attempted to maintain control through accommodation, sponsoring political careers of selected minority candidates and negotiating and managing change."

In 1966 Joseph Lockridge became the first African American elected to the Texas state legislature from Dallas (Graff 2008, 295), and in 1972 Eddie Bernice Johnson was elected to the Texas House of Representatives as the first African American woman elected to public office in Dallas County (Graff 2008, 296; Payne 2000, 384). In 1967 Dr. Emmett Conrad, a Dallas surgeon, was the first African American elected to the Dallas School Board (Payne 2000, 387; Graff 2008, 295). In 1968 George Allen, supported by the DCC, received an appointment to one of two new city council posts where he won formal election in 1969. Allen later became mayor pro tem (Hazel 1997, 58–59; Payne 2000, 386) and was succeeded in 1975 by seventy-three-year-old NAACP veteran civil rights activist Juanita Craft (Payne 2000, 412; Hazel 1997, 59). Anita N. Martinez, also endorsed by the DCC, became in 1969 the first Hispanic elected to the Dallas City Council (Graff 2008, 295; Payne 2000, 384 and 387; Hazel 1997, 58). In 1973 Lucy Patterson became the first African American woman elected to the Dallas City Council (Graff 2008, 296; Hazel 1997, 59).

In 1971 a group of African American and Mexican American residents of Dallas filed suit in the United States District Court for the Northern District of Texas (437 U.S. 535, 538) claiming that the Dallas city charter's at-large electoral process unconstitutionally crippled the ability of minority residents to elect leaders representative and responsive to the needs of minorities (Sweany 2005, 51; Payne 2000, 408; Find Law for Legal Professionals 1978). The complaint was dismissed for failure to state a claim, but the Court of Appeals for the Fifth Circuit Court disagreed and remanded the case to the District Court (*Lipscomb v. Jonsson*, 459 F.2d 335 [1972]) (Find Law for Legal Professionals 1978; U.S. Court of Appeals 1976; U.S. Supreme Court Center 1978). On January 17, 1975, after an evidentiary hearing, the District Court orally declared Dallas's at-large system of elections unconstitutional, and the city council, as a legislative body, had to prepare a plan that was constitutional (Hazel 1997, 59; Find Law for Legal Professionals 1978; U.S. Supreme Court Center 1978; Graff 2008, 296).

On January 20, 1975, the Dallas City Council passed a resolution for a new electoral plan, which allowed eight council members to be elected from single-member districts in addition to three at-large seats, including the mayor (Graff 2008, 296; Payne 2000; Hanson 2003; Find Law for Legal Professionals 1978). The plan was presented to the District Court on January 24, 1975 (Find Law for Legal Professionals 1978). The District Court held a remedy hearing to determine the constitutionality of Dallas's reapportionment plan. After an extensive hearing the District Court announced in an oral opinion delivered on February 8, 1975, that Dallas's new reapportionment plan was constitutional (Find Law for Legal Professionals 1978; U.S. Supreme Court Center 1978). Two days later, the Dallas City Council formally enacted the new ordinance incorporating the eight/three plan of electing council members, and on March 25, 1975, the District Court issued a written opinion that sustained the plan as a valid legislative Act (Find Law for Legal Professionals 1978). The Court of Appeals (United States Court of Appeals, Fifth Circuit. 551 F.2d 1043) reversed the judgment and held that the District Court erred by only evaluating city actions under constitutional standards rather than applying the teachings of *East Carroll Parish School Bd. v. Marshall* (424 U.S. 636), which held that, absent extraordinary circumstances, judicially compelled reapportionment plans should employ only single-member districts (Find Law for Legal Professionals 1978; U.S. Court of Appeals 1976; U.S. Supreme Court Center 1978). The case was then remanded to the District Court requiring that the city reapportion itself into the appropriate number of single-member districts (U.S. Supreme Court Center 1978; Find Law for Legal Professionals 1978). Dallas voters "approve[d] a 10-4-1 plan, although 95 percent of African-Americans and more than 75 percent of Hispanics oppose[d]" the measure (Graff 2008, 296).

The case was appealed to the Supreme Court and argued before the Court on April 26, 1978 (U.S. Supreme Court Center 1978). On June 22, 1978, the Supreme Court rendered its decision that the city of Dallas did its duty, as requested by the District Court, to create a substitute plan of electing council members by enacting the eight/three ordinance (Find Law for Legal Professionals 1978; U.S. Supreme Court Center 1978). The District Court reviewed Dallas's proposal as a properly, legislatively enacted plan and held it constitutional, despite the use of at-large voting for three of the council seats (Find Law for Legal Professionals 1978; U.S. Supreme Court Center 1978). The Supreme Court found that the Court of Appeals erred in evaluating the case under principles applicable to judicially devised reapportionment plans. Additionally, the Dallas City Council, in enacting the new reapportionment plan, did not claim to amend the charter but only to exercise its legislative powers after the charter provision had been declared unconstitutional (Find Law for Legal Professionals 1978; U.S. Supreme Court Center 1978).

Furthermore, "*East Carroll Parish School Bd., supra,* does not support the conclusion of the Court of Appeals that the legislative plan presented by the city must be viewed as judicial, and therefore as subject to a level of scrutiny more stringent than that required by the Constitution, rather than legislative" (Find Law for Legal Professionals 1978; U.S. Supreme Court Center 1978). The court found that the Dallas City Council met its responsibility of replacing the invalid apportionment provision with one that could withstand constitutional scrutiny. The Supreme Court subsequently reversed and remanded the case back to the Court of Appeals suggesting it consider the Voting Rights Act of 1965 (Hanson 2003, 287), which became applicable to Texas while this case was pending on appeal but was not appropriately considered and dealt with earlier by the Court of Appeals (Find Law for Legal Professionals 1978; U.S. Supreme Court Center 1978).

In 1988 then-Mayor Annette Strauss convened a tri-ethnic group of stakeholders, including business and minority leaders, called Dallas Together to formulate a plan that addressed the inequities in education, employment, and minority representation in Dallas city government (Hanson 2003, 287; Hazel 1997, 61). In the early '90s, during the time the Dallas Together report was in the implementation stage, civil rights leaders Roy Williams and Marvin Crenshaw filed suit in federal court challenging Dallas's eight/three ordinance (*The Dallas Morning News* 2004; Hazel 1997, 62; Hanson 2003, 287–88). They argued that the city's system of electing at-large council members prevented minorities from participating as equals in citywide politics (Hanson 2003, 287–88; Leslie 1964; Blumenthal 2004; Hazel 1997, 62). In an effort to quash the lawsuit, the city council appointed a charter advisory committee to address the eight/three system by recommending revisions to the current council election system to allow for a more representative government that could go before voters in the upcoming election (Hanson 2003, 288–89). To meet this deadline, committee chairman Ray Hutchison had to fast-track the work product of a diverse group of constituents with disparate goals and outside agendas (Hanson 2003, 288–89). After much discourse, disagreement, political posturing, a secret caucus, and a recess that caused the committee to miss the original report deadline, a final plan was approved: chairman Hutchison's original 10-4-1 plan (Hanson 2003, 292; Hazel 1997, 62).

The referendum went before Dallas voters in an August 1991 special election. The 10-4-1 proposition was approved "in a racially polarized vote" (Hazel 1997, 62) where white North Dallas voters were in favor and minority South Dallas voters in opposition (Hanson 2003, 294). A dissatisfied Williams and Crenshaw pressed their lawsuit to the federal district court (Hanson 2003, 294; Hazel 1997, 62) while the Dallas City Council forwarded the newly amended charter to the U.S. Department of Justice for compliance review under the the 1982 amendments to the Voting Rights Act (Hanson 2003,

294). The Department of Justice could not issue a ruling without applying the 10-4-1 system to the 1990 Census data. Because the 10-4-1 system had not yet been adopted, Dallas city officials were forced to defend the current 8-3 system, knowing it discriminated against minorities (Hanson 2003, 294). The federal district court ruled that Dallas's electoral system was undemocratic and required the council members to run in their own districts only. After bitter political and legal debate and discourse, Dallas replaced the existing eight/three ordinance with a "14-1" election system (*Dallas Morning News* 2004; Hazel 1997, 62; Hanson 2003) with fourteen council members elected from single-member districts and the mayor elected at large. The 14-1 plan is widely credited with increasing the number of African Americans and Hispanics elected to the city council.

For the first time in its history, Dallas began to get meaningful input from the African American and Latino communities through the election of council members who represented those neighborhoods (Graff 2008, 233; Sweany 2005, 51; Hanson 2003, 315). From 1993 to 1998 John Ware served as Dallas's first African American city manager (Hanson 2003, 229; Payne 2000, 490) and was succeeded by Dallas's first Hispanic city manager, Ted Benavides, who served for six years (Payne 2000, 490–91). In 1995 Ron Kirk, a prominent lawyer and community activist, was the first African American elected as mayor of Dallas (Graff 2008, 241 and 298). Regardless of the success of a representative city council, the Citizens' Alliance's money and influence was still present in the election for mayor fostering the belief that the mayor could generally keep a majority of council members on his or her side. During the 1990s and the first half of the 2000s, the 14-1 election plan with each elected official "looking out for their own turf instead of the whole city" (Falkenberg 2005, A5), added complexity to Dallas's city government. Critics claim that with a fourteen-member city council pulling in different directions amid constant disagreement and discord, Dallas has missed opportunities like the Boeing relocation, which ultimately went to Chicago (Curry 2005), the Dallas Cowboys stadium (Aaron 2008), and the Texas Motor Speedway, which went to neighboring cities (Falkenberg 2005, A5).

## Origins of Dallas's Form of Government Change Effort

For the past nearly two decades, Dallas has endured scandal by city council members, questionable school district leadership and fiscal responsibility, an unfair school tax, high crime, and poor road conditions that have driven corporations north to the incentive-friendly suburbs, and a recalcitrant city council whose "micromanaging self-interests . . . make it nearly impossible for developers to do business in the city" (Curry 2005).

Over time established leadership from the business community, once all-powerful and influential, began to lose its stronghold on city elections; the "old mix of business and politics in Dallas [was] changing" (Mobley 1988). In its place came smaller, more specialized groups with specific issues and agendas to promote and a city council of diverse interests and priorities. Other organizations, such as the Central Dallas Association, Greater Dallas Chamber of Commerce, Dallas Urban League, Community Council of Greater Dallas, and United Way of Greater Dallas, began to assert more influence and power (Hanson 2003, 263–67). The Dallas Citizens Council, still tangentially involved in city government, found its influence declining and its membership becoming more representative of the citizenry of Dallas (Payne 2000, 414–15).

The complexity of leading a large, diverse city became a task of managing myriad disparate interests, dealing with racial tensions, and placating a disapproving public that watched city government struggles for power between the mayor and the council members and among council members daily in the newspaper and on the television news. Ennis (2005, 70) noted: "If this sounds like an incipient municipal meltdown, it is: A once bright-eyed ingénue is now in danger of becoming the nation's most myopic and risk-adverse big city, desperately seeking leadership in the shadow of a patriarchy whose patriarchs vanished a generation ago."

Hassett and Watson (2007, 4–5) explained, "Changes in governmental form are most likely to occur when there are transformations in a community's basic values, often resulting from underlying shifts in demographics and economic factors." The change in the electoral system from at-large to districts brought dramatic shifts in the way Dallas was governed. However, despite the turmoil and dysfunction, a majority of Dallas citizens apparently continued to believe in the council–manager form of government although the limited power of the mayor in the council–manager form of government became a contentious issue.

In 2004 the *Dallas Morning News* commissioned the first comprehensive assessment of the city's operations, structure, and quality of life to determine the effectiveness of city government. The report, "Dallas at the Tipping Point," identified Dallas's decline with key indicators, such as increased crime rates, declining air quality, poor public schools, and an antiquated city charter of city government (Clyde et al. 2004). The report's prescription: Dallas needed change.

## Dallas's Strong-Mayor Movement

R. L. Thornton, formally elected to the office of mayor in 1953, began a period in Dallas history of strong mayoral leadership where "nobody had any doubt who was in charge" (Allison 2005, 14). On November 22, 1963, near the spot where John Neely Bryan first settled, President John F. Kennedy was assassinated. As noted earlier, after the assassination of President Kennedy, civic leaders approached J. Erik Jonsson, one of the founders of Texas Instruments, to ask him to become mayor. Once mayor, Jonsson, a keen businessman, assessed the city and began making decisions to invest heavily in Dallas's infrastructure. Within months construction began on the Dallas North Tollway. Within a few years building began on the Dallas/Fort Worth (DFW) airport, despite Dallas voters rejecting the proposition in 1967. By 1974 the airport was open. Thornton and Jonsson were considered strong mayors, not in the formal sense but because of the facilitative leadership that they provided for a growing city

(Svara 2008), one helping Dallas recover from the negative stigma resulting from Kennedy's assassination and the other preparing Dallas to compete economically on a global scale.

On March 7, 1991, State Representative Steve Wolens, husband to future Mayor Laura Miller, filed a bill (H.B. 2238) during the regular session of the 72nd State Legislature that would shift the duties of the city manager to the mayor; however, action was never taken at the state level regarding the proposed legislation other than the House hearing testimony on April 25, 1991 (Texas House of Representatives 1991; the *Dallas Morning News* 2004; Sweany 2005, 51). Wolens's push for a strong-mayor form of government in the Texas House of Representatives is indicative of a long-standing belief in Dallas that a stronger mayor might overcome some of the challenges facing Dallas (Sweany 2005, 51). In 1997 Mayor Ron Kirk, a former lobbyist and employee of the Citizens' Alliance, promoted a "strong-mayor, strong-council" plan to strengthen the mayor's hiring and firing power. However, the Dallas City Council did not support any changes in the existing power and governance structure (Hanson 2003, 318–19).

Council member Laura Miller, as a candidate for mayor in 2002, called for renewed discourse regarding Dallas's need for a strong-mayor form of government (Gurwitt 1993); however, the city's Charter Review Commission believed her request lacked citizen interest. In 2004 then-Mayor Miller's desire for a strong-mayor system of government became obvious, as she clashed publicly with the city manager, who retired partly because of the constant attacks on him by the mayor. In the end "those proposals went nowhere, the political equivalents of a snowball in a fireplace" (Sweany 2005, 51).

## First Change Effort: The Blackwood Proposal

In fall 2004 Dallas attorney Beth Ann Blackwood launched a petition drive to place the strong mayor proposition on the ballot. Blackwood, citing her frustrations with the inefficiencies, delays, distractions, and infighting at city hall, ran for city council, stating, "If you look at how things have been working on the City Council, they don't work quickly, they don't work efficiently, and they don't work effectively. . . . I don't think that's the fault of the people who are down there. I think that's the system they're trying to work with" (Sweany 2005, 48). To achieve her goal of changing Dallas city government for the better, Blackwood formed a nonprofit corporation she named Citizens for a Strong Mayor. Consulting the Local Government Code in the Texas statutes, Blackwood discovered she could get an item on the ballot if she collected twenty thousand signatures from eligible voters (Sweany 2005, 49). Blackwood collected tens of thousands of signatures getting the proposal on the ballot, something uncommon in Dallas (*Dallas Morning News* 2004). Proposition 1, otherwise known as the Blackwood Proposal, called for revamping sections of the city charter, among other things, to eliminate the city manager form of government, and replace it instead with a strong-mayor system common in big cities such as New York and Chicago (Falkenberg 2005, A5; Webb 2005).

Under the proposed Blackwood amendment, the newly empowered mayor would serve as the chief executive officer of the city, assuming powers previously held by the city manager; would have hiring and firing control over the police chief and other top posts; and would have greater control to issue rules and regulations governing city departments (Curry 2005; Webb 2005). "If the referendum passes, Ms. Miller would have the biggest patronage operation this side of Chicago," according to one opponent (Jeffers 2005a, B4). However, the council would still be responsible for setting policy, making laws, passing ordinances, allocating money, and dealing with constituent issues. Additionally, the city council would receive additional checks and balances to include the power to conduct an independent audit and vote to impeach or remove the mayor with a two-thirds vote on grounds of misconduct (Curry 2005). Blackwood's version of the strong-mayor system was much stronger than the version Mayor Laura Miller proposed to the city council. While Miller attempted to have the city council place her version before the voters, Blackwood followed the petition route. Blackwood found funding for this massive petition campaign from power brokers, financial backers, and wealthy donors who live in the Park Cities, a wealthy enclave north of downtown. In December 2004 the city secretary certified Blackwood's proposal to be placed on the May 7, 2005, ballot (Levinthal 2005a, B8; Ramshaw 2005a, B1).

Despite the fact that talks of governance change had swirled around city hall for decades, Blackwood's proposal raised the ire of many at city hall who considered her a pawn of big business and drew the admiration of others who were proponents of change to the current form of government. "One year ago, few people outside of legal circles had heard of her. Now she is one of the most talked about people in Dallas, a figure some see as the savior of city government and others as its curse" (Sweany 2005, 48). The unassuming Blackwood was considered an upstart, an interloper, and an outsider despite having lived in parts of Dallas for sixteen years (Sweany 2005, 49). What angered her detractors most was not her call for a new system of city government but her ability to maneuver around the city council and, through the citizens directly, get her proposal to change the city's charter on the May 7 ballot. Blackwood's success in going to the voters with one simple question, "Do you want to eliminate the office of city manager and transfer those powers to the mayor in an effort to create accountability at City Hall?" unwittingly challenged the city council's decision, made after the 2003 Charter Review Commission findings, to oppose changes in the city charter (Sweany 2005, 51).

Blackwood methods followed those used by the founders of many of our nation's governing documents, including the Declaration of Independence. Each was created by smaller groups of our founding fathers, which were then taken to the people for support (Curry 2005). Blackwood noted that the Dallas amendment was a near carbon copy of Houston's strong-mayor charter, which had been in existence for more than fifty years (Curry 2005). Further, she asserted that Houston, unlike Dallas, with a better employment picture and a growing downtown tax base, had not been the focus of Justice Department civil rights cases over its charter (Curry 2005). Blackwood asserted, "There's always the old knee-jerk reaction against change. I've heard comments from people who say this is extreme, this is radical, or this is way out there.

Frankly, those people either haven't read the charter, or they've read it and didn't understand it, or they have another agenda" (Sweany 2005, 49).

Laura Miller, who served on the city council before succeeding Kirk as mayor, said the Blackwood Proposal was "the tonic needed to pull the city out of its doldrums" (LaMasters 2005). Miller argued that a strong mayor would gain the needed political capital through her power to formulate budgets and name department heads strategically and effectively to create and implement a new vision for the city. "With the power of the chief executive, the mayor can move decisively," according to Sweany (2005, 51).

However, Miller endorsed the Blackwood plan only after council members rejected her own strong-mayor proposal. Miller called the current system "an inefficient bureaucratic traffic jam that promotes deadlock, mediocre leadership and stifles progress" (Falkenberg 2005, A5). Miller's constant frustration was that the only leader elected citywide that the citizens could hold accountable, the mayor, was virtually powerless. Instead, Miller asserted the city manager, a nonelected career administrator, was in fact the person with power. Further, Miller stated, "You've got elected officials who are idealistic and frisky and making lots of promises on the sad shape of the city and they come in and it's a complete clash between the elected folks and the bureaucrats" (Falkenberg 2005, A5). Miller, a frequent critic of city hall and its workers, as a journalist, a member of the city council, and then as mayor, was considered by many to be abrasive and unnecessarily aggressive. She, much like Blackwood, stated that she was frustrated with the lack of accountability in Dallas's current system of government. Miller stated, "I spent the first two years as mayor trying, trying to get a better city manager, and no one on the council supported me . . . and that manager hired an idiot to be a police chief without even interviewing anybody" (LaMasters 2005).

As a vocal proponent of the strong-mayor initiative, initially Miller was supportive of the Blackwood Proposal, particularly once it gained recognition, support, and momentum, something Miller never expected. Soon after, however, she changed her mind and blasted the proposal as "unworkable and too extreme" and announced the formation of her own committee, called Stronger Mayor, Stronger Dallas (Sweany 2005, 51). According to Brian Sweany, writer for *D Magazine*, "There was no way [Miller] was going to let Blackwood take all the credit, should the measure pass" (2005, 186). However, when Miller unveiled her own strong-mayor plan to the council, the plan was "dead on arrival" as her plan incited feelings that "ran so high at the Horseshoe that a shouting match broke out, uniting the members of the Council in such a way that happens as often as an 800-year flood" (51).

In the end Miller, overshadowed by Blackwood and feeling she had to make the issue her own, supported the Blackwood Proposal because she had no other choice; it was the only proposal on the ballot. "Because this goes into effect in September, there's only one person in the city who can talk about how it's going to work, and that's me," Miller stated (Sweany 2005, 186). One thing was clear: both Blackwood and Miller, having hired the most powerful political consultants in town, Bryan Eppstein and Rob Allyn respectively, were not working together; however, they were working toward the same goal (Sweany 2005, 186).

On May 7, 2005, voters in the city of Dallas went to the polls to let the mayor and city council know whether they supported the strong-mayor form of government over the council–manager system. Feelings about the strong-mayor proposal divided Dallas voters economically, racially, and geographically. The decision to maintain the current council–manager system or significantly increase mayoral power also closely followed ethnic, regional, and economic divisions. The referendum, designed by lawyer Blackwood, was overwhelmingly rejected at the polls by a 62 to 38 percent margin (Ramshaw 2005e). This loss came primarily as a result of unprecedented voter turnout in the southern sections of Dallas, which are primarily minority; many North Dallas whites favored the measure while most blacks in southern Dallas were opposed (Curry 2005).

## Arguments on Both Sides

The city of Dallas was divided on what form of government was needed. Many felt the current council–manager plan adopted in the early '90s worked well and were afraid of what could happen under a strong-mayor form of government. Others called for a shift to a mayor–council form of government. Each side had staunch supporters and constituent support.

### Pro-Strong Mayor

Supporters of the strong-mayor form of government believed it was exactly what Dallas needed to rid itself of its high crime rate, rebuild downtown, attract new business, and stimulate a city, "hollowed by suburban development," back onto a trajectory of growth (Falkenberg 2005, A5). The Citizens for a Strong Mayor campaign argued that Dallas needed change; a switch from Dallas's deadlocked council–manager form of government where the city operated as "14 mini-cities with 14 mini-mayors demanding attention" (Curry 2005). Royce Hanson, former dean of the School of Social Sciences at the University of Texas at Dallas, now professor at George Washington University, in Washington, D.C., and the author of *Civic Culture and Urban Change: Governing Dallas*, stated, "This is a fairly straightforward strong-mayor proposal" that "strikes a good balance between the powers of the mayor and the Council" (Sweany 2005, 51). Hanson noted an unusual feature in the Dallas proposal, one not normally found in strong-mayor governments: the mayor would remain part of the city council. Hanson stated, "[Keeping the mayor as a member of the city council] has the advantage of giving the Council more influence. . . . It has a salutary effect because the mayor has to face their questions. Mayors sometimes have a tendency to take themselves too seriously, and this assures that they are working with the Council" (Sweany 2005, 51).

The strong-mayor proposal garnered support from more than thirty thousand citizens, primarily from the business community and North Dallas residents (Ramshaw 2005a, B1). E. Edward Okpa II, who owns a real estate business in Dallas, contributed $10,000 to the proposal because he believed Dallas needed to elect a leader voters can hold accountable for successes and failures (Falkenberg 2005, A5). *D Magazine* editor and publisher Wick Allison along with Robert Decherd, the chairman, president, and CEO of Belo Corporation, which owns the *Dallas Morning News,* supported the strong-mayor proposal; a "strange pairing, given that Allison's two favorite pastimes are fly-fishing and lobbing grenades at the *News"* (Sweany 2005, 51). Miller and former mayor Ron Kirk agreed that the mayor should have more power, despite the rebuff they both received when they asked their respective city councils to create a plan allowing the mayor to hire and fire the city manager (LaMasters 2005).

Miller, one of the most visible supporters of the Blackwood Proposal, argued that the current system was mired in conflict and needed a strong-mayor system that would hold the council accountable to the public as well as improve the delivery of services. Miller wrote in a letter to supporters that she wanted to see a strong mayor in charge of making city services work, a government solving rather than politically debating issues (Curry 2005). Many Dallas citizens, in interviews and letters to the editor, said that they supported the Blackwood Proposal because it would allow voters to have a direct voice in the person who runs the city while also providing accountability to the public; if the "strong mayor" is unable to carry out campaign promises, the voters will have one person to hold responsible (Curry 2005).

According to the Citizens for a Strong Mayor campaign, "Not one person [in the current system] can ever be held accountable when mistakes and wrong decisions are made. The council points to the mayor, who points to the city manager, who points back to the mayor, etc. This leaves the citizens of Dallas with nothing but to accept the status quo, which is raising property and crime rates coupled with a failing economy and downtown tax base" (Curry 2005).

A poll conducted by Rob Allyn, Mayor Miller's political strategist, in late January, showed Miller with a 62.5 percent approval rating among Dallas residents most likely to vote. At that time, the poll indicated 50.5 percent said they would vote for the initiative with 38 percent opposed, and 11.5 percent undecided. These numbers indi-cated, and supported Miller's belief, that she could win the strong-mayor referendum, even if the city council was against the measure (Sweany 2005, 186). Certainly, atti-tudes and opinions about Miller played heavily in voters' decisions on the proposition. Support for Miller was closely aligned with voter preference on the referendum; those who said they would vote for the proposal also voted for Miller in 2003 (Curry 2005). Her combative style, however, resulted in strong opposition to her in the minority communities and among most members of the city council. She was clearly not a facilitative leader.

## Opponents of Strong Mayor

Beth Ann Blackwood, author of the proposed strong-mayor charter amendment, asserted during a debate with local businessmen that "Dallas is in crisis," with the nation's highest crime rate and a declining downtown tax base (Curry 2005). Max Wells, a banker and former city councilman for nine years, opposed the amendment because the Blackwood Proposal "goes too far," gives "too much power to one person," was created without citizen involvement, and would "lead to lengthy litigation" from civil rights violations under federal and state law as well as conflicts with the city charter (Curry 2005).

All fourteen council members publicly opposed the Blackwood Proposal, finding its changes to the city charter too sweeping. Minority leaders were concerned that a strong-mayor form of government would diminish minority influence at city hall, thereby allowing one well-established group to again take over Dallas politics (Jeffers 2005c, B1). Councilman James Fantroy, who disagreed with the potential shift to a strong-mayor form of government, said, "The devil is running loose in Dallas . . . in the form of a petition drive to eliminate the city manager and expand the power of the mayor. . . . It's a slap in the face to minority representation" (Sweany 2005, 48). For African American members of the council, the Blackwood petition mirrored past attempts to suppress the rights and voices of the minority population (Levinthal 2005b, B8; Jeffers 2005c, B1). Fantroy maintained that Dallas's current government works well citing several recent accomplishments, including the Trinity River Project, the Victory Park development, and the creation of a University of North Texas satellite campus in South Dallas (Sweany 2005, 48).

In an election that many saw as a referendum on Mayor Laura Miller, some political analysts said the final outcome indicated that Dallas residents did not trust her to take on greater authority. Some felt the mayor was a polarizing figure with "her hands in too many places, leaving open the opportunity to install cronies and yes men" (Sweany 2005, 51). "It's a referendum on her leadership," said Rufus Shaw Jr., a political analyst specializing in southern-sector Dallas issues. "She has not done a good job of dealing with her own council, the city management staff, and especially, the African-American community" (Ramshaw 2005e). One leading businessman said, "It's not that they don't like the idea of a strong mayor, they just don't like the fact that Laura Miller probably is going to end up as the first strong mayor of Dallas" (Falkenberg 2005, 5A).

Miller, a former journalist-turned-politician, is known for her sharp tongue, unfiltered responses, and go-it-alone style. She was credited with ousting the city's first black police chief, whom the city manager fired for poor job performance, because of her constant public criticism of him. Miller referred to Bolton as "an idiot" during a strong-mayor debate (Falkenberg 2005, A5). Many of the opponents of the switch to mayor–council government felt that Laura Miller was the problem (Sweany 2005, 48). "She got people scared, that's what it is. They don't know what she might do," said Carl Simon, a barber in Dallas's predominantly black southern sector who voted against the proposal in the May 7 election. "Would you get you a dog that bites and put him in your house?" (Falkenberg 2005, A5).

Initially, the Dallas Citizens Council, an organization consisting of leadership from Dallas's more than one hundred largest businesses, remained silent. However, by January 2005, the Dallas Citizens Council began to use its influential membership, including former mayor Ron Kirk, to oppose the strong-mayor proposal. The DCC launched a fundraising campaign headed by influential Dallas business leaders to raise money to support the Coalition for Open Government, a political action committee formed in an attempt to defeat Blackwood (Jeffers 2005a, B4). The DCC became active in the campaign against strong-mayor government because it believed it would lead to patronage and public corruption (Jeffers 2005b, B1).

Former mayor Ron Kirk, an earlier advocate for a strong-mayor form of government who debated against Miller on the Blackwood Proposal, called it a "radical reconstruction of our entire constitution" (Falkenberg 2005, A5). He described the proposal "as a divisive, almost diabolical plan that would push the city over a cliff" (LaMasters 2005) and asserted the Blackwood version was "the most unhealthy concentration of power in a mayor than anything I've seen anywhere" (Falkenberg 2005, A5). Kirk believed the proposal gave the mayor too much power, lacked adequate checks and balances, diminished the city council's power, and "came to voters through a petition drive, rather than through council negotiations" (Falkenberg 2005, A5).

Further, Kirk, as a member of the Dallas Citizens Council and long-time advocate for Dallas's minority communities, said, "the Blackwood proposal would confirm the fears of minority residents who say the plan would diminish their clout at City Hall" (LaMasters 2005). "We would return to the days when a handful of people get into a room and make the decisions for the rest of us. . . . If Blackwood passes, they [minorities] would be right. . . . I want us to go for a strong-mayor form of government, but I want us all to go together," Kirk said (LaMasters 2005). Five other former Dallas mayors joined him in expressing opposition.

The Greater Dallas Chamber of Commerce's Executive Committee and Charter Review Committee, after studying the arguments for and against the Blackwood Proposal, concluded that the Blackwood amendments, as designed, would make "sweeping changes to the way the City of Dallas would be governed" (Ramshaw 2005c, B1) and asserted that the amendments were "flawed" (Greater Dallas Chamber of Commerce 2005). The Chamber was "specifically concerned with the amount of power concentrated in one position, inadequate checks and balances, conflicts with state law, issues with the federal Voting Rights Act, and the amount, cost, and duration of litigation which could be expected if these amendments were to pass" (Greater Dallas Chamber of Commerce 2005; Ramshaw 2005c, B1). Further, the Chamber added, "The City Charter is the constitution of the City of Dallas. We hope the citizens of Dallas will amend it in a way that provides our charter with the dignity it deserves" (Greater Dallas Chamber of Commerce 2005). The DCC joined efforts to commission a report that legally challenged the proposal, citing conflict with state and federal laws (Jeffers 2005a, B4; Ramshaw 2005b, B1).

As the campaign continued, other coalitions, such as the Dallas Future Political Action Committee, the Committee for a Responsible Change, and Citizens for a Better Dallas, began to form and join the collaborative effort between the DCC and the Dallas City Council. For African American residents, the message spread by the Dallas Future Political Action Committee, subsequently funded by the DCC, spoke of fairness, justice, and opposition to Mayor Laura Miller. Hispanic residents heard a particular message from the Coalition of Open Government, also funded by the DCC, forecasting the loss of their seat at Dallas's political table. The message of a strong mayor split white voters and essentially muted their voice in the election. In the end, Dallas voters sent a clear message to retain council–manager government.

The nonprofit African American Pastors' Coalition (AAPC) said it opposed the proposed strong-mayor charter amendment and would mobilize its fifty thousand congregates to vote against it (Webb 2005). "After carefully studying the issues, we have determined that this proposal does not help make Dallas a better city," said Dr. Jerry L. Christian, president of the nonprofit and senior pastor of Kirkwood Temple CME Church in Oak Cliff (Webb 2005). The AAPC argued that the proposal conflicted with the Voting Rights Act of 1965 because it would weaken the single-member district system already in place (Webb 2005). The AAPC Coalition also expressed its strong support for the position of city manager and believed that the current system had dealt with minority issues fairly over the years (Webb 2005).

## Dallas's Second Attempt at Strong Mayor

While the various business groups opposed the Blackwood Proposal, they were not opposed to a change to strong-mayor government. Further, the city council opposed the Blackwood Proposal partly because it viewed its defeat as a mandate to put forth its own charter amendment to expand the powers of the council members. Supportive of the strong-mayor concept, the DCC and other Dallas business leaders urged Dallas's fourteen council members to pledge their support to the initiative by signing a document to place their resolution on an upcoming agenda (Levinthal 2005c, 1B). Dallas Citizens Council chairwoman Elaine Agather stated the DCC would ensure the Blackwood proposal would fail, because if the council's proposal failed, the DCC would seek out the necessary signatures itself to get the petition on the ballot (Levinthal and Ramshaw 2005, B15).

One month before the May 2005 election on the Blackwood Proposal, a majority of the city council approved holding a nonbinding referendum on an alternative plan should Proposition 1 be defeated. In an attempt to impede the Blackwood Proposal, the DCC gave the Coalition for Open Government $200,000 to counter the effort (Jeffers 2005d, B9; Levinthal 2005c, B1), thereby providing the opposition with double the amount of money as those who supported Blackwood's proposal (Ramshaw and Levinthal 2005, B13). The second referendum called for a November 2005 vote on a proposal that would have made additional, more moderate changes than the proposal rejected by Dallas voters in May 2005 (*Governing* 2005; Ramshaw 2005d, B11) and would also include giving the mayor power to appoint and remove the city manager or allowing a council majority to terminate the manager.

Additionally, a coalition of Dallas City Council members and local business leaders designed Proposition 1 in spring 2005 to persuade voters to defeat the May referendum that would have eliminated the city manager position and increased mayoral power (Ramshaw 2005e). Proposition 1, endorsed by the Dallas Citizens Council and the Greater Dallas Chamber, was designed to give the mayor authority to hire and fire the city manager as well as to draft the budget in coordination with the city manager. The city council would have been empowered to fire the manager with a simple majority and hire a budget oversight officer to counterbalance the mayor's fiscal power (Ramshaw 2005e). However, the AAPC, with its seventy-strong ministerial membership of more than fifty thousand congregation members, opposed the Dallas City Council's plan for an alternative plan to the strong-mayor amendment. The AAPC recommended allowing the findings of a June 2003 charter review commission be the starting point for any further deliberation. The 2003 charter commission effectively left all authority with the city manager while only marginally strengthening the city council (Webb 2005).

Interestingly, once Proposition 1 was on the ballot for the November referendum, several Dallas City Council members pulled their support, including Mayor Pro Tem Don Hill and council member Ed Oakley, both originators of the plan. Oakley and council member Bill Blaydes withdrew their support for the proposition after Miller attempted to derail a council-supported tax abatement for businessman Ray Hunt. Oakley maintained, "It was a turning point for me. And it angered people to the extent that they got engaged in this campaign. . . . They saw what too much power in the hands of one individual with a personal agenda could do" (Ramshaw 2005e). Additionally, an opposition campaign began to gain ground weeks before the vote, sending out mailers and drawing defecting council members into its ranks.

In November 2005, for the second time in six months, Dallas voters defeated a ballot measure designed to increase mayoral power (*Governing* 2005; Ramshaw 2005e) with 49,020 (46 percent) voting for and 57,487 (54 percent)[2] voting against Proposition 1. "Trounced at the polls—the result of unprecedented voter turnout in the southern sector and deep divisions in north Dallas," the defeat of the November referendum sent a forceful message that the citizens of Dallas were either satisfied with the city's form of government or afraid of the alternative (Ramshaw 2005e; Jeffers 2005e, A1). According to the mayor pro tem, Don Hill, the defeat was "an earthquake event in this city, and it means the southern sector will be a very big player in the next mayoral election" (Ramshaw 2005f, A22). According to the Dallas County elections administrator, Bruce Sherbet, voter turnout was high at 17 percent for a constitutional amendment election with no candidates on the ballot (Ramshaw 2005e); however, Sherbet attributed the increase to a contentious statewide gay-marriage-ban proposal, not Proposition 1. Still, Sherbet maintained that voters were apathetic on the issue as ballot vote totals were well below those in the earlier May election. Sherbet stated, "It's just a different animal completely" (Ramshaw 2005e). However, Sherbet maintained the voter breakdown between the November 2005 and the earlier May election was similar with southern-sector voters strongly opposed to, and northern voters divided on, the change-in-form proposition (Ramshaw 2005e). Ultimately, "the Dallas Citizens Council was the big loser. It put tens of thousands of dollars behind Proposition 1, mobilized long before the opposition and still saw voters defeat it" (Ramshaw 2005e).

For some citizens of Dallas, the vote had nothing to do with the wavering city council, while others wondered why they should champion a referendum "orphaned by its authors," the city council (Ramshaw 2005e). One voter said, "The council just broke and ran over the last couple of weeks, and that led voters to say, 'If you're not confident in this, neither are we.' . . . The council's erratic behavior has engendered doubt in Dallas voters" (Ramshaw 2005e). However, many voters simply did not trust the mayor and the increased powers and authority she would be granted. One Dallas voter said, "I really can't bring myself to vote for any strong-mayor proposal, especially with our mayor at this time" (Ramshaw 2005e).

*Governing* online (2005) noted: "Mayor Laura Miller, a supporter of a strong mayorship, may have sunk the referendum by clashing with her city council in recent weeks. She would have been better served if she had followed the example of Richmond, Virginia Mayor Doug Wilder: create a strong mayorship, THEN get elected mayor and ONLY THEN clash with the city council."

Miller, however, rejected the idea that the election was a referendum on her performance because, as she stated, "Ron Kirk campaigned for this, not me" (Ramshaw 2005d, B11). Kirk, who helped craft and campaign for the second referendum calling for a stronger-mayor proposal, said, "I think those of us that felt it was time for Dallas to take a different approach now have to accept that and take a step back to digest it" (Ramshaw 2005d, B11). Miller agreed, saying, "Voters have had two bites at the apple now, and have voted twice for the status quo" (Ramshaw 2005d, B11).


## Conclusion

Dallas presents an interesting case in the battle for form of government in one of the nation's major cities because the source of its strength is the minority community. In the early years of council–manager government, the Dallas city government was closely aligned with the business community. Dallas adopted council–manager government initially out of a desire to remove politics from city hall and have a professional city manager run the day-to-day affairs of the city. Certainly, the partnership between city hall and the business community, primarily through the Dallas Citizens Council, lasted until the federal courts mandated that the at-large system be abandoned and that fourteen council districts be formed to ensure minority representation on the city council.

Most observers in Dallas believe that the first fifteen years under the new district system has been a difficult adjustment for the community. For the first time, African American and Hispanic voters chose representatives of their neighborhoods to serve on the city council. Rather than having a small council of like-minded citizens making decisions on the allocation of resources and major policy matters, the city council now had a relatively large, diverse group governing for the first time. In addition the business community had lost much of its clout under the new system, and many of its leaders felt that the democratic process that played out in the newspaper and on television was too messy and inefficient and impeded Dallas's progress.

There were several factors that led to the defeat of both proposals.

1. Mayor Laura Miller was a polarizing figure who battled constantly with other members of the city council and with the city manager. She had been a crusading journalist who was highly critical of the city council before she ran for the council. While serving on the council, she continued to be outspoken in her criticism and opposition to many of her fellow elected officials. Although many voters

admired her courage and, as a result, elected her as mayor, she was not a facilitator but a divider. Many of her targets were minority council members who made no secret of their dislike for her. Her constant criticism of the city manager, who was Hispanic, and the police chief, who was African American, also created problems for her in the minority communities. The minority communities voted overwhelmingly against both the Blackwood Proposal and the DCC-backed plan because of their dislike and distrust of Mayor Miller.

2. Blackwood was an outsider who single-handedly decided to take on the establishment by circulating a petition calling for the change in form of government. While the mayor and city council members sparred over the wording of a plan to empower the mayor, Blackwood usurped their roles as leaders of the effort to change the form of government. In addition, her plan included several objectionable provisions that would give the mayor significant powers in his or her relationship with the city council. As a result, former mayor Kirk, as a member of the DCC, decided that the Blackwood plan was not a good one for Dallas. Kirk had advocated greater powers for the position when he was mayor, but he did not want to eliminate the city manager. He desired for the mayor to be able to appoint the city manager and have other executive authority but not to the extent envisioned by Blackwood.

3. The city council united with the DCC to oppose the Blackwood Proposal during the first referendum. The DCC pledged $200,000 to a PAC to oppose Blackwood, which was twice as much as the Blackwood supporters had to promote it. The agreement with the council to oppose Blackwood was based on the understanding that the council would place on the ballot in November its own plan to change to a strong-mayor system. After Blackwood was defeated, the council did place the matter before the public in a form that more nearly reflected former mayor Kirk's earlier proposal. However, actions by Mayor Miller, as cited above, and the uneasiness in the minority communities to change a system that had worked well for them led to defection by council members. A majority of the council opposed the very measure that they had placed on the ballot in light of the overwhelming opposition to it in the minority communities.

In conclusion, the issue of form of government in Dallas was not decided on the merits of council–manager government. It was decided for reasons of political power— dislike of Mayor Miller by minorities, influence of council members in the decision-making process, and fear by minority leaders that the strong-mayor system would return power to the white majority living primarily in the northern neighborhoods of Dallas. Apparently, council–manager government had worked for minority neighborhoods despite the apparent public contentiousness of the political process.

# Notes

1. U.S. Census Burea. 1960 dataset.

2. From Dallas County Elections Department. Accessed November 27, 2008, from www .dalcoelections.org/archiveresults/november82005/UPDATES.HTML.

# References

Aaron, Kimberly. 2008. A new stadium, a new city: The Dallas Cowboys' quest for a new playing field. In *Building the local economy: Cases in economic development*, by Douglas J. Watson and John C. Morris, 175–89. Athens, GA: Carl Vinson Institute of Government.

Allison, Wick. 2005. Strong mayors built Dallas. *D Magazine*, March 1.

Blumenthal, Ralph. 2004. The heady days of J. R. and Landry are history in humbled Dallas. *New York Times*, December 20. www.newyorktimes.com/2004/12/20/national/20dallas.html (accessed October 2, 2008).

Clyde, Andrew, Bob Lukefahr, Harry Quarls, and Keo Rubbright. 2004. *Dallas at the tipping point.* Commissioned Work, Dallas: Booz Allen Hamilton.

Curry, Kerry. 2005. Association sponsors strong-mayor debate. *Dallas Business Journal*, March 17.

*The Dallas Morning News*. A history of Dallas governance. *The Dallas Morning News*, December 12, 2004, 12B.

Ennis, Michael. 2005. What's the matter with Dallas? *Texas Monthly*, July 5.

Falkenberg, Lisa. 2005. Dallas mayor's proposal scares, splits voters. Associated Press, May 1.

Find Law for Legal Professionals. 1978. *U.S. Supreme Court—Wise v. Lipscomb, 434 U.S. 1329 (1977)*. June 22. http://laws.findlaw.com/us/434/1329.html (accessed March 12, 2008).

*Governing*. 2005. 13th Floor: Dallas "strong mayor" vote fails narrowly. November 8. http://13thfloor.governing.com/2005/11/dallas_strong_m.html (accessed September 11, 2008).

Graff, Harvey J. 2008. *The Dallas myth: The making and unmaking of an American city.* Minneapolis: University of Minnesota Press.

Greater Dallas Chamber of Commerce. 2005. *Greater Dallas Chamber opposes Blackwood charter amendments.* March 2. http://news.dallaschamber.org/e_article000366817.cfm?x=b11,0,w (accessed April 5, 2008).

Gurwitt, Rob. 2006. Can Dallas govern itself? *Governing*. Congressional Quarterly. August. www.governing.com/archive/2006/aug/dallas.txt (accessed September 22, 2008).

———. 1997. Nobody in charge: When everyone seems to be running a city, there's a good chance it isn't being run at all. *Governing*. Congressional Quarterly. September. www.governing.com/archive/1997/sept/cities.txt (accessed September 20, 2008).

———. 1993. The lure of the strong mayor. *Governing*. Congressional Quarterly. July. www.governing.com/archive/1993/jul/mayor.txt (accessed September 22, 2008).

Hanson, Royce. 2003. *Civic culture and urban change: Governing Dallas.* Detroit: Wayne State University Press.

Hassett, Wendy L., and Douglas J. Watson. 2007. *Civic battles: When cities change their form of government.* Boca Raton, FL: PrAcademics Press.

Hazel, Michael V. 1997. *Dallas: A history of "Big D."* Austin: Texas State Historical Association.

Jeffers, Gromer. 2005a. Citizens Council could tip strong-mayor debate. *Dallas Morning News*, February 1.

———. 2005b. Kirk joins strong-mayor debate—He's working to defeat the Dallas plan, and he might offer alternative. *Dallas Morning News*, February 15.

———. 2005c. Strong mayor sticky for blacks on council—With districts against any plan, support for option could fuel fallout. *Dallas Morning News*, March 21.

———. 2005d. Voters, prepare to be educated. *Dallas Morning News*, March 22.

———. 2005e. Latest setback fuels zeal to unseat Miller—Potential foes see failed plans as ammo for '07, but mayor unbowed. *Dallas Morning News*, November 10.

LaMasters, Byron. 2005. *Ron Kirk, Laura Miller debate strong mayor.* April 8. http://www.burnt orangereport.com/archives/003666.html (accessed September 20, 2008).

Leslie, Warren. 1964. *Dallas public and private: Aspects of an American city.* New York: Grossman Publishers.

Levinthal, Dave. 2005a. It's official: Dallas mayor behind vote—Miller considers own strong-mayor fundraising effort. *Dallas Morning News,* January 4.

———. 2005b. Lipscomb likens Miller to Nazis—Ex-council member blasts strong-mayor effort as a power grab. *Dallas Morning News,* January 6.

———. 2005c. Council to craft own strong-mayor plan—Members to vote on nonbinding resolution; specifics not released. *Dallas Morning News,* March 9.

Levinthal, Dave, and Emily Ramshaw. 2005. Miller: Don't credit me for strong-mayor plan. *Dallas Morning News,* March 20.

Mobley, Jane. 1988. Politician or professional? The debate over who should run our cities continues. *Governing.* February. www.governing.com/archive/1988/feb/managers.txt (accessed September 22, 2008).

Payne, Darwin. 2000. Big D: Triumphs and troubles of an American supercity in the 20th century. Rev. ed. Dallas, Texas: Three Forks Press.

Ramshaw, Emily. 2005a. Strong-Mayor foes are a diverse mix—Some fear differing strategies will hurt efforts to keep system. *Dallas Morning News,* January 9.

———. 2005b. Conflicts cited with mayor referendum—Details may violate state, federal laws attorneys say; sponsor defends proposal. *Dallas Morning News,* February 18.

———. 2005c. Council urged to budge on charter—Plans presented would strengthen mayor but retain city manager. *Dallas Morning News,* March 2.

———. 2005d. Mayoral power vote is stirring up less of a fuss—Dallas: This election so far lacks campaign blitz that accompanied May's. *Dallas Morning News,* September 27.

———. 2005e. Dallas rejects strong mayor: Some say second defeat in 6 months signals lack of trust in Miller. *Dallas Morning News,* November 9. ww.dallasnews.com/sharedcontent/dws/news/localnews/stories/110905 dnmetnudalmay or.332a8bc.html (accessed September 20, 2008).

———. 2005f. Southern Dallas shows muscle—Northern sections, for 2nd election in a row, sent mixed signals. *Dallas Morning News,* November 10.

Ramshaw, Emily, and Dave Levinthal. 2005. Latest donors help strong-mayor foes dwarf funding for supporters—Council candidates also report where their war chests stand. *Dallas Morning News,* April 30.

Svara, James H. 2008. *The facilitative leader in city hall: Reexamining the scope and contributions.* Edited by James H. Svara. Boca Raton, FL: CRC Press (Taylor & Francis, Ltd.).

Sweany, Brian D. 2005. Can a strong mayor save Dallas? *D Magazine,* March 1.

Texas House of Representatives. 1991. *Texas Legislature Online.* April 25. www.legis.state.tx.us/BillLookup/History.aspx?LegSess=72R&Bill=HB2238 (accessed March 14, 2008).

U.S. Court of Appeals. 1976. *U.S. Court of Appeals—Cases and Opinions.* http://cases.justia.com/us-court-of-appeals/F2/551/1043/43795/ (accessed March 12, 2008).

U.S. Supreme Court Center. 1978. *U.S. Supreme Court Cases and Opinions—Wise v. Lipscomb, 437 U.S. 535 (1978).* June 22. http://supreme.justia.com/us/437/535/case.html (accessed March 12, 2008).

Webb, Cynthia D. 2005. Pastors' coalition opposes strong mayor proposal. *Dallas Business Journal,* April 4.

CHAPTER 11

# CINCINNATI

## Charter Conflict and Consensus

JOHN T. SPENCE

The truth is that there is no magic in a mechanism of government and no salvation in a charter alone. Forms of government may and do aid in the formulation and realization of the people's will, but the fundamental thing is the spirit and temper of the people, their alertness, their commonsense, their leadership, their energy, and their determination to establish sound standards of city government.

—Charles E. Merriam, *Commercial Tribune*, 1924

## The Dynamic of Charter Change

PROPOSALS FOR SYSTEMIC CHANGE to the processes of local government are efforts to create institutional structures anticipated to be better able to respond to challenges to a city's vitality. In Cincinnati proposed changes have reflected either a community decision (petition by voters) or a decision by the ruling elite (petition by the council) to place charter amendments before the voters. Successfully adopted charter amendments often have resulted in shifting political power, and like any other political resource, a city's charter can be manipulated and used to protect and enhance the power of one set of actors or used to move power toward an alternative set of political actors, each with a different prescription for what ails a city's vitality.

Arguments for charter change may be more or less able to galvanize a majority of the voting public at any one point in time; the larger social and economic context within which the argument for change is taking place is also influential. In Cincinnati it has often taken a prolonged period of argument and counterargument among political actors, with social and economic factors often providing the tipping point sufficient for the public to support a charter change.

Particularly since the 1980s, proposed charter change in Cincinnati has reflected "a disposition to tinker with rather than overhaul the political and governmental system" (Miller 1997, 33). Although the community faced major challenges to its economic vitality and social stability, partisan interests focused their energies on modifying the structure of city government in order to increase their political influence. Simultaneously, individuals and special interests wanted to change the rules of the game to achieve their particular political goals. The intensity and longevity of this political conflict resulted in incremental, politically feasible, charter changes rather than more comprehensive and perhaps more appropriate changes to addressing larger community concerns.

Charter amendment proposals were many and varied, and attempts to create a more concerted vision for structural reform were generally unsuccessful, particularly in the 1990s. Not only were the different visions conflicting but they were also often viewed as potentially having negative consequences. For example, Charterites opposed any reform that was seen as diminishing city manager status, African American groups opposed reforms seen as potentially reducing their political clout, and Democrats and Republicans did not trust one another's motives.[1]

The consequence of this extended period of political conflict was a perception that Cincinnati government was unable to resolve important community challenges because it was self-absorbed with what was seen as trivial politics. When, with each new reform effort, the public did not see progress toward solutions to these community challenges, criticism of city hall increased. The recognition that substantive reform was necessary, however, became pervasive, and eventually the focus of reform became centered on empowering the mayor.

## Historical Reform in Cincinnati

Council–manager government in Cincinnati was adopted in the 1920s after a prolonged period of political conflict between a Republican Party–led boss system and political reformers composed of independent Republicans and Democrats who eventually formed the City Charter Committee.

Upon the adoption of council–manager government in 1924, the City Charter Committee essentially transformed itself into a political party and, in 1926, asked voters to adopt another charter amendment, further refining the changes made two years earlier. This new charter called for the mayor to be selected by the council, preside at meetings, be the ceremonial head of government, and have the power to appoint some members of city boards and commissions. The city manager was charged with organizing the administration of city government, appointing and managing department heads, developing an annual budget, and serving as a nonvoting member on the Planning Commission.

Though the city experienced many political changes over the decades following the adoption of council–manager government, including an increasing independence of council candidates from their political parties, the mayor's selection by the members of the council was unaffected. However, with growing social and economic problems associated with demographic changes in the city and upheavals in race relations, ideas for developing a stronger political leadership or an elected executive to address these challenges began to surface. In 1976 Republicans sponsored a charter amendment providing for the direct election of the mayor. The rationale for the proposed change was explained by John Hermanies, the Hamilton County Republican executive committee chairman: "People are tired of not knowing who is going to be mayor after a council election . . . people look for the mayor to be a leader, and there is no leadership when the mayor serves for a year" (Bauer 1976). The Charterite and Democrat Coalition reacted by proposing that the mayor be the top vote-getter in the council elections. However, that alternative failed to make the ballot, and the Republican effort failed at the polls. Meanwhile, the city's population fell by 200,000 during the 1970s, and much of the downtown business community left for the suburbs (Miller 1997, 33).

Cincinnati entered the 1980s with a political system primed for change. The city was set to enter a prolonged period of social and political conflict, eventually resulting in significant charter change.

## Looking for Leadership

In 1985 the city's three political parties created a nine-member charter review committee with three members representing each party. It was charged with determining how Cincinnati's governmental structure could be better organized to meet the city's growing challenges, but the committee failed to agree on any recommendations as every vote kept splitting 3-3-3 along party lines (Horstmann and Moloney 1995).

As further evidence of deep political divides, no political party gained a majority in the 1985 council election. The ruling majority on the council became known as the Gang of Five, a conservative group composed of two Democrats and three Republicans, all of whom were endorsed by a conservative political action committee on the city's west side. This majority named Charlie Luken, a Democrat, mayor. The new majority favored the direct election of the mayor.

However, in 1987 voters were asked to pass an indirect method for electing the mayor. The Top Vote Getter (TVG) charter amendment meant that the council candidate receiving the most votes would automatically be named the mayor. TVG created a situation in which no candidate and all candidates were running for mayor simultaneously. The last mayor named by the council, Charlie Luken, also became the first mayor elected under the new TVG system.

Unlike in the decades following adoption of a council–manager government, when Charter and the Republican Party competed in a true two-party political system, the political jockeying of council members between parties and the varying composition of council majorities contributed to the 1980s and 1990s being considered a period of a de facto no-party system composed of independent voters, candidates, and office holders (Miller 1997, 33). The combative and competitive council environment of the 1980s and 1990s, exacerbated by a mayoral selection process that pitted every member of the council against the other and that seemed to overstimulate the personal interests of each council member to be seen as the council's leader, helped paint a portrait of a city in political disarray.

## The Perfect Storm of Discontent

Dissatisfaction with the Cincinnati City Council did not emanate from any one issue. Although the TVG system for electing the mayor was widely viewed as the cause of the city's political problems, discontent was a consequence of many pressures placed upon a political system that was seemingly incapable of responding to them. Throughout the late 1980s and the 1990s, myriad charter proposals were introduced into the political arena by citizen activists, special interest groups, political parties and individual council members, each seeking to find the right structural change that would enable the city to successfully respond to the political and social challenges it faced.

In addition to questions about government and electoral organization, a number of other highly charged issues were debated by the council, in the press, and among the public, which resulted in many more charter amendment proposals. In varying degrees all the proposed amendments generated conflict among council members, raised the ire of the public and media, and contributed to the general lack of confidence reported by the media in Cincinnati's council–manager system. Underlying the intense political conflict in the city was the general acknowledgment that no one at city hall could be held accountable for the rancor or for the lack of progress in resolving the city's challenges.

The city council became the primary focus of ire. As Sharon Moloney of the *Cincinnati Post* posited:

> People look at city hall these days, and to many of them it indeed appears to be broken and in need of fixing. Half the members of Cincinnati City Council seem to want to be mayor and are spending two years campaigning for the job. Too many council members will sabotage any proposal, no matter its benefit, if it is put up by a political opponent. And these days, a political opponent as often as not belongs to the council member's own party. Council takes weeks and months to pass the simplest of proposals. . . . it seems more than time to take a look at the city's governing policy, the city charter. (1994)

The council became famous for disorganization. The council was accused of wanting to not only set policy but also run the city. What had been a part-time job had over time been transformed into a full-time job but without full-time duties, and as a consequence the council "which once met for a couple of hours a week, now drags meetings on for hours almost every day, getting up to all sorts of legislative and administrative mischief" (Moloney 1999). In addition, the council had difficulty in setting policy on critical issues, meaning that the city manager was often on his own in determining the appropriate course of action in a given situation.

## The Winkler Committee and the Strong-Mayor Gambit

In an effort to bring order to the various issues raised and proposals made to change Cincinnati government's structure, its electoral process, and bureaucracy, a new charter review commission was organized in 1994. Motivated by criticism that seemed to come from all quarters and unable to move forward with an ordinance to directly appoint the commission, the Cincinnati City Council approved a resolution calling for the chairs of the city's three political parties to form the commission. Chaired by former University of Cincinnati president Henry Winkler, each political party appointed three members. The rest of the sixteen-member committee was composed of representatives from a variety of politically active organizations from throughout the city.

The Winkler committee's charge was to conduct a comprehensive review of the city's charter including "how the city elects the mayor, the length of council terms, council pay, the city administration, [and] Cincinnati's independent boards and commissions" (*Cincinnati Post* 1994).

By April of 1995 a majority of the Charter Review Committee had determined that they supported the direct election of the mayor, but they did not agree on a process. Everyone did agree, however, that the mayor *should not* be elected via TVG. The committee also recommended that the mayor's powers be somewhat expanded and that the council should be elected at large, not be term limited, and have four-year terms (Moloney 1995a).[2]

The charter review committee left the critical decisions of how to implement its recommendations to the city council and almost immediately a citizen's group, Vote for Leadership, announced it would begin a petition drive to ask voters to approve the direct election of the mayor. The proposed charter amendment would also award the mayor with new powers; the city manager would report to the mayor, and the mayor would have responsibility "for running city government, producing a leadership agenda . . . and have veto power over all legislation" (Moloney 1995a). Although the mayor's veto could be overturned by six members of the council, this proposal was a call for an executive mayor. The proposal eventually included expanding mayoral and council terms to four years.

What gave the Vote for Leadership proposal credibility was that it counted among its chief supporters, and organizers, the Cincinnati Business Committee (CBC), whose seven co-chairs were all representatives of important businesses in the city. Critics of the proposal, including the chairman of the Hamilton County Democratic Party, labeled it the end of city manager government in Cincinnati (Moloney 1995b).

By the end of July of 1995 the strong-mayor proposal had been certified for inclusion on the special election ballot of August 30 as Issue 1, and the Hamilton County Republican Party had endorsed the CBC-backed proposal. However, an alternative to Issue 1 was introduced with the expectation that it would be on the ballot the following November. The alternative was developed by Cincinnatians for Constructive Change (CCC), a coalition of several civic groups and the city's mayor, Roxanne Qualls.[3] The principle difference between the two plans was how much power would be given to the mayor.

An executive mayor would effectively make the city manager a chief administrator, not the city's chief executive officer. Some suggested the proposal would potentially bring back the bad old days of political patronage associated with Boss government. The *Cincinnati Post* went on record as preferring the alternative plan because Issue 1 did not provide incentives for the mayor and the council to work together. In an editorial just prior to the election, the *Cincinnati Post* noted its opposition to Issue 1 because "it leaves virtually unchanged . . . the very aspect of city government most in need of a good shakeup: City Council" (*Cincinnati Post* 1995a).

Having two proposals for reorganizing Cincinnati's government further divided the community and the city council. Five members of the council were reported to have preferred to cancel the special election scheduled for August while four wanted the election to proceed.

About 26 percent of Cincinnati's voters went to the polls on August 30, and just over 64 percent of them voted down the strong-mayor plan; Issue 1 failed in 25 of the city's twenty-six wards. While credit for its loss was justifiably given to the grassroots effort organized by a multiplicity of the city's civic groups opposed to the plan, the publication of the Issue 1 campaign's preelection finance report just prior to the election may have had the most dramatic effect on voter opinion. Of the $382,393 raised on behalf of Issue 1, much of which was spent on an aggressive television and radio advertising campaign, all but one contribution came from twenty-seven local corporate political action committees. Meanwhile, Issue 1 opponents raised $82,451, which came from a broad spectrum of Cincinnati's civic community. Most donations were for less than $1,000 and the single largest donation, $9,025, was made by the International City and County Management Association.

As an editorial in the *Cincinnati Post* explained, because the CBC-backed strong-mayor plan was put together "behind closed doors, with no input from the civic sector" the public did not buy in to the idea and it came across as a power play by the city's business elite to buy city hall (*Cincinnati Post* 1995b). African American leaders echoed the frustration. "There was an arrogance on the part of the CBC," explained Reverend James Milton, chairman of the Coalition of Clergy that opposed Issue 1 (Horn and Moloney 1995).

## A Community Forum

The strength of the voting public's rejection of the CBC plan, however, did not diminish the general perception that Cincinnatians wanted change. With the defeat of the executive mayor proposal, various groups in the city renewed their individual efforts to push their particular interests. At the urging of several community leaders, Mayor Roxanne Qualls called for a summit to try to find a middle ground among the various interests; even those who had supported Issue 1 were open to participating. Finding a compromise position, however, appeared to be a Herculean task; the groups participating in the summit held contradictory positions.

Mayor Qualls invited seventeen community leaders to attend the summit held in September of 1995, and as a result of this discussion a coalition of groups asked Cincinnatians for Constructive Change to refrain from putting their proposal on the November ballot. Instead they were asked to work to expand the number of voices participating in the summit; particularly from the African American community (Moloney 1995c).

The result of the summit was the creation of the Cincinnati Forum for Charter Reform (Forum), involving twenty diverse organizations including representatives of the city's three political parties, labor, African American ministerial groups, women's organizations, neighborhood councils, and the Chamber of Commerce. After nine months of discussion, eighteen of the twenty groups involved in the Cincinnati Forum agreed upon a plan for reorganizing Cincinnati's government.[4] They proposed a partisan primary and a directly elected mayor, with a four-year term, whose status would be elevated by being designated as the city's official ambassador and who would be able to appoint city council committee chairs. The city manager would remain the chief executive of the city. Term limits were also retained in the plan, but the eight-member council would be elected via preferential voting for four-year terms in a system where voters would rank order their choices.[5]

The effort to have the Forum plan placed on the ballot was organized by Cincinnatians for Charter Reform (CCR), largely a coalition of civic activists who had been opposed to Issue 1 and been members of Cincinnatians for Constructive Change. Their goal was to have the proposal on the primary ballot in May 1997. However, the group was unable to get sufficient signatures to do so. There was also evidence that several groups, including some who had participated in the Cincinnati Forum for Charter Reform summit, had not been excited about the CCR charter amendment proposal and were not displeased that it failed to make the ballot. As a result of the criticism the proposal received, it was further simplified. The new amendment called for the direct election of the mayor through a nonpartisan primary followed by a run-off election between the top two finishers. The plan also gave the mayor power to appoint the chairs of council committees and, with the council, serve a four-year term.

CCR mounted a new petition drive in late 1997, seeking to make a March 1998 deadline for putting the modified issue before voters in that year's May primary election. However, after submitting their petitions for review (and two days prior to the deadline) a group of Republican activists charged that the initiative had failed to gather sufficient valid signatures. The board of elections eventually found the petition to lack 171 valid signatures to reach the minimum needed for certification. Amendment supporters saw the move to discredit their initiative as "a defeat of a people's grass-roots effort" and asked the Cincinnati City Council to use its authority to vote to put the proposal on the ballot despite the board of elections ruling (Moloney 1998a). In a 5-to-2 vote, the council declined to do so. The majority on that vote, both Democrats and Republicans, opined that they should not go against the ruling of the elections board. The two council members voting for the measure were Bobbie Sterne, the council's only Charterite, and Mayor Qualls.

## Build Cincinnati and the Stronger Mayor Compromise

During the summer of 1998, Hamilton County Democratic Party Chairman Tim Burke; the new Hamilton County Republican Chairman, Mike Allen; and the president of Cincinnati's chapter of the NAACP, Milton Hinton, formed a new committee to examine governmental change in the city. Coming on the heels of the last failed attempt to reform Cincinnati's government, this effort, Build Cincinnati, did not imbue many with optimism (Moloney 1998b).

Throughout the rest of 1998, Build Cincinnati held public meetings and heard from more than seventy community organizations. Based upon myriad recommendations and cognizant of the inherent political conflict in pushing a broad reform agenda, Build Cincinnati decided to focus its reform effort upon how to elect, and what powers to give to, the mayor. Initially the group considered at least two different reform proposals, but after Mayor Roxanne Qualls (D) and council member Phil Heimlich (R) began to meet with Build Cincinnati, a single revised proposal emerged that was presented to the Cincinnati City Council to discuss. The proposal provided for a nonpartisan primary, the direct election of the mayor from between the top two primary finishers, and a four-year term for the mayor. The mayor would preside at council meetings and have the power to veto legislation, which could then be overridden by six votes of the nine-member council, but the mayor would not be a member of the council. The mayor would name the vice mayor and council committee chairs, assign work to council committees, and be able to comment on the city budget. The city manager would report to both the mayor and the council, and though the mayor could recommend to hire and fire the city manager, the final decision to do so would rest with the council. The city manager would continue to develop the budget and be able to introduce legislation. Council races would stay the same, at large and by the 9X system, and council terms would remain two years. The plan, dubbed the Stronger Mayor proposal, would go into effect in 2001 if adopted.

Despite the apparent support for the proposal from the disparate groups who had been negotiating to achieve reform around the Build Cincinnati proposal, there were ongoing challenges from civic groups and reversals of support among those on the council that inhibited the process of adopting the measure and getting it to the ballot. A large number of African American groups, as well as three African American council members, expressed misgivings about the plan to directly elect the mayor. When the measure came up for a vote in early March 1999, council Democrats were split on the issue, while Republicans were united in their support for a stronger mayor. On a 6-to-3 vote, the council adopted the measure and sent it to voters to determine its fate (Osborne 1999a).

Following the vote, only Qualls and Heimlich indicated that they would take an active role in helping to pass the Build Cincinnati "Stronger Mayor" plan, but despite the support of these two prominent members of the council, the reform amendment (Issue 4) faced serious obstacles. Both the Charter and Democratic Parties were split on the issue. Charter opponents saw the proposal as a threat to the city manager form of government because of the amount of power that would be given to the mayor; many African American leaders opposed it because they believed it would make election of an African American mayor more difficult.

In an editorial following the council vote, the *Cincinnati Enquirer* declared that the reform proposal was good news from a city hall that too often had operated like a circus and had "become a regional punch line, a handy example of disorganized, back-biting political chaos." The way council members finally arrived at an agreement, it continued, "with backflips and leaps through hoops of fire . . . was itself a compelling case for a better system." The "Strong Mayor" [sic] amendment, the editorial argued, would finally give Cincinnati "leadership and accountability" (*Cincinnati Enquirer* 1999a). (See figure 11.1.)

Despite initial concerns that African Americans could not be elected mayor under the Build Cincinnati proposal, the first African American group to publicly support the plan was Cincinnati's chapter of the National Association for the Advancement of Colored People (NAACP). This was an important endorsement as African Americans reportedly composed 40 percent of Cincinnati's voting population, and the NAACP was one of the three organizations that had sponsored Build Cincinnati's reform study. An editorial in the *Cincinnati Enquirer* emphasized that the NAACP endorsement rein-forced the comments of African American councilman Charlie Winburn (R) that the plan was race neutral (*Cincinnati Enquirer* 1999b).

During the next two months, additional groups and individual stakeholders began announcing their support for, or opposition to, Issue 4. The leadership of the Republi-can, Democratic, and Charter parties all supported the plan, but some prominent Char-ter members, African American organizations, and the Cincinnati Democratic Committee joined the anti–Issue 4 campaign. Both sides sought strategic endorsements "considered the key to winning the hearts and minds of Cincinnati voters" (Osborne 1999c).

**Figure 11.1   Editorial Cartoon**

*Source: Cincinnati Enquirer*

Reported reasons for opposition or support varied. Although women's groups favored the direct election of the mayor, they felt the power of the stronger mayor would block average citizens from being able to be heard or to gain political access to city hall. They also believed that the proposal favored the wealthy, particularly because they thought the campaign costs for separate mayoral races would be so much higher. Labor organizations opposed Issue 4 because they felt it was bad for workers. Supporters of the plan, on the other hand, argued that the proposal "was a hard-fought compromise among the city's political factions" and had "the best chance of ending political gridlock and jockeying among City Council" (Osborne 1999b). Aaron Herzig, chairman of the pro–Issue 4 campaign, said this effort was the best option and opponents were not being realistic to think that another, better proposal would come along: "Those groups have been convinced there's some pie-in-the-sky plan out there in the future" (Osborne 1999b).

The *Cincinnati Enquirer* supported Issue 4 because its editors thought the city suffered from "weak leadership" and needed a stronger mayor instead of a "cardboard cutout that is propped up at ribbon cutting . . . ceremonies" (*Cincinnati Enquirer* 1999c). The argument was that a stronger mayor would improve accountability and give the city manager one boss instead of nine, and that a four-year term would allow the mayor to start a project, see it through to completion, and be held accountable should the project not be successful. The *Enquirer* posited that the city had outgrown the weak-mayor, council–manager system and needed stronger leadership.

Opponents to Issue 4 were led by council member Tyrone Yates (D) who argued that the plan would undermine the council's authority and turn the city manager into a puppet. Opponents believed the proposal was yet another attempt to ensure that the wealthy would control city hall. Compromise was not easily achieved between the various partners in the Build Cincinnati reform effort. Unlike the previous business-sponsored executive mayor proposal, Build Cincinnati appealed to a broad range of community groups.

## Few Voters Wrought Historic Change

The most important change to Cincinnati's council–manager government since the 1924 and 1926 reforms was made with relatively few voices. Just 18 percent of Cincinnati's 215,340 registered voters turned out for the election, and Issue 4 won by just 2,277 votes (53 percent), thanks in large measure to the city's Republican-dominated wards. Most heavily in opposition were the city's African American, strongly Democratic, wards which went 2-1 against the stronger mayor proposal. The vote clearly illustrated the deep divisions within the Charter and Democratic parties over the issue.

Despite the decade-long community discussion, the intensity with which the issue was debated in the press, the multitude of community groups that either worked for, or against, the proposal's passage, and the fact that a week before the election the city had spent $47,000 to mail copies of the Issue 4 ballot language to all of the city's registered voters, less than 40,000 of the city's voters went to the polls. One explanation for the low turn-out was that, for most Cincinnatians, the council had become "irrelevant" (Wilkinson 1999a). With its passage, the stronger mayor was scheduled to go into effect in 2001.

The last city election under TVG (1999) was greatly affected by the knowledge that in two years voters would choose a stronger mayor. Certainly being an incumbent would be an advantage in that race. The term-limit charter amendment, introduced and adopted in 1991, also influenced the 1999 election season. Two council seats were open as a result of two Democrats, Tyrone Yates and the mayor, Roxanne Qualls, being term limited. Surprisingly, the Hamilton County Republican Party announced its intention to seek five seats on the council in an effort to form the majority they had not been able to achieve for almost three decades. Seven incumbent council members sought reelection (three Republicans, three Democrats, and the council's lone Charterite). Of the thirteen challengers, one in particular stood out: Democratic former congressman, council member, and mayor, Charlie Luken. One month after voters passed Issue 4, Luken left his position as a local television news anchor and announced his candidacy. Based upon his name recognition and that he had previously been mayor under TVG, "[H]e immediately became the front-runner for mayor" (Wilkinson 1999b).

In November, as expected, Luken received the highest number of votes in the 1999 council election and was, again, elected mayor. His had been an anti-incumbent campaign, running television commercials that displayed the council as "chubby, old-time wrestlers body-slamming each other" (Wilkinson 1999c). He had argued that the council needed to be controlled as it was spending its time on "goofy things" (1999c). Following the 1999 election, it was widely acknowledged that in 2001 Luken would also almost certainly be the city's first "stronger mayor."

## A Time of Upheaval and Change

Cincinnati began the new century facing continued economic development challenges, ongoing racial tension between the African American community and the police, and a council in conflict with the city manager. In the interim, politics at city hall saw a continuation of conflict surrounding charter proposals to extend council terms, implement campaign-spending limits, and reform the city's civil service.

In the summer of 2000, a charter amendment was submitted to the city council that would extend council terms from two to four years. However, a majority of council members did not support the motion. Opponents charged that the change would lessen the council's accountability to voters and allow members to serve up to ten years in office, going against the spirit of term limits. After several months of debate, the motion was withdrawn, as consensus on the issue was not possible.

Among the two charter amendments on the 2001 ballot was a call for civil service reform.[6] Proposals for civil service reform in the past had focused on bringing more oversight to the police, including allowing the city manager to have more discretion in hiring the police and fire chiefs and assistant chiefs. Introduced several times in the past, most recently in a 1997 charter amendment, reform efforts had failed to gain sufficient voter support. After the city experienced a violent racial conflict, sufficient support came from the community to overcome resistance to reform. The city's response to this conflict had the effect of also deepening support for a "stronger mayor."

In April, following the shooting of an unarmed African American man by a white police officer and a bellicose meeting of the council two days later, the city erupted into three days of rioting. At the council meeting an angry crowd shared its frustrations with their elected officials. So contentious was the meeting that the mayor walked out and council chambers were cleared. Protestors then took their concerns to the street and marched on police headquarters. At first city hall was slow to respond, however, on the third day of rioting, Mayor Luken used his emergency powers and placed the city under a curfew. As a result of the rioting, more than 800 people were arrested, more than 100 Ohio state troopers were deployed in the city, and 120 businesses reported being damaged; it was the worst civil unrest the city had seen since 1968, following the death of Martin Luther King.

The crisis provided the impetus to reform the city's civil service system, and it thrust the mayor into a leadership role as he took the reins of the efforts to deal with the underlying causes for the city's civil unrest. The Cincinnati Black United Front, involved in a lawsuit with the city over alleged police harassment of African Americans, demanded that police reform be the city's top priority. The Front's membership included Ohio's secretary of state, the city's vice mayor, several state representatives, and former council members. City hall's neglect of long-simmering racial problems contributed to the riots, they argued, and now was the appropriate time to conduct a review of the police department, place a charter amendment on the ballot to reform the city's civil service system, and expand economic opportunities for African Americans. Luken responded by working with the city council to place civil service reform, Issue 5, on the November ballot. Voters approved the change by a narrow margin, thus removing from civil service status the fire and police chiefs, as well as assistant chiefs and other department heads at city hall. Shortly thereafter, the council also voted 5 to 4 to accept mediation to try to resolve the lawsuit filed against the city accusing the police of racial profiling.[7]

In the weeks following Luken's declaration of a state of emergency and the imposition of a citywide curfew that quelled the rioting, Luken was "unquestionably the focal point of activity at City Hall" (Wilkinson 2001a). Luken's own analysis of the situation was that someone had to step up in a time of emergency and that his actions were an indication of what the newer, stronger mayor would look like.

While the months following the rioting enabled Luken to exhibit his leadership capabilities, there was also considerable public dissatisfaction with the mayor. The fall primary was considered a referendum on the riots and resulted in mayoral challenger, Courtis Fuller, an African American recruited by the Charter Party and with no previous political experience, outpolling Luken 54 percent to 38 percent (Korte 2001a).

A heavy turnout of African American voters in the primary helped Fuller beat Luken by almost a 6-to-1 margin in some of the city's largely African American neighborhoods, but Fuller also did well in other wards because of his Charter connection.

Between the primary and general election, Luken had an opportunity to reverse the criticism city hall had received for its perceived slowness to act during the April riots. In September a judge acquitted the police officer for the shooting that had touched off the riots in April. At the ensuing council meeting, Luken "was polite yet firm with protesters . . . then declared a state of emergency and imposed a citywide curfew at the first sign of trouble" (Korte 2001b). Luken's quick actions received plaudits, and pundits asserted that his second chance to exhibit his leadership qualities helped to strengthen perceptions that he was already the city's stronger mayor.

## Cincinnati Gets Its Stronger Mayor

The election was too close to call before election day. Upon reflection, however, Luken's solid victory was understandable.[8] "There's no question it was a vote along racial lines," said Gene Beaupre, a political science professor at Xavier University in Cincinnati. "You could see it coming" (Wilkinson 2001b). As with the primary, turnout in predominantly African American wards was higher than usual, but that was offset by a relatively large turnout in predominantly white, westside wards. The result was that "whites voted overwhelmingly for Mr. Luken, while blacks did the same for Mr. Fuller" (2001b). Even in the city's less politically conservative eastside neighborhoods, Luken received big numbers, winning three of the larger wards with 80 percent or more of the vote.

The 2001 council elections further solidified the Democratic majority on the council, raising their number from five to six seats. Luken, a veteran Democratic politician, took office on December 1 as Cincinnati's first so-called stronger mayor. As was predicted, his experience relative to the council further added to his new title and lent more credence to the idea that a new era of mayoral leadership had begun at city hall.

John Shirey, who resigned as city manager on the day Luken assumed office, suggested that as a result of the mayor initiating the manager-hiring process, future managers would be "in some way especially indebted to the mayor" (Horstman 2001). Shirey, who had survived as Cincinnati's city manager for eight years, called the city's government "fractious" and identified two key factors, progress in race relations and economic development, particularly in the downtown, as largely determining whether the stronger mayor system would be a success (Osborne 2001).

Despite concerns by some that the stronger mayor would dominate the council, its institutional powers remained considerable. The council ultimately controlled the budget, and still played a major role as an interface between the public and the city's administrative bureaucracy. Many actions taken by city hall during the Luken administration would result from the policy leadership of council members.

Many believed that the stronger mayor contributed to a new civility on the council, whereas others credited the new mix of personalities, "including several political newcomers with business backgrounds" as being responsible for most of the change (Osborne 2002). Most likely, both factors contributed. Early in 2002 new rules for council conduct were adopted unanimously. These rules not only provided a way for the first stronger mayor council to distance itself from the troubled councils of the 1990s but they also gave the public an alternative picture of a functional council.

Cincinnati had hardly caught its breath from more than a decade of political conflict over mayoral power when further charter changes were proposed, including district elections and further strengthening of the mayor's office. In mid-2003 Mayor Luken and the vice mayor, Alicia Reece, proposed that a citizen advisory panel be organized to examine the potential for ward elections for the council and giving the mayor executive authority. The Cincinnati Election Reform Commission's thirteen members represented each of the city's three major political parties (three members each), while four members were appointed by the mayor.

In October of 2003 backers of an alternative proposal for district elections, the District Election Committee for a Greater Cincinnati, a bipartisan group, announced their intent to bypass the city-sponsored process and put on the ballot in March 2004 a proposal calling for a twelve-member council composed of nine members elected by district and three at large. The Cincinnati Election Reform Commission was reported, meanwhile, to be focusing on "strengthening the power of the mayor and returning city council to the role of a part-time policy-making body divorced from day-to-day municipal operations" (*Cincinnati Post* 2004).

There was little consensus on the council for any one of the myriad proposals that it had to consider. At the end of June 2004, and as a result of the confusion between which of the various options presented to the council should be supported, the chairman of the Cincinnati Election Reform Commission, Don Mooney Jr., asked the council not to place any charter amendment on the ballot. Instead of presenting the public with a large number of contradictory amendments, Mooney argued, it was preferable to only allow amendments to be placed on the ballot if they had the support of the public through the petition process. Since no petition surfaced, the November elections came and went without presenting voters the opportunity to make their opinion known on any of these proposals.

## The Stronger Mayor Survives

In August 2004 Mayor Charlie Luken announced that he would not seek reelection. Luken's criticism of the city council had become more aggressive following the failure of the council to place an executive mayor amendment on the ballot in 2004 suggesting that if there was any "dysfunction" at city hall during his term as the city's stronger mayor, it could be found in the council chambers, not in his office. "I think that the people have got to give great thought to their council and who they elect," Luken said. "Good people can make a bad system work, and bad people can make a good system fail" (Horstman 2004).

However, in his State of the City speech the following February, Luken said that the principle reason he would not seek reelection was the city's "bad government structure" (Osborne 2005a). The mayor stated that he would not seek the mayoralty of Cincinnati "so long as the system does not allow the mayor to be the real boss, the person who hires and fires department heads, and is permitted to bring in his or her own team, top to bottom" (2005a). Luken said that Cincinnati needed to "grow up and become a big city," and it was the only one in America "with this goofy way of running city government" (Korte 2005a). He hoped that in the future a charter amendment would be approved by voters giving the mayor of Cincinnati executive power.

Vice Mayor Alicia Reece, who had not yet announced her intention to run for mayor, responded to Luken's remarks by saying that she was "confused. . . . There aren't too many things the mayor's submitted that the council didn't support. I do think under this [stronger mayor] system, we can get some things done"[9] (Korte 2005a). Other council members pointed out that it was the city manager, Luken's handpicked candidate, that made staffing decisions and if there were problems he should work with her to solve them.

With Luken out of the race, the election to become the city's next stronger mayor was wide open. Republicans announced in June of 2005 that their candidate in the upcoming mayoral elections would be conservative former council member, Charlie Winburn, an African American, "known for his flamboyant oratorical style" (Osborne 2005b). Winburn would face three Democratic candidates in the spring nonpartisan primary—State Senator Mark Mallory, council member David Pepper, and Vice Mayor Alicia Reece—and three independent candidates; three of the four major party candidates were African American. The two candidates receiving the highest number of votes in the September primary would compete in the partisan general election in November 2005.

The primary results not only reflected the city's diminishing Republican voting strength but also illustrated that race continued to be an important factor influencing voting behavior. Only 20 percent of registered voters cast a ballot in the primary, and two Democrats, Pepper and Mallory, finished first and second respectively, each with about 31 percent of the vote and 215 votes separating them. Both agreed that they also could work within the stronger mayor system. An analysis of the primary results by the *Cincinnati Enquirer* revealed a voting pattern that emphasized race, with Mallory's strength coming from predominately African American precincts and Pepper's coming from predominately white precincts (Korte 2005c).

Republicans supported efforts at charter change that would create an executive mayor as a way to gain control over an alternative power to the council, but the changing nature of Cincinnati's politics showed that the city's demographic profile highly favored Democrats with the result that even the mayoralty seemed now beyond their reach. Mark Mallory won the general election contest for mayor in a very close race.[10] Again, voting strongly suggested that race was an important aspect of the election. In predominantly African American wards, Mallory won three to eight times as many votes as David Pepper, who won in predominantly white wards. However, it was the white liberal Democrats who enabled Mallory to win the majority (Cook 2005). Mallory's ability to speak to those who wanted to put behind them the city's racial divide may have been the key to his ability to build a successful electoral coalition. Pepper, according to some analysts, suffered from his association with city hall as a member of the council; however, one of the principal differences between the candidates was Pepper's focus on an issues agenda and Mallory's emphasis upon a vision of the mayor as the leader of a movement to unite the community. As one Democratic Party activist explained, "leadership trumped program in this case" (2005).

## The Future of Charter Change in Cincinnati

Mark Mallory, the new stronger mayor, had campaigned on a pledge to end the chaos at city hall. While council candidates had indicated that they would take their lead from the mayor, once elected, the council did not idly await the mayor's direction. Despite the relative inexperience of its members, the council readily challenged the mayor. As a result, Mallory, who had indicated that he was going to wield the powers of the stronger mayor more aggressively than his predecessor, faced a council with considerable political muscle. Following the 2005 election five members of the council—two Republicans, two Democrats, and a Charterite—formed a majority coalition that frequently submitted alternative legislative proposals to those put forth by the mayor.

Some informed observers interpreted the council's flexing of its muscle as an indication that power at city hall had shifted away from the stronger mayor back toward the council, and Mallory's leadership style may have partially contributed to that perception. His extensive legislative experience prior to being elected Cincinnati's mayor no doubt influenced his leadership style.[11] As a member of a Democratic minority, Mallory, having had to work across party lines to be effective, was well practiced at the art of compromise. Like Charlie Luken before him, Mallory did not reign in the council by exerting strong mayoral power. He instead generally practiced facilitative leadership, attempting to work with the council and respecting the council's interest and role in policy-making. In fact, it could be argued that Mallory has been even more adroit in practicing the art of facilitative leadership than his predecessor (Spence 2008).

As a consequence of the mayor's facilitative leadership, there was a palpable lessening at city hall of political conflict and a lessening of pressure for more institutional change in the city's political structure. The results of the 2007 council elections evidence this point. For the first time since before the adoption of the "stronger mayor," voters returned all nine incumbents to the council. "They must be happy," concluded Mallory, noting that voters were pleased not only with the direction in which the city was headed, but also with him and the council (Prendergast 2007). In addition to voters, key community stakeholders appeared generally satisfied with the progress the city had made recently, and Mallory received considerable praise for his performance as mayor (Klepal 2006).

Substantial progress on the twin issues of race relations and economic development also contributed to positive perceptions of city hall. Frustrations with the police, particularly among African American leaders, were calmed by a citywide effort (begun under Luken) to improve police community relations. Several actions, including the creation of the Citizen Complaint Authority, gave the public a stronger voice in matters pertaining to the police, and civil service reform, long supported by African American groups in the city, increased the accountability of the police and fire services to the city manager. In addition, a modified hiring system improved chances that African American candidates could enter upper management.

Changes in the administration of city government also added to the easing of race relations. Luken hired an African American city manager and supported her hiring of several African Americans for high-level management positions in the city. Mallory continued and added to Luken's successes, selecting an African American city manager and giving priority to, in his speeches and in his support for budget allocations, programs designed to improve job training and social program delivery to the city's poorer neighborhoods, many of which are predominantly African American.

Substantial progress was also made in solving some of the more conflicted economic development issues in the city, which had the effect of lessening the aggressiveness with which the business community pushed for further structural reform.

However, some critics of city hall see any conflict between the council and the mayor as an indication that the city's government is in "a state of incoherence that cries out not for a tweaking, but for a sweeping overhaul" (Hurley 2006). Despite Mallory's seeming comfort with constructive collegial differences between the council and himself, he sees the executive mayor as the logical evolution of structural change. According to Mallory, and several members of the council agree, "The only change that would make any sense is to move to an executive mayor system" (Wessels 2006). Further calls for reducing council power and increasing mayoral power, although muted, continue to be heard in the community, and the commitment to continue the stronger mayor system is apparently not shared by all groups, including some elected officials.[12]

In the summer of 2008 the city council was presented yet another proposal to adopt an executive mayor system with the argument that such a move would more clearly enunciate lines of accountability. Council members John Cranley, a Democrat facing term limits; Chris Monzel, a Republican; and Roxanne Qualls, the former mayor and Democrat reelected to the council in 2007 as a Charterite, supported the proposal.[13] Despite also having the mayor's tentative support, the issue failed to garner enough council support to be placed before voters in the general election.

In a pluralistic political setting, charter amendments are sold through a strong, focused message that convinces voters that sufficient cause exists for change. When the message does not find resonance in public perceptions, or when there are diverse messages confusing perceptions of problem and resolution, charter change is less likely. In Cincinnati multiple factors coalesced at one point in time to create the momentum for change. Much of the political conflict since 1990 focused upon identifying the kind of structural change that could meet the perceived challenges the city faced (particularly in race relations and economic development). As alternative proposals were made and failed, the principal question became to what extent the council–manager form of government would be modified, not whether it would be replaced. Cincinnati's unique political past and its resultant political institutions remain an important point of departure for any discussion of charter change. The adoption of the stronger mayor was a true compromise between various interest groups in the city. Although most, if not all, of these interest groups believed that change was needed, there was sufficient support for the existing institutions that the change was an incremental modification, not a complete replacement, of the existing structure.

Since 2000 there has only been one charter amendment on the ballot that modified the institutional structure of city government, the civil service reform measure approved by voters in 2001. Although a number of other charter amendments have passed, no further effort to modify Cincinnati's mayoral powers or reorganize the council has had enough support to make it to the ballot. This does not mean that change in Cincinnati is over. Although many of the points of conflict in the community seem to have been resolved for the present, the allure of the executive mayor is still strong. A crisis in leadership, a particularly troublesome council, a renewal of true partisan competition, another shift in the political demographics of the city, or a gifted and popular politician who is focused on acquiring the power of a strong mayor could create the momentum necessary to convince voters to support additional charter change.

## Notes

The author wishes to express his appreciation to Colleen O'Toole, PhD, for editing assistance; to Martha Cutter-Wilson of Xavier University for helping with background research; and to Jim Bergman for use of his political cartoon.

1. The Charter Committee was organized as a reform movement in the 1920s. After introducing council–manager government, the Charter Committee functioned much as a political party, representing a variety of interest groups, developing a platform, and recruiting, sponsoring, endorsing, and funding candidates (Charterites). For the sake of clarity, the Charter Committee is referred to in this analysis as the Charter Party (or Charter) to differentiate it from other charter reform committees or reform movements.

2. To obtain sufficient votes on the committee to support the recommendation that the mayor be elected directly, compromises had been made that removed support for giving the mayor the power to hire and fire the city manager with the advice and consent of council and having the manager report only to the mayor.

3. Qualls had been elected mayor of Cincinnati in 1993 when she received the highest vote in the council elections.

4. The Republican Party objected to the proposal to return to proportional representation, and the League of Women Voters did not support partisan primary elections in the mayor's race (Fox 1999).

5. Preferential voting is similar to proportional voting. The system was a compromise between those who supported district elections for the council and those who preferred the at-large system.

6. The other charter amendment was a proposal for campaign finance reform.

7. The rioting also made final what many had been expecting regarding the relationship of the council with the city manager. In a 5 to 4 vote, council moved to accept Shirey's resignation effective December 1, the same day that the new stronger mayor would take office.

8. Luken received 47,755 votes (55 percent) while Fuller received 38,494 votes (45 percent).

9. When Reece did announce her candidacy for mayor, she stated that she would have more of a "hands on role in the city's day-to-day operations than Cincinnati's city manager form of government had historically allowed" (Korte 2005b).

10. More than 73,000 of Cincinnati's 212,000 registered voters, just over 34 percent, went to the polls. Mallory received just over 52 percent of the vote, getting 37,206 votes to Pepper's 34,268 (48 percent).

11. Mallory served in the Ohio legislature, both as a representative (1995–1998) and as a senator (1999–2005).

12. Council's ability to challenge the mayor is part and parcel of the stronger mayor compromise. The fear was that a strong mayor might have no constraints. Council members, however, who are full-time, paid well, have staff, chair committees, have access to the media, and run in at-large elections requiring a broad-based constituency, have the ability to offer constraints to mayoral power in the stronger mayor system.

13. Ironically Qualls had led the fight against the executive mayor proposal placed before voters in 1995.

# References

Bauer, David. 1976. Direct mayoral election proposed. *Cincinnati Enquirer*, February 24.

*Cincinnati Enquirer*. 1999a [Editorial]. March 7.

————. 1999b. Thumbs up [Editorial]. March 20.

————. 1999c. That's not my job [Editorial]. May 2.

*Cincinnati Post*. 1994. The right way to do a review. July 9.

————. 1995a. Fix what's broken. August 26.

————. 1995b. Bad plan defeated. August 31.

————. 2004. Changing the charter again. February 26.

*Commercial Tribune*. 1924. City charter workers vote at dinner to make committee a permanent organization. November 20 1924.

Cook, Tony. 2005. Mallory wins tight race. *Cincinnati Post*, November 9.

Fox, John. 1999. The politics of politics. *City Beat*, March 4.

Horn, Dan, and Sharon Moloney. 1995. Big bucks go bust. *Cincinnati Post*, August 31.

Horstmann, Barry M. 2001. Luken ushers in new era at city hall today. *Cincinnati Post*.

————. 2004. Luken on Luken. *Cincinnati Post*, August 7.

Horstman, Barry M., and Sharon Moloney. 1995. Reform efforts: A long history of failure. *Cincinnati Post*, January 18.

Hurley, Dan. 2006. Cincinnati does not have 'strong mayor' system. *Cincinnati Post*, July 14.

Klepal, Dan. 2006. Mallory sees an end to chaos. *Cincinnati Enquirer*, March 10.

Korte, Gregory. 2001a. Campaign 2001: The race for mayor. *Cincinnati Enquirer*, September 13.

————. 2001b. Analysis. *Cincinnati Enquirer*, September 28.

————. 2005a. Frustration theme of Luken speech. *Cincinnati Enquirer*, February 3.

————. 2005b. Reece seeks higher job. *Cincinnati Enquirer*, March 7.

————. 2005c. Racial pattern seen in primary. *Cincinnati Enquirer*, September 15.

Miller, Zane L. 1997. Thinking, politics, city government: Charter reform in Cincinnati, 1890s–1990s. *Queen City Heritage* (Winter): 24–37.

Moloney, Sharon. 1994. Committee is poised for a run at Cincinnati charter reform. *Cincinnati Post*, July 13.

————. 1995a. Charter committee can't decide on electing mayor. *Cincinnati Post*, April 14.

————. 1995b. Vision: mayoral muscle. *Cincinnati Post*, April 29.

————. 1995c. City reform: New voices summoned. *Cincinnati Post*, September 2.

———. 1998a. Political pros are not daunted by grassroots sentimentality. *Cincinnati Post*, March 11.

———. 1998b. Yet another charter reform is headed for Cincinnati ballot. *Cincinnati Post*, December 2.

———. 1999. City council is blaming Shirey for problems that it has caused. *Cincinnati Post*, June 30.

Osborne, Kevin. 1999a. Mayoral election on ballot in May. *Cincinnati Post*, March 4.

———. 1999b. Women's groups oppose mayoral reform. *Cincinnati Post*, April 10.

———. 1999c. Issue 4 splits city, political allies. *Cincinnati Post*, May 3.

———. 2001. Dear John. . . . You're outta here. *Cincinnati Post*, December 1.

———. 2002. Luken and city adjust to new role. *Cincinnati Post*, May 28.

———. 2005a. Luken: No new goals for city. *Cincinnati Post*, February 3.

———. 2005b. Winburn to be GOP's mayor candidate. *Cincinnati Post*, June 15.

Prendergast, Jane. 2007. Mayor: That's vote of confidence. *Cincinnati Enquirer*, November 8.

Spence, John T. 2008. Charting progress of the empowered mayor: The 'stronger mayor' in Cincinnati, Ohio. In *The facilitative leader in city hall: Reexamining the scope and contributions*, ed. James H. Svara. Boca Raton, FL: CRC Press.

Wessels, Joe. 2006. Strong mayor faces test. *Cincinnati Post*, June 27.

Wilkinson, Howard. 1999a. Politics. *Cincinnati Enquirer*, May 9.

———. 1999b. Republicans salivating over council possibilities. *Cincinnati Enquirer*, September 5.

———. 1999c. Analysis. *Cincinnati Enquirer*, November 3.

———. 2001a. The mayor. *Cincinnati Enquirer*, May 8.

———. 2001b. Election analysis. *Cincinnati Enquirer*, November 8.

# PART III

# CHANGE FROM MAYOR–COUNCIL TO COUNCIL–MANAGER

CHAPTER 12

# EL PASO

## Professionalism over Politics in the Shift to Council–Manager Government

LARRY TERRY

IN RECENT YEARS cities across the United States have undergone a shift in municipal government form—most notably those considered to be "large cities" with populations exceeding two hundred thousand—by abandoning the professionally oriented council–manager structure for its more politically responsive mayor–council counterpart. However, the nation's twenty-first largest city, El Paso, Texas, went against the reform current in 2004 as its citizens democratically amended its city charter and appointed Joyce Wilson as its first city manager. With a city population of 609,405 reported in 2005, and the Greater El Paso–Ciudad Juarez metropolitan area population of nearly 2.4 million, the governmental modification seems counterintuitive from a representative democracy perspective considering the logic behind the managerial-based form; in smaller cities, where politics, public accountability, and public service responsibility are comparatively limited in scope when compared with larger cities, it is significantly more feasible to allow a nonelected, professionally trained official to manage a city's administrative affairs. Why then, would El Paso and its citizenry approve a change in government that might be grounded in professionalism yet susceptible to enhanced political scrutiny? It is toward this end that this chapter aligns its analysis.

To understand the dynamics behind El Paso's shift in government structure, the following chapter is divided into three primary sections: first, a brief discussion on El Paso's history, primarily as it relates to the growth of its municipal government and political landscape. The second section examines the contemporary political and administrative antecedents that led to the shift from a mayor–council to a council–manager government. This portion of the case study is particularly significant because, as mentioned above, the recent trend in large cities has leaned toward aligning city leadership with a strong, politically accountable executive who has the power to execute a municipality's administrative affairs. What was unique to the "Sun City" that propelled it to make the change in 2004? Finally, this chapter concludes by detailing the implications of the shift in municipal government form since 2004, namely, whether organizational restructuring, the inculcation of a customer-service approach to governance, and the development of new institutional roles for the mayor and city council has improved El Paso's efficiency, effectiveness, and responsiveness in public service delivery. In total, this survey of El Paso's shift to council–manager government concludes that while a "depoliticized" and professionalized environment has yielded some resistance within the city and from the community, overall it has provided the vehicle for long-awaited reform grounded in the public interest.

## Historical Background

The evolution of the isolated, nineteenth-century desert settlement called Franklin into the international metroplex that is now known as El Paso can largely be attributed to the city's origins as an old West outpost and its alignment along the United States–Mexico border. The city's development compares with many across the United States following the Civil War, as previously uninhabited or minimally populated northern cities and regions across the western frontier witnessed substantial growth at the end of the nineteenth century and beginning of the twentieth. Franklin's population grew significantly after 1881 when three railroad lines converged at the settlement, bringing merchants, miners, bankers, and transients to the settlement. While the railroad's expansion is credited with bringing Franklin and El Paso County out of isolation and creating new opportunities for its growing population, this expansion also presented a number of deleterious side effects that were exacerbated by an unstable political environment and an inadequate governmental structure. According to Vowell (1952), between 1850 and 1880 the rule of law was fragile at best as El Paso proved to be fertile ground for widespread theft, frequent raids on settlers by Native tribes, and other forms of unchecked aggression that frequently led to the murder of El Paso citizens. The most notable series of violent events were related to what was known as the Salt War, where a conflict over property and political power resulted in the deaths of a number of elected officials and other prominent public figures in 1877.

The political corruption and subsequent violence during the early periods of El Paso's development was in part due to a disorganized, inconsistent, and unreliable municipal government. The city was incorporated and elected its first mayor in 1873, Ben Dowell, and six city council members in August, only to replace four of them three months later because they resigned early. In August 1875 M. A. Jones defeated the incumbent Dowell for the position of mayor, and three new aldermen obtained seats on the city council. This shift in leadership did little to expand the scope of the council's activities beyond "the passage of ordinances concerning the public good . . . [such as prohibiting] spitting or throwing articles into the acequias" (Vowell 1952, 79). In September 1875 the council held its last meeting and ceased to exist until the election of 1880 established new municipal leadership. There has not been a lapse in government since.

Events such as the Salt War, the disintegration of the municipal government in 1875, and fraudulent elections like the controversial 1889 election proved to be early antecedents for governmental reform in El Paso history. The expanding population and economic boom that brought prosperity to the old frontier border settlement had simultaneously created a situation where a largely Hispanic citizenry was under the indiscriminate control of opportunistic politicians, carpetbaggers, and genuine crooks. Coupled with an increase in public health issues related to an increasingly dense urban area, such as poor water sanitation, citizens began demanding a more responsible and responsive government. This reform movement carried El Paso into the twentieth century, with citizens and reformist politicians battling elitist conservatives who desired to keep the city's unruly, yet profitable nature intact. Between 1905 and 1915 reformers made progress by outlawing gambling, developing a consistent garbage collection and street-paving program, reorganizing the police department, and implementing a tax rate increase to generate sustainable revenue for city services (Vowell 1952).

## Twentieth-Century Politics, Government, and Local Economics

According to Staudt and Stone (2007), "machine-style, mostly conservative . . . party politics made political control by the few and quiescence by the majority the norm in El Paso" (88), and as such, the border city's internal battle between reformers and the elite Anglo minority continued into the early years of the twentieth century. During the years surrounding World War I, conservatives and reformers alike began championing a more efficient, less political municipal administration; promises of "more business, less politics" or "a clean, progressive, and businesslike administration" that guaranteed equalized taxes and better services for all citizens reflected a nationwide trend toward stabilizing city government (Vowell 1952, 140). In the years following World War II, the expansion of Fort Bliss brought soldiers and other dependents to El Paso, while the developing industrial economy (copper smelting, oil refining), and other low-wage jobs that brought Hispanics from both sides of the border, accelerated the city's overall growth and urban sprawl.

With urbanization and an expanding population came an increase in political opportunities for Hispanics, despite the common thread of Anglo elitism maintaining a stranglehold on mainstream business and government. The election of El Paso's first Hispanic mayor, Raymond Telles, in 1957 was "initially disturbing to the Anglo elite" because of Telles's focus on dismantling partisanship in government in favor of professionalism (Staudt and Stone 2007, 88). In fact, a study of El Paso elite in 1948 asserted that "the election of a Spanish-name person as mayor was acceptable in principle, and that it should and would happen, but they were not prepared to have it happen in their lifetime" (Timmons 1990, 253). Telles would, however, become one of the city's most revered public figures and continued a distinguished public service career following his tenure as mayor, serving in both the Kennedy and Johnson administrations.

The 1960s in El Paso was a microcosm of the broader social movements occurring across the United States, with minority students at the University of Texas at El Paso demanding a more representative faculty and student body on campus, while the decade of the 1970s centered on bringing more business to El Paso so it could mirror the development of other southwestern cities, like Phoenix. The newly formed El Paso Development Corporation indicated that "the western tip of Texas has always depended on copper, cotton, cattle, and climate, and more recently on the clothing industry as the basis of livelihood for the people living here," but if the city was to reach its full growth potential, it needed to acquire new industry (Timmons 1990, 262). And with this newfound focus on luring a diversified economic base to El Paso, government was handed a number of fresh challenges. In the 1980s downtown revital-ization became of greater concern to the business community, and the city council designated an eighty-eight-block zone of downtown as a tax increment financing dis-trict, drawing legal action from a number of concerned entities that questioned its constitutionality (Timmons 1990). But it was the North American Free Trade Agree-ment (NAFTA) in the 1990s that caused the most disruption for the El Paso municipal government, as a significant amount of factory relocations into Mexico disturbed the local economy and forced elected officials to deal with the loss of its most stable indus-tries and large amounts of displaced workers.

As the twenty-first century dawned on the City of El Paso, it was addressing new-age problems with an ineffective, unprofessional, and inefficient government. Despite conventional wisdom and national precedent that indicated that a continuance of the mayor–council government was optimal for the expanding border town, the misguided political leadership and unstable bureaucracy ultimately led to the elite community in El Paso calling for a more expertise-laden government. The following section details this development and provides further understanding regarding the shift to the council–manager form.

## Professionalism, Politics, and Civic Capacity

According to Protasel (1988), a multitude of theories attempt to explain why cities undergo shifts in government form. The political development model posits that "as small mayor-council towns grow into middle-size towns they begin to encounter critical resource management problems that require the professional skills of full-time manag-ers. Thus, these cities abandon the mayor-council form of government and reform their governmental structures by adopting the council-manager plan" (Protasel 1988, 808). Furthermore, as middle-sized cities grow into larger cities, they abandon the council–manager and readopt the mayor–council form as a result of an increase in political volatility. As El Paso grew from a small to medium-sized city over the course of the twentieth century, it maintained its strong-mayor form. Interestingly, despite the city's maturation to a large city, rather than maintaining the mayor–council form as predicted by the political development model, the citizens of the City of El Paso approved the initiative to hire its first city manager in 2004.

Although Protasel (1988) posits that larger cities with city managers may have adapted to the increasing political demands on municipal government, making the need for a strong mayor less urgent, El Paso's centurylong quest for professionalism—coupled with a weak civic culture—made the shift less susceptible to political backlash.

From a professionalism standpoint, the exigencies can be analyzed from an internal and external perspective. Within city departments, administrators readily contended that the two-year term for city council and mayor (which also was amended to a four-year term in 2004) not only produced inconsistent policy agendas and ineffective implementation but also allowed politically ambitious amateurs unfamiliar with municipal management to run the city for brief periods. City staff also lamented the confusing, inefficient structure, where duplication and redundancy were partnered with an ambiguous chain of command. Externally, the business community crafted similar arguments for the governmental shift but also asserted that an experienced city manager brings the professional leadership necessary to develop a vibrant commercial environment.

El Paso's weak civic capacity also made the transition from a strong, directly accountable executive to a professional appointed manager a minimally debated topic within the community. Unlike large politically active municipalities such as Oakland and San Diego, which recently readopted the mayor–council form, government in El Paso has historically been guided by elite political and economic enclaves that have faced little organized opposition from the largely Hispanic citizenry. Previous attempts to professionalize the government were not quelled by issue-based voluntary associations or citizen-driven resistance movements but rather by having no one in the elite political or economic community to advocate for a change in form. The following sections discuss each of the antecedents for change in greater detail.

## Internal Demand for Professionalism and Cohesion

The February 2004 election proposed two charter amendments aimed at ameliorating the lack of continuity, cohesion, and professionalism that had plagued the City of El Paso for generations. Amendment 1 changed the election of the mayor and city council representatives from two- to four-year staggered terms, while Amendment 4 "changed the City of El Paso from a 'strong mayor' form of government to a 'council-manager' form of government and outlines the duties and authority of the Mayor and City Representatives" (City of El Paso 2006, 19). According to Patricia Adauto, deputy city manager of development and infrastructure services, "Before the shift, there was a general feeling that projects and plans got started but not completed. For example, there was once a transportation initiative on the table, which aimed to upgrade our transit system in an attempt to move the city away from cars. After a $750,000, comprehensive report was put together, a new city council was elected, and based on their political agenda, they did not want to take on the project" (Adauto 2008).

With respect to the El Paso's executive office, since 1989 when Jonathan W. Rogers finished his four-term tenure as mayor, of the six mayors elected to office only two served more than one term, and none served more than two. Deputy City Manager of Quality of Life Debbie Hamlyn provided some insight to the effects this political reality had on administration, noting that because elected officials were bound by two-year terms, "turnover was difficult to deal with. The mayor and council were involved in policy and administration, and many times the individuals elected were businessmen or other wealthy individuals who were not familiar with administration. It was hard to have a high performance organization without a [permanent] professional in place" (Hamlyn 2008). Under the mayor–council system, not only were mayors and council members moving in and out of office with relative frequency, but the task of administering the city's public policies was being conducted by quasi-political, unprofessional public servants. Deputy City Manager Adauto added, "The elected positions did not pay much. Most politicians had their own wealth, and were only interested in keeping things status quo. They ran government like a business from the basic standpoint of trying to balance the budget. There was no long-term planning approach" (2008).

Under El Paso's mayor–council government, there was a general perception that the executive was too powerful and that his influence could carry over into the administrative realm. This political power tool was enhanced in 1981 when at-large elections were replaced by district elections, which allowed for a more diversified, pluralistic council base. According to Richard Fleager, a member of the El Paso Chamber of Commerce since 1997 and chair of the City Charter and Bond Election Task Force, services and funds were readily "withheld from districts if they went against [the mayor's] agenda" (2008). In part El Paso made the shift from the mayor–council form to the council–manager form because while the political give-and-take and power brokering of policy development is immutable in municipal government, it is counterbalanced by a neutral administrator appointed by the entire elected body, and not politically dominated by a single individual or his agenda. While a small group of vocal citizens were cautious about the shift because it would hand over administrative tasks to an appointed city manager, the El Paso Chamber of Commerce and other "advocates for the change pointed out that the manager served at the pleasure of the mayor and council and could be removed from office by five voting members of the council" (Blodgett 2008, 212).

Interestingly, despite the perceived intent of mayors to protect their powers under the former charter, the movement for the shift to a council–manager form of government was actually spearheaded by Joe Wardy, who was elected to the executive office in 2003 by defeating incumbent Ray Caballero. Caballero (who opposed the shift to the council–manager form) was a political lightning rod who "shook his finger at generations of 'good old boy' elitism . . . [which had] left El Paso the fifth poorest city in the country and the only one in Texas that lost jobs because of NAFTA" (Nathan 2003, 5). Unlike his predecessor, whose political aspirations for a second term were in part negated by his aggressive attacks on the business elite, Wardy's platform for municipal reform was more inclusive and collaborative, and certainly less adversarial in that he attempted to "educate and gain buy-in from key players in the community" (Okubo 2005, 5). He acknowledged the internal deficiencies of the city's form and structure and "told people that if they were happy with the way things were run the last twenty-five years to go ahead and vote no [on the amendment]" (Okubo 2005, 5).

From a structural standpoint, many within the city believed its organization under the mayor–council form was inefficient and frequently produced administrative redundancies. Prior to the shift in 2004, the CAO was directly responsible for the city attorney, the Fire and Police departments, the municipal clerk's office, and the City–County Health District, and presided over five deputy chief administrative officers aligned

along the following common service areas: community services, financial and administrative services, municipal services, building and planning services, and transportation
services.

This structure, coupled with the intertwined policy–administration relationship
shared by the mayor and CAO, affected administrative operation within the city for a
couple of reasons. First, this structure was predicated on a centralized, top-down
approach whereby administrative action was initiated by the mayor and CAO. For
instance, as Debbie Hamlyn observed, "Constituency issues used to come directly from
the CAO, and then filter down through the related departments" (Hamlyn 2008). In
other words departments were not responding to citizen complaints and concerns as
they received them from the street level but rather were waiting for them to trickle
down from the top of the organization. From an efficiency standpoint, with decision-
making authority residing primarily with the mayor and CAO, it often took extensive
periods of time to resolve administrative issues, from citizen complaints to the hiring
and firing of employees. Second, the mayor–council form permitted the chief executive
to directly infiltrate departments to request information or initiate orders, without having to go through a deputy CAO first. While it is certainly clear that an administrative
task initiated by the mayor would hold supremacy over a conflicting order charged by
the deputy CAO, the potential for confusion, redundancy, and decision making based
on political premises rather than professionalism or expertise was greatly enhanced.
Perhaps more important, with the administrative body serving the direct will of the
mayor, the democratic principles and benefits of the administrative principles that support democracy—fairness, consistency, and equal access—and the judgment afforded
by an independent, professional implementation apparatus were also neglected.

The orientation of city government under the council–manager form could be
expected to be different for two reasons. First, without the internal demands of administrative responsibilities, the mayor of El Paso could provide a more constructive, calculated form of leadership for cross-border issues with Ciudad Juarez, which Saint-
Germain (1994) noted was a problem due in part to the city's previous form of government. According to Svara's study of mayoral leadership in council–manager cities, this
is certainly possible because, beyond serving as a ceremonial figurehead, "the mayor is
the single most important agent of cooperation in relations among officials" (Svara
1987, 213) and can be extensively involved in forming external partnerships. The may-
or's leadership draws on strong linkages to the council, the city manager, and the
public. Second, city managers recognize the need for administrative cooperation with
neighboring jurisdictions and are actively involved in developing operational agreements with other jurisdictions (Frederickson 1999).

*External Exigencies for Municipal Reform*

The internal organizational factors that led to the shift in municipal government form
in the City of El Paso were complemented by several external and environmental considerations. The business community harbored a number of the same concerns public

servants within the city held regarding a lack of cohesion and professionalism, although for different reasons. While municipal workers yearned for the consistent leadership and direction afforded by the council–manager form, the business sector advocated a change because it wanted economic development to be cultivated based on expert knowledge, sound management, and proven planning principles. However, considering the previous discussion regarding the political nature of large cities and their propensity for adopting or maintaining the mayor–council form, the business community's push for the form change exhibits not only their continued influence on municipal affairs, but perhaps more importantly, that El Paso's weak civic capacity may have aided in the success of the charter amendment. Unlike cities where "a heterogeneous population contributes to group conflict, the resolution of which is made more difficult by a complex and fragmented political structure," (Morgan and Watson 1992, 439) El Paso's largely Hispanic population has remained politically marginalized and wields very little organized power against the minority Anglo and economic elite. In this case, the lack of a legitimate competing theory on the potential ramifications of the council–manager was politically absent in El Paso, and ultimately led to an easy victory for advocates of the proposed charter amendment.

El Paso's push for a more efficient government was also unique because it occurred much later than other "big-city reforms" in the southwest region of the United States (Bridges 1997). After World War II, when cities such as Austin, Dallas, San Antonio, San Jose, San Diego, Albuquerque, and Phoenix were expanding in both square miles and population, much like in El Paso, political leaders "wrote the rules to restrict political participation and inflate the Anglo middle-class plurality in the electorate. The Anglo middle class was the favored constituency not because their working class fellow citizens were self-regarding or abided corruption happily but because the political wish list of the middle class was short and admitting other social groups posed the threat of redistribution" (Bridges 1997, 98). However, unlike the Charter Government Committee in Phoenix in 1959 or Albuquerque's Citizen Committee in 1962, which aggressively promoted reforming local government, the weak civic culture and abnormally inactive citizenry stalled the movement for a city manager nearly fifty years behind its regional counterparts.

While the movement for big-city reform was facilitated by the record expansion of southwestern cities in the postwar period, a sharp decline or loss of industries related to copper and textiles, in part, fueled the demand for a more professional approach to business development in El Paso. The Greater El Paso Chamber of Commerce, which was established in 1899 and has played a vital role in the city's politics for over a century, was one of the few community-based advocates of the shift in government form. This was not surprising considering Mayor Joe Wardy, a long-time Chamber member, served on a previous Chamber of Commerce Charter Review Committee in 1993. As the community organization leading the charter amendment movement, the El Paso Chamber of Commerce arranged a multitude of forums to educate the public on the benefits of the shift to the council–manager form. According to Okubo (2005), "The forums were well attended, with as many as sixty participants, and were informational rather than advocating for the change" (Okubo 2005, 5).

The Chamber's push behind Mayor Wardy's amendment initiative was largely grounded in matters of professionalism and the potential commercial benefits a trained administrator brings to municipal management and commercial development. Much like his public servant counterparts, Richard Fleager of the El Paso Chamber of Commerce noted that "mayoral issues often changed with the switch from one administration to another. It was hard to get programs implemented because there was no cohesive transition between mayors, and because of the two-year term limit, there was often a large learning curve in figuring out how the city works. From a business perspective, the mayors were not applying the best practices available, in zoning regulations for example, because they lacked the knowledge. A city manager brings an understanding of the right inducements for bringing in business" (Fleager 2008).

Not only were untrained politicians steering business development largely without the benefit of a city manager's knowledge, but in some instances, they were making a greater case for a politically neutral city manager by illegally awarding business contracts. In 2007 two former investment bankers pled guilty to federal bribery-related charges for schemes involving, among other elected officials, El Paso City Council members since 1999. The *El Paso Times* reported in December 2007 that the two members of Bear Sterns "allegedly devised a scheme to 'bribe elected members of [various] . . . boards and councils to secure their votes for certain vendors seeking to do business with the various public entities" (Bracamontes and Fonce-Olivas 2007). Incidents of corruption such as this undoubtedly shake the business community's confidence in its city government (Feiock, Jeong, and Kim 2003, 617), and lend credence to communitywide perceptions that decisions are largely politically grounded, rather than based on proven municipal management principles and the public interest.

In El Paso, however, it has historically been difficult to discern what is in the public interest. Since the city's early years as a small frontier settlement, El Paso's largely Hispanic population has retained a minimalist approach to civic affairs, even to the most basic citizenship responsibility of voting. According to Staudt and Coronado (2002), "power has been concentrated among the few and democracy has been limited at the U.S.–Mexico border. On the U.S. side, Anglo male elites have dominated economic decision-making . . . [and] people of Mexican heritage, faced obstacles in the exercise of voting rights. . . . Civic capacity is relatively weak, if civic capacity is measured in terms of the proportions of people who participate in public affairs through organizations, voting, and other means" (Staudt and Coronado 2002, 4). In order to understand this unique dynamic of El Paso city politics, it is helpful to appreciate the role its proximity to the border and local economics play in diminishing their civic culture.

The economic environment established by NAFTA in 1994 provided different opportunities for jobs, commerce, and the potential for an improved quality of life on both sides of the border. Yet, this long-standing formal and informal alliance has simultaneously yielded a politically passive citizenry in El Paso for a number of different reasons. In addition to the traditionally powerful economic and Anglo elite guiding the political agenda, as posited by Staudt and Coronado (2002), historically "migrants made up a critical mass of this population, and a fearful part of the population. Since the creation of the Border Patrol and periodic deportations, whether in the 1930's or the 1990's, immigrants' vulnerability and immigration profiling have undermined people's ability to organize and assert their rights. Many people prefer to maintain a low public profile to avoid surveillance and scrutiny" (Staudt and Coronado 2002, 31). Obviously Mexican citizens, legal or illegal, residing in El Paso are not eligible to vote in city elections. However, a strong familial culture often places those without voting rights in the same households with those able to cast their ballots during election time, and in many instances, the desire to remain detached from all public authorities keeps even those able to vote or participate in other arenas of governance, at home.

With respect to the charter amendment referendum in 2004, despite Okubo's contention (2005) that the citizenry played a pivotal role presenting the pros and cons to the change of form, there was little organized opposition to the amendment. There was only a small number of vocal citizens who were uncomfortable about the change. Their main concern focused on accountability, that the city manager was appointed and not elected and therefore citizens couldn't vote the manager out of office if he or she was ineffective. Knowledgeable citizens explained that five voting members of the council could remove the city manager or six members could override the veto of the mayor if the constituents felt the city manager wasn't doing a good job (Okubo 2005, 5). The "debate" over whether or not a change of government form never came to fruition, according to Kathleen Staudt, professor of political science and director for civic engagement at the University of Texas at El Paso (UTEP), because "people got used to not participating in civic politics. Early poll taxes and other forms of 'white is right' intimidation" have had a stranglehold on the broader Hispanic community's approach to public affairs (2008).

Prior to the election the *El Paso Times* urged citizens to participate in the political process by pledging its support for the shift in government and all other charter amendments on the ballot: "El Pasoans have an opportunity to change—and improve—the way their city is run . . . Amendment 4 would change the city from a 'strong mayor' form of government to a council–manager form. It would provide for a city manager who would have the expertise in running a city. That person would focus on day-to-day activities. Because that would free the mayor and council to focus on policy issues and also give the city more continuity, residents should vote 'yes' on this progressive move for El Paso" (*El Paso Times* 2004).

Although not historically low for El Paso elections, turnout was only 8 percent on February 7, 2004 (Okubo 2005), with 18,725 of 307,882 citizens casting their votes (Wilson 2004). Amendment 1 passed, providing the mayor and council with four-year staggered terms, while 54 percent of the voters approved Amendment 4, allowing the shift from a strong-mayor form of government to a council–manager form (Blodgett 2008, 213). Some citizens were uneasy with having the mayor relinquish a considerable amount of power, but the slim victory may have been a direct result of advocates noting the effectiveness of city managers in Texas and other parts of the southwest. As Gwen Pulido, formerly of the Greater El Paso Chamber of Commerce, noted, "Much of the advocacy for change was based on comparative assessments of city manager governments in the region. We looked at other cities in Texas and saw it as more efficient" (Pulido 2008). This analysis proved to be influential, as one citizen contended he voted for the city manager because "most cities in the United States have it, and it may work here as well" (Wilson 2004). Yet others remained slightly more skeptical, as another voter insisted before the election "I guess I'm more of a traditionalist. . . . The mayor should have had more power (in the charter proposal). I like the mayor having day-to-day oversight" (Wilson 2004). The final section of this chapter will examine the City of El Paso since the shift in government form.

## El Paso since 2004: Efficient, Professional, and Customer-Service Driven

Following the successful passage of Amendment 4 in February 2004, a transition team was established to assist in the government form change. Two council members, Mayor Joe Wardy's new executive assistant, and a governmental affairs staff member were initially charged with developing a smooth transition plan and finding an experienced city manager. According to Kathleen Staudt, "The [transition] committee wanted someone who could help professionalize city government, who could streamline operations, help with responsiveness with procedures like licensing, someone who could look at cost controls while keeping customer responsiveness. . . . Someone who could make things less political and look out for the broader interests" (Okubo 2005, 6). After a rigorous selection process, Joyce Wilson, the county manager for Arlington, Virginia, was selected as El Paso's first city manager. In addition to serving as county manager, Joyce Wilson was the assistant city manager for the City of Richmond, and she brought considerable knowledge about the problems relevant to the southwest as a result of time served as city administrator for Yuma, Arizona. According to Deputy City Manager Debbie Hamlyn, "initially the shift was difficult because [it required] a mindset change" by staff on how a city manager–based government operates. And while Joyce Wilson's hands-on managerial style has garnered some scrutiny from elected officials, city staff, and the broader citizenry, her accomplishments have greatly overshadowed any apprehensions about the shift to a council–manager government.

Feiock, Jeong, and Kim (2003) contend that "managers can best pursue the interests of citizens and the council by working toward professional goals rather than the political interests of the voters and council," and based on the previous examination of the antecedents for government form change in El Paso, it is clear that this contention served as the guidepost for the shift to a city manager. In identifying the need for a professional, stable administrative official, El Paso leadership executed the easy portion of the reform process. For Joyce Wilson the difficulty of restructuring an inefficient organization was met with an equally daunting task of inculcating a new organizational culture that challenged the previous norms, routines, and procedures of the mayor–council form; the shift also included an adjustment by the city council and the mayor to new institutional roles, and realigned the power structure within the city.

## Organizational Restructuring

With the continuity problem partially addressed through the passage of amendments 1 and 4, Joyce Wilson attempted to bring further clarity to El Paso's municipal government by reorganizing the city's structure. Deputy City Manager Debbie Hamlyn noted that much of the reorganization effort was geared toward streamlining and reducing city departments and functions in order to eliminate duplication, redundancy, and overall inefficiency. Before 2004 there were thirty-four independent city departments and related governmental entities, with the CAO directly overseeing the city attorney's office, the fire department, the municipal clerk, and police department. Below the CAO, five deputy CAOs were responsible for the service areas of Community Services,[1] Financial and Administrative Services,[2] Municipal Services,[3] Building and Planning Services,[4] and Transportation Services.[5] Deputy City Manager Patricia Adauto claimed that this arrangement produced "a lot of cross-pollination" (Adauto 2008).

In a presentation at the Texas City Managers Association Annual Conference in June 2006, Joyce Wilson addressed the streamlining effort undertaken in El Paso, noting that the downsizing of departments was one of the major accomplishments of her first year as the city manager. To eliminate the duplication and system redundancy that had muddled the city's efficiency under the mayor–council form, City Manager Wilson proposed cutting or consolidating a number of departments and reorganizing the remaining services areas by portfolios. Whereas under the mayor–council form there were five deputy CAOs responsible for the five service areas, the new organizational structure is predicated on four core service areas that operate under the city manager, with each of the following portfolios led by a deputy city manager: quality of life, finance and public safety, development and infrastructure services, and mobility services.

Community Services, which previously housed the Performing Arts and Cultural Resources, Community and Human Development, Library, Museums, and Zoo/Parks and Recreation departments transformed into the Quality of Life portfolio, led by Deputy City Manager Debbie Hamlyn. With the consolidation of the five deputy CAO service areas to four portfolios, this component expanded from five departments to six. The Museums Department was consolidated with the Performing Arts and Cultural Resources Department to form the Museum and Cultural Affairs Department, while the Community and Human Development and Library Departments remained autonomous entities. The City–County Health District, which was previously under the care of the chief administrative officer and managed anything from the control of sexually transmitted diseases to food inspections, was placed under the control of the City of El Paso exclusively as the Department of Public Health. The Zoo and Parks and Recreation departments became independently operated, and the Conventions and Visitors Bureau, which was previously deemed to be a core function of the Economic Development Department, moved from the Financial and Administrative Services realm to strategically focus on developing El Paso into a viable destination for tourism and professional conferences.

The Financial and Administrative Services of the mayor–council organizational structure endured a significant amount of reformation in its transition to the Finance and Public Safety portfolio. Currently under the leadership of Bill Studer, a native El Pasoan who was a finalist for the city manager position in 2004, this portfolio absorbed the Fire and Police departments, and the Municipal Clerk's Office, which were previously managed directly by the CAO. The new Financial Services Department consolidated the formerly independent Comptroller and Purchasing departments, while the Office of Management and Budget, Human Resources Department, and the Consolidated Tax Office each maintained their core responsibilities required under the mayor–council form.

The third portfolio developed under Joyce Wilson, Development and Infrastructure Services, was in essence a consolidation of the Municipal Services and Building and Planning Services components of the previous form and saw the most restructuring activity. Guided by Deputy City Manager Patricia Adauto's twenty-five years of experience within the City of El Paso, the Information Technology and Economic Development Departments, both of which formerly resided in the Financial and Administrative Services component, remained autonomous bodies under their new service umbrella. The Development Services Department, however, was created to combine the functions of the Building Permitting and Inspection Department and the Planning Department, rendering each to divisions within this new portfolio, along with the Customer Service and Business Center.

Next, the city minimized the Fleet Services Department by placing it under the supervision of the General Services Department as one of its three core divisions, while the Solid Waste Management Department was collapsed into the new Environmental Services Department, which also ensures environmental code compliance within the city and coordinates city beautification measures. The last major modification under this conglomeration divided the Street and Facilities Maintenance Department between two portfolios, with the former function becoming an independent department in Mobility Services, and the latter responsibility of preserving city's ninety-four buildings and work spaces falling under the management of the General Services Department.

Finally, Transportation Services became the Mobility Services portfolio, led by Jane Shang, a transportation expert of over twenty years. In expanding the breadth of this portfolio beyond traditional transportation-related issues (airport and public transit), this four-department division added an International Bridges Department to facilitate efficient and safe movement of people and goods across both sides of the border; and annexed the Street Department from the obsolete Municipal Services component in order to give this crucial infrastructural element independent, comprehensive attention.

With the structural realignment of portfolios by similar functions complete, Joyce Wilson and the four deputy city managers strategically addressed the lack of cohesion produced by an overloaded, unsystematic city organization chart. According to Deputy City Manager Patricia Adauto, despite the challenges inherent in "doing more with less," this aggressive effort to realign the city has proven to be extremely beneficial for the city's efficiency and effectiveness. "Do we have all the staff and resources we need—absolutely not. However, we are providing more services . . . [and] we have done more over the past three to four years than we had done over the past 20 to 25 years" (Adauto 2008). The city now consists of twenty-six independent departments, and each portfolio meets with its respective departments on a monthly basis in order to remain strategically aligned.

## New Institutional Roles—Mission, Policy, Administration, and Management

The introduction of a new city structure has done more than provide stability and rationality to the City of El Paso; it has also reshaped the institutional roles of both the city council and the mayor, established the city manager as a new player in the policy-administration game, and forced all three parties to adjust to the new relationship dynamic. This transition period had the potential to become muddled further by the spring 2005 elections, in which Joe Wardy and two of his allies on the city council were defeated, the former by councilmember John Cook. Cook, however, "gave Wilson his whole-hearted support during his campaign and has continued that strong backing since his election" (Blodgett 2008, 212).

Interestingly, in a presentation to the U.S. Consulate in October 2006 (City of El Paso 2006), Joyce Wilson applied Svara's (1985) seminal Mission-Management Separation with Shared Responsibility for Policy and the Administration (Dichotomy-Duality) model to describe the diversified, yet distinct role both the city council and the city manager play in determining the city's mission (what government should or should not address at the broadest level), policy decisions (how to spend government revenues, whether to initiate new programs or create new offices, and how to distribute services and at what levels within the existing range of services provided), administration (practices employed to achieve policy objectives), and management (actions taken to support the policy and administrative functions) (Svara 1985, 224–28). This is of great significance within the context of the City of El Paso, as the normative model described by Svara has proven to provide tremendous insight into Wilson's approach to her position, and perhaps the city council and mayoral reaction to the shift.

From a mission perspective, while the organization endured a great deal of consolidation and shifting within its structure, the general spectrum of government services provided by the City of El Paso changed very little if at all. Where Svara's early research on the Dichotomy-Duality Model indicated the city manager contributes minimally to a city's mission because defining the scope of city government is largely the "responsibility of elected officials. . . . This is clearly the normative requirement of democratic theory" (Svara 1985, 225), his work conducted nearly a decade later unearthed a shift in responsibilities that also seemed to be reflected in El Paso.

City managers contribute information about trends and conditions, help the council determine strategies, and contribute to the development of broader goals (Svara 1999). For instance, in 2006 City Manager Wilson started a neighborhood services program to revitalize and conserve many of El Paso's residential areas. While acknowledging the aesthetic benefits, Wilson had a broader vision for the program and the city, noting that "strong neighborhoods . . . tend to have low crime rates and to be more involved in the events around them" (Crowder 2006). The program has also made a concerted effort to involve the community in this program by including residents and the Center for Civic Engagement at UTEP in the comprehensive strategy—highlighting the city's newfound mission to enhance participatory governance.

Joyce Wilson's contribution to the mission and the development of city goals were reflected in other areas as well, reiterating Svara's findings that "administrators would prefer that council involvement decrease as activities shift from general and strategic to the specific and operational" (Svara 1999, 49). During the budget development process in 2005, City Representatives Eddie Holguin and Jose Alexandro Lozano drafted their own proposals. Noting the lack of attention given to debt service and operational costs in each of the proposed budgets, Wilson "pointed out serious errors in Holguin's offering" and was supported by City Representative Beto O'Rourke, who called the draft "arbitrary and irresponsible" (*El Paso Times* 2005).

She exhibited further leadership by developing six strategic goals that all city employees would assist in achieving: fiscal policy (ensuring long-term financial stability and sustainability); citizen involvement (to facilitate opportunities for citizens to be involved in local government); community development (to become the most livable city in the United States and be recognized as an international city); transportation (to establish a comprehensive transportation system); economic development (to become the city with the lowest unemployment rate and highest per capita wages in the United States); and customer service (to become a high-performing, customer-focused organization). The customer service focus is of particular interest with respect to the city's mission primarily because it is a calculated shift in the manner with which the City of El Paso aims to conduct government, despite the retention of the majority of services provided under the mayor–council form.

In addition to tackling the efficiency problem from a structural standpoint, Joyce Wilson was intent on reinventing the organizational culture (Rivera, Streib, and Willoughby 2000), and the city is now guided by the following mission statement: "Dedicated to Outstanding Customer Service for a Better Community" (City of El Paso 2008). According to Wilson, "We have instituted customer service standards for the entire organization and by department so that we can routinely measure our performance. We have various forms of informal and formal customer feedback loops so we can monitor areas where we need to pay more attention. . . . Overall we look at responsiveness, quality of service, feedback on service priorities as ways to gauge our performance and make appropriate adjustments" (*Newspaper Tree* 2008).

In the policy domain the city manager gains an increased level of input in comparison to mission-related tasks because the development of new programs or services is largely buttressed by the recommendations of administrators of all levels, and this appears to be the case in the City of El Paso thus far. According to Wilson, "I respect that city staff does not dictate policy. We take that direction from the City Council. We do have a responsibility though to provide recommendations and good research/information in areas of policy that are important to the Council and community so that informed decisions can be made" (*Newspaper Tree* 2008).

Within the administration realm, the level of task responsibility shifts largely to the city manager, leaving the council with the primary duty to address citizen complaints regarding service delivery and providing oversight of administrative performance. Svara

(1985) contends that "some specific implementing actions are carried to legislative bodies for final decision, such as application of a zoning ordinance to a particular case or approval of locations for scattered site housing" (226), but the development of the tools and techniques to be applied in such cases are within the confines of the city manager and the bureaucracy's expertise. This redistribution of tasks has improved the city, as Richard Fleager of the Greater El Paso Chamber of Commerce observed that "the city manager has allowed council to deal with more [traditional] issues such as gaining support for downtown development, the budget, and tax structures and fees" (Fleager 2008).

In placing the city council in a more traditional mission and policy-oriented role, the city manager has lightened the load for the city's elected body by taking over the decision-making process of how the City will achieve its policy objectives. For Joyce Wilson, citizen engagement has become a crucial component of administration. According to Gwen Pulido, formerly of the Greater El Paso Chamber of Commerce, this administrative enhancement has been one of the benefits of the shift. In her view, "Joyce Wilson has done a good job of informing the public through a network of neighborhood associations, church groups, Rotary Clubs, and community presenta-tions" (Pulido 2008) on the activities of government; perhaps more importantly, this component has been instituted to better understand and meet the needs of the community.

Within the management realm where functions include "controlling and utilizing the human, material, and informational resources of the organization to best advan-tage" (Svara 1985, 227), El Paso's city council was more involved in the past than it was under City Manager Wilson. As previously mentioned, the FBI probe that unveiled a wealth of corruption predicated on the delivery of contracts was one of the by-products of an excess of integration between politics and administration. With council members actively able to determine who received government contracts with the city without a professional check from a neutral administrator, special interests, not ratio-nal, public-interest driven expertise was utilized to award many projects. In applying a minimalist approach to the council's involvement in management-related issues, Joyce Wilson believes this "form of government has helped to insulate the City from some of the public corruption issues that have been ongoing over the past several years" (*Newspaper Tree* 2008).

In December 2007 this adapted management role was illuminated with Joyce Wil-son's "first high profile appointment since being selected as El Paso's first city manager" (Leon 2007). Deputy Chief Greg Allen was named interim chief of police over Assistant Chiefs Diana Kirk and Paul Cross, both of whom were a rank above Wilson's appoint-ment. While Allen's thirty years of experience in the police department left little room to question the appointment based on a lack of qualifications, some council members felt that City Manager Wilson ignored their interest in being included in the selection process. City Representative Steve Ortega "said he could not comment on Allen because he [did not have] the opportunity to meet him [prior to her appointment]. He said that Wilson did not approach him for suggestions as to who should be appointed as interim chief, although he did suggest to her that Cross become the interim chief" (Leon 2007).

According to Gwen Pulido, this issue reflects the council adjusting to less of a management role, and this in turn has generated some stress between the elected officials and the city manager. "There is some tension about Joyce's control over day-to-day operations, such as the hiring and firing of personnel. Sometimes she is perceived to have too much power, and in some instances she doesn't let entities discuss issues with the council" (Pulido 2008).

The mayor's office has also experienced a significant amount of institutional change since the shift in 2004. As mentioned on numerous occasions above, the mayor–council form in El Paso was disparaged in part because of an excessive and sometimes redundant bureaucratic structure and because of an overly active executive role in the administrative organs of the city. The shift to the council–manager government rectified the structural issues through the consolidation of departments and removed politics from the administrative hierarchy. Previous mayors often violated basic chain of command principles by initiating orders and demands around deputy CAOs and directly to departments, creating organizational confusion and frequent questions from staff regarding the merit of the requests.

As Gulick asserted over seventy years ago, "The rigid adherence to the principle of unity of command may have its absurdities; these are, however, unimportant in comparison with the certainty of confusion, inefficiency and irresponsibility which arise from the violation of the principle" (1937, 9). Now, according to Deputy City Manager Debbie Hamlyn, "the mayor can't just go to any department and request information or things to get done; he must go through a deputy city manager. This has definitely enhanced the checks and balances system" (2008).

The reduction in the mayor's responsibility in the policy and administrative arenas has in turn provided his office with an enhanced, more precise leadership role in both local and international issues. From a local standpoint, Mayor John Cook has adopted a function beyond a ceremonial figure and is serving as an educator in El Paso (Svara 1987). Among his multiple informative activities, he has implemented "Open Door with the Mayor," a monthly community outreach program intended to provide a direct avenue for citizens to discuss their concerns and get a better understanding of government activities. Mayor Cook is also exercising his role as promoter (Svara 1987) as a board member of the El Paso Regional Economic Development Corporation, a nonprofit organization, that facilitates business development in El Paso, southern New Mexico, and Ciudad Juarez. The business community has embraced the mayor's tailored leadership role because his position is allowing him to "take the lead in projecting a favorable image of the city and seek to 'sell' others on investment in it" (Svara 1987, 218). From an international standpoint, the mayor has become the focal point for improving cross-border cooperation with Ciudad Juarez. Although there are still problems related to the cooperation between the municipal governments of both cities, as Staudt notes, "Mayor Cook is paying legitimate attention to bi-national committees" and has established an intergovernmental relations office to centralize the organization's international efforts (2008).

## Conclusion

As this chapter has illustrated, the transition from the inefficient, inconsistent mayor–council form to the council–manager government has proven to be effective thus far on various fronts. Not only has Joyce Wilson and the institutional functions of the city manager brought cohesion and professionalism to the city's administrative body, it has also improved the ability for El Paso's elected officials to fulfill their traditional democratic roles without the worry of carrying out the law. There is widespread belief that the depoliticization and professionalization of the city has brought accountability and transparency to the administrative process because Joyce Wilson's autonomy, authority, and technical expertise allows her to "look under every rock" to ensure organizational effectiveness (Hamlyn 2008). While this has taken some getting used to for both tenured city staff and elected officials, the change has produced tangible and cultural results within the city organization that would garner the approval of an even more politically active citizenry.

Since her appointment, City Manager Wilson has made zoning laws more relevant, addressed flooding issues that have hampered the city for generations, and brought resolution to the police and firefighters' pension negotiations—and in doing so has provided a greater understanding of how a city manager is feasible in city the size of El Paso. According to Hamlyn, "A city manager government is democratically viable in a larger city because it is providing a check through professionalism. In El Paso it has balanced the political nature of the city and given us another steward of the public interest. Under the city manager form of government it is easier to figure out what the community wants and figure out what is the best way to do it" (2008). In 2006 the Texas City Management Association recognized El Paso for its improved performance as the city council received City Council of the Year honors, while Wilson was awarded Administrator of the Year (Blodgett 2008).

For the City of El Paso, the demand for professionalism and the transformation of politics has yielded a form of government that is tailor made to handle the uniqueness brought forth by its alignment along the U.S.–Mexico border. With the local, regional, and international problems constantly changing, perhaps the permanence of the city manager position has provided El Paso with the ability to maintain an accurate, impartial reading on these affairs and respond to them in a consistent manner. Whether or not the historically disengaged citizenry will one day find fault with the form due to its democratic deficiencies is uncertain; however, long-term administrative effectiveness and the willingness for the elected officials to adapt to their new, more concise institutional roles will go a long way in convincing El Pasoans of its sustainable value.

## Notes

1. Performing Arts and Cultural Resources, Community and Human Development, Library, Museums, Zoos/Parks.

2. Comptroller, Office of Management and Budget, Purchasing, Tax Office, Human Resources, Information Technology, Economic Development.

3. Fleet Services, Solid Waste Management, Street and Facilities Maintenance.

4. Building Permitting and Inspection, Engineering, Planning, El Paso Water Utilities, Metropolitan Planning Organization.

5. Aviation, Sun Metro, Metropolitan Planning Organization.

# References

Adauto, P. 2008. Interview by Larry D. Terry. July 2.

Blodgett, T. 2008. *City government that works: The history of council–manager government in Texas.* Texas City Management Association.

Bracamontes, R., and T. Fonce-Olivas. 2007. Bankers plead guilty to fraud, bribery in FBI Probe. *El Paso Times,* December 22. www.elpasotimes.com.

Bridges, A. 1997. Textbook municipal reform. *Urban Affairs Review* 33, no. 1 (September): 97–119.

City of El Paso. 2006. Understanding municipal government. http://www.ci.el-paso.tx.us/city_manager/_documents/Presentation-Joyce%20U.S.%20Consulate%2010–11–06.pdf (accessed June 2008).

———. 2008. Mission statement. www.ci.el-paso.tx.us/mission.asp (accessed June 2008).

Crowder, D. 2006. City manager brings many changes to El Paso. *El Paso Times,* December 25. www.elpasotimes.com.

*El Paso Times.* 2004. Amendments on February 7 ballot. January 18. www.elpasotimes.com.

———. 2005. Our views. August 4. www.elpasotimes.com.

Feiock, Richard C., Moon-Gi Jeong, and Jaehoon Kim. 2003. Credible commitment and council–manager government: Implications for policy instrument choices. *Public Administration Review* 63, no. 5 (September): 616–25.

Fleager, R. 2008. Interview by Larry D. Terry. June 27.

Frederickson, H. G. 1999. The repositioning of American public administration. *Political Science and Politics* 32, no. 4 (December): 701–11.

Gulick, L. 1937. Notes on the theory of organization. In *Papers on the science of administration,* ed. L. Gulick and L. Urwick. New York: Institute of Public Administration, Columbia University.

Hamlyn, D. 2008. Interview by Larry D. Terry. June 30.

Leon, R. 2007. Greg Allen named interim police chief. *Newspaper Tree,* December 6. www.newspapertree.com/politics/print/1887-greg-allen-named-interim-police-chief.

Morgan, D. R., and S. S. Watson. 1992. Policy leadership in council–manager cities: Comparing mayor and manager. *Public Administration Review* 52, no. 5 (September/October): 438–46.

Nathan, D. 2003. Who runs this city? *El Bridge* (Spring).

*Newspaper Tree.* 2008. Interview with Joyce Wilson. October 6. www.newspapertree.com.

Okubo, D. 2005. A time for change: El Paso adopts the council–manager form. *National Civic Review* 94, no. 3 (Fall): 3–9.

Protasel, G. J. 1988. Abandonments of the council manager plan: A new intuitionalist perspective. *Public Administration Review* 48, no. 4 (July/August): 807–12.

Pulido, G. 2008. Interview with Larry D. Terry. July 2.

Rivera, Mark, Gregory Streib, and Katherine G. Willoughby. 2000. Reinventing council–manager cities: Examining the role of city mangers. *Public Performance and Management Review* 24, no. 2 (December): 121–32.

Saint-Germain, M. 1994. *Border issues and public policy: Public managers on the U.S.–Mexico border.* Center for Inter-American and Border Studies, University of Texas at El Paso.

Staudt, K. 2008. Interview by Larry D. Terry. June 27.

Staudt, K., and I. Coronado. 2002. *Fronteras no mas: Toward social justice at the U.S.–Mexico border.* New York: Palgrave Macmillan.

Staudt, K., and C. N. Stone. 2007. Division and fragmentation: The El Paso experience in global-local perspective. In *Transforming the city: Community organizing and the challenge of political change,* ed. Marion Orr. Lawrence: University of Kansas Press.

Svara, James H. 1985. Dichotomy and duality: Reconceptualizing the relationship between policy and administration in council–manager cities. *Public Administration Review* 45, no. 1 (January/February): 221–32.

———. 1987. Mayoral leadership in council–manager cities: Preconditions versus preconceptions. *Journal of Politics* 49, no. 1 (February): 207–27.

———. 1999. The shifting boundary between elected officials and city managers in the large council–manager cities. *Public Administration Review* 59, no. 1 (January/February): 44–53.

Timmons, W. H. 1990. *El Paso: A borderlands history.* El Paso: Texas Western Press.

Vowell, J. C. 1952. *Politics at El Paso: 1850–1920.* Master of Arts Thesis, Department of History, University of Texas at El Paso.

Wilson, C. K. 2004. Voters OK city manager. *El Paso Times,* February 8. www.elpasotimes.com.

CHAPTER 13

# TOPEKA

## Council–Manager Redux Finding Balance in the Politics–Administration Dichotomy

R. PAUL BATTAGLIO JR.

## Introduction

TRUE TO THE THEME of the case studies in this collected work, this analysis turns to the city of Topeka, Kansas, which recently changed form of government to the council–manager[1] from mayor–council (also referred to as strong mayor). The discussion will shed light on the renewed interest in the progressive era form of government and the derisive local politics that resulted in the change in Topeka. Because the change in form has proven problematic, Topeka remains a city in transition, adapting structural forms to fit political purposes.

## A Concise History

Topeka, located in northeast Kansas, is the state's capital city and is the county seat for Shawnee County. The city had a population of 122,377 according to the 2000 Census and was projected to be just above that number by 2007 estimates (U.S. Census Bureau 2008). The city was originally founded by abolitionists in 1854 as a Free-State town after passage of the Kansas–Nebraska Bill, receiving its charter in 1857 (Hrenchir 2008c). In the immediate post–World War II era, Topeka enjoyed economic prosperity resulting from industrial investments made by the Defense Plants Corporation (Hrenchir 2008b). Topeka was also the source of the famous *Brown v. Topeka Board of Education* ruling by the Supreme Court declaring that separate schools for whites and African Americans were not equal and, therefore, were not legal (Hrenchir 2008c). During the 1960s Topeka experienced urban renewal resulting from federal economic development grants from the Johnson administration and an economic downturn along with the rest of the country as the 1970s ended. Beginning in the 1980s Topeka voters and politicians were confronted with a series of reforms aimed at changing the way the city was to be governed over the next twenty years.

Until 1984 Topeka was administered by a mayor–commission government. In the early twentieth century, Topeka was a latecomer to the commission form of government in Kansas, adopting the form at a time when it was seen as outdated by other governments in the region (Smith 2008a). Topekans were given the opportunity to switch from the commission form to council–management government in 1929, 1952, 1962, 1964, and 1969, rejecting the form of government each time (Hrenchir 2004g). In November 1984 voters in Topeka were given the chance to approve a change in city government form, opting out of their mayor–commission for the strong-mayor government. This change was prompted by concerns regarding the commission form as an impediment to economic and population growth. The commission form was seen as promoting indecision—a problem proponents felt could be improved by stronger leadership (Smith 2008a). The strong-mayor form took effect in 1985, with city government comprising a full-time mayor administrating the city and a governing body of nine council members elected by district (Smith 2008b). The elected mayor and his appointed chief administrative officer were responsible for day-to-day operations and the implementation of policies approved by the council. Mayor Douglas Wright served Topeka until 1989. In 1989 Harry L. "Butch" Felker III was elected mayor serving Topeka for one full term, then resigning in 1997 for health reasons. Felker later returned to office in 2001.

By the end of the twentieth century, Topeka politicians expressed dissatisfaction with the strong-mayor system put in place in 1984. Spearheaded by City Councilwoman Betty Dunn, reform-minded politicians advocated a change to the council–manager form of government. This effort was part of a larger political turmoil resulting from disagreement over economic policies between the mayor and city council members. In 1997 Joan Wagnon was elected the first and, until the present day, only female mayor of Topeka. Wagnon was an active member of the community, previously serving as director for the Young Women's Christian Association (YWCA) and state representative (Quinn 2000). However, Wagnon's tenure in office proved problematic as she struggled to reinvigorate a depressed Topekan economy. Wagnon was asked to discontinue presiding over city council meetings, with critics claiming she was too partisan and maintained a confrontational posture with the council (Hall 2001). Additionally, during her tenure the city's government form was once again reviewed. In 1988 an ordinance established the first form of government review committee, with subsequent reviews to be held every ten years (Hall 1998).

The 1988 review committee eventually recommended several changes to city government structure. Recommendations adopted were mainly aimed at reducing the power of the mayor and enhancing city council power (e.g., the council was given more input in the hiring and firing of the mayor's top administrators). Following ordinance policy, a charter review committee was appointed in late 1998. The committee was composed of members appointed by the city council (each council member had a single appointment) and three mayoral appointments (Hall 1998; McLean and Lassiter 1999). The committee's final report advocated increasing the mayor's administrative power while strengthening the city council's role in budgetary decisions. Further, the report recommended holding the elections for mayor and council members simultaneously in an effort to encourage discussions during the election cycle on issues affecting the city. The resulting ordinance entailing the committee's recommendations, however, failed to achieve the required support needed to pass the council. Councilwoman Dunn, along with other colleagues, blocked the measure, championing instead a council–manager form of government (*Topeka Capital-Journal* Editorial Board 1999).[2]

After rejection of the proposed ordinance strengthening the mayor and council's powers, bickering among council members and the mayor intensified over budgetary issues (Johnson 1999). Councilwoman Dunn and her allies again proposed a change to the council–manager form of government. The proponents for the council–manager form of government cited the many successes attributed to the form of government in other large cities in Kansas, including Wichita, Lawrence, Olathe, and Overland Park (McLean and Lassiter 1999). In fact, Topeka was the only large city in Kansas without a council–manager form of government. By summer 2000 Dunn and her allies were able to put an ordinance to a vote of the council that would change the current strong-mayor government to a council–manager government and replace the nine-member council with a seven-member council. Once approved by the council, the ordinance would then have to be placed on the next election ballot according to Kansas law (Kansas Statute [K.S.] 1976). As council members discussed the measure, objections to the plan gathered strength. Council members were particularly troubled by the fact that Councilwoman Dunn erroneously charged in the ordinance that the change in government would go into effect in sixty-one days unless a petition was circulated to put it on the ballot for Topeka voters (Hall 2000). The failure of the ordinance to include recourse for city voters ultimately doomed the passage of the measure. The council voted it down, 5 to 4.[3]

## Political Scandal for a New Century

Although the fate of city government reform seemed to end when the council–manager ordinance failed in 2000, political events in the first decade of the twenty-first century dictated otherwise. A series of political scandals in the mayor's office once again tempted politicians and voters to reconsider changing government form. The period surrounding the turn of the century saw Topeka's first female mayor (Joan Wagnon in 1997) as well as its first African American mayor (James McClinton in 2003). Topeka voters also returned Mayor Harry "Butch" Felker to office. Felker's term in office would be marred by a series of abuses related to his 2001 election campaign.

Felker first served as mayor of Topeka for seven years during the 1990s, winning election in 1989 (*Topeka Capital-Journal* Editorial Board 2008). Felker rose to public office from his position of parks and recreation commissioner for the city. Felker's tenure in the mayoral office, however, was cut short in 1997 because of health reasons. But Felker returned to public life, seeking the mayor's seat once again in 2001. During his later foray into public life, Felker encountered a number of obstacles that prevented him from continuing in office. Beginning in 2002 the Kansas Governmental Ethics Commission initiated an investigation into Felker's 2001 campaign dealings, subsequently charging him with six counts of violating state campaign finance laws (*Topeka Capital-Journal* 2005). The charges emanated from employees at the Topeka Convention and Visitors Bureau who alleged false travel expense reports were being filed. The money from the filings eventually made its way as a donation to Felker's reelection campaign—the sources of which were not properly documented by the campaign. Felker pleaded guilty in July 2003 to three ethics violations and was fined $7,500 (Hall 2008a). Two other ethics charges were subsequently dropped by prosecutors. Felker's violations, as well as suspected involvement in other misconduct, led to Shawnee County District Attorney Robert Hecht seeking his ouster from the mayor's office. Felker was suspended from work on October 10, 2003, with a trial set for November 17, 2003 (Fry and Moon 2003). The trial, however, never took place. Felker resigned from office on November 6 citing an inability to afford the legal expenses to defend his ouster (Moon and Henrikson 2003). During Felker's suspension and following his resignation, Deputy Mayor Duane Pomeroy assumed the role of acting mayor. A subsequent ethical complaint related to the incidents above was filed by the state disciplinary panel in 2005, alleging that Felker violated rules for professional conduct for lawyers (Carpenter 2005).

Along with Felker's alleged campaign misconduct, the mayor's office was also targeted for mismanagement of the city's purchasing card system (Moon 2003a). Under Felker's final stint as mayor, a number of city employees were disciplined for misuse of Topeka's purchasing card (P-card) system. Surrounding the controversy were allegations that employees were disciplined only after the wasteful spending practices were made public. Acting Mayor Pomeroy took the opportunity to investigate whether or not disciplinary action had taken place before the current publicity as Felker had attested. Pomeroy suggested that if necessary actions had not occurred before the recent events, he would target employees for disciplinary action. Pomeroy suggested the media attention that the P-card scandal gave city officials an opportunity to curb wasteful practices and put employees on alert (Moon 2003a).

During Pomeroy's short tenure as acting mayor, the city council began the difficult task of selecting a new mayor. According to the city charter, the city council was tasked with selecting Felker's replacement (Topeka, City Code 2008c). After vigorous hearings and debate, the council tapped former council member James McClinton from a field of forty candidates as Pomeroy's replacement (Moon and Henrikson 2003). McClinton became the first African American mayor of Topeka and the first mayor appointed by the city council. However, McClinton's ascendancy to the mayor's office was not without controversy. During the time leading up to the council vote, local YWCA officials accused McClinton of being "a batterer" stemming from domestic battery charges in 2002 that were subsequently dropped (Moon and Henrikson 2003). While a highlight of McClinton's mayoralty was presiding over the 150th anniversary of the *Brown* decision, his tenure in office was short lived. Even before McClinton's appointment, the push for a change to a council–manager form of government had been well under way. Council members Betty Dunn and Lisa Stubbs were fostering support for the change, using Felker's political scandal and ouster trial as a catalyst for citizen dissatisfaction (Johnson 2003). Both council members were keen to get the switch to the council–manager form of government on the 2004 ballot (Hrenchir 2004b). In the 2004 referendum Topeka citizens opted for the council–manager form of government, stripping the mayor's office of most powers in favor of a city manager. In 2004 McClinton decided not to seek election to a full term as mayor, citing the new "ceremonial" duties of the office as a reason (Goering 2006).

## Politics, Citizen Discontent, and the 2004 Council–Manager Referendum

Beginning in December 2003 city council members voted to conduct forums to assess the views of Topekans on the possibility of changing the form of city government (Hrenchir 2004b). The resolution called for any proposed changes to be placed on the November 2004 ballot (Moon 2003b). The forums were subsequently held in May 2004 at Washburn University, soliciting input from citizens in a town hall format. Washburn University officials compiled summaries of the forums for the city council to consider for change proposals (Hrenchir 2004a). By July 2004 city council members were ready to vote on the form of government measure. Reform was not, however, limited to just the change from strong-mayor to council–manager. City council members additionally considered a measure to encourage Kansas lawmakers to adopt legislation regarding the consolidation of the city of Topeka and Shawnee County. Not surprisingly, Mayor McClinton spoke against the council–manager form of government, citing recent evidence of its failure in Hartford, Connecticut, and Spokane, Washington, with both cities opting to return to the strong-mayor form (Hrenchir 2004b; Hassett and Watson 2007). However, based on the recommendations of the citizen forums, as well as overwhelming testimony in favor of the council–manager form from citizens, the Topeka City Council passed the measures on July 20, 2004, putting the vote for form of city government to Topeka citizens (Hrenchir 2004b).

The proposal for the 2004 ballot advocated several measures in favor of the council–manager form of government (Hrenchir 2004b, 2004c). Specifically, the ordinance called for rescinding the mayor's current power to hire and fire city department managers. The mayor's duties would then involve leading meetings, providing community leadership, promoting economic development, representing the city in intergovernmental relations, recommending legislation to the council, encouraging development programs, and serving as the city's ceremonial leader (Hrenchir 2004e). The mayor would also continue to be elected at large to a four-year term.

Essentially, the change measure would dramatically reduce the role of the mayor to serving simply as a figurehead with no real power over legislative matters before the council. The city's chief administrative officer, who reports directly to the mayor, would be replaced by a council-appointed city manager who would serve as Topeka's chief executive officer. The city manager would be responsible for hiring, firing, and supervising all city employees. Moreover, the city manager would administer all city administrative affairs and prepare the budget for approval by the council. The city manager would serve an indefinite term and could be hired or fired by a majority vote from the council, which would continue to set city policy. Elections for the nine city council members would continue to be staggered terms every four years from geographic districts.

However, the placement of the measure on the ballot was not without controversy (Hrenchir 2004c). Critics of the ordinance took issue with the change in form, citing lack of accountability, increased costs, and legal issues with the council–manager form. Councilwoman Lover Chancler urged voters to reject the council–manager form, citing the fact that citizens would no longer be able to hold their chief administrative officer accountable at the ballot box (Hrenchir 2004f). Councilman John Nave joined Chancler in her criticism, adding that increased costs attributable to salary and a severance package would accompany a move to the council–manager form (Hrenchir 2004f). Moreover, legal issues continued to surround the ballot measure as critics asserted that the council's 6–3 vote was null and void, falling short of the necessary two-thirds according to state law that requires the mayor's involvement as a member of the governing body.[4] Finally, critics argued that city managers tended to have short tenures in office and that this would negatively affect the city manager's ability to initiate and oversee necessary reforms.[5]

One sticking point regarding the change in form involved the legality of the measure. At issue was the role and authority of the mayor to vote and preside over council meetings. Critics asserted that the plan's approval would actually make the mayor part of Topeka's ten-member governing body, thus giving the mayor a vote on all measures considered by the council. Critics such as attorney J. Kevin Murphy and State Representative Bill Bunten suggested that the measure's flaws would lead to problems. One particular problem would be how the city would resolve ties if the mayor were given a vote, making the governing body ten (Hrenchir 2004c). City attorney Brenden Long countered such criticism by saying that while the mayor's office in the mayor–council form provides for his or her membership in the governing body (including the power to propose legislation and preside over council meetings), the mayor has no specific right to vote on council matters (Hrenchir 2004c). Long suggested that this practice would continue after passage of the change measure and that if a mayor were to assert greater voting rights city officials might simply amend the charter to curb such rights.[6] Thus, for Long and proponents of the form change, the November 2 ballot would constrain, if not remove, the mayor's voting powers, while his or her veto power would remain.

Rallying around Councilwoman Stubbs and her allies on the city council, proponents of the move to a council–manager form cited the advantages of professionalism, credibility, accountability, and its extensive use throughout the country (Hrenchir 2004e). Challenging critics' contention that the form lacks credibility, proponents countered that citizens in a council–manager government elect council members who have the authority to dismiss a bad city manager immediately as opposed to waiting for the next election cycle to remove a mayor. Councilwoman Stubbs asserted, "You elect the people who are the watchdogs for the city of Topeka. So it is their job to make sure that things are running the way they should" (Hrenchir 2004f). A city manager, advocates asserted, would provide professionalism to the city's management practices over the tendency of mayor to be more interested in the political affairs of staying in office. John Arnold, former chief administrative officer for Topeka, challenged the notion that the city manager's salary and benefits package would be a burden to the city. Arnold asserted that "a city manager will be able to find hundreds of thousands of dollars of savings, maybe even millions of dollars of savings in the organization" (Hrenchir 2004f). Such savings, Arnold contended, would more than outweigh any salary or severance package issues. In terms of credibility, proponents cited the recent study ordered by city officials and conducted by Cincinnati-based Management Partners, Inc., which criticized current management practices.[7] Moreover, the consultants argued that accountability would be improved through the dismissal powers of the council, whose members may fire a city manager at any time by a majority vote versus the need to wait for the next election when attempting to oust a mayor from office.

The campaign for the change in form of government was closely covered by the local media as voters weighed the issues for and against the council–manager form. Despite the many challenges, citizens opted for the council–manager form of government, replacing the nineteen-year-old strong mayor–council form (Hrenchir 2004g). The measure carried among Topekans with 66 percent in favor of the change and 34 percent against. Work on the change of government began almost immediately, with council members meeting to set salaries of elected officials, and that of the city manager at a later date. According to the ordinance, the council would meet on April 12, 2005, to appoint an acting city manager.

As part of the greater push for reform under way, city and county citizens were also asked on the November 2004 ballot to approve moving toward a consolidated government for the city of Topeka and Shawnee County. This measure also passed, 59 percent to 41 percent (Hrenchir 2004g). In opting for the consolidation measure, the voters of Shawnee County agreed to the appointment by state officials of a commission whose duties would include formulating a consolidation plan for city and county governments, or functions of those governments.[8]

## The Referendum's Aftermath

Shortly after the 2004 referendum, Topekans once again went to the polls in the spring of 2005 to elect a mayor under the new council–manager government along with several council seats.[9] The mayoral election pitted city councilwoman Lisa Stubbs, a proponent of the move to council–manager government, against long-time Kansas state legislator Bill Bunten (Hrenchir 2005a). Stubbs, one of the leaders for the move to council–manager government, gave up her district seat on the city council to seek the office she advocated changing during the push for the council–manager form. Bunten had previously run for mayor in 2001, losing to Butch Felker, and was among the forty candidates who sought the position after Felker's resignation. The thirty-year veteran of the Kansas legislature placed first in the March 1 mayoral primary, followed by

Stubbs. The two then faced off in a runoff election on April 5, with Bunten receiving 56 percent of the vote to Stubbs's 44 percent. Topekans also sent a message by choosing new city council members to represent four of the five seats that were up for election. Bunten was sworn in on the following Tuesday as the first mayor under the council–manager government—the same day the change in government form took effect. Bunten's salary is $20,000 as opposed to the $60,000 his predecessors were paid under the strong-mayor government (Hrenchir 2005a).

One week into his term, Bunten immediately went to work committed not to hold a mere ceremonial position. Bunten sought under the language naming the mayor as a member of the governing body the right to be a voting member on council committees. The council, however, was reluctant to give Bunten voting power, opting instead for providing the mayor with a nonvoting, advisory capacity on budgetary issues (Hrenchir 2005b). Given his thirty years in the state legislature handling budgetary affairs, Bunten felt his experience would be beneficial to city policymakers. The council's reluctance to provide the mayor with greater voting powers stemmed from the November 2004 ballot, which was not without legal debate. This legal issue continued to spark debate among council members apprehensive toward approving Mayor Bunten's requests for greater duties over the next three years.

In 2006 Mayor Bunten spearheaded efforts at the state level to establish a Topeka/Shawnee County Riverfront Authority (Hrenchir 2006a). Because Bunten pursued this without the council's permission, council members suggested amending the 2004 ordinance to diminish the role of the mayor. Council members had just hired Plainfield, New Jersey, city official Norton Bonaparte Jr. as city manager. replacing the acting city manager. While Bonaparte brought a thirty-year career in public administration that included manager of four cities, council members were clearly concerned that the city manager's authority might be usurped by such an active mayor (Hrenchir 2007). Indeed, Bunten challenged his detractors' interpretation of the charter, citing the legal challenges raised during the 2004 referendum suggesting the mayor's voting power came from previous ordinances naming him or her a member of the governing body (Goering 2006). Although council–manager proponents had intended to establish a weaker position of mayor, the ambiguous language in the charter unintentionally set up a struggle between the mayor and the council over policy issues. Bunten's challenge to the weaker role of mayor had grounding. State Attorney General Phil Kline ruled on August 4, 2005, in a nonbinding opinion that Topeka's mayor is a member of the city's governing body and as such is eligible to vote any time the council takes up questions that are fundamental to its formation (Anderson 2006; Hrenchir 2006a, 2006b). For Bunten, this meant voting on any future charter ordinances.

The legal challenge to the 2004 referendum continues to this day to plague city officials. While the mayor's voting power was later affirmed by the council's vote to amend the charter ordinance in March 2006, the mayor's battle to assume such powers faced an uphill struggle. During May 2006 the council was faced with a decision about changing the mayor's role in policymaking. The measure before the council would have allowed the mayor to continue voting on charter ordinances. Councilman Brett Blackburn, a former deputy mayor, was one of the members challenging the mayor's authority arguing, "I believe the people spoke clear and loud that they wanted the city manager to run this government" (Anderson 2006). Bunten supporters felt the need to curb the mayor's powers was unnecessary. Councilman John Alcala, one of the mayor's supporters on the council, suggested, "I think when the people voted, they knew you had a vote on charter ordinances and veto power" (Anderson 2006).

While the measure failed, the mayor was still able to retain his power to vote and veto matters before the council, a vestige of the strong-mayor form in place previously (Anderson 2006).[10] In the following two years the city council overrode several of Mayor Bunten's vetoes, further challenging the mayor's power over policy matters (Hrenchir 2008a). As late as October 17, 2008, Mayor Bunten was seeking changes to the charter to clarify the issues surrounding the mayor's powers under the current form of government (Hall 2008b). Specifically, Bunten was concerned with addressing the mayor's powers over legislative and administrative matters. Interestingly, Bunten suggested the charter created a "tyrant" by giving the mayor the power to veto legislation and the council no authority to override such a veto. Additionally, Bunten wanted the mayor to have a say over the tenure of the city manager, who reports solely to the council under the current charter language. The role of the mayor in city policymaking remains unresolved as of this writing (Smith 2008b).

## Discussion

While some other cities of comparable size examined in this volume have reverted to the mayor–council form, Topeka (along with El Paso) has instead opted for the council–manager government. Unlike some other large American cities, Topeka listened to its citizens' and political leaders' push for reform, but the reform sought here was a move to the council–manager government grounded in the politics-administration dichotomy. Topeka's divergent path raises a number of questions related to the choices citizens and political leaders face in choosing government forms.

Topeka, along with the other cities examined here, was faced with a choice between the major forms of local government. Clearly, local political abuses attributed to the political leadership in the mayor–council regime were a major factor in the decision to opt for a change in form. Butch Felker's tenure in the mayor's office, marred by allegations of abuse and fraud, clearly impacted the movement for a change in government form. The success attributed to the council–manager government in other Kansas cities and its perceived ability to ebb the corruptive tendencies of politics was important in the decision to switch forms of government. For Topekans, a government based on a strong elected executive was not as appealing as the traditional progressive reform prescription for a nonexecutive mayor and strong governing board buttressed by professional management.

Over the past two decades, corruption and political scandal in the mayor–council form highlighted a significant weakness in leadership and system performance in the case of Topeka. For Topekans, the consistent criticisms concerning the lack of leadership in the mayor–council system appeared to be a driving force for change. The lack of political accountability in the Topeka mayor–council system prompted citizens and city officials to opt for a more professional system. Although recent reforms have championed the administrative successes of strong-mayors and their professional staffs, the case of Topeka would suggest that the council–manager form is still quite attractive (see Nalbandian 1999, 192). Perhaps the allegations surrounding Felker and other perceived inefficiencies in the mayor's office led Topekans to question the executive's ability to govern and manage the city effectively. For Topekans and political officials, the professionalism advanced under the council–manager form served as a viable alternative to the self-serving tendencies of the previous mayor.

Yet the mayoral election shortly following the referendum on government form proved that the debate was far from over. While Topekans were clearly fed up with the corruption under Mayor Felker, their choice of Mayor Bunten over a key pro-council–manager candidate proved fateful. Mayor Bunten has successfully resisted efforts to sideline the mayor to a "ribbon-cutting" position. Due to ambiguous charter language, Mayor Bunten has sought to expand the scope of his leadership in a number of policy areas. This expansion in mayoral leadership has created a number of state constitutional and policy debates that have hampered progress under the new council–manager system. The transition to council–manager government in Topeka has proved complicated as the tension between the mayor and city council continues to unravel in policy and administrative matters.

Loran Smith, professor of political science at Washburn University in Topeka, provided insight into the impact of the recent government form change. Smith suggests that the authors of the current council–manager form did not use a template for guidance. Subsequently, the city has found managing the current form difficult. While the form made considerations for the council's role in the new government, very little was directed at articulating the mayor's role. According to Smith, the new form gave the mayor a veto; however, the language appears to have left out authorization for the council to override any mayoral veto (Smith 2008b). Moreover, the new city manager's job has proven to be complicated by the lack of clarity in the city charter regarding the new government. Mayor Bunten has taken this as an opportunity to inject himself into the policy process vacuum by providing leadership. However, this too has proven complicated as the mayor has discovered his power is also limited by the new government form. Smith stated that the dynamic political environment in Topeka has created a situation where citizens are not sure "what kind of government they have or what they want" (2008b). Meanwhile, Mayor Bunten's efforts to increase his office's powers were bolstered by the city's fire department union, which delivered a no-confidence vote for the newly appointed fire chief, signaling its rejection of the city manager's powers over administrative matters.

## Conclusion: Whither the Separation of Powers and Insulation of Administration from Politics?

Beginning with the separation of powers at the founding, the constitutional debate over the balance of power between the executive (mayor) and legislative (city council) branches of government continues. During the progressive era, institutional change and innovation led to the belief that administrative processes could be detached from politics (Svara 1990). The epitome of the politics-administrative dichotomy was the introduction of professional civil service systems along with council–manager forms of government (Frederickson and Smith 2003). As reformers focused less on issues of efficiency and waste, and more on political leadership, accountability, and responsiveness to the citizenry, council–manager forms of government came under fire in the mid-1900s with a gradual weakening of the form throughout the 1950s and 1970s (Wood 2002, 216). Initially, Topekans were poised to buck this trend by opting for the council–manager form as a means for strengthening cooperation between the legislature and executive on policy matters, while insulating council politics to a certain extent from administrative processes through the form (Montjoy and Watson 1995). Despite the switch, Topekans have not yet come to terms with the respective roles of the appointed and elected officials under the council–manager form as the current mayor seeks to play a more significant role in policy decisions.

Why did Topeka move away from the mayor–council form of government in 2004? Can we discern any trends across American cities that might explain this transition? Frederickson and Johnson's (2001) work on the "adapted city" might be useful in explaining the transition in Topeka. Their survey of American cities suggests that there is no discernable trend toward the abandonment of council–manager government but rather an upturn in the adoption of that form of government (Frederickson and Johnson 2001, 876). Furthermore, the authors note that there is notable instability in city government structures across America. They also note that cities are increasingly making modifications to city structures without totally abandoning the established form of government, with mayor–councils experiencing the most changes (Frederickson and Johnson 2001, 877). In many instances these changes to the mayor–council form are aimed at strengthening the mayor's powers in an effort to improve leadership capabilities (Frederickson and Johnson 2001, 881).

The Topeka case appears to be unique given the revitalized interest in mayoral systems elsewhere (see Sparrow 1985; Protasel 1988; Svara 1990). Revitalization efforts have tapped the mayor's office as a foundation for improved leadership through institutional arrangements (Frederickson and Johnson 2001). In many cities strengthening the mayor's office was deemed necessary in order to facilitate cooperation on political and community activities (Frederickson and Johnson 2001, 881). However, the case of Topeka appears to buttress the council–manager form for invigorating effective leadership and enhancing cooperation. Scholarship suggests that the council–manager form has evolved to support collaboration in civic authority and communitywide activities (Newland 1994; Montjoy and Watson 1995). The citizens of Topeka may have grown weary of the transactional politics of mayoral systems, opting instead for greater institutional strength through council–manager government.

Drawing from this edited volume's themes, the present analysis provides some important insights related to contemporary governance questions. First, both the media and civic organizations were active in the reform efforts in Topeka. Repeated forums and extensive media interest heightened public sentiment toward the change effort in

Topeka, awakening citizen discontent with politics as usual. As stated previously, Topeka's ordinance that the public and city officials review the form of government every ten years suggests that such interest will continue to factor into change efforts. An increasing awareness of the presence of both is essential to the governance question. Second, cities are still grappling with the balance of democratic responsiveness and administrative authority in their quest for "good government." The Topeka case suggests that citizens are drawn to insulating certain administrative prerogatives from politics (Montjoy and Watson 1995). Yet the continued debate over the mayor–council relationship suggests that the mayor's role in policy matters is reemerging. The confusion over the respective roles of the mayor, city manager, and council over policy issues suggests that citizens are tolerant of some political maneuvering but unclear as to policy responsibilities for each. It seems that Topeka would like to have its cake and eat it too. The city is merely applying more structural reforms to previous governments (Frederickson and Johnson 2001). While the city attempted to abandon the mayor–council form, that effort proved unresolved as the newly elected mayor continues to usurp power away from the city manager and council. It would appear in the case of Topeka that this debate is ongoing between the mayor and city council as each vies for power in the new governing arrangement. Topekans seem to be torn between longing for efficient government and eagerness for political leadership during turbulent times. This leads to the third point: the quest for "good government" is proving difficult as cities adapt common characteristics applicable to both strong-mayor and council–manager forms in an effort to appease everyone (Frederickson and Johnson 2001). The aftermath of the referendum effort in Topeka resulted in a complex governance arrangement where there are no clear winners or losers. Moreover, citizens as well as city employees and elected officials are not sure what form of government they really have (Smith 2008b). Perhaps, as Frederickson and Johnson (2001) suggest, a "formal legal description" of council–manager form is inaccurate for Topeka (882). Although in the case of Topeka this adapted structure was more accidental as the referendum has run afoul of previous institutional arrangements. The results of the referendum continue to be challenged by a mayor seeking greater authority. The result has blurred the lines of authority and created a system where shared-power is increasingly proving problematic. Future research will need to grapple with the strains that such complex arrangements place on effective governance.

## Notes

1. The council–manager form of government is also referred to as a city manager form of government. The media in Topeka often used the two terms interchangeably during the run up to the vote for a change in government form. For purposes of this research, the term council–manager is used throughout the text.

2. Small changes to city government form could be accomplished by having the council adopt new charter ordinances or regular ordinances. If, however, recommendations involve a change to a new form of government, such as council–manager, the measure would need to be approved by the city's voters (Hall 1998).

3. The Topeka city charter states that for matters before the governing body, "Five (5) members of the Council shall constitute a quorum. All actions by the Council shall be taken by the affirmative vote of five (5) or more members of the Council, unless a greater or lesser number of votes is required by this Charter Ordinance, by the Statutes of Kansas, or by the Constitution of Kansas" (Topeka, City Code 2008a). However, in the case of a charter ordinance, the mayor has a vote, making the total for an affirmative vote six as opposed to five for general matters (Topeka, City Code 2008b).

4. Proponents backed by city attorney Brenden Long responded by citing a 1992 case in which the state attorney general ruled that Kansas law did not allow Topeka mayors to take part in a council vote on whether to override a protest petition (Hrenchir 2004d, 2004e). Long asserted that this decision demonstrates that the mayor is not allowed to vote and the office's membership in the governing body should not be counted during voting.

5. Interestingly, recent research has refuted this notion of tenures cut short. In their analysis of 113 city managers, Watson and Hassett (2004) found that they were mostly long servers, lateral movers, ladder climbers, and single-city careerists. Indeed, their research suggests that city managers in the largest council–manager cities are commonly ladder climbers or single-city careerists, refuting the stereotypes cited by critics of the Topeka measure in 2004.

6. See footnote 2. It would appear that Topeka's mayor–council form of government in place before the 2004 change challenged the traditional notion of separation of powers, giving the mayor a vote on charter ordinances.

7. In 2004 Topeka paid Management Partners $125,000 in an effort to provide concrete proposals for improving city operations (Hrenchir 2008b). Management Partners's report included over 200 recommendations for a variety of city departments and services, including 22 affecting executive functions (Management Partners Recommendation Report 2004). Several of the measures sought greater coordination of city efforts under the city manager to facilitate strategic planning for the city's departments in an effort to enhance performance and productivity. As of April 2008 the city had implemented 107 of the 234 total recommendations (Hrenchir 2008b).

8. In the spring of 2005 Kansas lawmakers passed legislation creating a consolidation commission. The Commissioners released a preliminary plan in June, held numerous hearings seeking public input, with a final plan being approved on November 1 calling for the city council and county commission to be dissolved and replaced by a five-member elected body (Hrenchir and Anderson 2005). Voters were sent a mail ballot for the election to be returned on December 13. Topekans voted 70.5 percent to 29.5 percent for the plan; however, the measure failed as county voters who live outside Topeka rejected it, 60.1 percent to 39.9 percent (Hrenchir and Anderson 2005). The state legislation that created the commission mandated majority approval by both city and noncity voters for the consolidation to take effect.

9. According to the charter ordinance, elections for mayor are at large and if there are more than two candidates, there is a primary election. The two candidates receiving the most votes in the primary election then head to a general election. The same rules apply for city council members, although city council seats are elected from geographical districts versus at large (Topeka, City Code 2008e).

10. Currently the city charter calls for the mayor to preside as chair of council meetings but have no vote on legislation before the council—the only exception being charter ordinances. Moreover, the mayor's office was provided with veto and line-item veto power on appropriation ordinances. This veto power does not extend to charter ordinances (Topeka, City Code 2008d).

# References

Anderson, Ric. 2006. Mayor retains power. *Capital-Journal*, May 3. www.cjonline.com/ (accessed October 6, 2005).

Carpenter, Tim. 2005. Felker ethical complaint filed. *Capital-Journal*, February 16. www.cjonline.com/ (accessed June 13, 2008).

Frederickson, H. George, and Gary A. Johnson. 2001. The adapted American city: A study of institutional dynamics. *Urban Affairs Review* 36, no. 6 (July): 872–84.

Frederickson, H. George, and Kevin B. Smith. 2003. *The public administration theory primer.* Boulder, CO: Westview Press.

Fry, Steve, and Chris Moon. 2003. Felker quits: Mayor's decision ends ouster proceedings; district attorney says no charges will be filed. *Capital-Journal*, November 7. www.cjon line.com/ (accessed June 13, 2008).

Goering, Pete. 2006. Bunten playing by rules. *Capital-Journal*, March 5. www.cjonline.com/ (accessed June 13, 2008).

Hall, Mike. 1998. City government review committee to have organizational meeting today. *Capital-Journal*, October 17. www.cjonline.com/ (accessed October 3, 2008).

———. 2000. Charter ordinance falls short; city council discussed putting form of government question before voters. *Capital-Journal*, August 16. www.cjonline.com/ (accessed June 13, 2008).

———. 2001. Wagnon lost key precincts. *Capital-Journal*, March 4. www.cjonline.com/ (accessed October 3, 2008).

———. 2008a. Felker's career long, varied, controversial. *Capital-Journal*, January 4. www.cjonline.com/ (accessed June 13, 2008).

———. 2008b. Mayor proposes change in city charter. *Capital-Journal*, October 17. www.cjonline.com/ (accessed November 14, 2008).

Hassett, Wendy L., and Douglas J. Watson. 2007. *Civic battles: When cities change their form of government.* Boca Raton, FL: PrAcademics Press.

Hrenchir, T. 2004a. Council to study forum notes. *Capital-Journal*, May 25. www.cjonline.com/ (accessed October 3, 2008).

———. 2004b. Public to vote; officials agree to let citizens decide on government change. *Capital-Journal*, July 21. www.cjonline.com/ (accessed June 13, 2008).

———. 2004c. Ballot question may be flawed; critics: Change in government could let mayor vote with council. *Capital-Journal*, September 26. www.cjonline.com/ (accessed June 13, 2008).

———. 2004d. Lawyer protests ballot question; state constitution counts mayor in needed majority, Topekan says. *Capital-Journal*, September 28. www.cjonline.com/ (accessed June 13, 2008).

———. 2004e. Managers need background for job. *Capital-Journal*, October 11. www.cjon line.com/ (accessed June 13, 2008).

———. 2004f. Voters' rights at issue; opponents of switch in form say people should determine leaders. *Capital-Journal*, October 12. www.cjonline.com/ (accessed June 13, 2008).

———. 2004g. Topekans OK city manager; consolidation effort also approved. *Capital-Journal*, November 3. www.cjonline.com/ (accessed June 13, 2008).

———. 2005a. Bunten to lead city; statehouse veteran beats councilwoman. *Capital-Journal*. www.cjonline.com/ (accessed June 13, 2008).

———. 2005b. Council widens mayor's duties; Bunten tentatively allowed to advise budget committees. *Capital-Journal*, April, 17. www.cjonline.com/ (accessed June 13, 2008).

———. 2006a. Mayor's power at issue; two councilmen want to dilute authority of Bunten, his successors. *Capital-Journal*, March, 12. www.cjonline.com/ (accessed June 13, 2008).

———. 2006b. Mayor likely to retain some vote power. *Capital-Journal*, May 16. www .cjonline.com/ (accessed June 13, 2008).

———. 2007. Bonaparte reflects on his first year. *Capital-Journal*, March 13. www.cjon line.com/ (accessed October 6, 2008).

———. 2008a. Council's power questioned; Miller: Change of government ended ability to override vetoes. *Capital-Journal*, February 5. www.cjonline.com/ (accessed June 13, 2008).

———. 2008b. Your vision can help improve Topeka. *Capital-Journal*, May 4. www.cjon line.com/ (accessed June 13, 2008).

———. 2008c. Topeka's past and future—The 1950s. *Capital-Journal*, May 11. www.cjon line.com/ (accessed June 13, 2008).

Hrenchir, Tim, and Ric Anderson. 2005. Merger plan fails. *Capital-Journal*, December 16. www.cjonline.com/ (accessed October 6, 2008).

Johnson, Frederick J. 1999. People outweigh system. *Capital-Journal*, October 18. www .cjonline.com/ (accessed June 13, 2008).

———. 2003. Hasty change isn't advised. *The Capital-Journal*, October 19. www.cjonline.com (accessed October 3, 2008).

Kansas Statute 12–184, ch. 76, § 1; July 1 (1976).

Management Partners Recommendation Report. 2004. http://topeka.org/whatsnew/manage mentpartnerreport.pdf/ (accessed October 6, 2008).

McLean, Jim, and Kenneth Lassiter. 1999. Scrap mayoral form; Councilwoman Dunn proposes Topeka change to a city manager form of government. *Capital-Journal*, August 15. www.cjonline.com/ (accessed June 13, 2008).

Montjoy, Robert S., and Douglas J. Watson. 1995. A case for reinterpreted dichotomy of politics and administration as a professional standard in council–manager government. *Public Administration Review* 55, no. 3 (May/June): 231–39.

Moon, Chris. 2003a. Acting mayor calls for P-card accountability. *Capital-Journal*, November 4. www.cjonline.com/ (accessed October 3, 2008).

———. 2003b. Government form gains new life. *Capital-Journal*, December 6. www.cjon line.com/ (accessed October 3, 2008).

Moon, Chris, and Alicia Henrikson. 2003. McClinton elected; former councilman chosen in two rounds. *Capital-Journal*, December 6. www.cjonline.com/ (accessed June 13, 2008).

Nalbandian, John. 1999. Facilitating community, enabling democracy: New roles for local government managers. *Public Administration Review* 59, no. 3 (May/June): 187–97.

Newland, Chester A. 1994. Managing from the future in council–manager government. In *Ideal and practice in council–manager government*, ed. H. George Frederickson. Washington, DC: International City/Council Management Association.

Protasel, Greg J. 1988. Abandonment of the council–manager plan: A new institutional perspective. In *Ideal and practice in council–manager government*, ed. H. George Frederickson. Washington, DC: International City/Council Management Association.

Quinn, Tomari. 2000. Wagnon follows path of public service. *Capital-Journal*, December 26. www.cjonline.com/ (accessed October 3, 2008).

Smith, Loran. 2008a. Interview by author. November 3.

———. 2008b. Interview by author. November 4.

Sparrow, Glen. 1985. The emerging chief executive: The San Diego experience. *National Civic Review* 74, no. 11 (December): 538–47.

Svara, James H. 1990. *Official leadership in the city*. New York: Oxford University Press.

*Topeka Capital-Journal.* 2005. Complaint filed against Felker. *Capital-Journal*, February 15. www.cjonline.com/ (accessed June 13, 2008).

*Topeka Capital-Journal* Editorial Board. 1999. Change for a change. *Capital-Journal*, August 6. www.cjonline.com/ (accessed October 6, 2008).

———. 2008. Butch Felker, 1945–2008—For Topeka; former mayor's service to his hometown won't be forgotten, nor will his friendliness. *Capital-Journal*, January 4. www.cjonline.com (accessed June 13, 2008).

Topeka, City Code. 2008a. C.O. No. 94, § 10, 7–20–04; C.O. 96, § 2, 5–23–06/8–28–06. www.municode.com/ (accessed October 4, 2008).

———. 2008b. C.O. No. 94, § 16, 7–20–04. www.municode.com/ (accessed October 3, 2008).

———. 2008c. Ord. No. 18072, § 1, 8–19–03; Ord. No. 18381, § 6, 1–25–05. www.muni code.com/ (accessed October 3, 2008).

———. 2008d. C.O. No. 94, § 10, 7–20–04; C.O. No. 96, § 2, 5–23–06/8–28–06. www.municode.com/ (accessed November 14, 2008).

———. 2008e. C.O. No. 94, § 8, 7–20–04. www.municode.com/ (accessed November 14, 2008).

U.S. Census Bureau. 2008. Population finder. www.census.gov/ (accessed June 13, 2008).

Watson, Douglas J., and Wendy L. Hassett. 2004. Career paths of city managers in America's largest council–manager cities. *Public Administration Review* 64, no. 2 (March/April): 192–99.

Wood, Curtis. 2002. Voter turnout in city elections. *Urban Affairs Review* 38, no. 2 (November): 209–31.

# PART IV

# REJECTED CHANGE TO MAYOR–COUNCIL FORM FROM COMMISSION AND WEAK MAYOR

CHAPTER 14

# ST. LOUIS

## Déjà vu All over Again—Charter Reform Fails

ROBERT CROPF, TODD SWANSTROM, AND SCOTT KRUMMENACHER

IN NOVEMBER 2004 the citizens of St. Louis voted on four amendments to the city charter. In the classic tradition of good government reform these amendments would have strengthened the powers of the mayor, reduced the size of the board of aldermen, and broadened civil service protections. About a month before the election, billboards began appearing around the city equating support for the charter amendments with support for the confederate flag. Next to a depiction of the confederate flag, the billboards read: "A VOTE FOR CHARTER AMENDMENTS A, B, C & D EQUALS SUPPORT FOR THE CONFEDERATE FLAG. A VOTE AGAINST A, B, C & D PROTECTS YOUR RIGHT TO VOTE."

The billboards provoked howls of protest. The local chapter of the NAACP issued a statement saying that it was "totally outraged by the spectacle." It turns out the billboards were paid for by a thirty-three-year-old white man who worked in his family's bar, Colombo's, on the south side. A *St. Louis Post-Dispatch* editorial lashed out at the billboards as a "despicable" effort by "the feeder pigs [that is, the party politicians] who are now squealing and wriggling to keep their place at the public trough."

Even though the newspapers, four former mayors (two of whom were black), and nearly the entire business establishment supported the charter amendments (and funded an expensive pro-reform campaign), the charter amendments went down in flames, with no amendment receiving close to 50 percent approval, let alone the 60 percent needed to pass. Although the charge that charter reform was racist was clearly unfair, the evidence suggests that the mudslinging worked: the black wards voted overwhelmingly against charter reform.

What does the failure of charter reform in St. Louis mean for efforts around the country to strengthen the powers of mayors to deal effectively with the daunting challenges facing cities? We believe it speaks to two issues facing the strong-mayor reform movement—one having to do with the process of reform and the other addressing the substance of reform. As St. Louis native Yogi Berra would say, it was déjà vu all over again. The 2004 defeat of charter reform was remarkably similar to other defeats in 1911, 1950, and 1957. For nearly a century reformers in St. Louis have followed a debilitating pattern. In particular the downtown elite has stubbornly persisted in viewing city government as basically a poorly run business and has been unwilling to negotiate in good faith with party politicians and elected officials. The process of reform is top-down and controlled by elites, helping to create the perception among voters that strong-mayor reforms are injurious to the interests of minorities, as well as the poor and working classes.

If reformers initiated a more open dialogue with party politicians and elected officials (or "feeder pigs" as the *Post-Dispatch* derisively called them), it would result in a more diverse set of reforms that would aim to balance enhanced executive power with a more vigorous legislative branch, embracing the values of transparency, civic participation, and minority rights.

## Strengthening Mayoral Leadership through Urban Reform

There is a lively ongoing debate in this country over the forms of organization and the distribution of powers within local government, especially when it comes to the critical question of mayoral leadership. Increasingly scholars and practitioners are arguing that strong mayors are needed to provide a public face for city governance and establish direction for cities faced with a laundry list of difficult challenges—from foreclosures to rising unemployment to climate change. Reformers are again looking to institutional change as a way to enhance the mayor's leadership capacity. Several large cities with manager–council systems, such as New York and Los Angeles, strengthened the powers of the mayor and centralized executive authority in the past two decades. Council–manager systems too have taken steps to expand the role of the mayor. Svara (2008) notes the efforts by these systems to enhance the scope of the mayor's power. Reformers stress the need for political leadership that works across diverse coalitions and creates a vision for the city's future. Whereas earlier reform efforts called attention to the administrative powers of strong mayors, increasingly, successful reforms highlight the political and coalition-building roles of mayors in addition to their interest in managerial change.

The institutional arrangements of city government can aid or restrict the exercise of mayoral leadership. Several studies emphasize the role formal structures play in shaping the leadership style and behavior of mayors. Svara's (1990) study finds that municipal government structures support either executive or facilitative leadership styles by mayors. Executive leaders make use of their positional authority, while facilitative leaders work to overcome structural barriers by empowering others. Mayoral success depends on matching the appropriate style of the leader (executive or facilitative) to the right municipal structure (manager–council or council–manager). Expanding on Svara's framework, Wheeland (2002) identifies several subsets that emerge from these two leadership styles in manager–council and council–manager settings. Wheeland notes that in St. Louis, for example, leadership is constrained by institutional arrangements that limit the mayor's power to appoint department heads and prepare the city budget.[1]

Other scholars emphasize how structural barriers can present challenges for mayoral leadership that can only be overcome through the use of political skill and coalition building (Pressman 1972; Sonenshein 2004; Stein 2002). In mayor–council cities, for example, mayors and city councils regularly clash on a range of issues. City councils can reflect ward-based interests that clash with mayoral leadership on citywide issues (Stein 2002). Beyond major shifts from one government structure to another, such as a shift from mayor–council to council–manager, subtle differences in the distribution of executive powers can constrain or facilitate leadership. Even when mayors have significant executive power, structural arrangements spelled out in municipal charters can present leadership barriers (Schragger 2006; Wheeland 2002). Frederickson, Johnson, and Wood (2004) note that incremental adjustments in these arrangements can enhance political leadership without shifting from one municipal form to another.

The idea that formal limits on executive power weaken the ability of mayors to lead politically has become a salient theme in recent calls for municipal reform (Svara 2008). Indeed, this point has been a guiding rationale for the strong-mayor reform movement in large cities (Schragger 2006; Mullin, Peele, and Cain 2004). As Mullin, Peele, and Cain (2004) put it, "There appears to be growing agreement among political actors within big cities that institutional constraints on the formal authority of the mayor's office are an important obstacle to getting things done" (20).

This is not to say that mayors cannot be effective without significant formal powers; consider the case of Chicago. Nor do structural changes necessarily lead to effective mayoral leadership. Pluralist scholars have long emphasized that effective governance involves more than the use of the formal channels of municipal government, and regime theorists argue that political skill is necessary to create lasting coalitions (Dahl 1961; Stone 1989). But insights into the effects of municipal structures on local leadership provide a context for understanding both the impetus for, and the effects of, recent reform efforts. Raphael Sonenshein (2004) put it best: "What we are only beginning to learn is the *chemistry* by which institutional change, or reform, occurs. Institutions shape behavior, but people make choices with imperfect information and uncertainty about whom to trust. Reforms are not abstract ideas. They are competing proposals that require elite and mass constituencies, and which may in the hands of different leaders activate different constituencies. Successful reform is a mixture of lofty ideals and effective politics" (6).

Executive leaders constrained by their institutional arrangements can, and often do, seek changes that enhance their ability to govern. The latest wave of urban reforms aimed at strengthening the power of the mayor reflects this tendency. Manager–council cities have seen the rise of the what Sonenshein (2004) calls "new mayors" who have moved beyond the partisan political struggles of the past. Influenced in part by the reinventing government movement of the 1990s, mayors like New York's Michael Bloomberg are political moderates who emphasize competition, managerial competence, and pragmatic problem-solving (Flanagan 2004a; Sonenshein 2004; Schragger

2006; Svara 2008). Urban reform efforts in these cities reflect a push to overhaul government bureaucracy and maintain a pro-business atmosphere. Although Progressive Era reformers had once opposed the strong-mayor system as corrupt and wasteful, executive power is now championed as a way to improve government operations. The new mayors have been largely successful in building a winning base of support among key, often competing, interests and framing the reform effort as part of an attractive vision for the city's future. New mayors have been able to blend a managerialist agenda with a transcendent politics that creates space for the building of reform coalitions (Flanagan 2004a).

## Barriers to Reform

The difficulty for many reform efforts, however, continues to be the way leaders forge alliances and galvanize public support to approve changes in municipal governance structures. Successful urban reforms aimed at strengthening the power of the mayor must build coalitions across a broad range of interests. These alliances can be difficult to form in the modern context where political power is widely distributed across a range of competing interests. Although business interests remain influential, growth coalitions are only one of many possible alliances that can be established (Elkin 1987). Large-scale immigration in a number of U.S. cities has made coalition building more complex (Sonenshein 2004).

Reform efforts driven by good government groups and civic elites alone rarely have the capacity to produce change. As corporate headquarters relocate to other parts of the metropolitan area, corporate elites are declining as an influential force that can sustain significant change (Burns and Thomas 2006). Even formidable corporate leadership competes with a growing list of community organizations, racial groups, labor unions, and nonprofit entities for control of the civic agenda. Other traditional bases of political power are transforming, as well. Labor unions have declined as an influential force in many cities. Racial politics has also been reshaped by demographic shifts that have helped to sever alliances between minority groups and liberal reformers (Sonenshein 1993). Neighborhood and ward-based interests continue to assert power over city governance and can become obstacles to strong-mayor reforms. Broad-based coalitions are necessary if municipal reforms are to succeed. Schragger (2006, 2554) notes that "when reformers have lacked support across the myriad of urban constituencies, strong mayor reforms have failed." Furthermore, Schragger argues, successful reform efforts require a certain level of citizen dissatisfaction with the status quo and a sense of urgency for change that gets the public's attention.

Finally, the size of the municipality plays a role in helping to determine the success or failure of charter reform efforts. Typically, the larger the city, the more public services it provides. In other words, the scope and substance of the functional responsibilities of larger cities tends to be on the whole greater and more diverse than those of smaller ones. For example, cities over 1 million spend much more on public welfare than smaller cities (Judd and Swanstrom 2010, 301). The substance of different functional responsibilities may provide impetus for changing the governance structures of municipalities (Stein 1990). In the case of St. Louis, city government assumed substantial responsibility for the city's economy, which had performed poorly for decades. The reformers' desire to improve the city's economy led them to consider significant modifications in the institutional arrangements that had long governed the City of St. Louis.

We now turn to the 2004 effort to reform the charter of the City of St. Louis, which illustrates both the motivation to strengthen mayoral leadership and the obstacles that stand in its way.

## The History of Charter Reform in St. Louis

Ironically, St. Louis, which has had so much trouble reforming its governmental structure, adopted the nation's first municipal home-rule charter in 1876. The peculiarity of this home-rule charter is that St. Louis became a combined city–county government. As such, its borders were set in concrete. This inability to annex suburban land has been a major cause of the city's population decline (from a high of 857,000 in 1950 to 348,000 in 2000). The county offices in St. Louis were mandated by the state of Missouri and excluded from the city's home-rule powers. Another peculiarity of St. Louis is that the city does not control the police department, which is run by a board appointed by the governor, with the mayor as an ex officio member.

By the early twentieth century, St. Louis was widely recognized as one of the nation's most corrupt cities. (St. Louis was the only city that merited two chapters in Lincoln Steffens's *The Shame of the Cities*.) Stung by criticism from muckrakers, the city's civic elite began to press for serious reform of municipal government. Over the years these reform efforts were led by the city's business and professional classes and opposed by the party politicians and ethnic voters. In the early years of the twentieth century, St. Louis's business leadership was known as the "Big Cinch." In *St. Louis Politics: The Triumph of Tradition*, Lana Stein relates how an effort in 1911 by St. Louis's Civic League, supported by the Big Cinch, to strengthen the powers of the mayor and to create a legislature elected at large was soundly defeated by the city's ethnic and working-class voters, supported by the unions and the socialists.

The one successful example of charter reform in St. Louis is instructive for how it differed from the others. In 1914 the reformers tried again to improve St. Louis's city government, except this time they did not attempt to install the classic Progressive reform model of that time (for example, strong executive, at-large council). Instead, knowing that the voters opposed strong executive leadership because of their fears and resentments of the Big Cinch, the reformers retained the city's weak-mayor structure of city government. To allay the fears of ethnic and working class voters, the reformers included rights to initiative, referendum, and recall, and the charter reform passed by a narrow margin. The 1914 charter continues to govern the city to this day. The success of the 1914 reform shows the need to appeal to populist sentiments among the voters.

The city's business establishment did not attempt substantial charter reform again until 1950. In that year a charter reform package, which included eliminating three elected offices and putting them under civil service, went down to defeat. In a now-familiar pattern, trade unions and Democratic ward politicians led opposition to the proposed reforms. The same thing happened in 1957 when a proposed charter that would have strengthened the mayor and reduced the number of aldermen (with half elected at large) was soundly defeated, winning less than 40 percent of the vote.

## The 2004 Reform Effort

The most recent attempt to reform St. Louis city government had its genesis in a special committee appointed by the city's first African American mayor, Freeman Bosley Jr., in 1993. Bosley asked the committee—chaired by George H. "Bert" Walker, chief executive of the municipal banking firm, Stiefel Niklaus, and cousin of President George H. W. Bush—to devise recommendations to halt the city's longtime decline. The mayor's advisory committee consisted of prominent citizens, public officials, elected representatives, civic leaders, and members of the local academic community. Many different options were advanced but only one commanded consensus within the group: strengthening the powers of the mayor.

In 1996, a subcommittee of the Bosley Committee issued a report that summarized the recommendations for reforming St. Louis city government. The chief recommendations of what came to be known as the Walker Report were to:

◆ Strengthen and streamline the executive by eliminating the elected office of the comptroller and replacing it with the appointed position of deputy mayor for fiscal management; in addition, the mayor would appoint a deputy mayor for administration and deputy mayor for development.
◆ Eliminate the Board of Estimate and Apportionment and transfer its budget-making powers to the mayor.
◆ Grant the mayor the authority to appoint county officers (for example, county clerk), instead of having them elected by the voters.
◆ Extend civil service protection to include all employees of municipal and county departments, with the exception of the highest-ranking employees in the county offices, who would be mayoral appointees.
◆ Return the jurisdiction of the St. Louis police department to the City of St. Louis, with full control of the city's police force restored to the mayor.

These recommendations reflected a traditional reform agenda of strengthening the chief executive and reducing the ability of party officials to distribute patronage. One exception is that the report recommended that the board of aldermen be strengthened, particularly the budget-making powers, in order to offset the newly enhanced powers of the mayor. The report also recognized the importance of empowering voters, but it was vague in this regard.

With the exception of returning control of the St. Louis police department to the city, which was deemed too controversial to tackle at the time, the other recommendations were overwhelmingly approved by the Bosley Committee. In an editorial on the report, the *St. Louis Post-Dispatch* (1996) asserted that the group's recommendations "offer forward-looking approaches to making city government more responsive and effective in the 21st century."

The Walker Report revived interest in charter reform, and this time the effort was led by an organization representing the interests of big business called Civic Progress. Mayor Joseph Darst formed Civic Progress in 1953 as an elite group representing the largest corporations in St. Louis in order to spur urban renewal. With membership later expanded to the largest thirty corporations in St. Louis, Civic Progress has been a key behind-the-scenes player in most, if not all, major initiatives in the region. Lana Stein (2002), a close observer of St. Louis politics, describes Civic Progress as "removed from view" and cloaked in an "aura of mystery," aspects of the organization that have over time led to the widespread perception that Civic Progress runs St. Louis (11).

Since its creation, nearly every major new program or policy in St. Louis has borne the imprimatur of Civic Progress. The organization is particularly adept at raising large sums of money on short notice for the causes that it favors. The political class in St. Louis views the reformers as tools of the corporate elite, represented by Civic Progress. Following the Walker Report, Civic Progress took up the cause of charter reform. In 1956 the Missouri Supreme Court had ruled that St. Louis did not have the power to change its county functions. In November 2002, Missouri voters passed an amendment to the state constitution that gave the city home-rule authority over its county functions. Civic Progress raised $770,000 to pass the amendment, the bulk of which was used to purchase a statewide television and radio campaign. In an early sign that charter reform would encounter resistance among St. Louis's African American voters, a *St. Louis Post-Dispatch* article written before the statewide vote reported that more than half of the city's thirteen African American aldermen opposed the home-rule amendment. The leader of the opposition on the city's board of aldermen, Irving Clay, called the home-rule effort an attempt by the "rich and the powerful" to exert greater influence on St. Louis politics and government.

## The Stakeholder Process and the Campaign for Adoption

Flush with its success in passing the state constitutional amendment, Civic Progress led the effort to reform the city's charter. The group raised more than $500,000 and assembled an organization called Advance St. Louis to lead the process. Established in May 2003, Advance St. Louis created a 150-person Stakeholders Assembly to review and revise the city charter. Advance St. Louis chose the stakeholders from hundreds of applicants who attended a citywide meeting in June 2003. The Assembly, designed to reflect the city's diverse population, included several ethnic minorities, and comprised almost an equal number of men and women and blacks and whites.

A total of eight Stakeholder Assembly meetings were held from September to December 2003. A typical meeting would begin with opening comments from a representative of Advance St. Louis, which would be followed by a presentation by the consultants (see below), and then breakout groups in which ten to twelve stakeholders would discuss questions prepared in advance by the consultants for about an hour. At the end of the allotted time, each group would report its agreements and disagreements to the entire assembly, and finally the consultants would summarize the evening's main point.

Advance St. Louis hired consultants from the National Civic League to, as Jason Hannisch, Advance St. Louis's executive director, said, "do the research, and design and run the process." The consultants focused largely on national trends in local government in their presentations to the group, and a few local experts were brought in to discuss specific aspects of St. Louis government and politics. These presentations were designed mainly to highlight the differences in governmental structures in St. Louis compared to other major American cities.

Stakeholder Assembly meetings were open to the public, with some media coverage. Closed to the general public and the stakeholders, however, were the meetings of Advance St. Louis and the national consultants in which stakeholder feedback was analyzed, Assembly meeting agendas developed, and discussion questions, "option memos," as well as other meeting materials prepared. As a result, some stakeholders made public their dissatisfaction with the top-down and overly controlled nature of the process, questioning how legitimate the process was to the population at large. Douglas Adams, one member of the stakeholder assembly, commented to us: "When I was asked to participate, the project was presented as a participatory process with the Assembly being a *deliberative* body. I discovered the actual process to be highly *orchestrated*" (emphasis added).

Perceptions that the process was tightly controlled by Advance St. Louis appeared to be strongest among the African American stakeholders. The *St. Louis Post-Dispatch* noted that a report was circulated at a political meeting reporting that blacks had left the process once it became apparent that their "voices did not matter." At the outset of the stakeholder process, African American representation was approximately equal to that of whites; however, according to the report, by the time the recommendations were voted on, it had declined to about 30 percent of the Assembly.

For the most part, at least according to newspaper accounts of the process, stakeholders were satisfied with the results of the process, even if they were not always satisfied with the way the actual process was conducted. A formal vote was held on December 10, 2003, in which the stakeholders approved four areas for changes in the current charter: (a) fiscal management, (b) organizational structure of the government, (c) the role and responsibilities of the board of aldermen, and (d) personnel administration. It is interesting that three of the four areas chosen by the stakeholders (that is, items one, two, and four) were also areas of the city charter identified for change by the 1996 Walker Report. Over the next four months, intensive discussions were held in order to draft a list of proposals for charter changes in the four areas listed above, which would be voted on by the residents of St. Louis in the November 2004 elections.

All the evidence points to the conclusion that Advance St. Louis already had a clear idea of what it wanted to recommend before the process began and the function of the Stakeholder Assembly was to build legitimacy and voter support for those recommendations. Representing the business community, Civic Progress was behind charter reform because it viewed the city's weak mayor system of government as harmful to investment. Clearly, aldermanic courtesy, the uncoordinated county offices, and the Board of Estimate and Apportionment often slowed down the process of development. Developers complained about having to buy off aldermen, not knowing where to go for permits, and simply having to wait for the antiquated gears of city government to move forward.

The forces of reform in St. Louis represented the classic economy and efficiency approach to governance: city government should be run more like a business, with the chief executive representing the unitary interest of the city as a whole in attracting capital investment. As they have for more than a century, reformers in St. Louis viewed themselves as representing the forces of progress. The implication is that the opponents of reform were parochial, selfish obstacles to the city's modernization, wanting only to protect their little fiefdoms. This explains both the harsh rhetoric directed at politicians and why the reformers refused to negotiate in good faith with the ward-based political interests. Needless to say, the animosity has been mutual: the political class in St. Louis viewed the reformers as tools of the corporate elite, with calls for greater efficiency being a cover-up for the real agenda, which was to bend city government to the needs of large corporations and away from the hard-won rights of neighborhoods and minorities.

This historical pattern of "machine" versus "reform" hostility was played out once more in the Stakeholder Assembly process and the subsequent effort to pass the proposals to change the city charter in 2004. In the beginning there was an indication that things might be different this time, but this proved to be short lived. Following the passage of the home-rule amendment to the Missouri state constitution, a resolution was introduced at a board of aldermen meeting that would have effectively ended any effort to change the city charter before the reformers had a chance to begin. Seeking to forestall this event, the reformers persuaded an alderman to table the resolution in his committee. It was the alderman's understanding, according to a newspaper account, that the aldermen would be allowed to take part in the Stakeholder Assembly process and thus be given an opportunity to shape the charter changes that would be voted on by the city's voters.

It quickly became apparent to the city's politicians that the proponents of charter change had no intention of opening up the process to the politicians. In fact, a Stakeholder Assembly rule specifically excluded elected officials from participating in the process. While the deliberations over changing the course of St. Louis city government continued through the spring of 2004, the city's politicians could only watch from the sidelines while their sense of disenfranchisement from the process increased. Editorials from the *St. Louis Post-Dispatch* (2004a), the city's only major newspaper, that referred to city government in such terms as "dysfunction junction" where "politics trumps progress" further undermined what little support for charter reform might have existed among the city's elected officials.

On April 29, 2004, the Stakeholder Assembly voted overwhelmingly to submit to the voters a package of far-reaching reforms of the structure of city government and to streamline city hall processes. The specific changes that the stakeholders agreed on were replacing the Board of Estimate and Apportionment with a new city finance department under the mayor, transforming the elected county offices into mayoral appointments, creating a chief administrative officer for the city (another mayoral appointee), and reducing the board of aldermen from twenty-eight to fifteen members. With the exception of the reduction in the size of the board of aldermen, the other three proposals followed exactly the 1996 recommendations of the Walker Committee.

## The Election: African American and Working-Class Opposition

In November 2004 the four proposed amendments to the city charter appeared on the ballot, requiring the support of 60 percent of those voting on the amendments to pass. In April 2004 polling by Citizens for Home Rule (CHR), which ran the campaign for Civic Progress, showed strong support for the general idea of reform. When citizens began looking at the specific reforms, however, those who would lose their jobs, or suspected they would, began to mobilize in opposition. By putting all four amendments up at once, including one that would have put half the aldermen out of a job, CHR tainted the cause of reform. With the process of reform having been run in a top-down fashion, reform became associated symbolically with the business elite and against the interests of working people and minorities. However, before the vote in November, polls by both supporters and opponents indicated that only half of the city's likely voters even knew about the ballot's questions (*St. Louis Post-Dispatch* 2004b). This fact along with the fractured support resulting from putting up all four amendments at the same time and the need to achieve 60 percent of the vote proved too tall an order for the CHR.

With African Americans constituting 51.2 percent of the city's population (2000), no charter reforms could pass without their support. An analysis of the vote for Proposition A, which won more votes than any other, shows that the city's minority voters were hostile to reform. For example, the eleven wards with the highest percentage of black population according to the 2000 census were the same eleven wards that gave the lowest percentage yes votes to Proposition A. Nearly every black alderman came out against the charter reforms. Much of this had to do with the fact that reform was linked with the white business elite.

Some wards with large minority populations supported the reforms, but this had more to do with class than race. As in past charter reform efforts, support for reform was strongest in the city's central corridor wards, historically where the city's wealthy and professional middle classes have lived. The map shows that there was a strong positive relationship between per capita income by ward and voting yes on the charter reforms.

Further evidence of working-class opposition to reform comes from the political leaders who opposed it. A number of city unions came out against the charter reforms, including the unions for the St. Louis police and fire departments, representing more than two thousand members, and locals representing the plumbers, carpenters, and

**Figure** 14.1    Yes Votes on City Charter Reform Compared to Per Capita Income

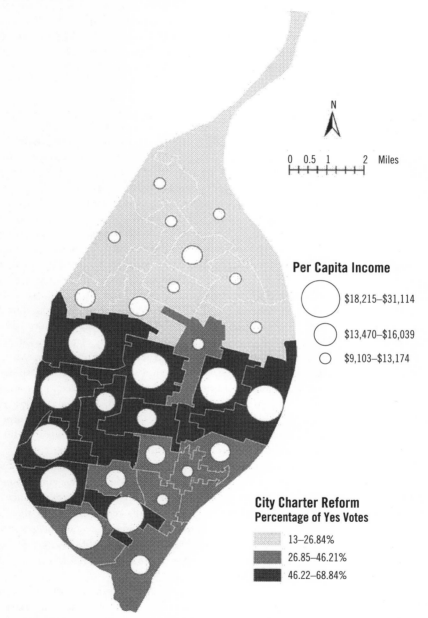

N

0  0.5  1        2  Miles

**Per Capita Income**

⬭ $18,215–$31,114

◯ $13,470–$16,039

○ $9,103–$13,174

**City Charter Reform**
**Percentage of Yes Votes**

▨ 13–26.84%

▩ 26.85–46.21%

■ 46.22–68.84%

*Source:* Robert A. Cropf and Todd Swanstrom, "Déjà Vu All Over Again: Charter Reform Fails in St. Louis," from *National Civic Review* 94(3) 2005: 16. Reprinted with permission from John Wiley & Sons, Inc.

electrical workers. Aldermanic President Jim Shrewsbury (2004) summed up the case against charter reform: "Corporate executives, attorneys, and out-of-town consultants are not going to get the job done. Charter change is supposed to be about what is best for the people, not about corporations getting the best deal possible. What has emerged from this decade-long endeavor is a disingenuous and contrived exercise in manipulation masquerading as grass roots."

## Conclusion: How Can Reform Move Forward

The St. Louis reform effort was motivated by a desire to strengthen mayoral leadership, a connection well documented in the scholarly literature (Svara 2008; Schragger 2006; Mullin, Peele, and Cain 2004). A strong argument can be made that the City of St. Louis would benefit from reforms strengthening the office of the mayor. Separately elected city and county officials can thwart the mayor whose appointment powers are anemic. Potential investors must get the approval of many different separately elected offices, and aldermen can veto almost any project in their wards. The mayor of St. Louis does not even control the police. Strengthening the office of the mayor would not guarantee dynamic mayoral leadership, but it would create levers of power that a skilled politician could use.

Given the obvious need for stronger mayoral leadership in St. Louis, why have reformers repeatedly failed to convince St. Louis voters to approve reforms? The St. Louis example demonstrates the barriers to reform identified in the literature (Burns and Thomas 2006; Schragger 2006). Publicly, competing visions of reform cast businesslike efficiency against minority and neighborhood representation. The mayor and civic elites were thus unable to match their view of reform to the broader constituency needed for successful change. When reforms do not make this connection, they are likely to be defeated by threatened interests (Sonenshein 1993; Schragger 2006). But reform is not impossible. The St. Louis defeat was a result of both the way reformers went about reform and the substance of the reforms they have recommended. A different process and a different mix of reforms could lead to a different result.

The most recent process for proposing charter reforms in St. Louis was run by a private group of citizens, Civic Progress, financially dependent on an elite business organization, most of whose members did not live in the city. To be sure, Advance St. Louis did create a group of over 150 stakeholders broadly representative of the city. But it is hard to avoid the conclusion that this group was designed to provide grassroots legitimacy to a set of proposals that were already laid out in the 1996 Walker Report. The Stakeholder Assembly was chosen by Advance St. Louis, not by the citizens of St. Louis, and it was not allowed to set its own agenda.

Most charter reform efforts around the country are organized and funded by the public sector. One common model is to have the mayor and council appoint a charter revision commission and then appropriate public monies to staff it. Once in existence, the commission is free to set its own agenda, with the commission choosing its staff—not, as was the case with Advance St. Louis, having the staff essentially choose the commission. Of course, having elected officials appoint the members of the commission means that many reforms that threaten their careers and material interests will be far less likely to find their way onto the ballot. However, a publicly orchestrated process will do a much better job of representing neighborhood and minority interests and co-opting elected officials into the process.

Equally important, a public process will be much more likely to propose reforms that can win voter approval. When Mike Jones, a respected African American political leader and aide to former mayor Clarence Harmon, said in the *St. Louis Post-Dispatch* after the city charter changes were defeated that "money, power, and privilege doesn't necessarily make you a winner on Election Day," he was simply stating a fact of political life in St. Louis. The proper role for Civic Progress, or any other private organization for that matter, would be to make its views known during the public meetings leading up to the drafting of charter amendments and campaigning for or against the amendments once they are put on the ballot.

Imagining a more democratic and transparent process for charter reform in St. Louis is easy. More difficult is the question of the substance of charter reform. For many years critics have charged that reformers were attempting to model city governments on the private corporation, increasing the power of the executive at the expense of elected representatives. The opponents of Propositions A, B, C, and D echoed these criticisms, charging that the reforms would make St. Louis less responsive to the concerns of ordinary voters. Were they right?

Following the logic of reformers who have long advocated a so-called short ballot, we believe a strong case can be made that reducing the number of separately elected county officials and putting them under the mayor would actually make city government more democratic, not less. Few voters can name even one of the county elected officials. Unaccountable to the voters, these county elected officers use the patronage at their command to construct their own mini machines. Putting most of these functions under the mayor, and eliminating the anachronistic Board of Estimate and Apportionment, would enhance the power of the mayor. The highly visible office of the mayor would be more accountable to the voters than the present confusing arrangement where voters have little idea where to assign responsibility.[2]

The problem with the proposed reforms is not that they would increase the powers of the mayor but that they did not include any provisions to check and balance the power of the mayor with a revitalized legislative branch. Since the Antifederalists, Americans have been rightly suspicious of too much executive power, and the U.S. Constitution embodies crucial checks and balances on executive power. In a city that is almost evenly divided between blacks and whites, putting so much power in the hands of the mayor risks alienating half the population. The representation of minority and neighborhood interests is essential to a healthy democratic government in St. Louis. And the key to this is strengthening the board of aldermen.

At present the board of aldermen in St. Louis does not check and balance the power of the mayor. Almost all legislation originates in the executive branch, which has the staff to research and draft complex legislation. Aldermen spend most of their time addressing service needs in their wards, such as fixing potholes and seeing that the garbage is picked up. Like most cities, St. Louis has a system of "aldermanic privilege" in which the board of aldermen defers to individual aldermen concerning developments that take place in one ward. The reformers have a legitimate point that the development process can be slowed down unnecessarily if an alderman takes a personal dislike to something or engages in petty corruption.

The challenge for charter reform is how to encourage the board of aldermen to become a more deliberative policymaking body. Clearly the board needs more staff and research capacity, and it needs more authority over the budget. In an age when government is perceived as impersonal and distant, the aldermen provide the kind of personal contact and responsiveness that the citizens of St. Louis crave.

One way to take some of the burden of day-to-day, ward-based service demands off the aldermen would be to create an ombudsperson to deal with simple complaints. Another way would be to incorporate neighborhood planning into the city government, as Los Angeles did recently in its charter reform. At present, neighborhood planning in St. Louis is often done by the aldermen with little input from the citizens. A transparent process that helped incorporate the neighborhood groups in the city into responsible governance would potentially enhance both civil society and government.

Reformers in St. Louis have alienated themselves from the political establishment by posing reform as only about increasing the efficiency of city government and making the city more attractive for investors. In fact, a healthy local democracy must balance a strong executive with a strong legislative body that can represent the diverse interests of minorities and neighborhoods. Ultimately, the well-being of the city as a whole depends on the well-being of its parts.

## Notes

1. Similarly, Flanagan (2004b) uses contingency theory to show how mayoral leadership is affected by the relationship of the mayor to the regime in power.

2. We do not believe the argument for reducing the size of the board of alderman is strong. The problem is not the size of the body; after all, the U. S. House of Representatives has 435 members. The weakness of the board of aldermen is its focus on ward-based services and patronage and its lack of a deliberative, citywide policymaking function.

## References

Burns, P., and M. O. Thomas. 2006. The failure of the nonregime: How Katrina exposed New Orleans as a regimeless city. *Urban Affairs Review* 41, no. 4 (March): 517–27.

Dahl, R. 1961. *Who governs? Democracy and power in an American city.* New Haven, CT: Yale University Press.

Elkin, S. 1987. *City and regime in the American republic.* Chicago: University of Chicago Press.

Flanagan, R. M . 2004a. *Mayors and the challenge of urban leadership.* Lanham, MD: University Press of America.

———. 2004b. Opportunities and constraints on mayoral behavior: A historical-institutional approach. *Journal of Urban Affairs* 26, no. 1 (February): 43–65.

Frederickson, H. G., G. A. Johnson, and C. H. Wood. 2004. *The adapted city: Institutional dynamics and structural change.* Armonk, NY: M. E. Sharpe.

Judd, D. R., and T. Swanstrom. 2010. *City politics: The political economy of urban America.* New York: Longman.

Mullin, M., G. Peele, and B. E. Cain. 2004. City Caesars? Institutional structure and mayoral success in three California cities. *Urban Affairs Review* 40, no. 1 (September): 19–43.

Pressman, J. L. 1972. Preconditions of mayoral leadership. *American Political Science Review* 66, no. 2 (June): 511–24.

Schragger, R. C. 2006. Can strong mayors empower weak cities? On the power of local executives in a federal system. *Yale Law Review* 115:2542–78.

Shrewsbury, J. F. 2004. Make charter change for the people, not the dealmakers. *St. Louis Post-Dispatch,* July 11, B3.

Sonenshein, R. J. 1993. *Politics in black and white: Race and power in Los Angeles.* Princeton, NJ: Princeton University Press.

———. 2004. *The city at stake: Secession, reform and the battle for Los Angeles.* Princeton, NJ: Princeton University Press.

*St. Louis Post-Dispatch.* 1996. Restructuring city government. September 9.

———. 2004a. Dysfunction junction. April 29. NewsBank online database (America's Newspapers). http://infoweb.newsbank.com (accessed February 3, 2009).

———. 2004b. Back up the bus. October 21.

Stein, L. 2002. *St. Louis politics: The triumph of tradition.* St. Louis: Missouri Historical Society.

Stein, R. 1990. *Urban alternatives: Public and private markets in the provision of local services.* Pittsburgh: University of Pittsburgh Press.

Stone, C. 1989. *Regime politics: Governing Atlanta.* Lawrence: University Press of Kansas.

Svara, J. H. 1990. *Official leadership in the city: Patterns of conflict and cooperation.* New York: Oxford University Press.

———. 2008. Strengthening local government leadership and performance: Reexamining and updating the Winter Commission goals. *Public Administration Review* 68, Special Issue (Dec.): 37–49.

Wheeland, C. M. 2002. An institutionalist perspective on mayoral leadership: Linking leadership style to formal structure. *National Civic Review* 91, no. 1 (Spring): 25–39.

CHAPTER 15

# PORTLAND

## "Keep Portland Weird"
## Retaining the Commission Form of Government

DOUG MORGAN, MASAMI NISHISHIBA, AND DAN VIZZINI

> How would you like to live in a state where the people can and do enact laws for
> the common good which their legislature has failed to enact for them, where they
> can nullify an obnoxious measure passed by the Legislature . . . a state where the
> party boss has been put out of business; a state in short where the people rule. . . .
> Such a state is Oregon.
>
> Eaton (1912, v)

HOW WOULD YOU LIKE to live in a city where this passion for citizen-centered control
over the destiny of the city and its governance process has been elevated into a slogan,
"Keep Portland Weird"? Such a city is Portland. Both the state and its major urban
center have become a national marquee for being different. The Portland metro area,
which is the home of 1,734,000 residents (more than one-third of the state's population), has been the driving force behind most of these innovative changes that are the
result of what has been characterized as populist liberalism (Clucas, Henkels, and Steel
2005, 16).

The city, like the state, has gained its own distinct national and international reputation for being different, even "weird," in at least four major respects. First, Portland
has acquired an international reputation in setting an example for urban sustainable
development. Second, social capital in Portland has grown at a time when it has been
decreasing in every other major city in the United States. Third, Portland is the only
city to retain the commission system of government. Fourth, upon closer examination,
even Portland's commission system looks weird to those who are familiar with this
form of government. Originally created to urge citizens to support local businesses by
"buying local," the slogan "Keep Portland Weird" has come to capture the unique
spirit of the city and is worn as a badge of honor. During the last election in 2007 to

alter the commission form of government established in 1913, opponents used the slogan as an argument to keep the commission system intact rather than replacing it with a strong-mayor form of government. This was the eighth unsuccessful attempt to replace the commission system with a more conventional form that clearly separates the executive and legislative functions of government.

In this chapter we provide a brief history of the commission form of government, a summary of Portland's particular application of the commission system, a documentation of the several efforts to replace Portland's commission system with a more executive-centered model, a summary of the factors that have enabled Portland's commission system to survive, and a discussion of the relationship between Portland's form of government and its international reputation for innovative sustainable development practices and high levels of civic engagement.

## History of the Commission System

The commission system was created in 1901 in specific response to a hurricane in 1900 that hit the island city of Galveston, Texas, killing six thousand people and creating millions of dollars in property loss. Influential business leaders of the community feared that the city might never recover its prosperity under the leadership of the incumbent city council, so they seized the initiative, prepared a plan, and requested that the governor appoint a commission to govern the city during the rebuilding period. To appease opponents who argued that appointed government was undemocratic, the plan was altered to provide for popular election of two of the five commissioners. Subsequent court challenges to the constitutionality of the partially appointive government led the legislature to make the office of all five commissioners elective, and in this form the commission plan became popular across Texas and the nation (Texas A&M University 2008).

The commission system was viewed by many of the business-oriented reformers of the day as the right answer to getting things done quickly, effectively, and efficiently. Experienced and knowledgeable business leaders could take control over a given functional area and mobilize the resources needed to complete a plan of action. At its peak in 1918, there were 500 cities that had adopted the commission system, but by 1984 the number had dwindled to just 177. The system gradually fell out of favor as it was replaced by the city–manager system, which was increasingly viewed as being much more effective in harnessing the growing and complex functions of local government under a single executive who had been specifically trained in the business of making government work. Galveston abandoned the system it became famous for creating in 1960 when it adopted the city manager form of government (Rice 1977; Texas State Historical Association 1996).

Ironically, the commission form of government fell out of favor for some of the very reasons that it was created in the first place. First, the commission system was criticized for its lack of professionalism. For example, a commissioner, who may have lots of private sector expertise in financial management and budgeting, may end up having oversight responsibility for transportation, police, fire, or other departments for which the elected official has no special competence, training, or experience. The city manager movement aggressively advanced the view that managing the public's business required special people who were committed to public service as a calling and who were schooled in the modern management tools necessary to transform this commitment into efficient and effective delivery of services carried out by technically trained career professional administrators.

In addition to assuming responsibility for hiring and managing a cadre of professional public administrators, proponents of reform argued that a city manager could do a much better job than a group of independent commissioners in coordinating all the complex activities associated with the delivery of local public services. While initially seen as a take-charge system that could get results in a hurry, the commission system came to be viewed as seriously defective in its ability to coordinate activities among diverse city functions each run by a semiautonomous commissioner.

Finally, in addition to the challenges of coordination posed by the commission system, there is also the problem of providing adequate representation to a diverse population. Because at-large balloting is intrinsic to the commission concept and since at-large elections may dilute minority voting strength, most southern cities were forced to abandon the commission plan because of suits brought under the Voting Rights Act of 1965 and subsequent amendments (Texas State Historical Association 1996).

Despite the multiple criticisms that have caused the commission system to be abandoned throughout the United States, Portland has remained steadfastly successful in its commitment. But in doing so, Portland has undertaken several changes to address some of the deficiencies inherent to the commission form of government.

## Portland's Commission System

In 1913 Portland eliminated the strong-mayor system that it had put in place in 1902 and adopted the commission form of government by only 292 votes out of a total of 34,342 votes cast. Piqued by the unwillingess of elected politicians to deal with prostitution and favoritism in award contracts, a group of prominent Portlanders mounted a well-publicized and well-funded campaign against the strong-mayor system in the months before the election. They hired the well-respected New York City Bureau of Municipal Research to provide a series of reports that documented the inefficiencies of the strong-mayor system in thirteen areas of functional responsibility (Lansing 2003, 290–91).

Once in place the system has remained intact (but as we shall see, substantially modified) despite eight major attempts to replace it. Like all commission systems, Portland's governance structure unites the legislative and executive functions rather than separating them into distinctly independent governing bodies. It does so by giving the mayor the authority to assign a portfolio of city bureaus to each city commissioner, much like a parliamentary system where cabinet ministers are appointed from parliament by the prime minister to provide executive oversight of the government's functional operations. This appointment model departs from the original commission form in which elected officials run to be commissioner of police, commissioner of roads, fire commissioner, and so forth.[1] In Portland commissioners run for office without portfolios, which are assigned by the mayor after their election.

The appointment power of the mayor to make bureau assignments is supplemented by the power to prepare and present the annual budget to the commission for adoption. In theory these two powers are significant and distinguish Portland's commission form of government from other commission systems, where these powers do not exist at the mayoral level. But in practice the dynamics of individually elected commissioners requires the mayor to gingerly exercise his or her special legal powers over the budget and bureau assignments in order to ensure that the mayor maintains at least the three votes needed to support his or her agenda. The need to maintain a voting majority makes the relationship among the commissioners an ongoing dance that depends on not only the personality of the commissioners but also the background music on the dance floor. As we elaborate more fully in subsequent sections, this music is Portland's civic culture and a political zeitgeist that prefers small, decentralized, and local governance.

The mayor, four commissioners, and the auditor make up the city's six elected officials. The mayor and the four commissioners together make up the city council, all of whom have an equal vote. All officials are elected at large on a nonpartisan basis and serve four-year terms. Elections are staggered, with the mayor and commissioners number one and four elected one year and the auditor and commissioners number two and three elected two years later. The staggered election schedule avoids a complete change of elected officials in any one year, except under unusual circumstances.

Following is a more detailed summary of the legislative, administrative, and quasi-judicial powers exercised by Portland's five-member commission.

*Legislative*—The city council meets weekly to conduct the city's legislative business. The council adopts the city budget and passes laws, policies, and regulations that govern the city. The mayor serves as chair of these legislative activities and has an equal vote to the other four members of the council. The legislative power of the city is shared with Portland citizens, who have the ability under state and city law to pass legislation through the initiative petition process. The council can also refer a legislative issue to a vote of the people through the referendum process.

*Administrative*—The mayor and commissioners serve as administrators of city departments, individually overseeing bureaus and carrying out policies approved by the council. The assignment of departments and bureaus is determined by the mayor and may be changed at his or her discretion. Bureau assignments do not necessarily correspond to departmental titles. For example, the commissioner of public works may not necessarily have any of the public works bureaus in his or her portfolio.

It is common practice during the annual budget deliberation process for the mayor to reclaim administrative oversight authority over all the bureaus, thus leaving the four commissioners without any executive responsibilities. During this process the commission functions mainly as a deliberative body with the exception of the mayor, who holds all the executive functions but only 20 percent of the deliberative control. This practice during the annual budget process is believed to encourage commissioners to act in the larger interest of the city as a whole, rather than merely serving as advocates for their respective bureaus. Since the mayor can redistribute bureau responsibilities differently after the budget process has been completed, the mayor's power during the budget process can be singularly important. However, there have been instances when the potential power of the mayor has been nullified by three members of the council who have formed an alliance to alter the budget priorities put forth by the mayor.

An important change was made to Portland's structure of government in 2000 when the council passed an ordinance creating a chief administrative office (CAO), who reports to the mayor and who has statutory authority over the Office of Management and Finance. The statutory power given to the CAO within the mayor's administrative portfolio helps to temper the argument that the commission system is especially weak in providing a unified approach to administrative planning and execution. In addition to the disproportionate executive authority exercised by the mayor through the CAO and the additional power given to the mayor during the budget process, it is common practice for mayors to assign themselves responsibility for those other administrative operations that are chief executive officer in nature (such as government relations, human resource management, planning, emergency management) and those bureaus that have important political stakeholders (such as police and economic development).

*Quasi-Judicial*—In addition to their legislative and administrative responsibilities, council members also act in a quasi-judicial capacity, which takes the form of hearing land-use and other types of appeals. There is nothing unique in the way this normal function is carried out by the city of Portland's commission system compared to the way it is carried out by almost all local government legislative bodies.

## Efforts to Replace Portland's Commission Form of Government

Portland's commission form of government has survived eight efforts to transform it into either a strong-mayor system or a city-manager/weak-mayor system (summarized in table 15.1).

The dissatisfaction with the commission system began shortly after it was adopted by a margin of only 292 votes in 1913. After two challenges in the first four years and two efforts to simplify the form in the 1920s—all unsuccessful—the citizens of Portland abandoned organized efforts to change the commission system until midcentury, when there were initiatives to adopt the council–manager form in 1958 and a mayor–council form in 1966. The former came within 6,538 votes of passing, with 47 percent of the votes cast; the mayor–council form was rejected by a 62 to 38 percent margin.

The next major effort to alter the commission system occurred in 2002 as a result of a concerted effort by a group of citizens to use the initiative process to change the form of government. There was increasing concern that commissioners elected at large disadvantaged Portland's growing minority communities. An initiative was placed on the May ballot in 2002 to change the commission form to a mayor–council system that would give all executive and administrative authority to the mayor and all legislative and quasi-judicial authority to a council of nine members—two elected at large

**Table 15.1   Summary of Proposals to Change Portland's Commission System to a Strong Mayor**

| Election Date | Purpose of Proposed Change | Vote Tally |
|---|---|---|
| May 3, 1913 | Provide commission form of government with a mayor and four commissioners elected at large. | YES: 17,317<br>NO: 17, 025 |
| June 4, 1917 | Abolish commission form of government and replace it with a mixture of the commission and council–manager form of government. | YES: 14,196<br>NO: 32,086 |
| June 4, 1917 | Repeal commission form of government and replace it with a council–manager form of government. | YES: 12,647<br>NO: 32,796 |
| November 2, 1926 | Simplify and retain commission form of government by giving the mayor more powers to run day-to-day government operations. | YES: 27,388<br>NO: 29,087 |
| June 28, 1927 | Simplify and retain commission form of government by giving the mayor more powers to run day-to-day government operations. | YES: 7,459<br>NO: 38,454 |
| May 16, 1958 | Replace the commission with an appointed city manager responsible to eight council members elected at large. The city manager would select all department commissioners. | YES: 55,283<br>NO: 61,821 |
| May 24, 1966 | Replace the commission with a strong-mayor form of government with a part-time council. | YES: 41,848<br>NO: 68,158 |
| May 21, 2002 | Replace the commission with a strong-mayor system; expand the commission from four to nine, with two elected at large and seven from districts. | YES: 29,730<br>NO: 94,179 |
| May 15, 2007 | Create a chief executive officer appointed by the mayor and confirmed by the council. | YES: 18,880<br>NO: 60,608 |

*Source:* Data cited from www.portlandonline.com/auditor/index.cfm?c=27132&a=5456.

and seven elected from geographically defined districts. The mayor would have been given veto power over legislative actions, subject to council override. This proposal was overwhelmingly rejected but set the stage for the 2007 contest.

The 2007 referendum occurred as a result of the creation of a charter review commission supported by the city council at the urging of Mayor Tom Potter, who was the former police chief (City of Portland 2007). Measure 26-91 called for the elimination of the commission form of government and the institution of a mayor–council form, with a strengthened CAO. Under the proposal the role of the city's CAO would be expanded to oversee and coordinate management of the city's bureaus, operations, and finances—a role currently performed by the city council. The CAO would be appointed by the mayor, subject to confirmation by city council, and accountable to the mayor. The mayor would be the city's chief elected executive official, have veto power over council actions, and have ultimate authority and political accountability for city operations, including the authority to fire most city employees. City council members would focus on legislative oversight of city operations and management, policy development, long-term strategic planning, and constituent representation.

The influential City Club of Portland once again appointed a research committee to undertake a detailed evaluation of the proposed changes. Because the City Club had dramatically reversed its historical opposition to the commission system by adopting the minority report that extolled the virtues of the commission system in the 2002 referendum, the outcome of the City Club research analysis of the 2007 proposal to created a CEO appointed by the mayor was far less surprising.[2] The committee concluded the following:

> While the proposed change in the form of government would likely promote greater efficiency in city government, the changes would also jeopardize the innovation and resiliency that benefit Portland under the current form. By granting considerable authority to each commissioner, the current form attracts strong leaders to run for city council and offers commissioners real opportunities to implement innovative policies and projects through their assigned bureaus. Furthermore, by spreading authority broadly among commissioners, the current form not only offers citizens greater access to city leaders, it ensures that diffuse leadership can serve as a bulwark against an ineffectual or reckless mayor. (City Club of Portland 2007, 25)

Grassroots organizations, former elected officials, and unions lined up in agreement, while members of the business community were steadfast in their traditional view that the commission system contributed to inefficiency and ineffectiveness in managing the city's business (Money in Politics Research Action Project 2007).

One of the complicating factors in the 2007 debate over commission reform was continued city council rancor over the mayor's leadership style. Mayor Potter was accused by his fellow commissioners of not being collaborative, of taking initiatives without consultation. This included efforts to push through a strategic planning process in addition to seeking changes in the city charter that would enhance his power. To some, Potter appeared to be a hardheaded bully who didn't like to listen very much before acting. These charges were seized upon by the mayor's opponents to characterize his desire to alter the commission system as merely a personal power grab.

With all of the citizen advocacy groups and unions lined up against altering the commission system, the ballot measure went down in defeat by 70 percent, by far the largest margin in history. There are reasons to believe that the 2007 ballot measure vote solidified support for the commission system that had been building slowly over the last forty years of Portland's history. The City Club report foreshadowed a growing belief that the commission form of government might somehow be responsible for Portland's growing international reputation for cutting-edge sustainable development practices and high levels of civic engagement. The increasing tendency to associate Portland's urban development success with the commission form of government is troubling to good government advocates who continue to believe that Portland's commission system suffers from lack of professionalism, inadequate coordination of city functions, and inability to represent minority racial and ethnic diversity. How has Portland's commission system sought to deal with these criticisms? In the following section, we seek to answer this question.

## What Enables Portland's Commission System to Survive?

Portland's commission system survives in large part because the majority of citizens believe the city is living up to its motto, "The City That Works." They point to the city's reputation for exemplary urban sustainable development practices, its high levels of civic engagement, and "good government" reforms to make Portland's commission system more effective, responsive, accountable, and efficient.

### Exemplary Urban Sustainable Development Practices

Portland has been recently described as "a paragon of healthy urban development" (Langdon 1992, 134), "a West Coast success story," and a model for "successful mass transit" that possesses "some of the best architecture in North America," which attracts delegations from around the world "looking for inspiration" (*Economist* 1990, 24–25).

Steve Johnson (2006, 2), one of the leading scholars on Portland's development over the last thirty years, provides the following summary of the city's sustainable development kudos: best bicycling city in North America (*Bicycling* magazine); the best walking city (*Prevention*); city with the most sustainable policies (SustainLane); one of the most wireless cities in the world, America's most vegetarian-friendly large cities, and the second most "enlightened city" in America (*Utne Reader*); and sixteenth most attractive destination for well-educated and creative young people.[3]

### High Levels of Civic Engagement

In addition to its reputation for leading-edge urban planning and development, Portland has become internationally well known for being an exception to the long-term and systematic decline in civic participation and social capital in the United States (Putnam 2000). In a dissertation published in 2002, Johnson documented a transformation in Portland's civic culture over a thirty-year period between 1960 and 1990. In *Better Together* Robert Putnam and his colleagues found Portland to be a significant exception to the decline in civic and social involvement across the cities in the United

States. They observed that Portland experienced a "positive epidemic of civic engage-ment," which they characterized as "an extraordinary civic renaissance" (Putnam, Feld-stein, and Cohen 2003, 241–42).[4]

## *"Good Government" Reforms Make Portland's Commission System More Effective*

Portland's commission form of government has survived in part because it has been responsive to good-government reform initiatives especially during the past thirty years. After providing a summary overview of these reforms, we assess the ongoing criticisms that the existing system results in inefficient and ineffective coordination of activities among semiautonomous bureaus headed up by independently elected commissioners, inappropriately diminishes the role of professionals in providing administrative over-sight, and results in inequitable representation of minorities as a result of at-large elec-tion of commissioners.

### OVERVIEW OF REFORMS

Since 1942 there have been thirty charter amendments and two council-initiated ordinances to reform government or alter the balance of power at city hall. All but eight of these initiatives have been adopted. We have provided a summary of these reforms from 1980 to 2009 in table 15.2.

The list of twenty-four adopted reforms since 1980 is impressive when viewed in totality over a twenty-nine-year span. During a period that has been marked by a significant decline in public trust of government, Portland has demonstrated high levels of trust and adopted measures to ensure higher levels of efficiency and accountability by rejecting term limits for the mayor, auditor, and commissioners; giving greater power to its elected officials to control Portland's urban development agency (Portland Develop-ment Commission) and to hire and fire bureau directors; authorizing independent audits of government performance and police investigations; internalizing its civil ser-vice system within a professional Bureau of Human Resources; centralizing administra-tive support services; and introducing public financing of political campaigns. The thirty-two reform initiatives since 1942 reflect a combination of concern for high levels of responsiveness and accessibility to the city's governing processes as well as concern for increased performance efficiency and effectiveness of all governmental units. But the success of these reforms has not reduced criticisms that the existing system is (a) inefficient and ineffective in coordinating activities among semiautonomous bureaus headed up by independently elected commissioners; (b) results in a diminished role of professionals within the policy development and implementation process; and (c) pro-vides inequitable representation of minorities as a result of at-large election of commis-sioners. In the following sections, we describe the ways in which Portland has sought to specifically address each of three major criticisms.

### COORDINATION AND EFFICIENCY ISSUES

As we have already seen, Portland's commission system has been criticized from its very inception for its woeful lack of coordination and resulting inefficiencies. In its

**Table 15.2   Portland "Good Government" Reforms, 1980–2009**

1. Require Vacancies in Office to be Filled by Election (PASSED, May 1980).
2. Establish a Police Internal Investigations Auditing Committee (PASSED, November 1982).
3. Require Residency for Civil Service Employees (PASSED, November 1982).
4. Require City Residence for Officers and Employees (PASSED, March 1983).
5. Require City Auditor to Be a Certified Public Accountant (PASSED, May 1984).
6. Require One-Year City Residence for Elective Office (PASSED, December 1984).
7. Authorize Auditor to Conduct Performance Audits (PASSED, May 1986).
8. Centralize Personnel Oversight by Personnel Bureau (PASSED, November 1986).
9. Increase Exemptions from Classified Civil Service (FAILED, November 1986).
10. Revise Charter Listing of Successors to Council Seats in Emergency (PASSED, May 1988).
11. Eliminate Mandatory Residency Requirements from City Charter (PASSED, May 1988).
12. Adopt Term Limits for Mayor, Commissioners, and Auditor (FAILED, May 1996).
13. Ordinance to Centralize Administrative Service Functions (PASSED, April 2000).
14. Exempt bureau directors from Civil Service system (PASSED, November 2000).
15. Eliminate Two-Election Process (PASSED, May 2004).
16. Adopt Campaign Financing for Elected City Offices (PASSED, May 2005).
17. Provide Periodic Review of the Charter (PASSED, May 2007).
18. Civil Service Reform (PASSED, May 2007).
19. Increase Powers of City Council over PDC (PASSED, May 2007).

2002 *Research Report* on a proposal to replace Portland's commission system with a strong-mayor form of government, the City Club of Portland collected abundant testimony of these inefficiencies. Steve Bauer, former director of the Office of Finance and Administration (1986–95), described Portland's commission system as a "big, robust, energetic, feudal system with lots of palace intrigue." Bauer estimated, in round figures, a 25 percent loss of efficiency resulting from the lack of unified executive authority in Portland's commission form of government—Bauer referred to this as "friction loss" (City Club of Portland 2002, 33). Vera Katz, two-term mayor and former speaker of the Oregon House of Representatives, characterized the system as "Byzantine and dysfunctional." She observed that the commission system is especially problematic when dealing with complex municipal issues that necessarily require the collaborative involvement of many bureaus, such as the cleanup of the Willamette River.

The testimony of Mayor Katz and former budget director Steve Bauer point to two inherent problems with the commission system that Portland has struggled to overcome. First, when conflicts arise between bureaus and the bureau managers that cannot be resolved, there is no incentive or structure within the commission form of government to resolve the problem. As a result there is a tendency for such problems to go unnoticed or unattended without much involvement by others, thus delaying resolution and thereby making the problem harder to solve than it otherwise should be. Second, when there are multiple goals of a given project, the commission system has no center that enables the differences and priorities to be reconciled. In the face of such disagreements, bureau staffs do not invest much energy in reconciling the differences (City Club of Portland 2002, 33). Defenders of the existing commission system have responded by disputing the evidence of their opponents, by calling attention to the political advantages of the commission system that actually increase efficiency, and by citing various reforms that have been made to achieve greater administrative efficiencies.

*1. Commission inefficiencies are overstated.* Former city auditor Gary Blackmer argues that over the past twenty-five years of doing in-depth performance audits, he has never encountered the kind of inefficiencies cited by Steve Bauer in his 2002 testimony to the City Club. "While there may be some loss of efficiency," Blackmer said, "the commission form allows five elected officials to each drive initiatives with their bureaus, accomplishing more than a centralized administration."[5] In its 2002 report, the City Club received testimony from those who pointed out that the five commissioners, or "five mayors," do not necessarily compete with one another. "They collaborate, cooperate, and compromise. They do not always and necessarily do this willingly but this feature of the commission system is one of its best attributes: the required consensus building and process of compromise is a strong check and balance against the will of a single politician or a faction" (City Club of Portland 2002, 33). The City Club and Blackmer's focus on the political efficiencies of the commission system is a common theme of defenders of Portland's system.

*2. Unique political advantages to Portland's commission system have increased efficiency.* In addition to arguing that the commission system encourages a collaborative approach to problem solving, the defenders of Portland's system have cultivated the mantra that "too much power in the hands of one person is dangerous." This was the core argument by opponents in 2007 to the proposal to replace the existing commission with a strong-mayor form of government. They successfully argued that it doesn't make sense to wrap "all the power around one person, with a layer of protection by a chief administrative officer" (Northwest Labor Press 2007; see also comments of neighborhood activist Chris Smith in Budnick 2007). The *Oregonian* had already concluded in the previous decade that "in Portland's history, the commission form traditionally has dispersed power, making the government remarkably free of corruption" (Lane 1988, B1).

*3. Administrative reforms have increased efficiency.* Over the past two decades various Portland mayors with support from the city council have undertaken initiatives to strengthen the central coordinating role of the city's Budget and Finance Office. The most ambitious of these initiatives was undertaken in 2000 when the city council embarked on a major effort to increase administrative efficiency and reduce the costs of city government administrative services by creating a new Office of Management and Finance (OMF). The new office was created by merging the existing Office of Finance and Administration, the Bureau of General Services, and the Bureau of Purchasing. At the same time, the city council also created a new position of a CAO who serves at the pleasure of the full city council but reports directly to the mayor. The council put the CAO in charge of OMF with responsibility and authority to coordinate the administrative service functions of the city, to suggest improvements for the "productivity, responsiveness and effectiveness of the services and programs of the OMF and to provide the city council with a detailed annual work-plan for improving city administrative services" (City of Portland, City Code 2009, Title 3.15.010).

Soon after creating the CAO with enhanced powers for centralized administrative coordination, it became clear that the principle of commissioner independence would at least temper, if not trump, centralized coordination efforts. The first task assigned to the CAO by the city council was to undertake an administrative services review (ASR). The council set a goal of a 10 percent cost reduction in administrative services citywide for the 2000–2002 biennium. OMF prepared framework plans for each service area. The process was completed in February 2001, and the CAO recommended a strategy of greater centralization of administrative services, beginning with human resources and information technology services citywide. The city council agreed and directed the CAO to implement the centralization of human resources and information technology services by April 2001.

But less than one year after the completion of the ASR and OMF's initial centralization of services, city bureaus and their commissioners began to push back. In January 2002 four bureau directors released a memo—referred to as the mutiny memo—that criticized the effectiveness and efficiency of OMF's centralization program. The memo was sent by the directors of four bureaus (Bureau of Environmental Services, Portland Department of Transportation, Office of Planning and Development Review, and Water Bureau) to their respective commissioners in charge.

CAO Tim Grewe responded with a memo in which he argued that many of the recommendations in the mutiny memo were made without adequate context and based on erroneous or insufficient information. Grewe wrote that many of the recommendations would result in "decreased council oversight of financial and citywide system integrity." Grewe noted that the bureau directors suggested that he cut the number of his financial analysts from ten to five while the bureaus would retain seventy-four analysts. He warned that these reductions would reduce OMF's ability to provide effective oversight of city operations (as cited in City Club of Portland 2002, 38). In the view of former city auditor Gary Blackmer (2009), "Grewe was defending the council policy but the mutineers were right in all their arguments. The quality of services to the public suffered when those support functions created bottlenecks. Grewe had no accountability to provide the timely responsive services that the bureau directors were supposed to deliver. This is the classic argument of centralized versus decentralized."[6]

We cite this mutiny memo to illustrate that Portland's commission system creates a limit on the possibilities for undertaking centralization of administrative functions in the name of efficiency. This limit is defended in part as a necessary check against excessive power at the center and in part as a way to preserve multiple points of leadership creativity and initiative in the system.

## PROFESSIONAL OVERSIGHT OF ADMINISTRATIVE OPERATIONS: "WE DON'T WANT 'EXPERTS' RUNNING THE GOVERNMENT. WE WANT TO HAVE 'PEOPLE' CONTROL THE GOVERNMENT."

As we pointed out in the first section of this chapter, the commission system lost popularity in the face of increasing calls for trained professionals with technical expertise to direct and manage the administrative functions of government. While this concern is still frequently heard in Portland, especially from members of the business community and career administrators, defenders of the commission system argue that there are three reasons why this concern is largely unfounded.

*1. High levels of civic engagement increase administrative efficiency.* The accusation that Portland pays a high price for the lack of administrative expertise of elected commissioners has been stood on its head by civic engagement activists who contend that Portland's most admired "civic jewels . . . did not emanate from elected or bureaucratic leaders, but from citizens" (Johnson 2006, 13–14). The alleged successes of citizen-centered leadership include strong neighborhood associations, a vital downtown business area, public transportation, recycling, and protection of public lands.

In addition to the results achieved by high levels of civic engagement, others cite the advantages of the process. As one long-time career administrator observed, "public engagement has moved quickly in Portland from being simply a part of 'public relations management' to being an integral part of policy implementation." In doing so, "it has increased government efficiency rather than diminished it."[7] Together the processes of civic engagement and the results achieved by these processes "established Portland's philosophy of urban livability—the idea that cities are for people, not just for commerce and cars" (Young 2005).

In addition to cementing the idea that "cities are for people, not just for commerce and cars," the civic engagement movement has successfully cultivated the mantra that "we don't want 'experts' running the government; we want to have 'people' control the government." On its face this mantra seems to mirror Andrew Jackson's famous observation that "the duties of public office, are, or at least admit to being made, so plain and simple that men of intelligence may readily qualify themselves for their performance" (Richardson 1902, 448). But there is an important difference that shapes the way in which the culture of civic engagement affects the operation of Portland's commission form of government.

The Jacksonian infatuation with the "common man" was both anti-expert and anti-elitist (Morgan et al. 2008, 65–69). Portland's culture of civic engagement, while appearing to be anti-professional, is largely the result of the involvement of upper-middle-class elites, who themselves are professionals. Thus, the civic engagement culture in Portland frequently results in a battle of warring experts, which has required career administrators to get good at structuring and staffing citizen engagement processes.

**2. Getting good at civic engagement and citizen participation.** As viewed from the Portland Building, city bureau directors and program managers look out on a network of ninety-plus neighborhood associations that extend to the far corners of the city and are linked through coalition offices and committees organized to influence public policies and programs. A similar network of business district associations represents the city's commercial centers and neighborhood business nodes. Both of these networks of city-sponsored associations are complemented by venerable civic organizations such as the League of Women Voters, the Portland City Club, labor unions, Chambers of Commerce, commercial and industrial associations, watershed councils, organizations representing immigrant and minority interests, social service nonprofit groups, civil rights activists, advocates for local schools, political associations of every kind, and environmental advocacy organizations. In the day-to-day operations of city government, managers and employees rub shoulders with legions of volunteer citizen advisers who serve on city boards, commissions, working groups, roundtables, and task forces. Like the air we breathe, civic engagement in Portland is a kind of plasma that envelopes, embraces, and energizes every aspect of public life.

Portland's strong culture of civic engagement means that city commissioners, bureau directors, and program managers diminish the role of community stakeholders and citizens at their peril. The city's history is replete with cases where the city failed to engage stakeholders and the general public, mismanaged the engagement process, or took a course of action that ran counter to public sentiment despite extensive public involvement. And Portlanders rarely make any distinction between public policy and program initiatives that are completely discretionary and those that are mandated by law, court injunction, or regulation.

Many cases of public policy decisions illustrate an active civic culture in Portland that can quickly mobilize grassroots campaigns in response to perceived and actual excesses of their city government. Public controversies involving citizen groups often are accompanied by battles of warring professionals, placing a premium on high levels of competency on the part of career administrators to deal effectively with citizen activists, neighborhood associations, and other grassroots groups. For example, in the Mid-County Sewer Project starting in 1988 and the Southwest Community planning process starting in 1994, there were initial public engagement missteps. Once these were corrected, however, the city and community developed new approaches to the respective projects that ensured successful outcomes. Most city bureaus have experienced failures of public engagement like these and have altered their approach to citizen outreach, sometimes adding community facilitators to their staff, enhancing the flow of information to external stakeholders, and writing civic engagement requirements into their contracting processes.

Portland's commission form and the accessibility of city commissioners to citizens and advocacy groups appear to be a perfect fit for Portland's civic culture. The willingness of Portland to trade off administrative efficiency for responsiveness at city hall is borne out by the high levels of public satisfaction registered in annual citizen surveys conducted by the city auditor. In the 2008 survey 61 percent of residential respondents graded overall city government performance as good or very good, and the level of satisfaction has averaged around 57 percent since 1999. Residential satisfaction with Portland's livability is even higher, averaging 78 percent since 1999 and topping out at 82 percent in the 2008 survey. And satisfaction levels increase even further regarding the livability of the respondent's neighborhood, reaching 86 percent in the most recent survey and averaging 83 percent since 1999 (City of Portland 2008a).

**3. The adoption of reforms that enhance professional oversight of administrative operations.** We mentioned in our discussion of administrative coordination and effi- ciency in the previous section the important steps taken in 2000 to provide greater administrative oversight of central city operations by a chief administrative officer. An important additional step Portland has taken to ensure professional accountability in the management of city operations is the creation of performance auditing oversight by the city auditor's office. The elected auditor is required to be a licensed professional who answers to the public, not to other elected officials, which ensures that the work is done in an impartial fashion. As a result of the expansion of the office's responsibili- ties in 1986 to undertake internal performance audits of city bureaus (in addition to just financial audits), successive auditors have taken the initiative to make recommenda- tions for improving the quality of city services, saving money, and ensuring public access to city information. In doing so the independently elected city auditors and their expert professional staff over the past two decades have developed a national and grow- ing international reputation for the excellence of their performance audit work (City of Portland 2008b).

In the public debate over whether Portland's commission system meets the govern- ment efficiency test, it is clear that civic engagement proponents have won the day in elevating the importance of the political efficiencies of access, participation, and collaboration over the administrative efficiencies of cost savings and timely project com- pletion. But in sacrificing some classical administrative efficiency that comes from high levels of political participation, Portland's auditor's office has played a key leadership role in elevating the importance of professional performance standards.

HOW PORTLAND'S COMMISSION SYSTEM ADDRESSES THE ISSUE OF MINORITY REPRESENTATION: "WE NEED 'ACCESS' AND 'RESPONSIVENESS' MORE THAN JUST 'REPRESENTATION.'"

Some critics of the commission system argue that citywide elections for commission- ers do not provide representation to certain segments of the population, especially minority groups. As noted above in our brief history of the comission form of govern- ment, many cities switched from the commission system after courts ruled that the districtwide elections diluted minority voting power and, hence, violated the federal Voting Rights Act. These rulings were made on the principle that district-based council members provide better access for citizens residing in each district as well as providing better representation for more citizens (*City of Mobile v. Bolden* 1980; Davidson 1984). Although methods of electing council members are not an inherent feature of a given form of government, the commission form presumes that the commissioners will be elected at large. This is because elected officials are expected to manage administrative portfolios on behalf of all the citizens, not just those from a given district. This contrasts with mayor–council or council–manager forms, which may have council members elected from districts, at large, or some combination of the two methods. This flexibility is not an easy option for the commission form of government because of the consolidation of the legislative and executive functions.

Still, Portland's commission system has not been widely or consistently criticized for its lack of representativeness.[8] Various reasons explain why this has occurred. First, Portland is the most white city of its size in the United States (Hammond 2009, A9), and nonwhite residents, who account for 22 percent of the population, are scattered throughout the city.[9] Thus, a district-based system of election will not necessarily produce greater representation for minorities. Second, the commission system provides minority community members with equal access to all of the commissioners, which may have become more important than so-called minority group representation. Building multiple sources of support for the agenda of minority groups is a sine qua non for success in Portland's small and geographically dispersed minority community. Finally, ethnic and cultural minority groups have had some success in obtaining minority group representatives on the city council, even under the citywide election system and even in the face of a relatively small minority population compared with other cities.[10]

Portlanders in recent years have become more self-conscious of the need to embrace diversity and combat the state's overtly racist history (McLagan 1980; Taylor 1998). The state's history in dealing with race has become a growing embarrassment for Portland's large liberal community and its political leaders, who work hard to erase the injustice of this past and recognize the need to make special efforts to address the concerns and needs of Portland's diverse urban population. Current mayor, Sam Adams, the second openly gay mayor of a major U.S. city, observes that because Portland is so overwhelmingly white, it means "we have to work that much harder to make sure that nonwhite Portlanders have unfettered access to social and economic opportunities." For Adams this means reestablishing the city's human rights commission, supporting minority contractor requirements, and battling what he calls "shamefully" high dropout rates of youth (Hammond 2009, A9).

In Portland the commission system has avoided the criticisms the system has received elsewhere in the United States for its inability to respond to the needs of minority communities. This is likely to continue for the foreseeable future. Portland's minority community is not growing very rapidly largely because affordable housing is not easily available, and Portland's demographic makeup will require political leaders to remain highly responsive to the diverse needs of minority groups within the city. These conditions bode well for those who advocate retaining Portland's commission form of government.

## Explaining the Paradox of Portland's Commission System

One of the striking findings in undertaking research for this article is the relatively small amount of evidence or speculation by scholars and citizen activists on the relationship between Portland's commission form of government and the city's international reputation for high levels of civic engagement and sustainable development practices. The city is cited as a model for urban sustainable development and for its civic engagement but not for its form of government. There is strong agreement among scholars that there is a close connection between Portland's high level of civic engagement and its success in being on the cutting edge of transportation and sustainable development planning. As one scholar concludes, "as America changes and as lessons from Portland's experiment emerge, it is becoming increasingly evident that metropolitan Portland's governance structure, civic engagement processes, planning approaches, and community health innovations are a harbinger for sustainable metropolitan developments" (Nelson as cited in Ozawa 2005).

Steve Johnson, a longtime activist who has undertaken the most definitive study of changes in Portland's civic infrastructure, argues that the "exceptionalism of Portland's civic life is one significant reason for the city's reputation as a well-planned city with a lively downtown and a strong creative community." But Johnson attributes this exceptionalism in civic life to "learned behaviors," not to Portland's form of government (2006, 13–14).

Putnam and his colleagues seem to be in agreement with Johnson's observations about the connections between high levels of civic engagement and Portland's successes on the urban development front, but they are more generous with respect to the role of governing institutions and leaders. They conclude that while "there is no way to sum up Portland's experiences of access and participation in a single formulation . . . many of the appealing things in Portland—the parks and open spaces downtown, the successful light-rail system, the thriving inner neighborhoods—are fruits of the cooperative work of government and citizen activists guided by a shared vision of a livable city in a healthy environment" (Putnam, Feldstein, and Cohen 2003, 265).

The one book that is singularly focused on trying to understand "what policies and processes put in place in the Portland, Oregon, region" account for its success does not discuss Portland's commission form at all and makes only three references to the city council in general (Ozawa 2005). The commission form of government is treated as a benign agent of change, neither much to be praised nor to be blamed for what has transpired over the last thirty years. It is almost as if Alexander Pope's epigram about the irrelevance of the forms of government is true in the case of Portland.

What are we to conclude about the role of the commission form of government in Portland's development? Let us begin with a summary of the claimed virtues of Portland's commission system:

1. It forces collaboration among different bureaus, departments, and government agencies, which is deemed more desirable by many than forced collaboration through the centralizing power of one individual. Portland's leading scholar on the city's urban development observes that he has "consistently opposed efforts to shift Portland to a strong mayor or council-by-districts system" in part because in "a relatively homogeneous city, at-large elections help to keep the city unified around something like a set of common goals" (Abbott 2008).

2. It encourages and gives credit to those who take leadership initiative. As the 2007 City Club report argued, "by granting considerable authority to each commissioner, the current form attracts strong leaders to run for City Council and offers commissioners opportunities to implement innovative policies and projects through their assigned bureaus" (25). Commissioners have an opportunity to build a constituency base for their work by courting the appropriate advocacy groups and, in the process of doing so, build a legacy that outlives their term of office. This has been the case for recent commissioners, who have taken on such causes as parks, a "children's agenda," building a bicycle-friendly city, light rail development, downtown revitalization, rebuilding neighborhood associations, and community policing.

3. The system ensures large amounts of transparency. While spreading authority broadly among commissioners may result in a reluctance to criticize the performance of bureaus under the supervision of their colleagues, the commission system makes it difficult to hide very much for very long.

4. When there are performance issues (as has been the case on numerous occasions), "the city can start anew with another commissioner, which cannot happen so easily in any other form of government." As former city auditor Blackmer observes, "in a strong mayor system, starting anew means voting him or her out. In the council-manager system, starting anew means firing the city manager. We sometimes take this notion for granted but it really is a great way to reboot the system and take a fresh start on a problem" (see note 6).

5. It ensures high levels of responsiveness by providing multiple points of access to citizens and advocacy groups. A former executive of one of the leading "tree planting" advocacy groups in Portland observed to one of the authors that when he finally understood how the system really worked, he was able for the first time to get money for his organization's tree-planting efforts from five separate bureau budgets: Parks and Recreation, Transportation, Water, Environmental Services, and the Office of Neighborhood Associations.

6. "It ensures that diffuse leadership can serve as a bulwark against an ineffectual or reckless mayor" (City Club of Portland 2007, 1).

The above list of virtues shows Portland's commission system has been a good fit for the liberal activist citizen professionals who have successfully used the system over the last several decades to put the city on the international map for innovative urban sustainable-development practices and high levels of civic engagement. This agenda has been supported by a set of state and regional policies and institutions that have facilitated growth while also protecting the environment (Seltzer 2000). The commission system deserves credit for being responsive to these changes in the citizen advocacy agenda that transformed Portland's development in the 1970s and 1980s. There was strong community consensus that produced commissioners who largely shared the community's vision. But the commission system also appears to be benefiting from a "cultural lag" phenomenon that gives the commission credit for previous successes even when the underlying rationale may be undergoing a decadelong change (Abbot 2001,

255; Johnson 2006, 8–16; Ozawa 2005, 304; Putnam, Feldstein, and Cohen 2003, 265–68).

Perhaps one of the best ways for understanding the role of the commission form of government in Portland's development over the last thirty years is to view the success as the result of a regime, not primarily the result of the form of government. We use the word *regime* to describe "the informal arrangements by which public bodies and private interests function together in order to be able to make and carry out governing decisions" (Stone 1993, 6; Lauria 1997; Leo 1998). A good example to illustrate what we mean by regime is provided by one of our key informants, Dick Feeney, retired TriMet director of public affairs.

Feeney pointed out that one of the unnoticed factors in Portland's success on the urban development front, especially with regard to transportation issues, is the professional network of planners, transportation experts, citizen advocates, elected officials, and urban specialists who over time have developed high levels of trust that cut across more than forty organization and jurisdictional boundaries within the Portland metropolitan area (see note 9). There is a rich web of professional, political, grassroots, formal, and informal relationships across organizational and jurisdictional boundaries that has accounted for Portland's success. This network has become "a way of life," which is the classical definition of what a regime means (Elkin and Soltan 1993). We think this lens provides the best way for understanding the role of the commission system in Portland's governing success.

Portland's regime consists of a strong commitment to urban sustainable development, high levels of civic engagement, a large population of engaged and "warring" professionals, a quirky predilection toward libertarian socialism, and a form of municipal governance that is dynamic, creative, collaborative, responsive, accountable, transparent, and constantly being fine-tuned to conform to community values. While the diffusion of power at city hall results in the sacrifice of administrative efficiencies and effectiveness found in stronger executive–centered forms, paradoxically this diffusion of power is essential to city hall's success. The system bestows great opportunities for leadership, experimentation, and external consultation while requiring extensive internal collaboration and compromise. The city council acts more as a council of elders than as a political organization in the classical American sense (Lansing 2003; McColl 1979).

The "regime perspective" gives more credit to both the form and processes characteristic of the commission system than is the case for most students of Portland's urban development. But it treats the commission as one of many key governing institutions within a larger array of elected officials and governing bodies working collaboratively with citizens, advocacy groups, and career public administrators to define a common vision and to transform this vision into an operational reality. Viewed from a regime perspective, the commission form of government can be changed without necessarily altering the fundamental way of life that Portland has built.

The commission form has survived through all manner of challenges, through painful economic contractions and spectacular expansions. But the combination of current challenges is unique in Portland's history. Economic decline and rapid demographic changes are occurring in the wake of Portland's growing national and international reputation for sustainable community practices. There is fundamental agreement that the city's future depends on the ability of public institutions to be responsive to active citizens, especially to the growing diversity of voices representing different socioeconomic, ethnic, racial, cultural, and ideological perspectives (Abbot 2001, 255; Johnson 2006, 8–16; Ozawa 2005, 304; Putnam, Feldstein, and Cohen 2003, 268). Without a strong community consensus, the commission form of government can quickly fall victim to its worst defects—stalemate, indecision, internal infighting—and the consequent losses of administrative efficiency and effectiveness that arise from such defects. For this reason advocates of the commission form of government are rightly concerned about the ability of Portland's relatively homogeneous community to maintain the strong working consensus that has made it so successful over the past several decades.

We shall see if the constant experiment that is municipal government in Portland is up to the test. The Portland City Club research report of 2007 reminds us that if there is a change, it will not come soon or easily. "Keeping Portland Weird" will likely remain Portland's marquee for the foreseeable future, and Portland's commission form of government is likely to remain near the top billing on this marquee.

## Notes

We would like to acknowledge the information obtained from review of the manuscript by three key informants: Carl Abbott, the leading scholar on Portland's recent urban development (1983, 1991); Gary Blackmer, former city auditor; and Dick Feeney, retired director of public affairs at Trimet.

1. Portland is the only commission form of government of its kind in the United States and the only commission form of any kind in a city over one hundred thousand in population. Both Bismarck and Fargo, South Dakota, have city administrators appointed by the commission, but neither has commissioners elected at large (Portland system) or commissioners elected to a predetermined portfolio of administrative responsibilities (classic Galveston model). Bismark and Fargo divide commission assignments among themselves by majority vote of the commission.

2. The City Club was formed in 1916 by a small group of well-educated citizens who were dissatisfied with the operation of the city's public institutions and government and wanted to foster a positive change in the community. It has undertaken research and produced reports on each charter review proposal to change the form of government (City Club of Portland 1933, 1961, 1963, 2002, 2007).

3. Planners regularly visit and study Portland for its urban planning practices including an urban growth boundary, effective mass transit system, and the only regionally elected government in America although these features were not created by Portland city government alone.

4. Robert Putnam documents that in the early 1970s metropolitan Portland looked virtually identical to other American metropolitan areas in civic terms. Two decades later Portland suburbs, by Putnam's measure, were roughly two to three times more civically engaged than comparable suburbs elsewhere (Putnam, Feldstein, and Cohen 2003, 242–44).

5. Personal e-mail from Gary Blackmer to Douglas Morgan, February 25, 2009.

6. Personal e-mail from Gary Blackmer to Douglas Morgan, February 21, 2009.

7. Interview of Dick Feeney by Douglas Morgan, January 19, 2009; personal e-mails to Douglas Morgan, February 17–18, 2009.

8. Portland's major African American business newspaper, the *Portland Skanner*, has consistently supported a strong-mayor form of government over the current commission system (*Portland Skanner* 2007). The reasons for doing so, however, seem to be the classic good-government arguments in favor of effectiveness and efficiencey rather than representational advantages that district-level elections provide to the minority community.

9. The City of Portland's population of 537,081 (2006) is predominantly Caucasian (77.9%) with the remainder composed of the following minorities: Hispanic (6.8%), Asian and Pacific Islanders (6.7%), black (6.6%), Other (2%) (U.S. Census Bureau 2006).

10. For example, African American commissioners Charles Jordan (1974–84) and Dick Bogle (1984–92) enjoyed successive terms of service on the city council.

# References

Abbott, Carl. 1983. *Portland: Planning, politics and growth in a 20th century city.* Lincoln: University of Nebraska, 1983.

———. 1991. Urban design in Portland, Oregon as policy and porcess: 1960–1989. *Planning Perspectives* 6:1–18.

———. 2001. *Greater Portland, urban life and lands ape in the Pacific Northwest.* Philadephia: University of Pennsylvania Press.

———. 2008. Personal e-mail. November 24.

Budnick, Nick. 2007. Group forms to oppose "strong mayor" proposal. *Portland Tribune,* February 8.

City Club of Portland, Oregon. 1933. *City manager plan for Portland.* Portland: City Club of Portland.

———. 1961. *Report on Portland city government.* Portland: City Club of Portland.

———. 1963. *Report on charter revisions for the city of Portland.* Portland: City Club of Portland.

———. 2002. *Portland's form of government: Ballot measure research study, ballot measure 26–30.* Portland: City Club of Portland.

———. 2007. *City club report on ballot meaure research 26–91.* Portland: City Club of Portland.

*City of Mobile v. Bolden.* 1980. No. 77–1844 (U.S. Supreme Court, April 22).

City of Portland, Oregon. 2008a. Auditor. Neighborhood survey results.

———. 2008b. *Service efforts and accomplishments: 2007–08.* Portland: Officer of the City Auditor.

———. 2007. *Charter review commission: Report to city council, a government for Portland's future.* Portland: City of Portland, Oregon.

City of Portland, City Code. 2009. Title 3.15.010. *City of Portland City Code.* Portland: City of Portland, January 19.

Clucas, Richard A., Mark Henkels, and Brent Steel. 2005. *Oregon politics and government.* Lincoln: University of Nebraska Press.

Davidson, Chandler, ed. 1984. *Minority vote dilution.* Washington: Howard University Press.

Eaton, Allen H. 1912. *The Oregon system: The story of direct legislation in Oregon.* Chicago: A. C. McClurg and Co.

*Economist.* 1990. Where it works. September 1.

Elkin, Stephen, and Karol E Soltan. 1993. *A new constitutionalism: Designing political instiutions for a good society.* Chicago: University of Chicago Press.

Hammond, Betsy. 2009. White in the face of change. *Oregonian*, January 18.

Johnson, Steve. 2006. How many citizens does it take to change a light bulb? Lessons from Portland's 35-year civic democracy experiment. *Letting Off Steam Conference.* Brisbane, Australia.

Lane, Dee. 1988. City Club studying whether to dump unique system: Portland commission again under scrutiny. *Oregonian*, March 6.

Langdon, Phillip. 1992. How Portland does it: A city that protects its thriving core. *The Atlantic Monthly*, November.

Lansing, Jewel. 2003. *Portland: People, politics and power; 1851–2001.* Corvallis: Oregon State University.

Lauria, Mickey, ed. 1997. *Reconstructing urban regime theory: Regulating local government in a global economy.* Thousand Oaks, CA: Sage.

Leo, Christopher. 1998. Regional growth management regime: The case of Portland, Oregon. *Journal of Urban Affairs* 20, no. 4 (December): 363–94.

McColl, E. Kimbark. 1979. *The growth of a city: Power and politics in Portland, Oregon, 1915 to 1950.* Portland, OR: The Georgian Press.

McLagan, Elizabeth. 1980. *A peculiar paradise: A history of Blacks in Oregon, 1788–1940.* Portland, OR: The Georgian Press.

Money in Politics Research Action Project. 2007. Press Release. April 12.

Morgan, Douglas F., Richard Green, Craig W. Shinn, and Kent S. Robinson. 2008. *Foundations of public service.* Armonk, NY: M. E. Sharpe.

Northwest Labor Press. 2007. Labor opposes strong mayor form of government. *Northwest Labor Press,* March 16. www.portlandonline.com/Leonard/index.cfm?a=150866&c=27435 (accessed January 19, 2009).

Ozawa, Connie, ed. 2005. *The Portland edge: Challenges and successes in growing communities.* Washington, DC: Island Press.

*Portland Skanner.* 2007. Editorial. *Portland Skanner*, May 10.

Putnam, Robert D. 2000. *Bowling alone: The collapse and revival of the American community.* New York: Simon and Schuster.

Putnam, Robert D., Lewis Feldstein, and Dan Cohen. 2003. *Better together: Restoring the American community.* New York: Simon and Schuster.

Rice, Robert. 1977. *Progressive cities: The commission government movement in America, 1901–1920.* Austin: University of Texas Press.

Richardson, James D. 1902. A compilation of the messages and papers of the presidents–Andrew Jackson. Vol. 2. Part 3. *Project Gutenberg.* January 1. http://onlinebooks.library.upenn.edu/webbin/gutbook/lookup?num=10858 (accessed Febuary 10, 2009).

Seltzer, Ethan. 2000. Portland and smart growth: What you can learn from the Portland experience. *Conference on cities in North America,* New York.

Stone, Clarence. 1993. Urban regimes and the capacity to govern: A political economy approach. *Journal of Urban Affairs* 15, no. 1 (Mar): 1–28.

Taylor, Quintard. 1998. *In search of the racial frontier: African Americans in the American West, 1528–1990.* New York: W. W. Norton and Company.

Texas A&M University. 2008. Charles Jordan-Corenlius Amory Pugsley Local Award 1995. *Texas A&M University,* December 19. www.rpts.tamu.edu/pugsley/Jordan.htm (accessed December 19, 2008).

Texas State Historical Association. 1996. Handbook of Texas online. *Texas State Historical Association,* January 1. www.tshaonline.org/handbook/online/browse/index.html (accessed January 19, 2009).

U.S. Census Bureau. 2006. Portland quick facts. *U.S. Census,* January 1. http://quickfacts .census.gov/qfd/states/41/4159000.html (accessed December 11, 2008).

Young, Bob. 2005. Highway to hell. *Willamette Week,* March 9. http://wweek.com/story.php? story=6110 (accessed December 19, 2008).

CHAPTER 16

# CONCLUSION

## Distinct Factors and Common Themes in Change of Form Referenda

JAMES H. SVARA AND DOUGLAS J. WATSON

THIS BOOK HAS BEEN INSPIRED by a desire to better understand the two major forms of city government based on different constitutional principles that are used in American cities. Although each of these forms and variations on them are used separately in other countries, in the United States they coexist, usually peacefully but with competition for favor in the court of public opinion or in the assessments of informed observers. In a relatively few cities, the adherents of each form directly confront each other in a contest over which form will be used in that city. The relatively small number of referenda does not diminish the interest generated by these contests or the implications of who is winning them. Of course, we are interested in the final outcome of the contests and how the game is played on each side. We also see the ideas generated by these contests as a valuable source of insights about the strengths and weaknesses of the forms themselves.

A major issue in the larger debate over form is whether the council–manager form is well suited to large, diverse cities, and these cities have been the focus of the case studies presented in this book. There is a widely and long-held perception that the form does not work well in these cities and that many large council–manager cities are shifting to the mayor–council form. The objection might be raised that a total of nine cities with over one hundred thousand in population making this change since 1990 does not constitute "many," especially when the same number of cities have rejected a change in form, and three cities have moved in the opposite direction. Still, something is going on that warrants close attention. The analysis presented in the opening chapter and in the case studies suggests that the issue regarding size and form of government should be reformulated. Given the growth in the number of large council–manager cities—a trend that will continue as more cities with this form grow into the large and larger city categories—the issue is no longer whether the form is suited for large cities. In large cities where problems are more complex, populations are more diverse, interests

303

are more numerous and better organized, and the media are a larger force, there are multiple political perspectives and wide-ranging debate. It is likely that the debate will focus not only on policy issues but also, in some places, on constitutional questions as well. The issue is whether the constitutional debate is going to be brought to the level of formal choice by the voters in large cities. When it happens, what arguments are raised, how appropriate are they to the conditions in these cities, and what points may be missing from the discussion? In this chapter we examine how general themes interact with the specific characteristics of a particular city to shape the outcome of the form of government referendum.

## Factors Related to Holding Referenda on Form and Their Outcomes

A range of factors can lead to efforts to change the form of government. Previous research has identified these as the following: an unsettled political climate, the politics of growth, the influence of business and the media, changes in other structural features, initiatives by political leaders, and shortcomings of city managers. The case studies are examined for evidence that is consistent with or departs from these factors.

### Is Form a Settled Issue?

As Hassett and Watson (2007, 141) observe, "In some cities, there is constant tension over the form of government, while in others the matter appears settled." They attribute inclination to change to the characteristics of the values of the electorate. If there is widespread adherence to a reinforcing cluster of values and familiarity with a prevailing political style, there is little tension over the form of government. For example, in large Northeastern cities, there is little discussion about changing the form of government. The roots of mayor–council government are very deep there, and no significant group is likely to propose a change to council–manager government. Likewise, in Arizona or North Carolina cities where council–manager government is firmly entrenched, it is unlikely for a pro-mayor–council group to be taken seriously if it proposes changing the form of government. We examine the content of the contrasting models of local governance later in the discussion, but the key point is that arguments for the "other" form do not connect with the attitudes and expectations that shape perceptions of and preferences for the governmental process in these settled cities.

In other cities, attitudes are unsettled as indicated by a history of challenge or change. Richmond, Hartford, and Spokane had relatively late adoptions of the council–manager form. Kansas City adopted early but experienced a continuation of machine-controlled politics until 1939. Topeka and St. Louis have frequently considered change in form, and in Oakland the change issue reappeared regularly starting in 1984. In Topeka the switch from the commission to the mayor–council form occurred in 1984, and the council–manager option was rejected five times between 1929 and 1969. After the change to the council–manager form in 2004, the commitment to the form was called into question by the first mayor elected under the new structure. Portland voters have frequently considered change but always reaffirmed its commission form. In all these cities, some could remember a time when a different form was used or could recall an earlier effort to change the form of government.

The remaining case study cities have become unsettled because of circumstances. The shift in attitudes may be prompted because of a positive example of a kind of leadership that is not associated with the existing form—for example, mayors Pete Wilson in San Diego, John Logie in Grand Rapids, or Joe Wardy in El Paso. Even in these cities, however, and the others that reconsidered what had been long-established patterns of governance, there was usually a combination of dissatisfaction with the governmental process or failure in performance that led significant groups to question the form of government in use. As Ehrenhalt (2004) has argued, shortcomings in city government lead some to want a change from whatever form they've got to a different structure. Success of the change effort, however, is not inevitable. The claims that deficiencies in the existing form are inherent and insurmountable do not necessarily carry the day. Once they have been expressed, however, and some become convinced of the superior features in the alternate form, the prevailing view may be uncertainty and wavering support for either form. Dissatisfaction with conditions and performance also contributes to the continuing cycle of reconsideration in cities that have frequently debated change in form. Some will advocate not just change within the form—for example, a new mayor or manager—but change in form.

In cities where a sizable percentage of the local electorate supports the form that is not in use, one can anticipate multiple attempts to change the form. In those cities the question of form is never settled, as Hassett and Watson (2007) have pointed out. In most of the cities that did change form, there had been a series of attempts at change that, in some cases, extended over decades. In cities that have experienced only one or two attempts, the adherents to the incumbent form should understand that the question is not permanently settled. For example, in the Dallas referenda, council–manager government benefited from the animosity of the African American and the Hispanic communities toward the incumbent mayor. In the future a more popular mayor may lead the effort to change form with the support of the business and minority communities. Oftentimes the issue of the day may influence voters to change forms, as it did in Spokane. Most voters do not understand the intricacies of form of government and base their decisions on a current negative environment or on a popular political personality, such as Jerry Brown in Oakland, Douglas Wilder in Richmond, or Eddie Perez in Hartford. In many of the cities, including Cincinnati, Grand Rapids, Kansas City, Portland, and Spokane, mayors pushed for charter amendments that would increase their powers.

*Growth*

Growth is likely to be a salient issue in referenda over form, but it is not clear whether it has special significance in comparison to other major policy debates. Either rapid growth or the lack of growth can cause tensions, and growth options are inherently divisive in many communities. Opposition to efforts to stimulate growth was a key factor in St. Petersburg where the council and manager were committed to this strategy, but the connection between the council–manager form and rapid growth is not automatic. In Sarasota, Florida, a city that retained the council–manager form in 2002, the same opponents to growth who were present in St. Petersburg defended the slow-growth orientation of the council–manager government and did not want to relax controls that would have limited development (Hassett and Watson 2007). Pro-development supporters in Sarasota hoped to have an executive mayor who would make the city bureaucracy more receptive to development and other growth-related interests. The community with many retirees was satisfied with the policies in city government and voted to retain the council–manager form. In St. Petersburg promoting a slower approach to growth meant changing the form of government. In San Diego pro-development interests were aligned with the strong-mayor forces, whereas controlled-growth supporters relied on district elections and were suspicious of change in form of government. In several cities, including Dallas and Richmond, business forces supported a change in the form because they felt they would be in a better position to influence pro-growth policies if they had to deal with a strong mayor rather than a diverse council. Both cities had small councils elected at large prior to federal court rulings that enlarged their councils with single-member districts.

The stakes in major development decisions are large, and failure brings recrimination. "Cities that are suffering economically seem to be ripe targets for a challenge to the form of government," as Hassett and Watson observe (2007, 143), and the same is likely to be true for cities that botch big development projects. St. Petersburg and Spokane had such projects, and there was general dissatisfaction with the pace of economic development in Cincinnati, Hartford, El Paso, Oakland, Richmond, and Spokane. There was a tendency to blame the existing form for the lack of progress. In several cities, such as Hartford, Oakland, and Richmond, there were dramatic changes in their economies over a relatively short period. All three were prosperous cities at the midpoint of the twentieth century, but by the end of the century, their economies were suffering, their tax bases were eroding, and their crime rates were some of the highest in the country. One of the reasons for this change in fortune for these cities was undoubtedly white flight to the suburbs. Rusk (1995) describes cities like Hartford, Oakland, and Richmond as inelastic, so that when whites moved to the suburbs, the central cities had nowhere to grow. Poorer people, who required more services and paid fewer taxes, remained in the core city. An accompanying result was that as the cities shrank in size, their commercial base moved to the suburbs as well.

## Business and Media

The business community and newspapers in cities have been highly interested in city government structure and often have been active participants in referenda either as advocates of change or defenders of the existing structure. In general these interests have been supporters of downtown development, centralization of influence in city government, and cleaning up and smoothing out the processes of city government. Formerly, they typically supported the council–manager form (Bridges 1997). This was still the case in El Paso. The major newspaper but not the business community opposed change to broaden the mayor's position in Grand Rapids and opposed the strong mayor in Portland. In Dallas the business community opposed the strong-mayor form in the first referendum but only because the city council promised strengthening the powers of the mayor. The *St. Petersburg Times* supported the council–manager form because the incumbent officials were pro-development. The *Oakland Tribune* opposed the mayor–council form in 1996 but supported it in1998. In all the other cities, the newspaper–business leadership combination supported the shift to the mayor–council form or the strengthening of the mayor as in St. Louis.

Most textbooks explain that historically businessmen, in addition to good government groups, were the main supporters of council–manager government. For example, in Dallas, the Dallas Citizens Council controlled the city government through at-large elections of a small city council. The city was successful, in their view, because it "ran like a business." However, after the federal courts ordered Dallas to move to fourteen single-member districts, the business community lost its grip on city hall. As a result, its support for council–manager government has weakened considerably. In Sarasota developers rebelled against the pro-neighborhood policies of the council–manager government when it supported a referendum calling for a change to a mayor–council system. Developers in Dallas and in Sarasota realized that it would be easier for them to elect a strong mayor rather than a majority of a large city council. An interesting question arises from the case studies: Has the traditional support from the business community for council–manager dwindled in the face of diversity and single-member districts?

*Other Structural Changes*

It appears that other structural changes altered the dynamics of the council–manager form in several cities that considered abandonment. District elections in Dallas, Richmond, and San Diego changed the orientation of council members and made the council process more contentious. Partisan elections in Hartford and strengthening the mayor in Hartford and in Kansas City may have contributed to the new conditions or a shift in attitudes that would lead to later efforts to change the form of government. In Cincinnati shifting from selection within the council to designating the top vote-getter as mayor was commonly viewed as a major cause of increased conflict among council members that was difficult for the council–manager form to handle. Cincinnati would empower its mayor after rejecting a change to the mayor–council form.

Each situation is unique, but two generalizations seem plausible. First, change in other institutions can affect the relationships among officials and the way a form of government operates or the way it is perceived by residents. Change in election institutions, however, typically does not fundamentally alter the form of government. Frederickson, Johnson, and Wood (2004) suggest that council–manager cities that elect mayors directly or choose council members from districts become more like mayor–council cities with chief administrative officers (CAO) than they are like other council–manager cities. Politicization makes the political process in these cities more like that in partially professionalized mayor–council cities. Svara and Nelson (2008) argue, on the other hand, that form still shapes roles, allocation of authority, and relationships, independently of electoral methods.[1] Furthermore, there is no indication that by itself the introduction of districts or direct election of the mayor leads to consideration of change in form. Grand Rapids has used district elections and elected its mayor since the 1920s. Over 80 percent of the 140 council–manager cities with more than 100,000 in population directly elect their mayor, and half elect a majority of their members from districts (32 percent elect all council members from districts). Of the twenty-four cities of over 250,000, all but six have a district majority. Still, the number of these cities that have had referenda on abandoning the council–manager form is nine for all large council–manager cities (plus nine that have changed to the mayor–council form) and four for the larger council–manager cities (plus five that have changed to the mayor–council form).

The retention of the traditional method of selecting the mayor from within the council may have affected two of the cities. The Richmond council and voters had approved direct election of the mayor in 1995, but the change was denied by the legislature—a decision supported by former governor Douglas Wilder. Council selection of the mayor from an all-district council presumably provides the weakest base for mayoral leadership in a council–manager city. In the case of Cincinnati, one might speculate that the failure to change the method of electing the mayor sooner contributed to the pressure for change and that the minimal alteration of designating the top vote-getter as mayor contributed to the contentiousness of the council on which all were automatically candidates for mayor.

Partisan elections added a divisive element in Hartford, and a three-party competition contributed to the fragmentation of the council in Cincinnati, but partisan elections are an uncommon practice in both mayor–council and council–manager cities and did not play a role in most of the charter contests over form of government in the cities covered in this study. There are two clear exceptions. The standard politics and charter reform politics in Hartford have been divided along partisan lines. In Cincinnati party difference was one of many characteristics that affected support for changing form of government or directly electing and strengthening the mayor. The Republican Party tended to support these changes, and the Democratic Party was split on the changes or opposed them. In St. Louis the efforts to change form were led by business and professional leaders and opposed by the party politicians, especially Democratic ward-level leaders. The absence of partisan forces is somewhat surprising in view of the increased party involvement in mayoral elections in large council–manager cities with nominally nonpartisan elections. It is consistent, however, with research that shows little impact of the mayor's party on the size of government (Ferreira and Gyourko 2009). If promoting strong mayors is perceived as the preferred approach of one party, it will be more difficult to put together coalitions to support change in form of government. Furthermore, the emphasis on combining civic leadership with professional leadership in council–manager cities makes it unlikely that supporting the council–manager form will have a strong partisan appeal. Thus, constitutional contests over form are likely to remain largely free of extensive party involvement or consistent partisan divisions.

## Political Leadership on Choice of Form

An important factor in the initiation and outcome of referenda on form of government is the nature of political leadership related to charter change. It is common for political leaders to push efforts to change the form of government from council–manager to mayor–council to expand their own influence in the government process. Mayor Rudolph McCollum in Richmond is one incumbent mayor who sought to continue the form. David Fischer in St. Petersburg favored the revamped council–manager proposal on the ballot rather than the strong-mayor proposal, although he would become the first strong mayor when the strong-mayor option was chosen and he was reelected. It is quite rare to find a mayor–council mayor who leads the effort to switch to the council–manager form—Joe Wardy in El Paso is the exception in the case study cities. Among incumbents Pete Wilson epitomized what a strong mayor could be like in San Diego and started the long process of rethinking that led to adoption of the mayor–council form. John Logie pushed the change but declared that he would not run for reelection to be the beneficiary of new powers, and Dick Murphy shepherded the change in form referendum through the council (after initially being opposed) although he did not subsequently run for the new office in San Diego. In St. Petersburg two mayors in the late eighties (and three managers) functioned as if they were strong mayors pushing the development agenda, so the change in form essentially confirmed what had been emerging in practice. Incumbent mayors in Cincinnati (Luken, before and after being elected as a stronger mayor), Dallas, Hartford, Kansas City, Oakland, and Portland sought to expand their own office. Some mayors, such as Harris in Oakland and Funkhouser in Kansas City, sought additional powers when they were unable to build a majority coalition on the council. Former Virginia Governor Doug Wilder led the campaign to change the form of government in Richmond and after the successful outcome announced that he would run for mayor. Jerry Brown, who sought expanded powers for the office he was seeking, may not have been the major reason for the trial adoption of the mayor–council form in Oakland, as Megan Mullin demonstrates, but he helped align leaders, organizations, and voters who were trending in the direction of a new form to support it. Kim and Wood observe, however, that two former mayors in Kansas City who sought to change the form of government while mayor now view the enhanced position of the mayor in the council–manager form as satisfactory and feel that no further change in the form of government is necessary.

The importance of the incumbent mayor can be an advantage or disadvantage depending on how the mayor is assessed. The failure of Proposition F in Oakland in 1996 was explained in part by the weakened position of Mayor Harris after six years in office. Many observers interpret the ballot questions in Dallas as a referendum on Mayor Laura Miller. She was not the person that many people wanted to be either a

strong or stronger mayor. Mayor Miller had alienated most of the city council, including all of the African American and Hispanic members, by her sharp attacks on them.
A number of observers of Dallas city government credit the mayor's unpopularity with
the two large minority groups as the main reason for defeat of mayor–council government. While she was succeeded by a facilitative pro-council–manager mayor, the issue
of form is likely not permanently settled. In Hartford Mayor Eddie Perez convinced
his supporters that he had to have the powers of a strong mayor if the voters were to
hold him accountable. Because Hartford had suffered through a series of ineffective
and political city managers, voters were willing to empower Perez in the hope that
change would improve the city's standing.

These cases suggest that the leader-centered model is likely to be attractive to some
of the kind of people who reach the top elected office in council–manager governments.
Mayors can achieve substantial results using a shared leadership style within the features
of the council–manager form (Svara 1994, 2008). The evidence indicates, however,
that some who become mayors in council–manager cities may decide to take the charter
change path to expanding leadership rather than focusing on facilitative leadership and
drawing on the contributions of other council members and the manager to develop a
shared vision for the city. This situation is likely to continue unless a different kind of
leader seeks the office or there is a different understanding of the leadership potential
in the council–manager form. Currently, assertive leaders who occupy or seek the may-
or's office may promote the expansion of their power through change in form, sometimes with success. They are more likely to want to be a powerful leader who is in
charge than a facilitative leader who blends his or her vision with the contributions of
others and ensures that the city has clear goals and strong performance.

## Shortcomings of City Managers

There are always serious implications when city managers fail to perform satisfactorily.
As professionals with specialized training and experience and with an ethical commitment to support the work of the city council and as persons selected through a process
intended to identify not only strong general qualifications but also background relevant
to the position to be filled, it is expected that managers will do a good job. If there are
problems, performance corrections can be identified through a review process. If the
needed changes are not forthcoming, the manager can be removed at any time. In some
cities the process of selection, assessment, and replacement does not work properly. For
example, in several cities council members did not seek highly qualified professional
city managers but rather chose local people with little to no prior city management
experience. As mentioned above, Hartford city councils over a number of years hired
city managers with little training or experience in city government. When city councils
are not committed to hiring highly qualified city managers, it is likely that the system
will not work as it is designed. In St. Petersburg and Hartford, there were rather serious
ethical lapses by the city managers that reflected poorly on the city management profession. Supporters of council–manager government cite the adherence by city managers

to a strict code of ethics as a major advantage of the form. When some managers do not adhere to it, it lessens the image of all city managers and detracts from the form.

As noted previously, when major projects are botched as they were in Spokane and St. Petersburg, citizens and the media are determined to hold someone accountable. Since the city manager is responsible for ensuring that projects are properly constructed or financed, he or she is often responsible. In other cases the city manager may generate controversy over the way he uses his authority as in personnel decisions in Spokane, the firing of the police chief without consulting the council in St. Petersburg, or the handling of the budgeting process and the pattern of fiscal mismanagement in San Diego. Some conclude that it is not enough to change the manager, but the form of government must be blamed and changed. An important exception was Robert Bobb in Oakland. He was respected, and the understanding that Jerry Brown would retain him as the de facto CAO (he retained the title of city manager) helped assure some voters that administrative competence would be maintained in the new form of government. Some managers have substantial support, and their misgivings about a structural change can contribute to its defeat, as in Grand Rapids.

## Regimes and the Question of Form

An important concept for understanding how leadership is organized across sectors in city government is the regime (Stone 1989, 1993). There are in many cities continuing partnerships between the leaders in the governmental arena and in the business and civic sectors that shape what broad strategies are pursued and adopted; these partnerships help overcome fragmentation of power (Mossberger and Stoker 2001). Morgan, Nishishiba, and Vizzini use the concept to consider how the commission form fits into the patterns of governance in Portland and to explain the support for continuing the use of the modified version of the form that Portland has developed. Building on their comments, we offer these preliminary observations.

Presumably, regimes coalesce behind and operate through the existing form of government. A challenge to the existing form may represent a weakening of an existing regime or at least the defection of key elements. In Portland the regime recoalesced around the commission form in 2007 after some indication of division between business and civic leaders in the 2002 contest. The replacement of a form probably indicates a shift in the preferences of a regime and the splintering of or a challenge to the existing regime. In St. Petersburg the growth regime closely aligned with the council–manager form was challenged by anti-growth elements that wanted a new policy orientation and argued that change in form was part of the way to achieve it.

The business/civic portions of a regime may persist but want a different configuration of the governmental partner. In El Paso the mayor-dominated government was perceived by business to be an unreliable partner because of corruption and inept performance, and in Spokane the council–manager form lost support of business leaders. Finally, a new leader may emerge on one political side who wants to change the governmental organization as a preliminary step in changing the regime, as in Oakland. Future research should more fully and explicitly consider the relationship between form, regimes, and constitutional change.

## Referendum Process and Constitutional Changes

Before turning to an analysis of the arguments used in form of government referenda, it is useful to briefly consider the nature of the referendum as a process for constitutional deliberations. Initiatives—issues put on the ballot through petition by citizens—in particular and referenda in general are frequently criticized as a policymaking process distorted by moneyed interests and simplistic arguments (Broder 2000). The outcome may reflect who can spend the most on a persuasive public relations campaign rather than a thoughtful assessment of alternatives by voters. Some assessment of how well the initiative and referendum process works is in order.

The literature of direct democracy indicates that the criticisms are overblown. Concerns that form of government referenda may leave important decisions about the constitutional framework of local government in the hands of an unrepresentative electorate unduly influenced by the paid advertising of interests with big bank accounts appear to be unfounded. The interests of minorities may be threatened in the arena of referenda, but the results of state referenda do not typically disadvantage minority groups (Tolbert and Smith 2006). Minorities were part of successful opposition to charter change in Dallas and St. Louis, and there was a division between African American leaders supportive of the strong-mayor form in Richmond and those who preferred retention of the council–manager form.

Money may get an issue on the ballot but does not usually determine the outcome, and this is particularly true in local referenda (Blanc and McCabe 2008). A common characteristic in referendum cities has been the pressure from the business community to change to the mayor–council form of government, and campaigns backed by businesses are likely to be well funded. The results are approximately an equal number of successes and failures.

There is new appreciation of the educative effect of referenda with increases in voter awareness, interest, and participation as a result of the use of ballot measures particularly in low salience elections (Tolbert and Smith 2009), and referendum campaigns can have a positive educative effect on voters (Smith and Tolbert 2004). Although it is expensive and disruptive to the local political process to have a referendum over changing the form of government, citizens may actually learn more about how their city is governed by having a referendum, and they are just as likely—consistent with the initiative and referendum research—to reaffirm their existing form as they are to jump on a high-priced bandwagon for change. Local circumstances rather than the referendum process appear to determine the outcome.

## Arguments Stressed in Campaigns—Old Themes with Modifications Live On

In chapter 1 a summary of potential arguments for and against the major forms was presented. When one analyzes the arguments that were made on each side of the contests in the case study cities, only some of these arguments were used. The range is narrower, and the arguments usually stress the traditional distinction between having a strong political leader, on the one hand, and an insulated professional manager, on the other. Both of these simple images are viewed in positive and negative terms depending on which form one prefers, but neither presents a complete picture of what their respective forms offer. This pattern is not quite the same as the argument that a city's preferred form represents a choice between two contrasting paradigms (Hassett and Watson 2007) or a tendency to accept political values or professional values (Box 1995) although aspects of those explanations persist.

There is no indication that the mayor–council advocates or their supporters expect that decisions will be made on political grounds, for example, particularism, special treatment, or patronage. Indeed, accountability and improved performance—traditionally major themes of the council–manager form—have been emphasized in campaigns for strong mayors (Ehrenhalt 2004). The emergence of strong mayors in the nineties who stressed reinventing government methods, such as Giuliani, Goldsmith, Rendell, and Daley, made it easier to make the connection between management reform and the strong mayors. On the other hand, corruption and failing governments in some strong-mayor cities, such as Providence (Stanton 2004), provided ammunition to the anti-strong-mayor groups. In our case study cities, the mayors in Richmond, Spokane, and Hartford under the new mayor–council form have been roundly criticized for abuses while in office, and the Oakland mayor has encountered a variety of difficulties, including the investigation of his chief administrative officer for charges of nepotism and interfering with a police investigation of an Oakland gang. In events since the completion of the case study (in late January 2009), Mayor Eddie Perez in Hartford faced bribery and other charges related to home renovations done by a contractor who performed millions of dollars of work for the city. The mayor was found guilty on five charges in June 2010.

The St. Louis referendum evolved into a contest between strong executive, "government-as-a-business" advocates versus defenders of a decentralized system with access to favors and patronage offered by leaders in the party and ward organizations. Council–manager supporters, on the other hand, generally emphasized standard good government arguments for a governmental process dominated by a professional city manager. A typical justification was used by the advocates of council–manager government in many of the cities. Generally, it was "no boss mayor" that would rule autocratically to the detriment of democracy. Ironically, the clearest support for the value of shared authority among elected officials came from the commission city of Portland.[2]

As indicated in table 16.1, proponents of the strong mayor–council form assert that the form brings strong political leadership with greater accountability and less likelihood of a contentious city council that cannot make clear or bold decisions. An extension of the fragmented council argument is the claim that authority is diffused in the council–manager form. Ironically, there were also cases in which the manager was criticized for being too powerful, and the council was faulted for not setting a different direction or properly supervising the manager. Back to the disorganization theme, there was the experience with or fear of managerial turnover. Finally, in cities where there

**Table 16.1    Major Themes in Support of the Mayor–Council Form by City**

| *Positive Arguments/Claims for the Mayor–Council Form* | |
|---|---|
| Strong leadership; mayor is in charge or "stronger" vis-à-vis council and manager; mayor can forge coalitions with use of incentives and sanctions. | Cincinnati, Dallas, Grand Rapids, Kansas City, Oakland, Portland, Richmond, St. Louis, St. Petersburg, San Diego, Spokane |
| One person who can be held accountable by voters. | Cincinnati, Dallas, Oakland, Richmond, St. Louis |
| Greater capacity to initiate major policy changes. | Dallas, Richmond, Spokane |
| CAO provides administrative expertise. | Grand Rapids, Oakland (1998) |
| *Arguments/Claims That Criticize the Council–Manager Form* | |
| Mayor is figurehead; does not have enough power to set direction, form coalitions, or overcome opposition. | Cincinnati, Dallas, Hartford, Topeka |
| City council is prone to dissension, and there is no one who can overcome it; potential for deadlock. | Cincinnati, Dallas, Kansas City, Richmond, Spokane |
| Diffusion of power and accountability; too many masters. | Cincinnati, Dallas, Kansas City, Richmond |
| City manager acquires too much influence; is not properly supervised. | St. Petersburg, San Diego, Spokane |
| City manager turnover; city council can arbitrarily remove manager. | Hartford, Topeka |
| Having city manager does not guarantee competence and high ethical standards. | Hartford, Richmond, St. Petersburg, San Diego, Spokane |

were significant shortcomings in performance or failure in initiatives, the city manager was held up as a contributor and the claim of professional managerial competence was questioned.

In addition, several other arguments were articulated in specific cities. Oakland mayors complained that the city manager could ignore the mayor, although this position can be restated to assert that the manager is responsible to a majority of the council and cannot have a special responsiveness to the mayor alone. Critics of the council–manager form in Topeka argued that city managers are expensive to hire and costly to remove because of severance packages often included in manager contracts.

Some additional arguments that might have been advanced appear not to have been important in these contests. Traditional criticisms include the charge that the city manager is narrowly focused on improving efficiency and ignores broader values, that the city manager is an outsider whose decisions do not reflect community values, and that the form is efficient in small matters but not effective in taking on major initiatives (Banfield and Wilson 1963). Each of these points can be challenged with considerable anecdotal and research evidence, and perhaps they are dropping out of common usage. City managers focus on a wide range of public service values (Keene et al. 2007). Watson and Hassett (2003) noted that a high percentage of city managers in the cities of over one hundred thousand in population were hired from within the city organizations. When this is the case, the traditional argument against the city manager as outsider disappears. Council–manager cities including Charlotte, Kansas City, Phoenix, and Raleigh have taken on major development initiatives.

As indicated in table 16.2, proponents of the council–manager form assert that the form brings strong administrative leadership by a qualified professional who is continuously accountable to the council. Other traditional advantages are a more effective city council and less likelihood of abuse of power by a strong mayor.

In selected cities arguments based on the positive qualities of the mayor and council were advanced, although they were not strongly emphasized. In Grand Rapids and Kansas City, defenders of the council–manager form noted that current mayors had demonstrated that they could be leaders, but the general assertion that the form permits a distinctive kind of facilitative and visionary leadership appears to be missing. The advantage of having a council whose members including the mayor share leadership was identified in some cities, including Portland.[3] The city manager was recognized for advancing values beyond efficiency in cities where minority representation was strong on the city council, but only fairness was identified. Just as common as arguments that identify strengths of the council–manager form were criticisms of the mayor–council form—lack of continuity, bossism and excessive reliance on power, weak professionalism, waste, and ignoring minority groups.

There are additional arguments that were not often or clearly expressed. Academic research demonstrates that city managers provide policy advice based on knowledge, experience, and objective assessment of trends, needs, and community goals, but this contribution is largely ignored and the focus remains on the manager's role in managing day-to-day affairs. The cooperative relationship among the mayor, council, and manager was not stressed. This condition that is commonly found in council–manager cities has been overshadowed by the disagreements that emerge in some cities. Little attention is given to the record of council–manager cities in establishing long-term goals, maintaining continuity of commitments, and introducing innovative practices. Among criticisms of the mayor–council form, the weaker performance of the council as a governing board and its domination by the mayor was noted in Grand Rapids, but conflict between the mayor and council and the risk of impasse between the two seats of power appear to be rarely mentioned. In Richmond after mayor–council government was instituted, there were constant battles between Mayor Wilder and the city council. There is little discussion of the relationship of separation of powers to shortcomings in accountability, an issue discussed further below.

The defense of the commission form and the weak-mayor form was supported by additional arguments not included in the tables that are rooted in democratic values.

**Table 16.2    Major Themes in Support of the Council–Manager Form**

*Positive Arguments/Claims for the Council–Manager Form*

| | |
|---|---|
| Mayor is leader; a visionary who provides facilitative leadership and builds partnerships; leader of the council and symbol for the community. | Grand Rapids, Kansas City |
| Council is a governing board that focuses on coherent policymaking and oversight of administrative performance. | El Paso, Grand Rapids, Portland |
| Shared leadership is valuable; better than centralized power. | Portland, Richmond |
| Decisions reflect universal values such as equality, fairness, social equity, inclusiveness, responsiveness, efficiency, and effectiveness. | Dallas and Richmond (fairness to minorities) |
| City manager brings professionalism to day-to-day operations and stresses effectiveness and efficiency. | El Paso, Oakland |
| City manager is continuously accountable to the council for performance. | El Paso |

*Arguments/Claims That Criticize the Mayor–Council Form*

| | |
|---|---|
| Performance of form is too dependent on one person; effectiveness can rise and fall with qualities of the mayor; lack of continuity; when faced with obstacles, mayors seek more power; strong mayor weakens council. | El Paso, St. Louis |
| Mayors have excessive power and are more prone to cronyism, favoritism, and corruption. | Cincinnati, Dallas, El Paso, Grand Rapids, Spokane, Topeka |
| Mayors will strengthen business, downtown power. | Cincinnati, Dallas, Portland, Richmond, St. Louis |
| Political inference in administration; no CAO or professionalism of the CAO depends on whom the mayor appoints; mayor can bypass the CAO and undercut his or her professionalism. | El Paso, Grand Rapids, Oakland (1996), Spokane |
| Promotes waste and inefficiency. | El Paso |
| Centralized power weakens minority groups and neighborhood groups and offsets their representation on the council. | Dallas, Richmond, St. Louis, St. Petersburg |

In Portland the advantage of having elected officials as directors of administrative functions to balance the influence of experts was identified. As noted in table 16.2, there is a clearer articulation of the value of shared leadership in Portland than there is in most council–manager cities where the same characteristic is found. The standard criticisms of the commission form—lack of political leadership, weakness in administrative standards, and a lack of centralized review of the performance of independent commissioners—have been offset by the unique authority given to the mayor in Portland. Similar to a cabinet form of government in some European cities, the mayor assigns and during the budget season reclaims the administrative portfolios of commissioners, and the mayor oversees the work of the chief administrative officer in directing budgetary and management systems. Unlike the cabinet form with backbenchers who are not part of the cabinet, there is no division between the elected officials responsible for the administrative work of government and those responsible for legislative oversight of their performance.

In St. Louis the proponents of the strong mayor in the civic elite articulated the position of reformers that predate the emergence of the council–manager form. Strong mayors can improve performance, increase efficiency and economy, offset ward-based fragmentation and patronage, and strengthen the unitary interest of the city as a whole. In contrast, maintenance of the current structure is supported by the political elite in order to protect the ability of party officials and ward leaders to distribute patronage. There is also support for maintaining the power of the council to check the power of the mayor. Changes need to be made to increase the power of the council and strengthen it as a deliberative, policymaking body. There appears to be an acknowledgment that the council as well as the mayor is weak in this structure with fragmented authority that goes beyond standard separation of powers.

## The Missing Discussion of Constitutional Features

The analysis of the case study cities reminds us of the importance of approaching issues of local government structure from a constitutional perspective. Strong and weak mayor–council cities are based on separation of powers and checks and balances among different branches of government. Council–manager and commission cities are based on the principle of unified authority and shared leadership. There is little explicit discussion of the implications of choosing one constitutional basis or the other for organizing government. The debate between forms still perpetuates the disagreement about the traits associated with each form in the past as well as a new debate over performance and accountability. Council–manager advocates stress reform versus corruption and efficiency versus waste. Mayor–council advocates stress initiative versus stability and responsiveness versus remoteness. Both tend to give excessive attention to the elected political–executive mayor versus the appointed professional–executive manager in comparing the forms.

In contrast, discussing the constitutional principles of form of government focuses attention on all officials, their respective level of authority, and how they relate to each other. Direction flows from the unitary source of authority in the council to the executive and administrative staff and advice is provided from the top administrator to elected officials in the council–manager form and related cabinet and parliamentary systems. The mayor and council determine policy and exercise oversight without resistance from an executive with separate powers and usually receive the support of the city manager in carrying out these functions—a conclusion based on research of the actual relationship and reinforced by professional norms. In a separation-of-powers structure, the mayor and council must reach agreement on policy. Although the mayor is the executive and responsible for the faithful execution of the laws, the mayor's control of resources can support discretionary interpretations by the mayor of what "faithful" execution means as well as provide the opportunity to shift focus or priorities independently of the council. The flow of professional analysis and advice is to the mayor, who may decide what information is conveyed to the council.

The veto, a nearly universal check that mayor–council mayors have, may be used to both stop policy initiatives and to set aside instructions to the mayor about the use of executive power. The council may override in either situation, but this means that a supermajority is needed to set policy or give instructions to the executive over the mayor's objections, compared to a simple majority in unified-authority settings. On the other hand, a simple majority of the council in a mayor–council city can deny the mayor authorization to undertake a new program or spend funds, creating the possibility of impasse between the mayor and council. In a council–manager city, the majority is decisive.[4] The substantial authority of the council makes its level of cohesiveness critical to the proper functioning of the government in the council–manager form.

The mayors in the two structural settings play different roles, but both can make substantial leadership contributions. Both are leaders of the community and represent the unity of the people. The strong mayor is the policy initiator and the chief executive. The mayor in the council–manager city is the policy visionary and leader of the council. The executive mayor can attempt to be in charge whereas the council–manager mayor is responsible for the successful performance of the government. The mayor–council mayor has more freedom to undertake initiatives because individuals can act more flexibly than collective leaders, but the council–manager mayor is able to fashion broader support based on a full and fair-minded consideration of the options presented by the manager and the backing of the council.

Finally, a comparison of structure offers insights into accountability—a major issue in the current debate about form of government that is subject to divergent interpretations (Svara 2009). Advocates of the mayor–council form argue that it makes one person accountable for the performance of government, and some mayors have substantially reoriented the performance of their governments (Flanagan 2004). The claim implies that there is someone to blame if things go wrong. This is true in the sense that the mayor is the chief executive and can direct subordinates to alter performance that is deemed to be unsatisfactory. The claim has limited validity, however, if it implies that the mayor can unilaterally make a policy or allocate new resources to address a problem. It does not mean that the mayor necessarily is accountable to a majority of the council. In these respects, separation of powers creates unclear lines of responsibility. Although the mayor is directly chosen by the voters, the review of the mayor's performance in elections is infrequent and absent for lame-duck mayors, and the emphasis on electoral success makes the mayor more accountable to supporters than to all voters. Howard and Williamson (2008, 13) in their examination of Richmond conclude that switching to the mayor–council form can be a "step in the direction of accountability" by allowing voters to determine whether the mayor will remain in office—"the ultimate expression of being held accountable in a democratic system." It is not clear, however, whether the mayor–council form can produce meaningful accountability as a "more regular feature of day-to-day governance, not just something that happens every four years on Election Day."

Unified authority means that direction comes from one source and performance is reviewed by the same source. Beyond the broad goals and specific policies set by the council in council–manager governments, it is more common than in mayor–council cities for goals to be established for the organization, for the parts of the organization to be integrated, and for performance measurement systems to be utilized. The city manager is continuously accountable to the council and can be removed at any time if performance is not satisfactory or problems are not corrected. As in any principal-agent relationship (Niskanen 1971; Banks and Weingast 1992), the reviewing body is dependent on information from the subordinate, but councils overwhelmingly give managers good ratings in providing information to support their oversight and assessment. Mayors in council–manager cities can express frustration that citizens hold them responsible for actions they do not control, for example, a complaint heard in Kansas City and Oakland, but the mayor is in fact responsible for the clarity of policy direction coming from the council and the quality of review through administrative oversight and appraisal of the city manager's performance. A different kind of problem arises if the city manager needs political power as well as administrative authority to control strong department heads that have supporters on the city council. The deeper problem here is conflicting expectations coming from the city council. As in setting policy direction, the governing board must be clear and consistent in its performance expectations. Likewise, city managers must understand and practice their proper role in the council–manager system. In some cities, such as St. Petersburg and Hartford, city managers acted inappropriately either in gaining personal benefits or engaging in electoral politics.

The choices that ultimately determine the charter changes that occur in a given city are based not just on the standard features of major forms of government. The exact terms of the successful changes reflect the balancing of contending forces and political compromise between partisan, neighborhood, racial, business, and other interests as much as the expression of constitutional principles or seeking institutional balance. As Spence observes about Cincinnati, the change in the charter occurred because it was possible politically and could secure a majority of referendum votes. Oakland's compromise in 1998 broke through the resistance that had held back previous proposals.

Revised charters differ in the extent to which they reflect the standard features of the major forms of government. Still, constitutional principles provide the basis for

comparing forms of government at a conceptual level and point to issues of performance that may be missed when considering the standard arguments pro and con. Cities
do not always behave as their charters might predict, but structural arrangements still
provide a frame of reference for assessing performance that is worse or better than
might be expected from the form that is being used. Constitutional choices have political implications for who will be advantaged and disadvantaged. They affect which values are given precedence over others. A principled case can be made for each of the
major constitutional models. The bottom line is that the choice of the model makes a
difference.

## Final Word

As noted at the beginning of this chapter, the issue is not suitability of forms to large
cities but whether the constitutional debate that is more likely to occur in larger places
is going to be brought to the level of formal choice by the voters in large cities. The
review of the cases indicates that a referendum could result from performance problems,
personal failings of leaders, or disagreements about development strategy—whichever
form is used. Three other factors, however, make a referendum more likely to occur in
council–manager cities.

First, the attitude of business coalitions and the media has shifted in favor of the
mayor–council form in many cities. Supporters of the council–manager form are challenged to make the case to these interests that effective political and professional leadership can be expected with the form.

Second, even more common is the preference of assertive political leaders to have
the powers of the strong mayor at their disposal. Such leaders are likely to push for
abandonment of the council–manager form or to defend the mayor–council form.
There is often not the same focal point of leadership for the shift to the council–
manager form in a mayor–council city. It would take an examination of large cities with
no substantial movement backing the mayor–council form to determine whether positive
leadership from mayors defuses the discussion of abandoning the council–manager
form.

Third, there are more council–manager cities that grow into the large city category
and experience constitutional contests. The outcome, however, is not clear. In all the
large city charter change efforts since 1990, nine of twenty-three have favored the
strong mayor–council form, and fourteen have not; that is, the result was the rejection
of change to the strong mayor–council form or adoption of the council–manager form.

Two generalizations about the preference of groups in the original adoption of the
council–manager form need to be revised when examining attitudes about the retention
of the form. We have already noted that business leaders are often prime supporters of
strong mayors whereas they typically supported the original adoption of the council–
manager form. Minority groups that often opposed the form and the use of at-large
elections that usually accompanied it have been supporters of the council–manager
form in a number of cities. These groups seek to preserve the representation they have

secured on the council and the evenhanded treatment they receive from professional city managers. Although the council–manager form was originally part of a conservative regime, it is not necessarily found with such regimes today.

When referenda occur, the debate over form is still largely expressed through the old themes of corruption versus competence, responsiveness versus efficiency, and executive mayors—savior or boss depending on one's perspective—versus professional managers—reformer or bureaucrat. It is time to compare forms based on an assessment of all officials—the kinds of mayors, councils, and administrators that are likely to emerge in both forms—and the full record of performance in the short term and the long term and in both policy and administrative actions.

Broadening the terms of comparison and the expanding scope of evidence will not only improve the level of discourse in the few cities that have referenda on change of form but will also help improve the quality of the governmental process in the vast majority of cities that will not experience a constitutional contest. Some cities will debate the question "which form is best?" General features of forms and the circumstances found in a particular city—history, quality of campaigns, assessment of current leaders, and so forth—will determine how that question is resolved. More cities should confront the question "how do we get the best performance from the form we have?" There are no magic bullets or automatically successful forms of government. Governing is difficult. The time and resources invested in an effort to change the form may not produce the change that is hoped for. Building on the strengths and offsetting the weaknesses of each form of government within the context of a specific city can be the shared goal for all those interested in enhanced local governance and may achieve more positive results.

## Notes

1. An exception to this generalization is the commission form of government as noted in chapter 15. The commission form presumes that the commissioners will be elected at-large since they are expected to manage administrative portfolios on behalf of all of the citizens, not just those from a given district.

2. In the view of the case study authors, Portland's commitment to a "shared power" model is similar to the civic republican tradition of the Anti-federalists in its emphasis on a communitarian-centered antipathy to strong-executive-centered government. But unlike the Anti-federalists, the commitment is more white collar than blue-collar.

3. Hassett and Watson (2007, 152) found this expression of support for shared leadership in Sarasota, Florida: "When the opponents [of the council–manager form] charged lack of political leadership, the No Boss Mayor group made its central argument that the quality of life in the community could be jeopardized by a powerful mayor who was in the pocket of the development community. Having a broad-based group of elected officials where power was not concentrated was put forward as a virtue."

4. The rare council–manager mayor who has the veto can block a policy decision but cannot block an instruction to the mayor as an executive.

# References

Banfield, E. C., and J. Q. Wilson. 1963. *City politics*. New York: Vintage Books.

Banks, Jeffrey S., and Barry R. Weingast. 1992. The political control of bureaucracies under asymmetric information. *American Journal of Political Science* 36, no. 2 (May): 509–24.

Blanc, Tera, and Barbara McCabe. 2008. Under pressure: Does the threat of citizen initiative impact local development decisions? Paper presented at the 69th ASPA Annual Conference, Dallas, Texas.

Box, R. C. 1995. Searching for the best structure for American local government. *International Journal of Public Administration* 18, no. 4:711–41.

Bridges, Amy. 1997. *Morning glories: Municipal reform in the Southwest*. Princeton, NJ: Princeton University Press.

Broder, David S. 2000. *Democracy derailed: Initiative campaigns and the power of money*. New York: Harcourt.

Donovan, Todd, Caroline J. Tolbert, and Daniel A. Smith. 2009. Political engagement, mobilization, and direct democracy. *Public Opinion Quarterly* 73, no. 1 (Spring): 98–118.

Ehrenhalt, A. 2004. The mayor–manager conundrum. *Governing*, October. www.governing.com/archive/2004/oct/assess.txt (accessed June 2008).

Ferreira, Fernando, and Joseph Gyourko. 2009. Do political parties matter? Evidence from U.S. cities. *Quarterly Journal of Economics* 124, no. 1 (February): 399–422.

Flanagan, R. M. 2004. *Mayors and the Challenge of Urban Leadership*. Lanham, MD: University Press of America.

Frederickson, H. G., G. A. Johnson, and C. H. Wood. 2004. *The adapted city: Institutional dynamics and structural change*. Armonk, NY: M. E. Sharpe.

Hassett, W., and D. Watson. 2007. *Civic battles: When cities change their form of government*. Boca Raton, FL: PrAcademics Press.

Howard, A., and T. Williamson. 2008. Richmond, Doug Wilder, and the move to a strong mayor system: A report on a political experiment in progress. Paper delivered at the Annual Meeting of the Urban Affairs Association, Baltimore.

Keene, J., J. Nalbandian, R. O'Neill Jr., S. Portillo, and J. Svara. 2007. How professionals add value to their communities and organizations. *PM* 89, no. 2 (March): 32–39.

Mossberger, Karen, and Gerry Stoker. 2001. The evolution of urban regime theory: The challenge of conceptualization. *Urban Affairs Review* 36, no. 6 (July): 810–35.

Niskanen, W. 1971. *Bureaucracy and representative government*. Chicago: Aldine.

Rusk, D. 1995. *Cities without suburbs*. Princeton, NJ: Woodrow Wilson Center Press.

Smith, Daniel A., and Caroline Tolbert. 2004. *Educated by initiative*. Ann Arbor: University of Michigan Press.

Stanton, M. 2004. *The Prince of Providence: The rise and fall of Buddy Cianci, America's most notorious mayor*. New York: Random House Trade Paperbacks.

Stone, Clarence N. 1989. *Regime politics: Governing Atlanta*. Lawrence: University Press of Kansas.

———. 1993. Urban regimes and the capacity to govern: A political economy approach. *Journal of Urban Affairs* 15, no. 1 (March): 1–28.

Svara, J. H. 1994. *Facilitative leadership in local government: Lessons from successful mayors and chairpersons in the council–manager form*. San Francisco: Jossey-Bass.

———. 2008. *The facilitative leader in city hall: Reexamining the scope and contributions*. Boca Raton, FL: CRC Press.

————. 2009. Are elected executives needed to achieve accountability to citizens? Performance issues and form of government in large U.S. cities. In *Public Sector Leadership,* J. Raffel and P. Leisink, ed. Northampton, MA: Edward Elgar Press.

Svara, J. H., and K. L. Nelson. 2008. Taking stock of the council–manager form at 100. *PM* 90, no. 7 (August): 6–14.

Tolbert, Caroline J., and Daniel A. Smith. 2006. Representation and direct democracy in the United States. *Representation* 42:25–44.

Watson, D. J., and W. L. Hassett. 2003. Long-serving city managers: Why do they stay? *Public Administration Review* 63, no. 1 (January/February): 71–78.

# CONTRIBUTORS

**R. Paul Battaglio Jr.** is an assistant professor in the public affairs program in the School of Economic, Political, and Policy Sciences at the University of Texas at Dallas. His research and teaching interests include comparative policy and administration, public human resource management, and comparative political attitudes. His work has appeared in the *Journal of Comparative Policy Analysis, Public Administration Review*, and the *Review of Public Personnel Administration*. He earned an MPA from Louisiana State University and a PhD in public administration from the University of Georgia. Before entering academic life, Dr. Battaglio served for six years in the governor's office in Louisiana.

**J. Edwin Benton** is a professor of political science and public administration in the Department of Government and International Affairs at the University of South Florida. He has published widely, with his scholarly works appearing in a wide range of journals and edited volumes. In addition, he is the author or coauthor of over forty technical reports for various state and local governments, civic groups, and nonprofit organizations. His most recent books include *Counties as Service Delivery Agents* (Praeger, 2002) and *Government and Politics in Florida*, 3rd ed. (University of Florida Press, 2008). He is currently working on a manuscript titled *Financing Local Governments: Where Does the Money Come From?* He is a recipient of the Aaron Wildavsky Book Award (Policy Studies Organization) and the Manning J. Dauer Award by the Florida Political Science Association for his sustained research contributions to scholarship on government and politics in Florida. He earned his PhD in government from Florida State University.

**Robert Cropf** is an associate professor and the chair of the Department of Public Policy Studies at Saint Louis University. His recent publications include "Creating an Accelerated Joint BA-MPA Degree Program for Adult Learners" in the *Journal of Public Affairs Education* (Spring/Summer 2007) coauthored with Jennifer Kohler, and "E-Government in Saudi Arabia: Between Promise and Reality" in the *International Journal of Electronic Government Research* (April–June 2008), coauthored with Maher Al-Fakhri, Patrick Kelly, and Gary Higgs. His textbook *Public Administration*

325

*in the 21st Century* was published by Pearson-Longman in 2007. His research interests include urban government and politics, e-government and e-democracy, and public administration pedagogical theory.

**Wendy L. Hassett** has over twelve years of experience in local government management. Currently, she is a clinical associate professor of public affairs in the School of Economic, Political, and Policy Sciences at the University of Texas at Dallas. Her scholarly work has appeared in *Public Administration Review, Public Performance and Management Review, Review of Public Personnel Administration, Journal of Public Budgeting, Accounting and Financial Management,* and other journals. She is coauthor of *Civic Battles: When Cities Change Their Form of Government* (PrAcademics Press 2007) and coeditor of *Local Government Management: Current Issues and Best Practices* (M. E. Sharpe 2003). She earned her PhD in public administration and public policy at Auburn University.

**Karen M. Jarrell** has over twenty-two years of experience in higher education administration. Currently, she is a clinical associate professor of public affairs in the School of Economic, Political, and Policy Sciences at the University of Texas at Dallas. She also serves as the university registrar and assistant vice president for student financial aid and academic records at the University of Texas at Dallas. Her scholarly work has appeared in the *Review of Public Personnel Administration.* She has presented at conferences across the nation on issues affecting higher education, contingency and succession planning, leadership, and public management. She earned her PhD in public affairs at the University of Texas at Dallas.

**Scott Krummenacher** is visiting assistant professor of public policy studies at Saint Louis University. His recent works include "Regional System of Greenways: If You Can Make It in St. Louis, You Can Make It Anywhere" coauthored with Todd Swanstrom and Mark Tranel in the *National Civic Review,* and coeditor of "ICT and Virtual Public Spheres" forthcoming from IGI Publishing. His research interests include regional governance, civic engagement, and e-democracy. He received his PhD in public policy studies at Saint Louis University.

**Donald C. Menzel** is president of Ethics Management International and served as the 2005–06 president of the American Society for Public Administration. He is emeritus professor at Northern Illinois University. He has published widely in the field of public administration with particular interest in local government management and ethics and has lectured on these subjects in China, Thailand, France, Germany, Portugal, and Italy and at numerous professional conferences in the United States. His most recent books are *Ethics Moments in Government: Cases and Controversies* (2010) and *Ethics Management for Public Administrators: Building Organizations of Integrity (*2007). He holds a PhD in political science from the Pennsylvania State University. He served in the U.S. Air Force from 1962 to 1967.

**Doug Morgan** is a professor of public administration and director of the Executive Leadership Institute in the Mark O. Hatfield School of Government at Portland State University. He has studied the leadership role of career administrators in the U.S. system of separation of powers and checks and balances. He has authored more than two dozen articles and book chapters on ethics, administrative discretion, and public service. Current projects include a handbook on public budgeting and a monograph with Craig Shinn on the foundations of American public service. As director of the Executive Leadership Institute, Morgan coordinates and participates in the delivery of more than a dozen leadership development programs to senior-level leaders for more than thirty federal, state, and local public agencies in the Pacific Northwest.

**Megan Mullin** is assistant professor of political science at Temple University. She specializes in American politics and public policy, focusing on how institutional rules and structures affect political participation and policy outcomes. Her work has appeared in the journals *American Journal of Political Science, Political Analysis, State Politics and Policy Quarterly,* and *Urban Affairs Review* as well as in several edited volumes. She currently is completing a book manuscript titled *Governing the Tap: Specialized Governance and the New Local Politics of Water,* which examines the effect of governmental organization on policies for the sustainable use of water resources in American communities. Her research has been supported by grants from the National Science Foundation and the Haynes Foundation, and she has received three Best Paper awards for work presented at the American Political Science Association's annual meetings. She received her PhD from the University of California–Berkeley in 2005.

**Kimberly Nelson** is an assistant professor of public administration at Northern Illinois University, where she teaches in the master of public administration program. She researches in the areas of municipal economic development, local government management, and form of government. She has developed the Municipal Structure Dataset covering 95 percent of cities over ten thousand in population. She is coauthor with James Svara of "Adaptation of Models versus Variations in Form: Classifying Structures of City Government," in press with *Urban Affairs Review.* She received her PhD in public administration from North Carolina State University.

**Masami Nishishiba** is an assistant professor of public administration and assistant director of Executive Leadership Institute in the Mark O. Hatfield School of Government at Portland State University. She has taught graduate courses in organizational theory, organizational behavior, diversity in the workplace, intercultural communication, research methodology, and statistics. In addition she has been active in community-based research and professional training for public agencies in Oregon, Washington, and Japan. Recent work includes a coauthored Japanese/English bilingual book, *Project Management Toolkit: A Strategic Approach to New Local Governance,* and an article in *Journal of Public Affairs Education* based on the Civic Capacity Initiative research at PSU, funded by the U.S. Department of Education Fund for Improving

Post Secondary Education (FIPSE). She received her PhD in public administration and policy from Portland State University.

**Darryl Paulson** is emeritus professor of government at the University of South Florida (USF)–St. Petersburg, specializing in political parties and elections, and Florida and Southern Politics. He is the recipient of a National Teaching Fellowship and two undergraduate teaching awards from USF. He was selected as a Salvatori Fellow at the Heritage Foundation in Washington, DC. He has served as an expert witness in state and federal court cases and participated in the U.S. Civil Rights Commission Hearings after the Florida 2000 presidential election. He has been interviewed more than seven thousand times by the print and broadcast media. He is currently writing a book for the University Press of Florida on *From Cramer to Crist: The Emergence of the Modern Florida Republican Party* (in press, University Press of Florida). He received his PhD from Florida State University.

**Glen W. Sparrow** is emeritus professor of public affairs at San Diego State University. His areas of specialization include state and local government management, metropolitan/regional governance, intergovernmental relations, and border governance. He was executive director of the Sacramento and San Francisco charter commissions, and spent a year on the staff of a member of the California Assembly, a member of the San Diego City Council, and a member of the Sacramento County Board of Supervisors. He provides consulting assistance to cities and counties in California in the areas of incorporation, fiscal management, and public–private partnerships, and he was instrumental in the drafting, campaign, and implementation of the mayor–council form of government for San Diego. He received his PhD in government from Claremont Graduate School.

**John T. Spence, AICP,** is a lecturer in political science at Thomas More College. His primary research focus is municipal government, electoral and voter behavior, and civic engagement. He is the author of a study on mayoral leadership in Cincinnati included in *The Facilitative Leader in City Hall* edited by James Svara. He served two terms on the Covington (Kentucky) Board of Commissioners, one of five elected officials responsible for overseeing a city government of more than three hundred employees and a $50 million budget. He received his doctorate from the University of Cincinnati in 2003.

**James H. Svara** is professor in the School of Public Affairs at Arizona State University and director of the Center for Urban Innovation. In his research and teaching he specializes in local government politics, management, and ethics, and he has a special interest in the roles and responsibilities of elected and administrative leaders in local government. He is the author of numerous books, chapters, and journal articles that examine leadership by mayors, council members, and city managers. The books he has authored include *The Facilitative Leader in City Hall* (CRC Press, 2008), *The Ethics Primer for Public Administrators in Government and Nonprofit Organizations* (Jones &

Bartlett Publishers, 2007), and *Leadership at the Apex: Politicians and Administrators in Western Local Governments* (University of Pittsburgh Press, 2002) with Poul Erik Mouritzen. He is a fellow of the National Academy of Public Administration and an honorary member of the International City/County Management Association.

**Todd Swanstrom** is professor of public policy at Saint Louis University where he moved in 2001 after serving as a professor of political science in the Rockefeller College of Public Affairs and Policy at SUNY–Albany for nineteen years. He is the author or coauthor of six books and more than twenty-five scholarly articles. His applied policy work includes serving as a neighborhood planner for the City of Cleveland and as staff director of strategic planning for the City of Albany. Together with Peter Dreier and John Mollenkopf, he coauthored *Place Matters: Metropolitics for the Twenty-first Century*, rev. ed. (University Press of Kansas, 2005), which examines the relationship between urban decline and suburban sprawl. Recently, he has published research, sponsored by the Brookings Institution, on the prospects for alliances between central cities and distressed suburbs and on economic segregation among municipalities. His current research focuses on regional approaches to equity and theories of regional network governance. He is a member of the MacArthur Foundation's Building Resilient Regions Network. He received his PhD in politics from Princeton University.

**Larry Terry** is an assistant professor in the School of Business, Public Administration, and Information Sciences, Department of Public Administration at Long Island University. His research and teaching interests include comparative public administration, the European Union and democratization, and public leadership. Prior to his academic career, he worked for the City of Santa Barbara and the County of San Diego, and as a doctoral student, he assisted in the establishment of the Center for Public Administration of Montenegro in Podgorica, Montenegro. He earned an MPA from San Diego State University and a PhD in Public Affairs from the University of Texas at Dallas.

**Dan Vizzini** is a principal financial analyst at Portland's Bureau of Environmental Services. His assignments include utility rate reform, infrastructure financing for new urban reserves, a stormwater marketplace feasibility study, intergovernmental and legislative affairs, and the development of bureau policies and administrative rules. He is the bureau's liaison with the city's Small Business Advisory Council. He joined the bureau in 1997. Prior to arrival at the bureau, he served as the city assessments manager in the Office of the Portland City Auditor. In addition to these positions at the City of Portland, he served as a budget analyst with the Multnomah County Tax Supervising and Conservation Commission from 1979 to 1985 and the New Jersey State Bureau of the Budget from 1976 to 1979. He earned a BA in economics from Boston University in 1976.

**Douglas J. Watson** retired in 2010 as a professor and director of the public affairs program at the University of Texas at Dallas. He is coeditor of *Local Government Management: Current Issues and Best Practices* (M. E. Sharpe 2003), *Spending a Lifetime: The*

*Careers of City Managers* (Carl Vinson Institute of Government, 2006), and *Civic Battles: When Cities Change Their Form of Government* (PrAcademics Press, 2007), and four other books. His work has appeared in *Public Administration Review, Review of Public Personnel Administration*, and other journals. Dr. Watson was a local government practitioner for more than thirty years (1971–2003) and served as city manager of Auburn, Alabama, for the twenty-one years of his tenure.

**Nelson Wikstrom** is professor of political science and public administration at Virginia Commonwealth University. He is the author of *Councils of Governments: A Study of Political Incrementalism* (Nelson-Hall, 1977), *The Political World of a Small Town: A Mirror Image of American Politics* (Greenwood, 1993), and *County Manager Government in Henrico, Virginia: Implementation, Evolution, and Evaluation* (Henrico County, 2003). He is also the coauthor, along with G. Ross Stephens, of *Metropolitan Government and Governance: Empirical Analysis, Theoretical Perspectives, and the Future* (Oxford University Press, 2000), and *American Intergovernmental Relations: A Fragmented Federal Polity* (Oxford University Press, 2006). Wikstrom has also contributed to a score of professional journals, including the *Public Administration Review, State and Local Government Review*, and the *American Review of Public Administration*. He received his PhD degree in political science from the University of Connecticut.

**Curtis Wood** is an assistant professor in the master of public administration program at Northern Illinois University, where he teaches courses and conducts research in public management, ethics, and regional governance. He is a coauthor of *The Adapted City: Institutional Dynamics and Structural Change* with H. George Frederickson and Gary Alan Johnson (M. E. Sharpe 2003). He has twenty years of municipal government experience, seventeen years as a finance director. He received his PhD in political science from the University of Kansas.

**Eric S. Zeemering is** an assistant professor in the Department of Public Administration at San Francisco State University. His research on local policymaking and urban service organization has appeared in *Public Administration Review, State and Local Government Review* and *Urban Affairs Review*. He is currently conducting research on the adoption, oversight, and abandonment of interlocal contracts among local governments in California. He completed his PhD in political science at Indiana University in 2007.

# INDEX

Note: Page numbers in italics represent figures and tables in the text.

council–manager form of government
(*continued*)

    16–17, 25–138; and corporate organization reform, 5; distribution among U.S. municipalities (1984–2008), 8, *9*, *10*; distribution among U.S. municipalities by population size, 8, *10*; increasing use in large cities, 11, 12, 255, 303–4, 320; and rejected change to mayor–council, 17–18, 141–222

Council of Neighborhood Association (CONA) (St. Petersburg), 28, 33

Craft, Juanita, 184

Cranley, John, 219

Crenshaw, Marvin, 186

crime, 72, 82, 93, 99

Cropf, Robert, 18–19, 263–77

Cross, Paul, 240

Crum, Roger, 48

Curtin, Edward M., Jr., 69, 76

Curtsinger, Ernest (Curt), 34–36, 38

Daines, Bernard, 53

Dallas, Texas (strong-mayor movement and survival of council–manager form), 17–18, 183–201, 305–12, *314*, *316*; the Blackwood proposal (Proposition 1 to put strong mayor proposition on ballot), 189–96, 197, 199; city council reapportionment plan and constitutionality of electoral process (1970s), 185–86; city population and demographics, 184; early strong mayors (1950s and 1960s), 188–89; factors leading to defeat of both strong-mayor proposals, 198–99; federal lawsuit regarding election of at-large council members (early 1990s), 186–87; the 14–1 election system, 187; mayor Miller's personality and leadership style, 198–99, 309–10; origins of the effort to change form of government, 183, 187–88; racial relations and African American representation in city

government, 183–87; the strong-mayor movement, 188–99

Dallas Charter Association, 184

Dallas Citizens Council (DCC), 184, 188, 194–99, 307

Dallas Express, 183–84

Dallas Future Political Action Committee, 195

*Dallas Morning News*, 188, 193

Dallas Together, 186

Dallas Urban League, 188

Darst, Joseph, 269

Davis, Ilus W., 147

Decherd, Robert, 193

Dellums, Ron, 134–35

DeSantis, V. S., 11

*D Magazine*, 191, 192–93

Dowell, Ben, 226

Dunn, Betty, 246–47, 248–49

Dunn, James W., 85

Edgerly, Deborah, 135

Ehlets, Vernon, 179n5

Ehrenhalt, Allan, 6, 305

11-Ward Committee (Grand Rapids), 165, 175

Ellegood, Wade, 95

Ellis, George, 164

El Paso, Texas (change to council–manager form), 18, 225–44, 305–9, 311, *316*; the business sector's push for change, 231–32; and Chamber of Commerce, 230, 232–33, 240; the charter amendment referendum (2004), 234–35; consolidation of deputy CAOs into four core service areas, 236; corruption charges against elected officials, 233, 240; customer service focus, 239; downtown revitalization and business community (1980s), 228; and economic effects of NAFTA, 228, 233–34; external exigencies for municipal reform, 231–35; Hispanic population, 233–34; historical

North American Free Trade Agreement
  (NAFTA), 228, 233–34
Novak, Terry, 48, 50–52, 54, 57

Oakes, Donald, 166, 167–68, 170, 171,
  177
Oakland, California (two measures for
  change to strong-mayor form), 17, 106,
  107, 121–38, 304–14, *314*, *316*, 319;
  and baseball stadium politics, 133; Brown
  and Measure X (1998), 124–34;
  campaign effects and elite influences
  affecting public attitudes, 128–32, 134;
  campaign spending, 128; and city
  manager role, 130; Dellum administration scandals, 134–35; different
  approaches in achieving goals of strong-
  mayor system, 129–31; different ballot
  measure campaigns, 128–29, 131–32;
  different timing of the measures and
  management of the campaigns, 131–32;
  the early council–manager form and
  mayors' efforts to reform charter,
  121–23; effects of incumbent mayoral
  support, 126–28, *127*, *128*, 136n4; elite
  opinion/elite influences, 129, 131–32,
  133–34; endorsements, 128–29; Harris's
  failed strong-mayor proposal on 1996
  ballot (Measure F), 123, 125–32, 136n7;
  importance of mayor's governing style,
  134–35; and mayor Brown's celebrity,
  124–25; Measure X's sunset provision
  and reauthorization of Brown's strong-
  mayor reform, 131, 132–34; the personal
  vote hypothesis, 124–28, *125*, *127*, *128*;
  precinct support for Measure F (1996)
  and Measure X (1998), *125*, 125–28,
  *127*, *128*, 135n3; precinct vote on
  Measure F (1996) and Measure X (1998),
  126–28, *127*, *128*; racial composition of
  voter precincts, 126–28, *127*, *128*,
  136n5; responding to arguments about
  potential abuses of power, 130–31

*Oakland Tribune*, 129, 130, 131, 133–34,
  307
Oakley, Ed, 197
O'Bannon, John M., 84
Obering, Robert, 30, 34
Okpa, E. Edward, II, 192
Okubo,D., 232, 234
Olson, Dave, *146*, 147–48, 149, 158n1
*Oregonian*, 289
O'Rourke, Beto, 239
Orr, Julian, 165, 175
Ortega, Steve, 240–41
Ozawa, Connie, 295

Pantele, William J., 95
Paquette, Lee, 69
Parks, Lyman, 169, 173, 179n8
Patterson, Lucy, 184
Paulson, Darryl, 16, 25–45
Pazniokas, Mark, 74
Peele, G., 265
Pelissero, J. P., 19n3
Pendergast, James, 143
Pendergast, Tom, 143–45, 148
Pepper, David, 217–18, 221n10
Perez, Eddie, 73–75, 77–78, 310, 313
Perry, Carrie Saxon, 70–71
Peters, Mike, 70–71, 72, 73, 74, 76
Phoenix, Arizona, 177, 232
Pinellas County, Florida, 25, 31. *See also* St.
  Petersburg, Florida
political leadership at the apex, 154–56,
  157–58, 158n3, 158n5, 159n6
Pomeroy, Duane, 248
Portland, Oregon (retention of commission
  form of government), 19, 279–301,
  305–7, 311, *314*, 315–17, *316*; adminis-
  trative powers/operations, 282–83,
  290–93; the CAO's enhanced administrative power, 283, 285, 290; the City
  Club's 2007 report, 285–86, 288, 289,
  296, 298, 298n2; city population and
  racial demographics, 294, 299n9; the

city's unique "weirdness" and populist
liberalism, 279–80; civic engagement
levels, 286–87, 291–93, 295, 298n4; the
commission system structure, 281–83,
298n1; coordination and efficiency
issues, 287–91; eight efforts to replace
commission with strong mayor, 281,
283–86, *284*; elections and staggered
election schedule, 282; explaining the
paradox of the commission system,
294–98; "good government" reforms
(1980–2009), 287–94, *288*; history of
the commission system, 280–81; legislative and executive functions united,
281–82; mayor's appointment power to
make bureau assignments, 281–82;
mayor's power to prepare and present
annual budget, 282–83; minority representation issue, 293–94, 299nn8–10; the
"mutiny memo," 290–91; Office of
Management and Finance (OMF),
290–91; professional oversight of administrative operations, 291–93; quasi-
judicial powers, 283; "shared power"
model, 313, 317, 321n2; the 2007 referendum debate, 284–86; and urban
sustainable development practices, 286,
295, 297, 298n3
Potter, Tom, 284–85
Powers, John, 51–52
Powers, John T., Jr., 57–58
preferential voting, 209, 220n5
professionalism: and commission form of
government, 280–81; and El Paso's
change to council–manager form, 18,
225–44, 305–9, 311, *316*; and forms of
government, 7–8; Topeka's council–
manager form, 250–51
Progressive Voters League (Dallas), 183–84
Protasel, G. J., 228–29
Providence, Rhode Island, 313
Public Parking Development Authority
(PDA) (Spokane), 50–51
Pueblo, Colorado, 12, 20n6

Pulido, Gwen, 234–35, 240–41
Pupo, Bill, 48, 50, 54–55
Putnam, Robert, 286–87, 295, 298n4

Qualls, Roxanne, 207–12, 213, 219,
220n3, 221n13

Rayner, Bob, 100
Reece, Alicia, 216, 217, 220n9
referenda campaigns for change of form
(distinct factors and common themes),
19, 303–23; business and media, 306–7,
320; city growth, 305–6; constitutional
features and local government structure,
1, 312, 317–20; council–manager form
(arguments/claims that criticize), 14,
*314*; council–manager form (major
themes in support of), 14–15, 315–17,
*316*; mayor–council form (arguments/
claims that criticize), 15, *316*; mayor–
council form (major themes in support
of), 313–15, *314*; the nature of political
leadership (and leadership styles),
309–10, 320; partisan elections and other
methods of selecting mayor/city council,
307–9; and question of form as settled
issue, 1–2, 255, 304–5; regimes and the
question of form, 311–12; shortcomings
of city managers, 310–11. *See also* urban
reform and strengthening mayoral
leadership
regimes: and commission form of
government, 297, 311; and the question
of form, 311–12
Reid, William Ferguson, 84
rejected change to strong mayor–council:
Cincinnati, 18, 203–22; Dallas, 17–18,
183–201; Grand Rapids, 17, 163–81;
Kansas City, 17, 141–61; Portland, 19,
279–301; retaining commission or weak
mayor, 18–19, 263–301; retaining the
council–manager form, 17–18, 141–222;
St. Louis, 18–19, 263–77

recommendations to strengthen mayor and council powers (1988), 246–47; under mayor-commission and strong-mayor (1980s), 246; the politics-administrative dichotomy, 254–56; and professionalism, 250–51; proponents'/critics' arguments over the ordinance and related controversies, 250–51, 257n4; proposed changes to role of mayor and CAO, 249–50; reasons for move away from mayor–council form, 255; the referendum's aftermath, 251–53

Topeka/Shawnee County Riverfront Authority, 252

Top Vote Getter (TVG) elections (Cincinnati), 205, 206, 207, 213

Tsebelis, G., 19n1

Tucson, Arizona, 12

Uberuaga, Michael, 112, 115

Uccello, Antonina P. "Ann," 68

Ukrop, James E., 90

Ulrich, Robert, 26, 31–33, 44n4

union opposition to strong-mayor reforms: Grand Rapids, 173; San Diego, 113; St. Louis, 267–68, 272–74

United Way of Greater Dallas, 188

University of Texas at El Paso (UTEP), 227–28, 234

urban reform and strengthening mayoral leadership, 264–67, 274–76; barriers to reform, 266–67, 274; broad-based coalition-building, 266; provisions to check and balance power of mayor, 275–76; role of mayors' leadership styles and behavior, 264–65, 276n1, 310; and size of the municipality, 266–67; structural barriers presenting challenges for mayoral leadership, 265; why a public process is more likely to win voter approval, 274–75. See also mayor–council form of government

U.S. Conference of Mayors (USCM), 51

U.S. Department of Housing and Urban Development (HUD) loans, 49, 51–52

U.S. Supreme Court, 185–86

Verner, Mary, 59–60, 61

Vizzini, Dan, 19, 279–301, 311

Vote for Leadership (Cincinnati), 207

Voting Rights Act (1965), 88, 91, 186, 195, 196, 281, 293

Vowell, J. C., 226

Wagnon, Joan, 246, 247

Walker, George H. "Bert," 268

Walker Report (1996) (St. Louis), 268–69, 272, 274

Ward, Terry, 152–53

Wardy, Joe, 230, 232–33, 235, 238, 305, 309

Ware, John, 187

*Washington CEO* magazine, 53

*Washington Post*, 68

Watkins, John C., 84

Watson, Douglas J., 1–22, 87, 98, 183, 188, 303–23, 315, 321n3; on city growth and form change, 306; and city managers' tenures, 257n5; on community paradigms and local policy decisions, 5; and governance form/structure as settled issue, 1–2, 304, 305

Wells, Max, 193–94

Welsh, George, 168, 169

West, James Elton "Jim," 58–59, 60

Wheeland, C. M., 264–65

Wheeler, Charles B., 147, 148, 149

White, Leonard, 144

Wikstrom, Nelson, 16, 81–102

Wilder, L. Douglas, 16–17, 82–100, 198, 309

Williams, Lawrence E., 91–92

Williams, Michael Paul, 93, 94

Williams, Roy, 186

Williamson, T., 319

Wilson, A. J., *146*

Wilson, J. Q., 5, 11